THE PSALMS IN HUMAN LIFE

The Psalms
in Human Life

ROWLAND EDMUND PROTHERO

SOLID GROUND CHRISTIAN BOOKS
BIRMINGHAM, ALABAMA USA

Solid Ground Christian Books
PO Box 660132
Vestavia Hills AL 35266
205-443-0311
sgcb@charter.net
www.solid-ground-books.com

THE PSALMS IN HUMAN LIFE
Rowland Edmund Prothero (1851-1937)

Taken from 1903 edition by John Murray, Abermarle Street, London

Cover image is taken from a photo by Ric Ergenbright
Sheep compete for the best grass near the Dallas Divide
in the San Juan Mountains in Colorado

Cover design by Borgo Design
Contact them at borgogirl@bellsouth.net

ISBN- 978-159925-193-6

"What a record that would be, if one could write it down—all the spiritual experiences, the disclosures of the heart, the comforts and the conflicts which men in the course of ages have connected with the words of the Psalms! What a history, if we could discover the place the Book has occupied in the inner life of the heroes of the kingdom of God!"
– Friedrich Tholuck (1799-1877)

PREFACE

SOME of the notes, on which the following pages are founded, were discussed with Dean Stanley in 1878. A list of historical instances of the use of the Psalms, made by the Dean himself, was sent to me in 1895 by the Right Rev. H. H. Montgomery, then Bishop of Tasmania. To it I am indebted for the reference (page 271) to the reopening of the Cathedral at Moscow, after the French invasion of 1812.

Since my collection of notes was begun, the ground has been partly occupied by the Rev. John Ker, D.D. (1886), and the Rev. Charles L. Marson (1895). But Dr. Ker's book was unfinished, and both he and Mr. Marson followed a method of treatment different from that which is adopted in the following pages.

In Appendix A will be found a general list of the principal authorities. Appendix B arranges the historical instances, which in the text are grouped, more or less, in order of time, under the particular Psalms that are quoted. The Index contains, in addition to the ordinary matter, references to the books from which the historical instances are derived.

For assistance in the preparation of Appendix A, and for the Index, I am indebted to Mr. G. H. Holden, Assistant Librarian of All Souls' College, Oxford, and to Mr. C. Nolan Ferrall. To Mr. Holden I owe Appendix B.

ROWLAND E. PROTHERO.

6th September 1903.

CONTENTS

CHAPTER I
GENERAL

	PAGES
The Psalms as the mirror of the human soul; their association with national and individual life; their universality; not limited to any age, nation, or variety of Christian creed; their translation into verse; their influence in literature; the first of religious autobiographies; power over human lives in all ages of history . . .	1-8

CHAPTER II
EARLY AGES OF CHRISTIANITY

The Psalms in services, ceremonies, and the catacombs; use in persecution—Crispin and Crispinian, Theodore the Martyr, the Saracen convert, the Emperor Maurice; in public worship; in ordinary life—Origen, the family of Gregory Nazianzen, Monica; on deathbeds—Basil the Great, Ambrose, Paulinus of Nola, Cyril of Alexandria; influence of the Psalms in Monasticism—the Egyptian Anchorites, Basil and monastic communities of the East, Athanasius and the West, Jerome and Paula, Martin of Tours; the Psalms in action—struggle between Church and State—Athanasius and Constantius, Basil and Valens, Ambrose and Theodosius; the Psalms in human thought—*Confessions* of Augustine . . 9-30

CHAPTER III
THE FORMATION OF NATIONS

The invasions of the barbarians; supremacy of moral power over brute force, Totila and Benedict; the Rule of Benedict; monastic missionaries; translation of the Psalms into Sclavonic; the Psalms in the lives of Columban, Gall, Patrick, Columba, Cuthbert; Irish and British Christianity—Battle of Mold, Kentigern, Bangor; Roman Christianity—the island of Death and Silence; Gregory the Great; coming of Augustine; introduction of Benedictine Rule; its foundation on the Psalms; its establishment in England—Benedict Biscop, Wilfrid, Neot, Dunstan; universality of the Rule . . . 31-51

Contents

CHAPTER IV
THE MIDDLE AGES

PAGES

The battle of Vouglé; the Psalms in ecclesiastical or semi-ecclesiastical history—(1) The Papacy and the Empire—Charlemagne, Gregory VII. and Henry IV., Anselm and William Rufus, Henry II. and Thomas à Becket, Alexander III. and Frederick Barbarossa; (2) pilgrimages; (3) the crusades, Abp. Baldwin, Richard I., Henry V., Abbot Adelme at the Tagus, Cardinal Ximenes, Demetrius of the Don; (4) the religious revival, Bernard, Stephen Harding and the Cistercian reform, Cîteaux and Fountains Abbey, Francis of Assisi and the Franciscans; the Psalms in secular history—William the Conqueror, Vladimir Monomachus, David I. of Scotland, Abelard and Heloïse, Louis IX. of France, William Wallace; in mediæval science; in mediæval literature—*De Imitatione Christi, Divina Commedia, Piers Plowman, The Golden Legend* 52-86

CHAPTER V
THE REFORMATION ERA

The influence of the Psalms among pioneers of the Reformation—Wyclif, John Hus, Jerome of Prague; among mediæval reformers—Savonarola; among Protestant leaders—Luther and Melancthon; among champions of the Papacy—the Emperor Charles V.; among discoverers of New Worlds—Christopher Columbus; among men of the New Learning—Erasmus, Pico della Mirandola, Sir Thomas More; John Fisher; John Houghton; among leaders of the Roman Catholic Reaction—Xavier and Teresa; among Protestant and Roman Catholic Martyrs—Hooper, Ridley, and Southwell . . . 87-109

CHAPTER VI
THE STRUGGLE BETWEEN PROTESTANT ENGLAND AND ROMAN CATHOLIC SPAIN

The Psalms in the vulgar tongue, the English Prayer-book version; metrical translations, Germany, France, England, Scotland; growth of the influence of the Psalms in the sixteenth and seventeenth centuries; Lady Jane Grey; the Duke of Suffolk; Counts Egmont and Horn; accession of Queen Elizabeth; the murder of Darnley; execution of Mary, Queen of Scots; the Spanish Armada; the Turkey merchantmen; the wreck of the *Tobie*; the Earl of Essex; Burghley; Bacon; Shakespeare; Richard Hooker; Bishop Jewel; George Herbert; Hooker on the Psalms 110-136

Contents

CHAPTER VII

THE HUGUENOTS, 1524–98

Marot's *Psalms* at Court; the distinctive heritage of the Huguenots; the power of the Psalms in the public and private lives of the Huguenots—Palissy the potter, Calvin, Theodore de Beza, Robert Estienne, Casaubon, Jean Rousseau; traces in modern France of the struggle between Roman Catholics and Huguenots; beginning of the persecution of Protestants—Jean Leclerc (1524), Wolfgang Schuch (1525); indecision of Francis I.; the Huguenot martyrs of Meaux, Jean Rabec, massacre of Vassy; commencement of the Wars of Religion (1562); Coligny at Noyers and Moncontour; Massacre of St. Bartholomew (1572); Henry of Navarre, flight from Paris to Alençon, battles of Courtras and Château d'Arques; Edict of Nantes (1598) 137-152

CHAPTER VIII

THE HUGUENOTS, 1600–1762 (*continued*)

The Roman Catholic Reaction—Vincent de Paul, François de Sales: changed conditions of the Huguenot cause; their effect on the character of the Wars of Religion, 1621–29—Henri de Rohan, sieges of Montauban and La Rochelle; the Roman Catholic triumph and maintenance of the strictest orthodoxy—Port Royal, Pascal, Madame Guyon; edicts against the Huguenots and the use of the Psalter: the Vaudois and Henri Arnaud; revocation of the Edict of Nantes (1685); persecution of the French Huguenots; the rising in the Cevennes—murder of François du Chayla, Cavalier and the Camisards, Bellot, Martignargues (1704), Salindres (1709); the Pastors of the Desert—Rang, Roger, Benezet, Rochette; effect of the Psalms on the virtues and defects of the Huguenots 153-172

CHAPTER IX

THE PURITANS, 1600–1660

The Pilgrim Fathers and Benjamin Franklin; the Psalms among the royalists—Jeremy Taylor, Bishop Sanderson, Strafford, and Laud; the Civil War—Marston Moor, John Hampden, Charles I. at Newark; Puritanism as a poetical, religious, and political force in Milton, Bunyan, and Cromwell 173-196

Contents

CHAPTER X

THE SCOTTISH COVENANTERS AND THE REVOLUTION OF 1688

PAGES

Progress of the Reformation in Scotland—George Wishart, John Knox, James Melville; the Solemn League and Covenant (1638); the restoration of Episcopacy (1661-4); popular discontent—the Pentland Rising, Hugh M'Kail, Drumclog and Bothwell Bridge, Richard Cameron, Donald Cargill, Baillie of Jerviswood, Alexander Peden, James Renwick, the Wigtown Martyrs; the Revolution of 1688; siege of Derry (1689) 197-224

CHAPTER XI

1688–1900

Changed character of the romance of religion: the Psalms in the lives of religious leaders—Baxter, Law, John Wesley, Charles Wesley, William Wilberforce, Keble, Manning, Newman, Thomas Arnold, Julius Hare, Neander, Charles Kingsley, Stanley, Chalmers, Irving; the Psalms in the lives of men of science—Locke, Humboldt, Maine de Biran, Sir W. Hamilton, Sir James Simpson, Romanes; the Psalms in literature—Addison, Cowper, Boswell, Scott, Byron, Hogg, Wordsworth, Tennyson, Matthew Arnold, Robert Browning, Elizabeth Barrett Browning, Fitzgerald, Ruskin, Carlyle 225-249

CHAPTER XII

1688–1900 (*continued*)

The Psalms in philanthropic movements—Prison Reform and John Howard; in missionary enterprises—John Eliot, David Brainerd, William Carey, Henry Martyn, Alexander Duff, Allen Gardiner, David Livingstone, Bishop Hannington; in ordinary life—Colonel Gardiner, Thomas Carlyle, Jane Welsh Carlyle; in secular history —Brittany and La Vendée, the execution of Madame de Noailles, the evacuation of Moscow in 1812, the Revolution of 1848, Bourget in the Franco-German War of 1870-1, Captain Conolly at Bokhara and Havelock at Jellalabad, Duff, Edwards, and " Quaker " Wallace in the Indian Mutiny, the Boer War 250-279

APPENDIX A.—PRINCIPAL AUTHORITIES 283

   ,,   B.—INDEX TO THE USE OF PARTICULAR PSALMS   302

INDEX 309

THE PSALMS IN HUMAN LIFE

CHAPTER I

GENERAL

The Psalms as the mirror of the human soul: their association with national and individual life: their universality; not limited to any age, nation, or variety of Christian creed; their translation into verse; their influence in literature; the first of religious autobiographies; power over human lives in all ages of history.

ABOVE the couch of David, according to Rabbinical tradition, there hung a harp. The midnight breeze, as it rippled over the strings, made such music that the poet-king was constrained to rise from his bed, and, till the dawn flushed the eastern skies, he wedded words to the strains. The poetry of that tradition is condensed in the saying that the Book of Psalms contains the whole music of the heart of man, swept by the hand of his Maker. In it are gathered the lyrical burst of his tenderness, the moan of his penitence, the pathos of his sorrow, the triumph of his victory, the despair of his defeat, the firmness of his confidence, the rapture of his assured hope. In it is presented the anatomy of all parts of the human soul; in it, as Heine says, are collected " sunrise and sunset, birth and death, promise and fulfilment —the whole drama of humanity."

In the Psalms is painted, for all time, in fresh unfading colours, the picture of the moral warfare of man, often baffled yet never wholly defeated, struggling upwards to all that is best and highest in his nature, always aware how short of the aim falls the attempt, how great is the gulf that severs the wish from its fulfilment. In them we do not find the innocent converse of man with God in the Garden of Eden; if we did, the book would for our fallen natures lose its value.

On the contrary, it is the revelation of a soul deeply conscious of sin, seeking, in broken accents of shame and penitence and hope, to renew personal communion with God, heart to heart, thought to thought, and face to face. It is this which gives to the Psalms their eternal truth. It is this which makes them at once the breviary and the viaticum of humanity. Here are gathered not only pregnant statements of the principles of religion, and condensed maxims of spiritual life, but a promptuary of effort, a summary of devotion, a manual of prayer and praise,—and all this is clothed in language, which is as rich in poetic beauty as it is universal and enduring in poetic truth.

The Psalms, then, are a mirror in which each man sees the motions of his own soul. They express in exquisite words the kinship which every thoughtful human heart craves to find with a supreme, unchanging, loving God, who will be to him a protector, guardian, and friend. They utter the ordinary experiences, the familiar thoughts of men; but they give to these a width of range, an intensity, a depth, and an elevation, which transcend the capacity of the most gifted. They translate into speech the spiritual passion of the loftiest genius; they also utter, with the beauty born of truth and simplicity, and with exact agreement between the feeling and the expression, the inarticulate and humble longings of the unlettered peasant. So it is that, in every country, the language of the Psalms has become part of the daily life of nations, passing into their proverbs, mingling with their conversation, and used at every critical stage of existence.

With our national, as well as with our private lives, the Psalms are inextricably mingled. On the Psalms, both in spirit (Ps. xx. 9), and language (Ps. lxviii. 1), is based our National Anthem. From the lion and the unicorn of Ps. xxii. 21, are taken the supporters of the royal arms. In all the Coronation Offices from Egbert to Edward VII., not only the services, but the symbolic ceremonies are based upon the Psalms—the oil of gladness above his fellows, the sword girded on the thigh of the most Mighty one, the crown of pure gold, the sceptre of righteousness, the throne of judgment. In Christian Art, as the conventional representation

General

of the Wise Men of the East as three kings is founded on the Kings of Tharsis, Saba, and Arabia of Ps. lxxii. 10-11, so the use of the Pelican as a symbol of Christ is guided by the comparison to the pelican in the wilderness of Ps. cii. 6. A Psalm (li., verse 1) supplied the " neck verse " of mediæval justice, which afforded the test of benefit of clergy. In the Psalms ancient families have sought their mottoes, such as the " Fortuna mea in bello campo " (Ps. xvi. 7) of the Beauchamps, the " Nisi Dominus frustra " (Ps. cxxvii. 1) of the Comptons, or the " Non dormit qui custodit " (Ps. cxxi. 3) of the Coghills. Ancient trade guilds have found in the Psalms the legend of their charter of incorporation, like the " Omnia subjecisti sub pedibus, oves et boves " (Ps. viii. 6-7) of the Butchers' Company. From the Psalms Edinburgh takes its motto of " Nisi Dominus frustra " (Ps. cxxvii., verse 1). From the same source the University of Oxford took its " Dominus illuminatio mea " (Ps. xxvii. 1), and the University of Durham its " Fundamenta ejus " (Ps. lxxxvii. 1). Under the sanction, as it were, of a text from the Psalms (" The earth is the Lord's, and all that therein is; the compass of the world, and they that dwell therein," Ps. xxiv., verse 1), was held the Great Exhibition of 1851. " Except the Lord build the house, they labour in vain that build it " (Ps. cxxvii., verse 1), is the verse chosen by Smeaton for the Eddystone Lighthouse. To innumerable almshouses, hospitals, public buildings and private houses, the Psalms have supplied inscriptions. To coins they have furnished legends, like the coins of the Black Prince in Guienne, " Dominus adjutor meus et protector meus," etc. (Ps. xxviii. 8); the florin of Edward III. in 1344, " Domine, ne in furore arguas me " (Ps. vi. 1); or the shilling of Edward VI. in 1549, " Inimicos ejus induam confusione " (Ps. cxxxii. 19). On sword-blades, trenchers, and rings, verses from the Psalms are inscribed. By texts from the Psalms, sun-dials all over the world enforce the solemn lesson of the passage of time. Here are the " Dies mei sicut umbra declinaverunt " (Ps. cii. 11) of San Michele at Venice, or Langen Schwalbach; the English version, " My days are gone like a shadow," at Arbroath, and St. Hilda's, Whitby; and the same idea, " L'homme est semblable à la vanité; ses jours sont comme une ombre qui passe" (Ps. cxliv. 4), at St. Brelade's, in Jersey.

With a psalm we are baptised, and married, and buried; with a psalm we begin, and realise to the full, and end, our earthly existence. With what strange power do the familiar words of the Book come home to us as we grow older! Here are verses, over which have stumbled, forty years ago, the childish lips of brothers, severed from us by years of change and absence, yet now, by force of association with the Psalms, seated once again by our side in the broken circle of home. Here again is a passage, which, with trembling voice and beating heart, we read aloud by the deathbed of one, with whose passing the light faded and our own lives grew grey, and void, and lampless. Yet still it is to the Psalms, even when they wound us most, that we turn for help and comfort. As life's evening closes round us, and as the winged thoughts, that we have made our own, sweep in from the horizon of our memories, no words come home to us with swifter, surer flight than those of the Psalms.

To weary travellers of every condition and at every period of history, the Psalms have been rivers of refreshment and wells of consolation. They alone have known no limitations to a particular age, country, or form of faith. In them the spirit of controversy and the war of creeds are forgotten: love of the Psalter has united the Anglican and Roman Catholic, Presbyterian and Nonconformist. Over the parched fields of theological strife the breath of the Psalms sweeps, fresh and balmy. For centuries the supplications of Christians, clothed in the language of the Psalter, have risen like incense to the altar-throne of God; in them have been expressed, from age to age, the devotion and the theology of religious communions that, in all else, were at deadly feud. Surviving all the changes in Church and State, in modes of thought, in habits of life, in forms of expression, the Psalms, as devotional exercises, have sunk into our hearts; as sublime poetry, have fired our imaginations; as illustrations of human life, have arrested our minds and stored our memories.

In the Psalms the vast hosts of suffering humanity have found, from the time of Jonah to the present day, the deepest expression of their hopes and fears. As our Lord Himself died with the words of a psalm upon His lips, so the first martyr, Stephen, had used the words thus hallowed. So also, in prison at Philippi, Paul and Silas encouraged themselves by singing psalms throughout the night. It was by the Psalms that the anguish, wrung from tortured lips on the cross, at the stake, on the scaffold, and in the dungeon, has been healed and solaced. Strong in the strength that they impart, young boys and timid girls have risen from their knees in the breathless amphitheatre, thronged with its quivering multitudes, and boldly faced the lions. Neither the rudeness of mosaic art, nor the lapse of sixteen centuries, has obliterated the radiant smile of triumph, with which St. Agnes and her companions, on the walls of S. Apollinare Nuovo at Ravenna, press forward to greet Him, for whose sake they gave their young and tender bodies to be tortured. With the Psalms upon their tongues, myriads have died—now in quiet sick-rooms, surrounded by all who have loved them best in life—now alone, and far from home and kindred—now hemmed in by fierce enemies howling for their blood. Thus in the Psalms there are pages which are stained with the life-blood of martyrs, and wet with the tears of saints; others, which are illuminated by the victories of weak humanity over suffering and fear and temptation; others, which glow with the brightness of heroic constancy and almost superhuman courage. Over the familiar words are written, as it were in a palimpsest, the heart-stirring romances of spiritual chivalry, the most moving tragedies of human life and action.

How much, or how little, of our religion is a matter of habit, or a personal acquisition, this is no place to inquire. But assuredly the Psalms gain in interest and power from their associations with human history, and from their use by our fellow-men in every form of trial which can confront humanity. They have inspired some of the noblest hymns in our language. Their rendering into verse has occupied many of the most gifted men in the history of our nation—knights of chivalry, like Sir Philip Sidney, aided by his sister, Margaret, Countess of Pembroke; men of science, like Lord Bacon, in whose version the philosopher overmasters the poet; classical scholars, like George Sandys, one of the most successful of early versifiers; courtiers, like Sir Thomas Wyatt; ambassadors, like Sir Thomas Smith, Sir Henry Wotton, or Hookham Frere; distinguished prelates, such as Archbishop Parker, or Bishop Ken, or Bishop Hall, or Bishop King; queens and kings, like Elizabeth, or James I.; sturdy Puritans, such as Francis Rous; Cromwellian captains, like Thomas, Lord Fairfax, or George Wither, whose sweet vein of early poetry was soured by the vinegar of politics and polemics; poets, like Crashaw, Phinehas Fletcher, Henry Vaughan, Burns, Cowper, or Milton, whose versions, with one exception, fall below the standard which we should have expected his lyric genius and devotional fervour to attain; parish priests, like George Herbert and John Keble; heroes of the Dunciad, like Sir Richard Blackmore and Luke Milbourne; masters of prose, like Addison; Methodists, like Charles Wesley; Nonconformists, such as Isaac Watts, whose version of Ps. xc., " O God, our help in ages past," is perhaps the finest hymn in the English language.

Poets and men of letters, like Dante and Camoens, Shakespeare and Cervantes, Wordsworth, Walter Scott, Carlyle and Ruskin, Heine and Herder, Pascal and Lamartine, have acknowledged the unrivalled charm of the Psalter. From the Psalms hymn-writers have drawn their most striking inspirations; to turn them into verse has been the occupation of men of all nationalities, professions, and pursuits at every period of history; their language, imagery, and ideas have fascinated men of the highest poetic genius. But besides the indirect influence which they have thus exercised on literature, the Psalms may be said to have created a literature of their own. Of all that mass of writings in which is recorded the inner life of Christians, they are the precursors and the pattern. They are the parents of those religious autobiographies which, even in literary and psychological interest, rival, if they do not surpass, the *Confessions* of Rousseau, or the *Truth and Fiction* of Goethe. From the Psalms are descended books like the *Confessions* of St. Augustine, the *Imitation of Christ* of Thomas à Kempis, the *Grace Abounding* of John Bunyan, the *Devotions* of Bishop Andrewes, the *Thoughts* of Blaise Pascal.

In the pages of such works the tone and spirit of the Psalms are faithfully represented; whether in devotional exercises, in guides to the spiritual life, in meditations and counsels on holy living and holy dying, or in the unconscious records of the personal history of religious minds, their influence is everywhere present. They are the inspiration of that soliloquy at the throne of God, in which Augustine revealed his soul before a world which is yet listening, as for fifteen centuries it has listened, to the absolute truthfulness of his *Confessions*. They are the wings which lifted Thomas à Kempis out of his white-washed cell, bore him above the flat meadows of St. Agnes, and floated heavenwards those mystic musings of the *Imitations* which thrilled with mingled awe and hope the heart of Maggie Tulliver. They lent their height and depth to the religion of Bishop Andrewes, whose private prayers, in their elevation above doctrinal controversies, in their manliness and reality, and in the comprehensiveness of their horizon, seem to translate, for individual use in the closet, the public worship of the Anglican Church. They were the live coal which touched the lips of John Bunyan, and transformed the unlettered tinker into a genius and a poet, as, with a pen of iron and in letters of fire, he wrote the record of his passage from death to life. They sharpened the keen sight with which Pascal pierced to the heart of truth, and nerved the courage with which he confronted the mysteries of the vision that his lucid intellect conjured up before his eyes. Thus the Psalms, apart from their own transcendent beauty and universal truth, have enriched the world by the creation of a literature which, century after century, has not only commanded the admiration of sceptics, but elevated the characters of innumerable believers, encouraged their weariness, consoled their sorrows, lifted their doubts, and guided their wavering footsteps.

So far I have spoken mainly of the influence of the Psalms on human thought. But their workings in the sphere of human action have been equally striking and equally universal. No fragment of the glorious temples at Jerusalem has survived the lapse of time; but the imperishable hymns of the Jewish worship rule the hearts of men with more than their pristine power, and still continue to inspire and elevate the conduct and devotions of successive generations of mankind. Fathers of the early Church, like Origen, Athanasius and Jerome, Basil, Ambrose and Augustine—apostles of British Christianity, such as Columba, Cuthbert, Wilfrid, Dunstan, and Bede—mediæval saints, like Bernard, Francis of Assisi, or Thomas of Villanova—statesmen, like Ximenes, Burghley, and Gladstone—have testified to the universal truth and beauty of the Psalms. With a psalm upon their lips died Wyclif, Hus, and Jerome of Prague, Luther and Melancthon. Philosophers, such as Bacon and Locke and Hamilton; men of science, like Humboldt and Romanes; among missionaries, Xavier, Martyn, Duff, Livingstone, Mackay and Hannington; explorers, like Columbus; scholars, like Casaubon and Salmasius; earthly potentates, like Charlemagne, Vladimir Monomachus, Hildebrand, Louis IX., Henry V., Catherine de Medicis, Charles V., Henry of Navarre, and Mary, Queen of Scots—have found in the Psalms their inspiration in life, their strength in peril, or their support in death.

To collect together some of the countless instances in which the Psalms have thus guided, controlled and sustained the lives of men and women in all ages of human history, and at all crises of their fate, is the purpose of this book.

CHAPTER II

EARLY AGES OF CHRISTIANITY

The Psalms in services, ceremonies, and the catacombs; use in persecution—Crispin and Crispinian, Theodore the Martyr, the Saracen convert, the Emperor Maurice; in public worship; in ordinary life —Origen, the family of Gregory Nazianzen, Monica; on deathbeds —Basil the Great, Ambrose, Paulinus of Nola, Cyril of Alexandria; influence of the Psalms in Monasticism—the Egyptian Anchorites, Basil and monastic communities of the East, Athanasius and the West, Jerome and Paula, Martin of Tours; the Psalms in action —struggle between Church and State—Athanasius and Constantius, Basil and Valens, Ambrose and Theodosius; the Psalms in human thought—*Confessions* of Augustine.

THOUGH the influence of the Psalms has been confined to no age, no nation, no class, and no creed, there have been special periods when they have spoken with peculiar force. This was been particularly the case in times of persecution, when circumstances gave to the words an immediate personal application. Such a period was the infancy of Christianity. Secretly, under cover of night, or at early dawn, children cast out by their parents, slaves oppressed by their masters, citizens suspected by their neighbours, subjects proscribed by their rulers, gathered for prayer and praise in the catacombs of great cities, in workshops, or in the upper rooms of retired houses on the outskirts of towns. Of their religious services the Psalms formed a conspicuous part, and special Psalms were soon appropriated to particular occasions, such as the 63rd for the morning and the 141st for the evening worship. These little companies of wool-workers, cobblers, fullers, craftsmen, and slaves—" the most vulgar and illiterate of mankind "—with whom assembled a handful of persons of higher rank, centurions, government officials, and ladies of noble birth, met together in danger of their lives. The ceremony which admitted them into this proscribed and perilous company found its symbol in a psalm. The hart

(Ps. xlii., verse 1) was the emblem of those thirsting souls who, in the cooling streams of the baptismal font, drank freely of the fountain of eternal life. Once admitted, they were as " sheep appointed to be slain "; but the Lord was their Shepherd, and their trust in Him, conquering their fears, still speaks in the rude pictures on the walls of subterranean Rome.

The language of the Psalms was ever on the lips of those who, in the early history of Christianity, suffered violent deaths for or in the faith. A Psalm (xxiii.) was fitly chosen by Augustine as the hymn of martyrs. It was in the words of Ps. cxv., verses 4 and 5, " Their idols are silver and gold," etc., that Christians defied the imperial order to sacrifice to Cæsar, and it was with a psalm that they met the torturer or the executioner. At Soissons, for instance, in the Diocletian persecution of 288, two brothers, Crispin and Crispinian, afterwards the patrons of shoemakers, suffered torture and death. For love of Christianity, they had renounced the honours of their birth, and made shoes for the poor. In their prolonged torments they were sustained by the words of Ps. lxxix., verses 9-10, " Help us, O God of our salvation, for the glory of Thy Name. . . . Wherefore do the heathen say, Where is now their God? " Their bodies, thrown into the river, were carried to the sea. The waves, so runs the legend, for love of the Blessed Feet which once had walked upon them, wafted the mangled bodies of His martyrs to the shores of Romney Marsh, where the inhabitants received them in joy, and built in their honour the church of Lydd. Theodore the Martyr, the young soldier who rashly burned to the ground the temple of the Mother of the Gods at Amasea in 306, found strength to endure the torture by chanting Ps. xxxiv., verse 1, " I will alway give thanks unto the Lord; His praise shall ever be in my mouth." Another illustration is the story told by Gregory of Decapolis. A noble Saracen, converted by a vision of the Lamb of God, sought a Christian teacher, learnt the Psalter by heart, and returned to his native land to preach the faith of Christ. But his countrymen refused his message, and stoned him to death. In his agony he repeated Ps. xiii., verse 3, " Lighten my eyes, that I sleep not in death." It was, again, a psalm that encouraged

Early Ages of Christianity

the Emperor Maurice to bow to the will of God. During the twenty years in which he had ruled the Roman Empire, he had shown many of the virtues which, in 582, marked him out to succeed Tiberius II. But the army turned against him, and in 602 he fled, with his wife and children, to Chalcedon, to escape the fury of the deformed and disfigured Phocas. He did not long remain in safety. By order of Phocas, he and his five sons were seized and executed. He was the last to die. As, one by one, the boys were murdered before his eyes, the father cried aloud, with each stroke of the sword, "Righteous art Thou, O Lord, and true is Thy judgement" (Ps. cxix., verse 137). Firm in his adherence to truth, he rejected the kindly fraud of the nurse, who gave her own child to save one of the royal princes, and thus supplied to Corneille the plot of *Heraclius*.

As Christianity spread and became a power, the Psalms occupy a larger, and still larger, space. Their use in public worship varied in different Churches. Custom prescribed the portions that should be read, or sung, or expounded; but they formed the substance of most of the daily services. "When other passages of Scripture," writes Ambrose, "are used in church, the words are drowned in the noise of talking. But when the Psalter is read, all are dumb." Still more striking was their use in daily life, as an expression of the feeling that God was everywhere present. Clement of Alexandria, in his *Stromata* (vii., sect. 7), says, "We praise God as we till our lands; we sing to Him hymns as we are sailing." Sidonius Apollinaris describes how the boatmen, toiling with bent backs to urge their laden barges against the stream, sang psalms till the river-banks echoed their hallelujahs. "Any one possessed of his five wits," writes Ambrose, "should blush with shame if he did not begin the day with a psalm, since even the tiniest birds open and close the day with sweet songs of holy devotion." "Of other Scriptures," says Theodore of Mopsuestia, "most men know nothing. But the Psalms are repeated in private houses, in streets, and market-places, by those who have learned them by heart, and feel the soothing power of their divine melodies." When Paula and Eustochium wrote from Bethlehem their famous letter to Marcella, they exhort her to flee from the tumults and distractions of Rome to the solitude of Christ's village. Here, they say, is the quiet of country life, unbroken save by the chanting of the Psalms. The ploughman, leaning on his plough-handle, sings in them his praises to God; the sweating reaper lightens his labours with the chanting of the Psalms; the vine-dresser, as he prunes his vines, raises one of the songs of David. "The Psalms are our poetry, our love-songs, our pastorals, our implements of husbandry." [1]

If any records were preserved, it would probably be found that the Psalms profoundly influenced Christian homes in the early ages of the Church. But glimpses of the inner life of families are as rare as they would be precious. In the boyhood of Origen, one significant fact is recorded which proves that the Psalms had their part in the education of children. Jerome says that the boy learnt Hebrew so well that he vied with his mother, who was possibly of Jewish origin, in the singing of psalms. Better known, perhaps, than that of any other Christian household, is the domestic life of Gregory Nazianzen, the poet of Eastern Christendom, and one of the greatest of its orators and theologians. Gregory's mother, Nonna, a woman of ardent piety, born of a Christian family, and carefully trained in the faith, was "a housewife after Solomon's own heart"—so her son describes her—"submissive to her husband, yet not ashamed to be his guide and teacher." It was Nonna's constant prayer that her husband, Gregory, should become a convert, for, though a man of high character and exemplary life, he was a pagan. A dream inspired by a psalm, helped her to gain her heart's desire. Pagan though he was, her husband seems to have known the Psalms, for he dreamed that he was singing the words, "I was glad when they said unto me, We will go into the House of the Lord" (Ps. cxxii.). The impression was too deep to pass away when he awoke. After a short preparation, he was baptised, and eventually became, and for forty-five years remained, Bishop of Nazianzus (329-74). Gorgonia, the daughter of Gregory and Nonna, though not baptised till a short time before her death, had lived a Christian life. She

---

[1] Hæc sunt in hac provincia carmina, hæ, ut vulgo dicitur, amatoriæ cantationes, hic pastorum sibilus, hæc arma culturæ.—"Letter to Marcella," *Palestine Pilgrims' Text Society* [12].

had long felt, says her brother, a desire to " depart and be with Jesus." So great was the longing, that it produced a presentiment of the approach of her death, and an anticipation of the time when it would take place. The looked-for day found her aged parents, her husband, and her daughter, gathered round her bedside. When she had taken her leave of each in turn, the bystanders thought she was already dead. But once more her lips were seen to move, and the watchers, stooping over the bed, heard the words, familiar by their use as an evening psalm, and fitted to the close of her earthly day, " I will lay me down in peace, and take my rest " (Ps. iv. 9). So died Gorgonia. The verse, it may be added, was loved by Luther. Writing from Coburg to Ludwig Seuffel, he asked him to compose for him a requiem. From his youth, he said, he had always loved the concluding verses of the 4th Psalm. But, as he learned to understand its full meaning, and as he hourly prepared for death, the last verse became more and more dear to him, and he would gladly sing, and hear sung, those soothing words, " Ich lieg und schlafe ganz mit Frieden."

Yet another instance is afforded by the death of Monica, the mother of St. Augustine, whose patient perseverance in prayer, and reward in the life of her son, have comforted thousands of mothers in all ages of the world's history. On Easter Sunday, 387, Augustine had been baptised by Ambrose at Milan. In the summer he set out to return to Africa with Monica. At Ostia they paused to recruit from the fatigues of their long journey, and prepare for the coming voyage. Mother and son were leaning on the ledge of a window, which looked upon the garden where they lodged. Alone together, away from the crowd, God in his secret ways having so ordered it, they talked of the eternal life of the saints, and of what sort it should be, " panting with the lips of our souls for those heavenly streams of Thy fountain, the fountain of life which is with Thee." It is the moment chosen by Ary Scheffer for his famous picture:

> " The dear consenting hands are knit,
> And either face, as there they sit,
> Is lifted as to something seen
> Beyond the blue serene."

To the mother it seemed that the purpose of her life was

achieved, now that she had seen her one longing gratified and her son baptised a Christian. Five or six days later, while they were still waiting to embark, Monica was struck down by fever, and died in the fifty-sixth year of her age. It was in the Psalms that Augustine found comfort in his sorrow. When the first gush of weeping was over, his friend, Euodius took up the Psalter, and began to sing, the whole household joining with him, Psalm ci. " My song shall be of mercy and judgement: unto Thee, O Lord, will I sing," etc.

Forty-three years later, in his own city of Hippo, closely besieged by the Vandals, Augustine himself died. " It was," says his biographer, Possidius, " a plain and barely furnished room in which he lay. The seven Penitential Psalms were, by his orders, written out, and placed where he could see them from his bed. These he looked at and read in his days of sickness, weeping often and sore." So, with his eyes fixed on the Psalms, Augustine passed to his rest, August 28th, 430. It was with the words of a Psalm upon his lips, " Into Thy hands I commend my spirit " (Ps. xxxi., verse 6), that Basil the Great breathed his last at Cesarea, January 1st, 379, his deathbed surrounded by citizens who were ready to shorten their own lives, if so they might lengthen the days of their Bishop. In 397, Ambrose lay dying at Milan. He had, as is well known, introduced into the Western Church the antiphonal method of chanting the Psalms which was practised in the East. Almost his last labour was a Commentary on Ps. xliv.: " It is painful to wait so long for the day when mortality shall be swallowed up of Life; but, happily the torch of the Word of God does not quit mine eyes." He died as he reached verse 23: " Up, Lord, why sleepest thou: awake and be not absent from us for ever." Paulinus, Bishop of Nola (353-431), as the hour for Vespers approached, and the lamps were being lighted in the church which he had built, stretched forth his hands and passed away, repeating the words, " I have ordained a lantern for mine Anointed." (Ps. cxxxii. 18). With the same words on his lips, in June 444, died Cyril, Archbishop of Alexandria, whose life-long struggle for the purity of the Christian faith has been overshadowed by his alleged complicity in the hideous crime of the murder of Hypatia.

But if we pass from domestic or deathbed scenes to episodes of a more public character, the recorded instances of the influence of the Psalms are multiplied. No figure in the early history of the Church is more attractive than that of Origen (185-253). The son of a martyr, the master of disciples who braved martyrdom, himself a confessor who endured imprisonment and the torture of the chain, the collar and the rack, he dominated the century as much by his character as by his genius. In his childhood, as is told above, he vied with his mother in singing the Psalms, and his commentary upon them, his notes, and his homilies bore witness to their abiding influence on his mind. During the persecution of Severus, his father, Leonides, was beheaded, encouraged by Origen, then a lad of seventeen, to die without thought of those he left behind. The lad himself was only prevented from sharing his father's fate by being imprisoned in his own home. In after years, the persecutions which he endured from the State as a Christian scarcely exceeded those which, as a heretic, he suffered from the Church. Yet friends were as enthusiastic as enemies were bitter. Even those who compared him to Satan paid homage to his gifts by admitting that, if he had fallen from Heaven, his fall was like the lightning flash. Driven from Alexandria, he travelled from place to place, fascinating some by the splendour of his teaching, terrifying others by the boldness of his speculations. So journeying, as the story is told, he came to Jerusalem. Somewhere in his wanderings, even his intrepid spirit had recoiled from dread of torture. He had consented to sacrifice to Cæsar; incense had been thrust into his hand, which was forced over the altar. Remorse overwhelmed him, when, at Jerusalem, he was entreated to preach. Taking the Psalter in his hand, he prayed, and, opening the book, read the words of Ps. l., verse 16, " But unto the ungodly said God: Why dost thou preach My laws, and takest My covenant in thy mouth? " He shut the book, sat down speechless, and burst into tears. " The prophet David himself shut the door of my lips," was his bitter lament, as he applied to his apostasy the verse (Ps. lxxx. 13), " The wild boar out of the wood doth root it up; and the wild beasts of the field devour it."

As the fourth century dawns, the long struggle between Paganism and Christianity entered its final stage. On the death-agony of the ancient faith, still enshrined among us by lingering superstitions and a thousand graceful fictions in art and literature, history is comparatively silent. But its downfall was marked by a period of moral relaxation and social corruption, which fostered the belief that it was the highest duty of a Christian to shun a polluted world. The longing to flee away and be at rest from the fury of persecution, and from the contamination of the heathen, encouraged the growing feeling. Solitude tempted some men as a refuge from spiritual danger; to others it appealed as a bolder challenge to the powers of evil; to yet another class it seemed to offer at once a shelter from the world, and the supreme test of self-denial. Of the ascetic principle, the most famous example was Antony (251-356), born in the lifetime of Origen, known throughout civilisation by the pictures of Caracci, Guido, and Salvator, and by the quaint legends that have gathered round his name. The influence which he and his followers exercised upon Christendom, and the impulse which they gave to the monastic life, are almost incalculable. A psalm was at once the weapon, the pæan, and the rule, of two of the earliest leaders in the new movement.

Rich, young, and an orphan, Antony gave all his possessions to the poor, and devoted himself to the ascetic life. Unlike the anchorites who had preceded him, he retired to a distance from his fellow-men. To combine in himself the special virtues, to which other ascetics had respectively attained, was his constant effort. To be as prayerful as one, as courteous as another, as patient of vigil and fast as a third—this was the rivalry on which his ambitions were centred. There were times, for he was still young, when his enthusiasm failed, his courage flagged, and the temptations of the world and the flesh swept over him with all their storms. Yet still his faith triumphed over every assault. The Psalms were the weapons with which he met the evil tendencies that, to his overwrought vision, presented themselves in material and often grotesque forms. It was, for example, with the words, " Some put their trust in chariots, and some in horses: but we will remember the Name of the

Early Ages of Christianity

Lord our God " (Ps. xx., verse 7), that he put Satan to flight. It was with a psalm that he sang his pæan of victory. So sorely beset was he within the ruined tower where he lived, so vehement were the sounds of the strife, that the multitude, which had gathered to see and hear him, believed that the saint was attacked by the people of the country. Suddenly the clamour ceased. High and clear rose the voice of Antony alone, as he chanted Ps. lxviii. in triumph at his victory over his spiritual foes.

Is Browning's use of the same words an echo of St. Antony? As Giuseppe Caponsacchi watches by the side of Pompilia, hears her moaning in her restless fevered dreams, and sees her wave away some evil spirit that threatens her, he cries:

> " Oh, if the God, that only can, would help!
> Am I his priest with power to cast out fiends?
> ' Let God arise and all his enemies
> Be scattered!' By morn, there was peace, no sigh
> Out of the deep sleep." [1]

Among Antony's most distinguished disciples was Pambo. Eminent for his austerities, he had taken for his special rule of life the words of Ps. xxxix., verse 1, " I said, I will take heed to my ways, that I offend not in my tongue," and, in his constant effort to keep the door of his lips, he is said to have excelled even Antony himself. Half in banter, half in earnest, Browning describes Pambo,[2] " arms crossed, brow bent, thought-immersed," from youth to age pondering over the verse, and finding in the seeming simplicity of the command enough to absorb every faculty of mind and body, so long as life endured.

The influence of Antony and other hermits spread from Africa to Asia. Monastic communities multiplied rapidly, and in their religious services the Psalms held the chief place. Of such communities in Eastern Christendom, Basil (329-79) was the chief organiser. The secluded place, in which he himself fixed his own temporary retreat, lay on the banks of the river Iris, near Neo-Cesarea in Pontus—a spot as beautiful in his eyes as " Calypso's Island." He describes the devotional exercises which his communities of monks

[1] *The Ring and the Book*, Giuseppe Caponsacchi, 1300-1304.
[2] *Jocoseria*, Pambo.

practised. While it was yet night, the brethren rose, as in the days of persecution Christians had risen for concealment, entered the house of prayer, and, after confession to God, turned to the singing of psalms. Now, divided two by two, they answered each other; now, one led the chant, the rest following. Thus passed the night till the day began to dawn. As morning broke, they all in common, with one mouth and from one heart, lifted to the Lord the Psalm of Confession (Ps. cxviii.). As the day began, so it ended.

Nor was the fame of the Egyptian anchorites confined to the East. It crossed the sea to Europe. In Roman society, as the fourth century advanced, two opposite tendencies were equally marked. A startling contrast was presented between the unbridled luxury of the Imperial City and its inclination to the solitude and severity of monastic life. From 340 to 343 Athanasius, an exile and a fugitive, had found a refuge at Rome. The spell of his master-mind, his enthusiasm for the monks of the desert, the life of Antony, and the presence of two Egyptian anchorites, seized the imagination of Roman patricians. Slumbering fire leaped into flame, as Athanasius revealed the grandeur of human self-abnegation, and he thus became, through Antony, the spiritual ancestor of Western monasticism.

A few years later, Marcella, a young and wealthy Roman widow, who had, as a child, heard from the lips of Athanasius descriptions of the Thebaid and of Antony, bade adieu to the world, and made of her palace on the Aventine Mount her cell, and of its garden her desert. Round her gathered a little knot of women, like-minded with herself, who devoted their lives to the study of the Scriptures, psalmody, prayer and good works. That they might sing the Psalms in the native tongue, they learned Hebrew; that they might study the Gospels, they learned Greek.

Among the most illustrious of these women was the high-born Paula, whose ancestors were the Scipios and the Gracchi, and in whose veins ran the blood of the half-fabulous rulers of Sparta and Mycene. She and her daughters, Blesilla, Paulina, and Eustochium, and her grand-daughter Paula, breathe and speak and move in the glowing pages of Jerome. To Paula's daughter, Eustochium, is addressed the first code of Christian virginity; to her step-daughter, Lœta, is penned the first treatise on the Christian education of women.

Of the family of Paula, Jerome was at once the spiritual guide and historian. Born in 346, at Stridon in Dalmatia, on the southern slopes of the Illyrian Alps, Jerome had studied at Rome. After his baptism he had settled at Aquileia, the Venice of the fourth century, the great seaport of the Adriatic, a city situated, as the Bordeaux Itinerary shows, on the highway by which pilgrims travelled from the West to the Holy Land. There his enthusiasm for study and his inclination towards asceticism grew stronger and stronger. His two favourite texts were, " But his delight is in the law of the Lord; and in His law will he exercise himself day and night " (Ps. i., verse 2); and, " O that I had wings like a dove! for then would I flee away, and be at rest " (Ps. lv., verse 6). Where, except in solitude, could he gratify his longing or follow the law of the Lord night and day? At last, as the Egyptian anchorites had fled from the lusts and anarchy of the world to find rest in the silence and discipline of the desert, so Jerome fled to the depths of the desert of Chalcis. In 382 he came to Rome, emaciated and weakened by the austerities of his life, but with his fiery impetuous spirit yet untamed. At Rome, he revised from the Septuagint the Latin version of the Psalms. There, too, he became the teacher of the devout ladies who assembled on the Aventine Mount at the house of Marcella.

In 385 he left Rome, where he had made many friends and not a few enemies. Convinced, as he says, that he had tried in vain to " sing the Lord's song in a strange land " (Ps. cxxxvii., verse 4), he embarked for Palestine. After him sailed Paula, heartbroken at the death of Blesilla, and with Paula went her surviving unmarried daughter, Eustochium. They met Jerome at Antioch, wandered through Palestine, visited the Solitaries in the Nitrian desert, and finally settled at Bethlehem. There were built a monastery, of which Jerome became the head; a convent, presided over by Paula; a church, and a *hospice* for pilgrims. At Bethlehem in his grotto—his paradise, as he calls it—close to the traditional site of the Nativity, Jerome laboured with persistent strenuous energy till his death in 420.

At Bethlehem, in this realised " City of the Saints," Paula and Eustochium lived and died. Their efforts to induce Marcella to leave Rome and join them in the Holy Land, had failed. In vain Jerome had supported their appeal with a letter, which closes with the words of Psalm lxxiii., verse 24, " For ourselves, who are here," he says, " we think it good to trust to God for all, to rest every hope on Him; that when we exchange the poverty of this world for ' the riches of Heaven,' we may be able to cry with David, ' Whom have I in Heaven but Thee? and there is none upon earth that I desire in comparison of Thee.' " But though Marcella still remained on the Aventine Mount, there gathered at Bethlehem a community of women, who sang the Psalter through in their daily services, and were pledged, among other rules, to learn it by heart. Gradually the strength of Paula failed. In 403 she lay on her deathbed. Her daughter, Eustochium, watched over her with the tenderest care, praying, while Paula slept, that she might depart from life before her mother. As her last moments approached, the watchers heard Paula murmur the words of those Psalms which were seldom far from her lips: " Oh how amiable are thy dwellings, Thou Lord of Hosts!" (Ps. lxxxiv. 1); " Lord I have loved the habitation of Thy house and the place where Thine honour dwelleth " (Ps. xxvi. 8); " I had rather be a doorkeeper in the House of my God, than to dwell in the tents of ungodliness " (Ps. lxxxiv., verse 11). When the last of the verses was ended, she began again with the first. To the end, with closed eyes, and faintly moving lips, she continued to repeat them, and so passed away on the 26th of January 404. Round the body gathered Christian Palestine. Monks and nuns from monasteries or convents, hermits from their solitary cells, bishops from the surrounding dioceses, the poor, the widowed, and the orphans, flocked to pay to the dead their last tribute of affection. Night and day, continuously for three days, the Psalms were chanted round the bier in Greek and Hebrew, Latin and Syriac. On the fourth day, Paula was buried in a rock-hewn grave, close to the birthplace of Our Lord and the grotto where Jerome laboured.

Sixteen years later (420), died Jerome himself. In the

interval Eustochium had died, but her place was taken by her niece, Paula, the grand-daughter of the elder Paula. Legend has fastened on the strange spiritual romance, which linked with Jerome three generations of a noble Roman family as the guardians of his life. In the fancy of mediæval art, the place of the three women is taken by the lion, whose wounded paw was cured by Jerome in the deserts of Chalcis, and who in gratitude became the healer's protector and faithful servant.

Years before the death of Jerome, Martin of Tours (316–96), whose influence on French history has been accepted by the most secular historians, whose fame not only spread to the most distant lands, but is commemorated in scores of quaint legends in provincial France, had founded a monastery in Gaul. The young soldier, who, at Amiens had divided his cloak with a naked shivering beggar, saw in a dream, Christ Himself clad in the halved garment. Accepting the dream as a call to religion, he was baptised, left the army, and enlisted under St. Hilary, Bishop of Poitiers, as a soldier of the Cross of Christ. During his friend's exile, he himself settled near Milan; but on Hilary's return to Gaul, Martin followed. In order to be near the bishop, and also in order to preach on the great Roman road from Poitiers to Saintes, he built the wooden hut at Ligugé, on the river Clain, five miles from Hilary's see, which is regarded as the earliest of French monastic institutions. By a strange coincidence, Rabelais, twelve centuries later, found refuge close to the Abbey Church of Ligugé, the cradle of that system which, in its decadence, he keenly satirised. From Ligugé the fame of Martin spread to Tours, whose inhabitants were eager to have him for their bishop. Enticed from his monastery by a trick, Martin visited the city. Crowds had collected for the election. The vast majority favoured Martin; a few led by a bishop, named Defensor, objected to the meanness of his personal appearance, his unkempt hair, his squalid garments. It was by a verse from the Psalms that the election was decided. A bystander, opening the Psalter at hazard, read the verse, " Out of the mouth of very babes and sucklings hast Thou ordained strength, because of Thine enemies; *That Thou mightest still the enemy and the avenger*" (Ps. viii., verse 2). In the version then in use, the words are, "Ut destruas inimicum et defensorem." The words were hailed as an omen. Defensor and his supporters were confounded, and Martin was consecrated Bishop of Tours (372). Two miles from the city he founded his *majus monasterium*, now Marmoutier, which eclipsed the fame of Ligugé, and became the most celebrated of French monasteries.

Thus in Africa, Asia, and Europe a great movement had begun which, every year, assumed larger proportions. In the fourth century, multitudes of men and women, in solitary cells or monastic communities, sought a retreat from a world of conflict, change and persecution. That this should have been the case is not surprising. The time was one when the *Te Deum* of victory alternated with the *Miserere* of defeat, when the secular power first accepted religion as its ally, then endeavoured to employ it as a servant, and finally acknowledged it as a master. Among the great ecclesiastics of the century no names stand higher than those of Athanasius, the impersonation of purity of faith; or of Basil, the upholder of order and discipline in the Church; or of Ambrose, the champion of ecclesiastical authority. With striking scenes in the lives of each, the Psalms are inseparably connected.

In October 346, Athanasius returned to Alexandria from his second exile. The people streamed forth to meet him "like another Nile." Every point of vantage was crowded with eager spectators. The air, fragrant with the smoke of incense, and bright with the blaze of bonfires, rang with cheers and the clapping of hands. Nearly nine years of peace followed in the troubled life of Athanasius. But the interlude was only the lull which preceded the storm. The Emperor Constantius was in the hands of his Arian courtiers; a great majority of the Council of Milan (355) had condemned Athanasius; and it became evident that some violence would be attempted against the archbishop in his own city of Alexandria. The Psalms had been his constant study. His *Exposition of the Psalms*, his *Titles of the Psalms*, as well as his frequent allusions to them in his writings, prove how deep was their hold upon his mind. His favourite Psalm was the 72nd. "Against all assaults upon thy body," he says,

Early Ages of Christianity 23

"thine estate, thy soul, thy reputation, against all temptations, tribulations, plots and slanderous reports, say this Psalm." So now, in the hour of his own and his people's danger, he turned to a psalm for help.

At midnight, on Thursday, February 8th, 356, Athanasius was holding a vigil in the Church of St. Theonas. The building was thronged with worshippers preparing for the service of the morrow. Suddenly the church was beset by soldiers, and the clash of arms resounded in the precincts. " I thought it not right," says Athanasius, " at a time of such disorder, to leave my people. Rather I preferred to be the first to meet the danger." At the extreme east end of the church was the archbishop's throne. Sitting down upon it, Athanasius ordered the deacon to read Psalm cxxxvi., and all the people to respond with " *For His mercy endureth for ever*," and then to withdraw to their homes. The act of faith was hardly finished, when the doors were forced, and the soldiers rushed in, discharging their arrows, brandishing their swords and spears in the dim light of the building, as they crowded up the nave. " The clergy and the people," continues Athanasius, " prayed me to escape. I refused to move till all were in safety. So I stood up, called for prayer, and bade the people leave. Many had gone; others were trying to follow, when some of the monks and of the clergy came to my throne and carried me away. So then I passed through the crowd of soldiers unseen, and escaped, giving thanks to God that I had not betrayed my people, but had secured their safety before I thought of my own." But Athanasius only describes that part of the scene which had passed before his eyes. In the buildings that surrounded the church, there were fighting and slaughter. The dawn of day revealed lifeless bodies, and blood-stained steps and passages; and Alexandria mourned not only the disappearance of the beloved archbishop, but the murder of many of her citizens.

Imperial tyranny failed to subdue the spirit of Athanasius, who confronted the world in order to assert the principle of the eternal Sonship of his Redeemer. Equally powerless was it against Basil, whose character inspired the genius of Hooker, and extorted the admiration of Gibbon. How great a share the singing of psalms held in the life of his monastic communities, has been already shown; and it was in part the awe that the sound of chanting inspired which saved him from the violence of Valens. On the feast of the Epiphany, 372, the emperor, surrounded by his guards, entered the chief church of Cesarea. At the eastern end of the nave, behind the altar, stood Basil, supported by his clergy. Tall, erect, his clear-cut features sharpened by his austerities, his bright eyes gleaming under his arched eyebrows, he faced the intruders with silent dignity. The emperor's presence was ignored. The service proceeded with the order and reverence which Basil had introduced. As the crowd of worshippers, who filled the building " with a sea of people," continued to chant the Psalms with an imposing volume of sound, the weak, excitable Valens almost fainted before the impression which the scene and sound created. The mind of the Arian despot was overawed, his eyes were dimmed, his nerves shaken, by the manifestation of a Divine Kingdom which was entirely regardless of his power. He abandoned the thought of violence, returned in peace, and, for a time, Basil reasserted over him the influence of his character.

Before the intrepidity of an Athanasius and a Basil, Constantius and Valens had recoiled. But though emperors had failed to subdue the spirit which great ecclesiastics represented, they had not acknowledged the supremacy of religion in the domain of conscience. That acknowledgment was made by Theodosius in the Cathedral of Milan, and in the words of a psalm his confession was clothed.

In 390, a well-known and popular charioteer had been imprisoned by the Gothic governor of Thessalonica. The populace, careless whether the sentence was just or unjust, clamoured for the release of their favourite. Their demand was refused, and a tumult arose, in which the governor and several of the magistrates were killed. Theodosius was determined that the punishment of the Thessalonians should be signal. The secret was well kept. The officials of the city summoned the inhabitants to the circus, as though they were to witness an ordinary spectacle; but, as soon as they were assembled in the arena, armed soldiers surrounded the place, and put to the sword every living being, man, woman, or child, who fell into their hands. In the massacre, seven thousand persons are said to have perished.

Horrified at the news, Ambrose, Bishop of Milan, wrote to the Emperor Theodosius, urging him to throw himself as a penitent on the mercy of God. "Sin," he pleaded, "is effaced neither by tears nor by penitence: neither angel nor archangel can remove its stain; God, and God only, can take away sin. You have imitated David in your crime; imitate him also in your repentance." For eight months Theodosius refused, and for eight months he was interdicted from the consolations of religion. At last he yielded. Conscience conquered pride, and he submitted to receive his sentence and his pardon from the Church. Prostrate on the floor of the Cathedral of Milan, with tears and lamentations, the emperor prayed in the words of the psalm (Ps. cxix., verse 25), "My soul cleaveth to the dust; O quicken Thou me, according to Thy word." The spiritual victory was complete, and its effect on the popular mind was deep and lasting. The new relations between the Church and the Empire were summed up by Ambrose in the trenchant phrase, "The Church is not in the Empire, but the Emperor is in the Church." The words were used of the religious sphere; but they might have been the text, on which the political and spiritual despots of the Middle Ages were the bold commentators, and to which the actions of a Gregory VII. or an Innocent III. form only the exaggerated conclusions.

In the sphere of human action, the power of the Psalms was great; but in the domain of thought, it would be probably found, if evidence could be traced, that their sway was equally universal. Take, for example, such a religious autobiography as the *Confessions of St. Augustine*, and through the first nine books, which end with the death of Monica, follow the influence of the Psalms. From the beginning of the *Confessions*, opening, as they do, with the quotations, " Great is the Lord, and marvellous; worthy to be praised." " Great is our Lord, and great is His power; yea, and His wisdom is infinite " (Ps. cxlv., verse 3, and cxlvii., verse 5), down to the " Prayer for his dead mother," with which the ninth book closes, there is scarcely a page without a reference to the same source.

"With my mother's milk," so says Augustine of himself, "I sucked in the name of Jesus Christ." Through all the wild excesses of his youth, the ambitions and intellectual wanderings of after life, the religious impressions of infancy remain distinct. His soul "longed after God"; it was "athirst" for Him. He never lost that passionate desire to know the living God, which bursts from his lips in the opening passage of the *Confessions* : "Thou madest man for Thyself, and the heart knows no repose till it rests in Thee."

Ever craving for something ideal and enduring, haunted by the solitude of his own mind, he obeyed the wild impulses of youth, pursued delights that appealed to his artistic or sensuous nature, sought distractions in objects pleasing to the eye, in games, theatres, or music, or in the indulgence of animal passion. Yet, tortured by reproaches of conscience, he reaped no harvest of repose; he only gleaned self-loathing. Ambitious of worldly fame, he pursued with eagerness his studies of literature, of rhetoric, of the sciences. Still restless, he turned to higher and better things. The *Hortensius* of Cicero inflamed him with a passion for wisdom, "for Wisdom alone, as she might reveal herself." Yet, even under the mastery of this longing, he "turned to flee back from the things of earth to God."

In his eager quest for wisdom and truth, he sought them among the Manichees, who claimed the possession of rational knowledge, and derided the Christians for their blind belief. For nine years Augustine wandered in the mazes of their speculations, his intellect subdued by their subtleties, his imagination charmed by their symbolical interpretations of nature. Here, too, he found no abiding happiness; his faith in their system was gradually undermined. When, in 384 A.D., he came to Milan as a teacher of rhetoric, he came embittered by a sense of deception, inclined to general scepticism, yet still asking of his soul the reason of its sadness and disquietude.

At Milan, Augustine fell under the influence of Ambrose. He loved the man, was charmed by his eloquence, and through his preaching learned to study the Old Testament.

Early Ages of Christianity 27

He was standing at the gate of the sanctuary; but a hard struggle was to be faced before he crossed the threshold. His mother Monica was now at his side. She had crossed the sea from Carthage to be with her beloved son, and her prayerful confidence in his ultimate triumph over doubt could not fail to influence his mind. Slowly the conviction came to him that the peace of God was not to be won by the mind alone. The lofty idealism of Plato turned his thoughts upward and inward; but it brought him no moral strength to raise himself from the earth. Then he gave himself to the study of the Bible, and especially to the study of St. Paul's Epistles. Here he learned the source of that power which enables men to embody high ideals in daily practice. In the pages of the Platonic writers he finds, as he says, no trace of the " humble and contrite heart," no " sacrifice of the broken spirit " (Ps. li. 17). No one sings there, " Truly my soul waiteth upon God; from Him cometh my salvation: He only is my rock and my salvation; He is my strong tower; I shall not be greatly moved " (Ps. lxii., verses 1, 2). " It is one thing," he continues, " to see afar off, from some tree-clad height, the fatherland of peace, yet to find no path thither, and, struggling vainly towards it, to wander this way and that among wilds beset by the ambushments of lurking runagates, with their prince, the lion and the dragon (Ps. xci., verse 13). It is another thing to tread securely on a highroad that leads directly thither, built by the hand of the Heavenly Emperor, whereon no deserters from the celestial host lie in wait to rob the traveller, for they shun it as a torment."

His struggle grew in intensity till it became an agony. The flesh lusted against the spirit; the law in his members warred against the law of his mind, and held him captive. But the supreme crisis was not far distant. It came in September 386, in the thirty-third year of his age. He had thrown himself down in a retired corner of his garden at Milan, and there under the shade of a fig-tree, poured out a flood of tears. " How long, O Lord, how long? " he cried. " How long wilt Thou be angry? Oh remember not our old sins! " (Ps. lxxix., verses 5, 8). As he prayed, he seemed to hear the voice of some boy or girl, which he knew not, repeating in a kind of chant, the words, *Tolle, lege! Tolle, lege!* "Take and read! take and read!" "I checked," he says, "the torrent of my tears, and raised myself to my feet, for I received the words as nothing less than a Divine command to open the Bible, and read the first passage on which my eyes lighted." Was not Antony, of whose life he had recently heard, converted by a similar oracle of God? Running to the spot where he had left his Bible, he snatched it up, opened its pages, and read the words: "Not in rioting and drunkenness, not in chambering and wantonness, not in strife and envying. But put ye on the Lord Jesus Christ, and make not provision for the flesh to fulfil the lusts thereof." The shadows of doubt were dispersed; the light of peace irradiated his heart; as he finished the sentence, he had neither desire nor need to read further.

The passage, as he read it in the ascetic spirit of the age, told him not only to renounce his wild life, but to forego his marriage, abandon the pursuits and honours of the world, and dedicate himself wholly to the service of Christ. The vintage holidays were at hand. As soon as they began, he resigned his office as a teacher of rhetoric, and withdrew to the hills above Milan to prepare for baptism. There he read and re-read the Psalms, spending half the night in their study, and finding in their words the expression of his own deepest feelings—the sad lament of penitence rising into the triumphant song of praise for the infinite mercy of God. "How, O God," he says, "did I cry unto Thee, as I read the Psalms of David, those hymns of faith and songs of devotion, which fill the heart against all swellings of pride. I was still but a novice in Thy true love, a beginner, keeping holiday in a country place with Alypius, like myself a catechumen, and with my mother—in garb indeed a woman, but in faith a man, in the tranquillity of age, full of a mother's love and Christian devotion! How did I cry unto Thee in these Psalms! How did they kindle my heart towards Thee! How did I burn to rehearse them all over the world, if so I might abate the pride of man!"

It was especially the 4th Psalm that worked upon his mind: "When I called upon Thee, Thou didst hear me, O God of my righteousness: Thou hast set me at liberty

Early Ages of Christianity 29

when I was in trouble; have mercy upon me, and hearken unto my prayer " (verse 1). As he read it, he mourned over the Manichees, pitying their blind rejection of the antidote which might have cured their madness;—" Would they could have heard, without my knowing that they heard, lest they should have thought it was on their account I spoke, what I cried as I read these words! In truth I could not so have cried, had I felt that they were watching. Nor, indeed, if I had used the very same words, could they have meant to them what they have meant to me, as they poured from my heart in that soliloquy which fell on Thine ears alone. For I trembled with fear, and I glowed with hope and great joy in Thy mercy, O my Father. Yea, joy and hope and fear shone in my eyes and thrilled in my voice, while Thy good Spirit turned to us, and said, ' O ye sons of men, how long will ye blaspheme Mine honour; and have such pleasure in vanity, and seek after leasing? ' " (Ps. iv., verse 2).

On Easter Sunday, April 24th, 387, Augustine was baptised by Ambrose at Milan, and at his baptism the 43rd Psalm was sung. Throughout his subsequent career his lifelong study of the Psalms may be traced. It is proved by his two commentaries on the book; by his vision of Ps. cxix., rising like a Tree of Life in Paradise; by the inscription of Ps. xxxii. above his bed, that his eyes might rest upon the words at the moment of waking; by the closing scene of his life in the bare room within the walls of beleaguered Hippo. As Gregory Nazianzen began his *Apologia* against the Emperor Julian with a quotation from Ps. xlix.; as Ambrose was moved to write his treatise on the Duties of the Clergy, by the patience, simplicity, and contempt for riches which marked Ps. xxxix.; so Augustine chose for the motto of his work on " The City of God," the words, " Very excellent things are spoken of Thee, thou City of God " (Ps. lxxxvii., verse 2). That noble treatise (413-26), written, as it were, in the glare of burning Rome, expresses with glowing eloquence, his sense of the eternal destinies of the City of God. The same intense conviction of everlasting endurance amid decay, speaks in the inscription — " Thy Kingdom is an everlasting Kingdom " (Ps. cxlv., verse 13)—which is written in Greek characters, unobliterated by time or enemies, above the portal of the church at Damascus, once a Christian cathedral, but now, for twelve centuries, a Mahomedan mosque. It is again the same conviction, that God's City, in the midst of an ephemeral world, stands firm for ever, which dictates the inscription in the Cathedral of Saint Sophia at Kieff, the oldest church in Russia, built by Yaroslaf in 1037. On the mosaics behind the altar is a colossal figure of the Virgin, bearing the inscription, " God is in the midst of her, therefore shall she not be removed " (Ps. xlvi., verse 5).

CHAPTER III

THE FORMATION OF NATIONS

The invasions of the barbarians; supremacy of moral power over brute force; Totila and Benedict: the Rule of Benedict; monastic missionaries; translation of the Psalms into Sclavonic; the Psalms in the lives of Columban, Gall, Patrick, Columba, Cuthbert; Irish and British Christianity—Battle of Mold, Kentigern, Bangor; Roman Christianity—The island of Death and Silence; Gregory the Great; coming of Augustine; introduction of Benedictine Rule; its foundation on the Psalms; its establishment in England—Benedict Biscop, Wilfrid, Neot, Dunstan; universality of the Rule.

MEN needed all their faith in the eternity of " the City of God " during the successive invasions which, in the fifth and sixth centuries, swept over Europe. The siege and capture of Rome (410) by Alaric and his Arian Visigoths, thrilled the civilised world with consternation. The news, as has been noted, stirred Augustine to write his *De Civitate Dei*, with a psalm for his motto. Jerome, in his cave at Bethlehem, wrestling with the difficulties of the Prophet Ezekiel, found in a psalm the best expression for a horror which, as he said, made him forget his own name: " O God, the heathen are come into Thy inheritance; Thy holy temple have they defiled, and made Jerusalem an heap of stones " (Ps. lxxix.). In rude contrast to the solemnity of this universal lamentation was the sensation of relief which, according to the popular story, the event produced upon the Emperor Honorius. " Rome has perished ! " cried the panic-stricken messenger, as he hurried into the emperor's presence. " Rome perished ! " replied the imperial poultry-fancier, who had a favourite hen called " Rome "; " impossible ! an hour ago she was feeding from my hand." It was explained that it was the City of Rome which had been destroyed. " But I thought," said the relieved emperor, " you meant that it was my bird, Rome, which I had lost."

Alaric and his Arian followers spared Christian churches and those who had found refuge within their walls. But what shelter was there from the savage glance of Attila's small bead-like eyes, as his squalid Pannonian hordes swept over Europe (441–51), leaving in their track a blackened and desolated waste? A panic-stricken world saw that the weapons of the Christian faith alone availed against the hosts of evil. Priests were not indeed always spared. Nicasius, eleventh Bishop of Rheims, was cut down by a Vandal in 407, as he stood on the threshold of the church, chanting the words, " Quicken Thou me according to Thy word " (Ps. cxix., verse 25). Paris may have owed security to insignificance rather than to the prayers of St. Genevieve. But there is better evidence to prove that Orleans was saved by St. Aignan, Troyes by St. Loup, and Rome by St. Leo. Divine interpositions on behalf of the Church and her saints were magnified by the legends which clustered round the name of Attila, the *Flagellum Dei* of theologians, the " Etzel " of the *Niebelungen Lied*. The inroads of the Huns stimulated the spread of Christianity, for the barbarian was awed by the priest alone, and the instruments of God's wrath trembled only before the agents of His mercy. It was then that Paganism lost its hold on the Imperial City, when Pope Leo refuted the plea that Rome owed her downfall to desertion of her ancient gods. It was then also, that the foundations of the Papal Empire were firmly laid, when the successor of Peter triumphed where the successor of Cæsar had ignominiously failed.

But among the barbarians and the native races, the sense of awe in the presence of the supernatural was thus deepened by the events of the invasion. Living examples of Christian charity, like Deo Gratias, Bishop of Carthage, or Cesarius, Bishop of Arles, who spent their substance in the redemption of captives, passed the comprehension, yet commanded the respect, of the invaders. Trusted mediators, like Epiphanius, Bishop of Pavia, won their confidence. An Odoacer bowed before the spiritual insight of Severinus of Noricum, the mysterious prophet and apostle of Austria. A Totila—as the story is told in Spinello's frescoes in San Miniato at Florence—paid homage to the saintly character of Benedict

The Formation of Nations

of Nursia; and the spell which the Patriarch of Western Monasticism cast over the all-conquering king testifies, with silent eloquence, to the supremacy of moral power over brute force, and strikes the prelude to the illustrious life of the Benedictine Order.

Driven from the wild gorges of Subiaco by the evil devices of his enemies, Benedict found a retreat at Monte Cassino. There he established among a pagan people the capital of the monastic order. The temple of Apollo was overthrown; the sacred wood was felled, and the faith of Christ preached to a people who, two centuries after Constantine, and in the heart of Christendom, still worshipped the gods of ancient Rome. Dante has told the story ("Paradiso," canto xxii.):

> " In old days,
> That mountain, at whose side Cassino rests,
> Was, on its height, frequented by a race
> Deceived and ill-disposed; and I it was
> Who thither carried first the name of Him
> Who brought the soul-subliming truth to man,
> And such a speeding grace shone over me,
> That from their impious worship I reclaimed
> The dwellers round about, who with the world
> Were in delusion lost."

"From the heart of the Benedict, as from a fountain-head of Paradise," flowed the monastic life of the West. Monte Cassino was, as it were, its Sinai. From it issued the famous Rule of St. Benedict (528), the code under which lived the vast majority of those who embraced the monastic discipline of labour and obedience.

Shortly before his death, the great monastic lawgiver saw in a vision, as Pope Gregory relates, the whole world gathered together under one beam of the sun. Five centuries later, it would be true to say that the vision was realised in the obedience of the monastic world to the Rule of Benedict. But for the moment, no uniformity existed. Here, as in Southern Italy, prevailed the Eastern Rule of Basil; here, as at Lerins, the Egyptian Rule of Antony or of Macarius; here, as in Spain, the Rule of Isidore. Gradually the continent was covered with monastic missionaries, who carried Christianity among the pagan provincials or heathen barbarians, bridged the gap between the old civilisation and the new, and, in countries devastated by wars and rapine, practised the arts of peace under the sanction of religion. In such missionary enterprises the Celtic saints were nobly distinguished. Now, in the spirit of Antony and the anchorites of the Egyptian deserts, the storm-beaten islands of the Atlantic Ocean were tenanted by eager solitaries, who, by day and night, from year's end to year's end, amid the roar of the waves and the wild screams of seabirds, sang the Psalms to God. Now, in another aspect of the same religious fervour, men left their wattled chapels, their stone oratories, and wooden shrines in Ireland and Scotland, to carry the Gospel message to the heathen. Columban at Luxeuil and Bobbio, Gall in Switzerland, Cataldus at Tarentum, Virgilius at Salzburg, Donatus at Fiesole, were among the Celtic saints who made their influence felt in Western Europe from Iceland to Southern Italy.

It was by a text from the Psalms that the first translation of the Scriptures into a language "understood of the people" was sanctioned by orthodox Christianity. Methodius and Cyril desired to construct an alphabet, and to translate portions of the Bible into the Sclavonic tongue. Their request was referred to Pope John VIII. in 879, and it was justified in his eyes by the words, "Let everything that hath breath praise the Lord" (Ps. cl., verse 6). In the Sclavonic language, and in the rude alphabet, which still witnesses to the Byzantine origin of the Russian religion and literature, the whole of the New Testament was translated. From the Old Testament the Book of Psalms alone was selected No one can doubt the meaning of the choice, or that it was wisely made. For missions, especially to pagan peoples, no book is better adapted. In the first place, Nature is treated in its unity rather than in its detail; it is contemplated in great masses: it is painted not as self-subsisting or glorious in its own beauty, but as the living expression of the one God, the embodiment of one overruling spiritual power. No book, again, appeals so strongly to the simple elemental feelings, the universal eternal emotions of mankind; no book relies less upon the special forms of human opinion to which different ages and varying circumstances have given their transitory mould. No book, again, is so calculated to

The Formation of Nations   35

encourage that sense of awe before the Divine invisible omnipresence which gives its sanction to the voice of conscience. In the poetry of Homer, the Deities of Olympus in three paces traverse the uttermost bounds of the earth; and to this material omnipresence Plato added moral grandeur by his conception of the ubiquitous supervision of Divine Providence. But the splendour of the thought, as imagined by the Greek poet or philosopher, is only a pale reflection of the sublimity of the idea as it is represented by the Hebrew Psalmist. In Psalm cxxxix. the beautiful blossom bursts into the full glory of the flower. On its language is modelled one of the earliest fragments of missionary teaching: " O Lord, my thoughts," it runs, " cannot elude Thy thoughts; Thou knowest all the ways by which I would escape. If I climb up into heaven, Thou dwellest there; if I go down to hell, there also I find Thy presence. If I bury myself in the darkness, Thou findest me there. I know that Thy night can be made clear as my day. In the morning I take flight; I flee to the ends of the sea; but there is no place in which Thy hand reaches me not," etc. The sentiment is that which prompted Linnæus, the Swedish naturalist, to inscribe over the door of his lecture-room, " Innocui vivite: Numen adest." It is the same also which, in an utilitarian, prosaic age, is coldly paraphrased in Thomson's " Hymn ":

> " Should fate command me to the farthest verge
> Of the green earth, to distant barbarous climes,
> Rivers unknown to song, . . . 'tis nought to me;
> Since God is ever present, ever felt,
> In the void waste as in the city full."

To learn the Psalter by heart was, in monastic life, the first duty of a novice. Among the secular clergy, knowledge of the Psalter was the threshold to preferment. A council of the Church and the capitularies of an emperor, provided that no one should be raised to any ecclesiastical dignity who could not recite the whole book. By the Psalms were sustained the lives and deaths of the men whose spiritual daring converted Europe to Christianity. Above the mists of legend, through the pictured veil of romance, one fact shines out with penetrating, steadfast light. It is the strength that, in solitude or danger, missionary and monk, secular priest and anchorite, derived from the Psalms of David. The words lived in his mind; they were ever on his lip; in them, his thoughts were unconsciously clothed; in them, his cry for help was naturally expressed. Take, for example, the stories, legend or truth, of two great continental missionaries, the Celtic saints Columban and Gall.

Like Francis of Assisi, Columban wielded a magnetic power over wild creatures. At his call squirrels leaped from the trees to nestle in his bosom, or chase each other in the folds of his white scapular; birds, as he knelt in prayer, fluttered round him and perched on his uplifted hands, or on his Bible as it hung by a strap from his shoulder; to him a bear gave up its cave for a retreat; a raven confessed its crime, and restored his stolen gloves. With a psalm, he and his colleague, Gall, the apostle of Switzerland, exorcised the demons of Bregenz. There the two Irish missionaries had established (*circa* 610) a little colony of Christians, living by the labours of their hands. The Lake of Constance swarmed with fish, and Columban made the nets, which Gall cast into the waters for a draught. One night, as Gall watched silently in his boat among his nets, he heard the demon of the mountains calling aloud to the demon of the waters:

" Arise! " he cried, " help to chase away the strangers who have driven me from my temples. It will need our united strength to thrust them forth."

" What can we do? " asked the demon of the waters. " Here is one upon the water-side, whose nets I have tried to break; yet have I never succeeded. He prays always, and never sleeps. Our labour will be but lost. We shall avail nothing against him."

Then Gall made the sign of the Cross, and, hurrying to land, roused Columban, who straightway tolled the bell for midnight prayers. Before the first psalm was sung through, the yells of the baffled demons echoed in fury from the surrounding hills, grew faint in the distance, and died away among the mountains like the confused sounds of a routed host.

Another incident in the life of Gall serves to connect with the Psalms the choice of the site of one of the most famous monasteries. Columban had left Bregenz (612), and Gall determined to seek another home from which to preach the Gospel. As he wandered through a forest, he came to a spot where the little river Steinach, falling from the mountain, hollows itself a bed in the rock. Here Gall, stumbling over a bramble, fell. His comrades strove to raise him; but he bade them leave him, for "This," he cried, "shall be my rest: here will I dwell, for I have a delight therein" (Ps. cxxxii., verse 15). So was founded the great monastery of St. Gall, renowned for its library, its learning, and its cultivation of the arts.

Coming nearer home, we find in the legendary history of St. Patrick a noble use of the verse, "Some put their trust in chariots, and some in horses; but we will remember the Name of the Lord our God" (Ps. xx., verse 7). Every third year, at the spring equinox, which closed the Celtic year, the festival of Tara was held on the great plain of Breg. Here were gathered the five kings of Ireland, the twenty-five tutelary kings, their attendants, their warriors, and their chariots. In nine triple circles, as night fell, they took their places round the huge flower-strewn pyre, which rose on the terrace of the palace of Tara. Throughout all Ireland, every hearth was cold. The people waited to rekindle their fires from the sacred flame which descended from heaven upon the pyre.

Suddenly, as the vast throng was hushed in anxious expectation, a bright light shone out on the extreme verge of the plain. "Who," cried King Laeghaire, in his rage, "has dared to commit this sacrilege?" And all the counsellors, the bards, the judges, and the nobles answered, "We know not." But the chief of the Druids cried aloud to Laeghaire, "O King, if that distant flame be not now extinguished, it will never be put out. Before it our sacred flame will pale, and the man who has lighted it will destroy thy kingdom. Over thee and over us he will bear rule, and he and his successors will reign for ever in Ireland." Then the king ordered the Druids to seize the sacrilegious wretch, and bring him to Tara. So the Druids, with their chariots, their horses, and their spearmen, set forth on their mission. They found that the light was shining upon a little altar set up in a rude hut, and before the shrine knelt white-robed men in prayer. They were St. Patrick, his twelve priests, and the boy, Benignus, who were celebrating their midnight service to welcome the dawn of Easter morning.

The Druids dared not enter. Standing without, they bade the men come forth. Patrick obeyed the summons, and followed the Druids to the palace of Tara, chanting as he went, " Some put their trust in chariots, and some in horses; but we will remember the Name of the Lord our God." Before the assembled hosts he spoke of the Kingdom founded by the King of kings, and of Him who reigns from the Cross. With words of such power did he speak, that nature was hushed in stillness; the ebbing tide ceased to sink; the branches stirred not in the woods; the eagle checked his flight; the white stag of Mulla, bending over the stream, forbore to drink. The power of the Druids was broken. As day dawned, the magic circles were dispersed, the sacred pyre was cold, and the only flame that shone through the twilight was the altar-fire which the Christians had kindled to hail the resurrection of their Lord.

In the career, both legendary and historical, of Columba, to whom, and to whose spiritual posterity, Northern Britain owed its Christianity, may be traced the power of the Psalms. Born in 521, at Gartan, in Donegal, Columba died in 597. His life thus spans the century which preceded the landing of Augustine in England.

On the stone of Lacknacor, in Donegal, Columba was born. As the great missionary gave up his native land for the love of God and of human souls, so those who sleep a night upon this stone are cured from that home-sickness which is the anguish of emigrants. When Columba knew only how to read the alphabet, he was able, as an old life of the saint records, to say the Psalms by heart. The priest, Cruithnechan, who had baptised him, was called upon at an ecclesiastical festival to recite the Psalm (ci.), " My song shall be of mercy and judgment." Memory and voice failed him; but, in the place of his guardian, the child repeated the Psalm, and thus " the names of God and of Columba were magnified by the miracle."

On the shores of Strangford Lough, Columba became a pupil of St. Finnian. There, so legend tells as, he copied his host's Psalter by stealth, shutting himself up by night in the church where the book was treasured, and writing by the light which streamed from his own hand. Finnian claimed the copy; Columba resisted the claim. The dispute was referred to the king at Tara, who, in homely phrase, gave his decision against Columba: " to every cow her calf ": to the book its copy. In defence of his treasure, Columba armed the clans, and Diarmid was defeated at the bloody " Battle of the Psalter." Under the name of Cathac, or "The Battler," the O'Donnells, for centuries, carried to their battles the silver case containing Columba's reputed copy of the Psalter as a pledge of victory.

In 563, Columba left his beloved oak groves of Derry, and with twelve companions, drove his hide-bound coracle on the shores of Iona, at the spot still known as " the bay of the osier bark." From Iona the " island soldier " pushed his missionary enterprises, for more than thirty years, among the Picts and Scots, and ruled the numerous churches which were founded in Ireland, Scotland, and Northumbria. In June 597, Columba had reached his 77th year. Worn with age and labour, he knew that his end was at hand. He had gone to bless a distant barn belonging to the monastery of Iona. As he rested on his road home by a wayside cross, on a little hill, there came to him a white pack-horse, which carried the milking vessels from the cow-sheds to the monastery. Laying its head upon his shoulder with many plaintive moans, it gazed into his face with eyes filled with tears. The attendant would have driven away the faithful mourner, but Columba forbade him, saying, " Let be; it so loveth me, that it poureth its bitter grief into my bosom. Thou, being a man, and having a rational soul, canst know nothing of my departure hence, save that which I myself have told thee. But to this brute beast, being devoid of human reason, the Creator hath revealed that I, its master, am about to leave it." So saying, he blessed the pack-horse, which went sorrowfully away.

Returning to his cell, he sat there transcribing the Psalter. When he came to the 10th verse of Ps. xxxiv., " The lions do lack, and suffer hunger; but they who seek the Lord shall want no manner of thing that is good,"—he laid down his pen. "Here," he said, "I make an end; what follows, Baithen will write." As Adamnanus comments, the last verse was fit for Columba, who should lack none of the treasures of eternity; and for Baithen, who succeeded him both as a teacher and as a writer, it was fitting that he should write the words that followed, "Come, ye children, and hearken unto me: I will teach you the fear of the Lord" (Ps. xxxiv., verse 11). After vespers, as was his wont, with the bare flag for his couch and for his pillow a stone, Columba passed the early hours of the night. As the bell tolled for the nocturnal office of the morning of Sunday, June 9th, he rose, and entered the church before the brethren. Diarmid, his faithful attendant, drawing near to the door, saw that the building was flooded with a heavenly light, which disappeared as his foot touched the threshold. Greatly wondering, he asked, "Where art thou, my father?" Then, groping his way through the darkness, he found Columba lying before the altar. He raised the saint's head, and sitting beside him, laid it on his bosom. Thus they were found by the brethren, and then, as Diarmid raised his master's right hand, Columba moved it in sign of blessing, and so passed away.

Iona became for the Celtic races the cradle of sacred knowledge, the nursery of bishops, the religious capital of Northern Britain, the burying-place of its kings. "Where is Duncan?" asks Ross of Macduff, and Macduff replies:

"Carried to Colme-kill:
The sacred storehouse of his predecessors
And guardian of their bones."[1]

On certain evenings, every year, St. Columba is seen counting the surrounding islands, lest any should have been sunk by the power of witchcraft:

"As Iona's saint, a giant form,
Throned on his towers, conversing with the storm,
Counts every wave-worn isle and mountain hoar
From Kilda to the green Ierne's shore."

Among the spiritual descendants of Columba, none is more famous than Cuthbert. As a shepherd lad, tending

[1] *Macbeth*, Act II., scene iv.

The Formation of Nations 41

his flock by night on the hills of Lammermoor, he saw the vision which determined his vocation. Suddenly the dark sky shone with a broad tract of light, down which descended a host of angels, who presently mounted heavenwards, bearing with them the soul they had sought on earth. Aidan, Bishop of Lindisfarne, had died that night (651). Thirteen years later, Cuthbert was drawn from Melrose, and appointed prior of the monastery of Lindisfarne, that he might reform the abuses of the house. After twelve years, he withdrew to the barren island of Farne, where he built an anchorite's cell.

Legend lingers lovingly round his name. The sea-fowl, whom he made his companions, are called the Birds of St. Cuthbert. The little shells that are found on the coast are known as the Beads of St. Cuthbert; and by night he may still be seen, so tradition tells us, fashioning them, with a stone for his hammer, and a rock for his anvil:

> "But fain St. Hilda's nuns would learn
> If on a rock, by Lindisfarne,
> St. Cuthbert sits and toils to frame
> The seaborn beads that bear his name."

From his dear solitude he was taken, against his will, to be made Bishop of Lindisfarne (685). Two years afterwards, he returned to his cell a dying man. He died March 20th, 687, having received the Sacrament at the hands of Herefrith, Abbot of Lindisfarne, who tells the story of his death. Near the landing-place of the island was a rude shelter, in which some of the brethren had passed the night in prayer and chanting. When Herefrith brought the news of Cuthbert's death, the monks were singing the 60th Psalm. By an agreed signal, the light of two torches, held aloft, proclaimed to the watcher on the mainland that the soul of Cuthbert had departed to the Lord. Hurrying from the tower to bear the news to those who worshipped in the church, the watchman found the assembled brethren singing the same Psalm.

The influence of Columba and his followers overran Scotland; it crossed the borders into England; it extended to the Midland Counties. Along the West, its Irish type came into contact with British Christianity. Kentigern, of whom the story runs that he began the day by reciting the Psalter standing breast-high in a running stream, was at once the beloved St. Mungo of Glasgow, and the founder of the monastery of Elwy, in North Wales.

Unlike the continental invasions which overwhelmed and submerged the native populations, the invaders of Britain fought their way, step by step, in face of stubborn resistance. Gradually the British were forced back into their mountain fastnesses, carrying with them the national forms of their Christian worship, which they jealously guarded as symbols of their independence. With fire and sword, heathen invaders swept away priests and people, and the wooden reed-thatched churches in which they worshipped. So ruthless was the destruction, that in it Bede, like Jerome, or like the historian of the Vandals in Africa, saw the words of the Psalm verified: " O God, the heathen are come into Thine inheritance," etc. (Ps. lxxix., verses 1-4). It is a period of darkness, with few and uncertain glimmerings of light. But among the legendary or historical records of the persecuted Church, the Psalms are associated with one signal triumph of the native Christians over their heathen invaders. In 429, Germanus, Bishop of Auxerre, and Lupus, Bishop of Troyes, were implored by the Britons to aid them against the Picts and Saxons. At Eastertide, so runs the story, the little army of newly-made Christians, " with the dew of baptism fresh upon them," was posted by Germanus in a defile, near Mold, in Flintshire, close to a spot still known as *Maes-Garmon*, " the field of Germanus." As the heathen host approached, the Britons, at a signal from the bishop, shouted three times the Paschal Alleluia.[1] Caught up and re-echoed among the hills, the sound struck terror into the Picts and Saxons. Throwing down their arms, they fled; and faith, unarmed, won a bloodless victory.

Among the national institutions of British Christianity were their colleges, partly religious, partly educational, in which the members were numbered by their thousands. The exact Rule which governed these establishments is uncertain. But, as in Columba's institutions, the object of study was the Scripture, and especially the Psalms, so the names of the Welsh colleges *Cor* (choir) and *Bangor* (high choir) may show that choral services were an essential part

[1] The Hallel of Ps. cxiii.-cxviii., or of cxxxiv.-cxxxvii.

The Formation of Nations

of their arrangements. At Bangor Iltyd, 100 of the members were engaged every hour in chanting, so that without intermission, psalms were rendered night and day. At Elwy, in North Wales, 365 of the brethren were devoted, day and night, to the singing of psalms and the divine offices, so that the praise of God from year's end to year's end never ceased. Another famous monastic institution in Wales was Llancarvan, of which Cadoc the Wise was the first abbot or principal. It was with a psalm that Gwynlliu the Warrior, father of Cadoc, turned from a life of violence to the austerities of an anchorite. Won to religion by the example of his son, the robber chieftain did penance for his sins, chanted Psalm xx., " The Lord hear thee in the day of trouble," retired from the world, and lived in such sanctity that he is commemorated as St. Woolos, the patron saint of Newport in Monmouthshire.

In the year of Columba's death (597), Augustine and his companions landed in Kent, to attempt the conversion of Saxon England. That event brought Roman Christianity into collision and conflict with the Irish and British types: it introduced the Benedictine Rule as a rival to the existing discipline of Celtic monasteries; it carried England once again into the circle of European life. How complete was the darkness which, in the fifth and sixth centuries, hung over England, may be gathered from the account given by Procopius (500-65) of the island of Brittia.[1] The island, he says, is the Island of Silence and the Dead. On the opposite coast of the mainland live subjects of the Frankish kings, fishermen and husbandmen, who hold their land free, except for one service. That service is to transport the souls of the dead from the mainland to the island coast. At midnight, an unseen hand knocks at their doors, and the voice of an unseen being summons them to their labour. How or why they are constrained to obey, they know not; they only know that they are so constrained. Rising from their beds, and hurrying to the shore, they there find boats that are not their own, loaded to a finger's breadth between the gunwale and the water; yet no forms are seen, no freight is visible. They push off; they bend to their oars; and, in one short hour,

[1] *De Bello Gotthico*, iv. 20.

they drive the strange barks upon the shore of the island, which, in their own boats, with oars and sail, they can scarcely reach in a night and a day. None are seen to land, or to leave the boat. But a voice calls each shadow by name, proclaiming its earthly dignities and parentage. When the voice is silent, the boat is now so lightly laden that only the keel is covered. · Thus the rowers perform their service, and return to the shore of the living.

To restore the Island of Death and Silence to Christian life, had been the cherished dream of Pope Gregory the Great, when he was still a humble monk in the Benedictine monastery of St. Andrew, which he had founded in his father's palace on the Cœlian Hill. In the familiar story of his conception of the dream, the Psalms have their place. The countrymen of the three angel-faced Angles, in their remote Yorkshire home, were to be plucked from the ire of God, and taught to sing their Alleluias in the realm of King Ælla. Gregory's love of the Psalms is illustrated by the picture of his mother Silvia, visible for centuries after his death, which he caused to be painted on the walls of what is now the Church of St. Gregory at Rome. In her left hand she held the Psalter, open at the words, " O let my soul live, and it shall praise Thee; and Thy judgments shall help me " (Ps. cxix., verse 175). It was with the words of a psalm that Gregory expressed his love of the monastic seclusion from which he was torn, to be made Pope (590). He lamented a change, which seemed to thrust him far from the face of God, and back into the world. " I panted," he writes, " for the face of God, not in words only, but from the inmost marrow of my heart, crying, ' My heart hath talked of Thee, Seek ye my face: Thy face, Lord, will I seek ' " (Ps. xxvii., verse 9). But when the choice fell upon him, he seized the opportunity to carry out the dream which, in his own person, he was not permitted to fulfil. As the Roman Senate, with Hannibal at the gates, sent forth its legions to Spain and to Africa, so Gregory, when Italy was ravaged by invaders, despatched his missionaries to Britain. It was over a country blackened by Lombard fires, that Augustine passed as he started on his mission. In 597 he landed in the Isle of Thanet, preceded by the Cross and painted banner, and followed by his companions, chanting Psalms and litanies.

With the landing of Augustine, the Benedictine Rule was introduced into England, and the religious history of Saxon England is to a great extent bound up in the progress of the Order.

"Hearken, my son!" are the words with which begins the Rule of "Holy Benet," and "Ausculta, O fili!" are the words which in Christian iconography are inscribed on the book placed in the hands of St. Benedict. The 34th Psalm (verses 12-15) strikes the keynote of the Rule. "The Lord," says Benedict, "who seeketh His servant in the midst of the people, still saith to him, ' What man is he that lusteth to live, and would fain see good days?' If at that word thou answerest, ' It is I,' then will the Lord say to thee, ' If thou wouldst have life, keep thy tongue from evil, and thy lips that they speak no guile. Eschew evil, and do good; seek peace, and ensue it.' And that being done, ' Then shall My eyes be upon you, and My ears shall be open to your cry. And, even before thou callest Me, I shall say to thee, Here am I.'"

On the Psalms are based many of the chapters of the Benedictine Rule, and in them the book is profusely quoted. With a psalm, novices were admitted into the Order. The child, whose hands had been wrapped in the white folds of the altar-cloth, grew up in the monastic school. To him at length came the desire to give himself to God: "Here will I dwell for ever" (Ps. xxiii., verse 6). He became a novice; and, the year of his noviciate ended, he took the vows to remain attached to the monastery; to labour, while strength lasted; to perfect himself in the state to which he was called; and, lastly, to obey the abbot. Then, with outstretched arms, he sang three times the verse which was the "Open Sesame" of the monastic life (Ps. cxix., verse 116), "O establish me according to Thy word, that I may live; and let me not be disappointed of my hope." Three times the community repeated the words, and added the *Gloria Patri*. Then, dressed in monastic habit, the new brother knelt at the feet of each of the brethren, asked for their prayers, received the fraternal kiss, and so became a monk, bound by the threefold cord of Obedience, Labour, and Humility. With the same verse from the Psalms, girls were received into the religious communities, which, like the company of Benedict's sister, Scholastica, followed the Benedictine Rule.

Once admitted to the Order, the lives of monks and nuns were to a great extent regulated by the spirit, if not by the letter, of the Psalms. On the words, " I said, I will take heed to my ways, that I offend not in my tongue " (Ps. xxxix., verse 1), was based the rule of silence. One of the first labours of the brethren was to learn the Psalter by heart. In such duties of monastic life, whether homely or sacred, as making bread for the altar, setting out the relics, attending the death-agony of a brother, taking places at the refectory, the weekly washing of feet, the beginning and end of readings during meals—psalms were sung or recited. In adorning copies of the Psalter with all the quaint and beautiful fancies of devotional imagination, monks spent prayerful years of solitude and silence. As shrines for the Psalter, their abbeys and churches were built, and to the chanting of a psalm (lxxxiv.) their chosen sites were sprinkled with holy water. A Psalm, " Praise the Lord with harp; sing praises unto Him with the lute, and instrument of ten strings," sanctioned the use of the organ in divine service. By verses of the Psalms (" In the evening and morning, and at noonday, will I pray, and that instantly," Ps. lv., verse 18; " Seven times a day do I praise Thee, because of Thy righteous judgments," Ps. cxix., verse 164; and " At midnight I will rise to give thanks unto Thee," Ps. cxix., verse 62) the canonical hours were regulated, and on the Psalms the services themselves were mainly based, so that the Psalter was sung through every week. To the singing of a psalm (cl.) their bells were cast, as the brethren waited at the furnace for the metal to be poured into the mould. With the chanting of the Psalms, monks traversed wild forests and mountain solitudes; or, like Stephen Harding, second founder of the Cistercians, as he journeyed to Rome, met the perils of the way by a daily recitation of the Psalter. In the words of a psalm, the monastic vocation came to men like Thomas Aquinas (Ps. lxxxiv., verse 11, " I had rather be a door-

The Formation of Nations 47

keeper in the house of my God, than to dwell in the tents of ungodliness "), and he obeyed the call to become a Dominican. With a psalm (Ps. cxiv., " When Israel came out of Egypt "), men like Francis Borgia, Duke of Gandia (1510-72), turned their backs on wealth and worldly honours to enter religious societies. With a psalm, like Gall, or Vincentius of Lerins (Ps. xlvi., verse 10), monks chose the sites of monasteries, and, as they reared the walls, exorcised the demons of mountain, lake or wood. In the spirit of the Psalms, monastic builders lavished their genius and devotion on arch and capital, altar-shrine and tower, portal and window, that they might beautify the habitation of God, and prepare a dwelling-place meet for His honour. Thus it was with Hugh of Cluni, who, according to his biographer, said within himself, with the Psalmist, " I have loved the habitation of Thy house, and the place where Thine honour dwelleth " (Ps. xxvi., verse 8); and whatsoever the devotion of the faithful gave, he entirely consecrated to the decoration of his church or to the good of the poor.

To the mediæval monk, the choir was the garden of the Lord, in which he laboured day and night; it was his paradise, where, in the cool shadow cast by his Redeemer, he might rest from the burning heat of the world. One of the contemporaries of Thomas à Kempis describes him, when he took part in the offices of the Church: " Whilst he was singing, he was to be observed with his face always raised towards heaven, as if inspired with a sacred enthusiasm, carried and borne beyond himself by the wonderful sweetness of the Psalms." This was the spirit of mediæval psalmody. As its tide rolled forth, night and day, from the convent or monastery, and swelled over hill and fen, midnight wayfarers, travelling in fear of their lives, felt that they were in the hands of God; and labourers, rising to their work at dawn, or resting at noon, or returning with night, knew, though they understood not the words, that their toil was consecrated in the sight of their heavenly Father.

As the Psalms presided over every part of a monk's life, so they were present with him in his death. When a brother lay dying, the haircloth was spread, the ashes were scattered, and in them a cross was traced. Here the sick man was laid. By blows on a board the brethren were summoned, and, wherever they were, or whatever their occupations, they ran to his side, and remained with him in his anguish, chanting the Penitential Psalms and Litanies. Thus, in the presence of the fraternity, in sackcloth and ashes, supported by the supplications of their brethren, with the words of the Psalms beating on their ears, as they had sounded throughout their lives, died thousands of " Knights of God "—members of the most powerful, and, with all their shortcomings, the most useful, of mediæval institutions.

With words of the Psalms in their ears, or on their lips, died three of the men who were most conspicuous in the establishment of the Benedictine Rule in England—Benedict Biscop (623-90), Wilfrid (634-709), and Dunstan (924-88).

To Benedict, England owes a vast debt. On his work rested much of the learning and culture of the eighth century. Studying the Benedictine Rule at Canterbury, at Lerins, and other continental monasteries, he established it in his monasteries of Jarrow and Wearmouth. Six times he visited Rome—now seeking architects, masons, and materials to beautify his churches; now bringing with him musicians or instructors in ritual; now gathering relics, pictures, images and vestments; now collecting the manuscripts which made his libraries famous. Worn out by labours, and paralysed in his limbs, he listened, through sleepless nights, to the repetition of psalms, in which he was himself too weak to join. He died January 12th, 690, when those who watched by him were repeating Ps. lxxxiii., " Hold not Thy tongue, O God; keep not still silence." Within the walls of Jarrow the Venerable Bede, the father of English history, the flower of the monastic schools, the true type of a Benedictine, was already harvesting the stores of learning which Benedict had collected, giving his whole energies, as he says of himself, to meditation on the Scriptures; delighting, amid the observance of the monastic rule and the daily ministry of singing in the church, either to learn, or to teach, or to write.

Widely different from the methods of Benedict Biscop were the means by which Wilfrid sustained the cause, of which both were zealous champions. Yet in their love of art they were at one, and the magnificence of Ripon rivalled

The Formation of Nations

that of Wearmouth or Jarrow. In the monastery of Lindisfarne, Wilfrid studied the Scottish usages, acquired fame for learning, and committed the Psalter to memory in the version of Jerome. But Rome exercised over him an irresistible fascination. His mind was set towards the Papal city, even during his stay at Canterbury, where once more he learnt the Psalter by heart—this time in the old Italic version, which was adopted there and at Rome. The years 652-8 were spent at Lyons and at Rome in studying the usages, ritual, and discipline, which he laboured all his stormy life to establish in Northern England. In his long conflict against Celtic Christianity, he suffered deposition, exile, imprisonment. But his purpose never wavered. Thrown into prison at Dunbar (*circa* 681), the bishop was deserted by his spiritual chief, separated from .friends and adherents, deprived of all that he possessed except his clothing, robbed even of his precious reliquary, which was the companion of his many journeys. Yet his guards heard the fallen prelate chanting the Psalms as cheerfully as if he were in his own monastery of Ripon or Hexham. His banishments were fruitful in labour. During one, he became the apostle of the Frisians; in another, the missionary of Sussex and the Isle of Wight. The last effort of his old age was the visitation of the monasteries which he had founded. Setting out from Hexham, now the centre of his See, and visiting Ripon on his way, he rode to the Mercian houses in turn. In October 709, he came to Oundle, in Northamptonshire. There he was seized with a fatal illness. Round the dying man gathered the whole community, chanting the Psalms which he had loved so well. As they reached the 30th verse of Ps. civ., "When thou lettest Thy breath go forth, they shall be made," his breathing ceased, and his stormy life was ended.

Up and down the country, in England as on the Continent, were scattered monastic institutions—links in the national unity, sanctuaries of religious life, centres of education and civilisation, nurseries of arts and industries, agricultural colonies which drained fens or reclaimed forests, treasuries in which were preserved the riches of ancient learning. Gradually the stern severity of the Celtic discipline yielded before the more human spirit of its Italian rival, which hallowed not only manual but intellectual labour. With the Danish invasions there came a check and a recoil. In the North, East, and centre of England, the invaders fell with special fury on the religious communities. They devoured the land like locusts. Fire and sword swept away, in a few hours, the fruits of the patient toil of a century. In the South and West, the defenders, though hard-pressed, held their own. With one signal triumph over the Danes, Saxon legend inseparably associated the Psalms in the person of St. Neot, who every morning said the Psalter through, and every midnight chanted a hundred psalms. The saint died, full of years and honour, among his countrymen. No man of equal sanctity had risen to take his place, when, in 878, King Alfred lay in his tent at Iley, on the eve of the battle of Ethendun. To the king appeared St. Neot, "like an angel of God; his hair white as snow, his raiment white, glistering, and fragrant with the scents of heaven." He promised Alfred victory. "The Lord," he said, "shall be with you; even the Lord strong and mighty, the Lord mighty in battle, who giveth victory unto kings" (Ps. xxiv., verse 8). As morning broke, the little band of Saxons fell on Guthrun and the sleeping Danes. So sudden was their onset, that at first they carried all before them. But gradually the tide of battle began to sway. It was turned again in favour of King Alfred, when a majestic figure, whom the Saxons recognised as St. Neot himself, seizing the royal banner, marshalled his countrymen to renewed effort, victory, and pursuit. So, for a time, peace came to the land, and Guthrun and his followers became Christians.

During this life-and-death struggle, it was not strange that morals relaxed, monastic fervour cooled, and heathen practices revived. With Dunstan, the statesman who laboured to unite England under King Edgar, the ecclesiastic who, as Archbishop of Canterbury, strove to revive monastic life—a new spirit was breathed into Church and State. As Abbot of Glastonbury, Dunstan had reformed the community which he governed. But the Benedictine Rule was then imperfectly known to him, and it was only after his exile in Flanders and his sojourn in the monastery of St. Peter at Ghent (956–57) that he realised its strength. A man of learning, he was attracted by its opportunities for education. To his kindly character it commended itself by its humanity. Himself skilled in music, painting, iron work and embroidery, it appealed to his artistic temperament. Keenly sensitive to the immorality of the times, he valued its example of the separation from all sexual relations. In its uniform adoption, he saw a powerful instrument for the moral reform of Church and State, for the unification and intellectual progress of the nation. Before his death, the Rule was practically universal in England. Almost his last public act was the coronation of Ethelred, in 978, at Kingston. Retiring from affairs of state, he passed his remaining years at Canterbury, occupied in business, in teaching, or the practice of handicrafts, constant in prayer by night and day, delighting in the services of the Church and in psalmody. In May 988, his strength failed him. He had received the " Viaticum," and died as he was giving thanks in the words, " The merciful and gracious Lord hath so done His marvellous works, that they ought to be had in remembrance. He hath given meat unto them that fear Him " (Ps. cxi., verses 4, 5).

At the close of the tenth century, the Benedictine Rule had conquered France; it had won Germany and Spain; it was established in England. The vision of Benedict was realised, and the monastic world gathered together under one beam of the sun.

CHAPTER IV

THE MIDDLE AGES

The battle of Vouglé; the Psalms in ecclesiastical or semi-ecclesiastical history (1) the Papacy and the Empire—Charlemagne, Gregory VII. and Henry IV., Anselm and William Rufus, Henry II. and Thomas à Becket, Alexander III. and Frederick Barbarossa; (2) pilgrimages; (3) crusades, Abp. Baldwin, Richard I., Henry V.—Abbot Adelme at the Tagus, Cardinal Ximenes, Demetrius of the Don; (4) the religious revival; St. Bernard; Stephen Harding and the Cistercian reform—Citeaux and Fountains Abbey; St. Francis of Assisi and the Franciscans; the Psalms in secular history—William the Conqueror, Vladimir Monomachus, David I. of Scotland, Abelard and Heloïse, St. Louis of France, William Wallace; in mediæval science; in mediæval literature—*De Imitatione Christi, Divina Commedia, Piers Plowman, The Golden Legend.*

As the centuries advance, the Psalms touch human life at points which grow more and more numerous, till the whole circle of thought and action seems to be embraced. Mediæval literature and science, as well as secular and ecclesiastical history, are permeated by their influence.

The strongest of the monarchies which rose on the ruins of the Western Empire was the Frankish Kingdom. Hitherto the youthful nations, whose vigour had scourged the effeminacy of the older world, if Christians at all, had been Arians. But the baptism of Clovis had for the first time arrayed force on the side of orthodox Christianity; alike against heretics, heathen, and Saracens, the Franks were its zealous champions. It was this fact that gave significance to the victory which Clovis won at Vouglé (507) over Alaric II. and his Arian Visigoths.

Blessed by Remy at Rheims, Clovis had marched towards the Loire. Encamping close to Tours, he sent to the church, in which rested the bones of St. Martin, to inquire whether any presage of victory would be vouchsafed to him. As his messengers entered the church, the choir were chanting the

The Middle Ages 53

words, "Thou hast girded me with strength unto the battle; Thou shalt throw down mine enemies under me. Thou hast made mine enemies also to turn their backs upon me; and I shall destroy them that hate me" (Ps. xviii., verses 39, 40). Encouraged by the omen, Clovis pressed on. A ford over the Vienne was revealed by a deer, and, as he advanced towards Poitiers, a bright gleam, shining from the church of St. Hilary as from a lighthouse, guided the movements of his troops. In the battle of Vouglé, Alaric was killed by the hand of Clovis; the Visigoths fled, and southern Gaul, from the Loire to the Garonne, fell into the hands of the Franks.

From the time of Clovis onwards, the growing power of the Frankish Kingdom had attracted the eyes of successive Popes, who saw in its rulers the destined heirs of the Roman Emperors of the West. The idea of an universal church, whose centre was Rome, rapidly approached its realisation. With it grew up the conception of its necessary counterpart, a conception which was bred partly of memory, partly of hope. The establishment of an universal monarchy in close alliance with the world-wide dominion of the Church, was the vision which fascinated the imagination of the noblest minds. At the head of this Christian commonwealth of nations, in its temporal character, was to stand the emperor; at its head, in its spiritual character, was to stand the Pope.

For the realisation of such a vision the ground was already prepared. The spell of the old Empire lay upon the barbarians themselves. Not only were they awe-struck by the stately ceremonial of the Christian religion; they were also impressed with a sense of the sanctity of the emperor, eager to preserve imperial institutions, anxious to perpetuate imperial methods of administration. Decrepit though the Eastern Empire might be, the West was familiarised with the idea of universal monarchy by the shadowy claims, waning powers, and insecure ascendency of the Byzantine Emperors.

In the eighth century the policy of the Papacy rapidly assumed a definite shape, and the first steps were taken to break the link which still bound the Popes to Byzantium. Already the aid of Pepin had been invoked against invaders; already the Papacy had lent a special sanctity to the corona-

tion of the King of the Franks; already it had received its
reward in the gift of the Papal States. Once more, at Pepin's
death, the Lombards invaded the possessions of the Church.
At the call of Pope Hadrian, Charlemagne swept away the
invaders, and added Northern Italy to the dominions of the
Franks.

With the penultimate stage of a vast change, a psalm is
inseparably connected. Leaving his army at Pavia, Charlemagne journeyed to Rome. Outside the city he was welcomed
by the Cross, which hitherto had only been carried beyond
the walls to greet the approach of the Exarch or the Patrician.
At the sight of the sacred symbol, Charlemagne dismounted
from his horse, and, entering Rome on foot, reached the
portal of St. Peter (April 2nd, 774). There Pope Hadrian
received him and took him in his arms. Together they
entered the basilica, which Constantine had erected on the
spot traditionally hallowed as the scene of St. Peter's martyrdom. Hand in hand, they advanced towards the semicircular apse, passed under the arch of victory, ascended the
long flight of steps, and prostrated themselves before the high
altar, while the multitude, who thronged the building,
chanted, "Blessed be he that cometh in the Name of the
Lord" (Ps. cxviii., verse 26).

On the next day, Charlemagne, hailed by the Pope as his
champion and by the people as their deliverer, was confirmed
in the title of Patrician and Consul of the Romans, promised
to protect the City and defend the Church, and in the tunic
and sandals of the Patrician, took his seat at the tribunal of
justice. For six and twenty years the final stage was postponed, while the Byzantine Emperor remained the titular
sovereign of Rome. On Christmas day, 800, the long revolt
was consummated. Western Europe disavowed the rule of
the Eastern Empire, when, in the basilica of St. Peter, Pope
Leo III. placed on the head of Charlemagne "the diadem of
the Cæsars," while the people prayed for long life and victory
to "Charles, the most pious Augustus, crowned by God, the
peace-giving Emperor."

Fourteen years later (January 28th, 814), Charlemagne,
whose favourite psalm was Psalm lxviii. ("Let God arise"),
died at Aix-la-Chapelle, repeating with his last breath the

words, " Into Thy hands I commend my spirit " (Ps. xxxi., verse 6). He had loved to be called among his friends by the name of David. Church music and psalmody were the delight of a man, who, in his terrible vengeance on his enemies, his political and ecclesiastical work, and the moral aberrations of his passionate nature, presents curious points of resemblance to the founder of the Jewish monarchy.

As time went on, the relations between the Papacy and the Empire took a different shape, and became a contest for supremacy between the temporal and spiritual powers. At Salerno, in the Cathedral of St. Matthew the Apostle, surrounded by the narrow, irregular streets, which still bear witness, through their varied architecture, to the Lombard occupation, the Saracen conquests, the Norman rule of Guiscard, and the ascendency of the Hohenstaufen, is the tomb of Hildebrand, the son of a carpenter at Soana, and, as Gregory VII., the vehement champion of the papal supremacy. It was Hildebrand who freed the Church from vassalage to the temporal power, and stemmed the flowing tide of priestly corruption. If, on one side of his career, he seemed the incarnation of spiritual pride, it should not be forgotten that, as a moral reformer, he roused the conscience of Europe. From the austere heights of his own self-discipline, he rebuked the vices of emperors and kings, and to his example men appealed, in after ages, when sin was once more rampant in high places:

" We need another Hildebrand to shake
And purify us." [1]

For a quarter of a century, during five successive pontificates, Hildebrand had guided the policy of the Papacy with strong hand and watchful eye. Tier by tier, he had raised the fabric of Theocracy, which, in its moral grandeur, was the inspiration of his life. If kings refused to recognise the eternal laws of divine justice, their rule was tyranny; if the people yielded no obedience to civil rulers, the result was anarchy. It was Hildebrand's aim to make the Church, purified, and independent, the arbitrator between the two, and the spiritual ruler of both. Elected Pope in 1073 under

[1] Longfellow, *The Golden Legend*, iv.

the title of Gregory VII., he entered on the struggle which lay before him with the serene conviction that, as the Vicar of Christ, he was the Divine instrument. His ambition was for the Papacy rather than for himself. His pride was not a peasant's vanity in his exalted station, but an assertion of his dignity as the earthly representative of God.

The history of his Papacy is full of dramatic episodes. It had its triumph when the Emperor Henry IV., in penitential garb, ascended the rocky path, and for three days, in hunger, cold and shame, waited at the gate of the Castle of Canossa (1077). It met its fatal reverse (1084) when the Pope, a prisoner in St. Angelo, was rescued by Robert Guiscard. Such a downfall broke the heart of Gregory. In the Castle of Salerno, under the protection of the Normans, he died on 25th May 1085. His last words, taken from Psalm xlv., verse 8, breathe the tragic fulness of his bitter disappointment, " I have loved righteousness, and hated iniquity;—and therefore I die in exile."

The great struggle between the Popes and the temporal rulers of Europe extended to England, though, during the reign of William the Conqueror, it was averted by the personal concert between himself and Archbishop Lanfranc. But when to William's wise, yet severe tyranny succeeded the savage licence of William Rufus, that struggle between Church and State at once began which lasted to the Reformation. In Archbishop Anselm were worthily embodied the spiritual claims of the Church. Tender-hearted and affectionate, he loved both man and beast. The well-known story of the hunted hare illustrates his feeling for dumb animals, and his habit of reading moral lessons into the ordinary events of life. As the archbishop rode from Windsor to Hayes, a hare was started and pursued by his retainers and their dogs. It took refuge under his horse, and Anselm bade the men call off their dogs, and let the trembling creature go. The hunters laughed. "Do ye laugh?" he said; "this poor beast is far from laughter. She is like a Christian soul ceaselessly pursued by demons, that would drag it down to eternal death. Poor soul in torture, looking round in sore distress, seeking with longing unspeakable for a hand to save!" Every instinct of his

The Middle Ages

nature impelled him towards the ideal rather than the practical aspects of life, or inclined him to study its spiritual rather than its temporal needs. Thought, not action, was the true sphere of the man whom Dante places among the doctors of the Church in the Heaven of the Sun. Transferred from the retirement of the Abbey of Bec to the publicity of the See of Canterbury (1093-1109), he likens himself to an owl, who, " when he is in his hole with his young ones, is happy; but when he goes out among crows and other birds, they hunt him and strike him with their beaks, and he is ill at ease." His office compelled him to be not only a great ecclesiastic, but a great feudal noble. It forced him, also, to choose between the Pope and the king. To his pure soul the solution of the difficulty would probably have been the surrender of worldly greatness, in order to increase his moral influence. But to a guardian of the gifts bestowed upon the Church of God, such a way of escape was impossible. When therefore the conflict began, his choice was inevitable; he made it with quiet courage, and adhered to it with invincible resolution. As the struggle dragged its slow length along, he stood alone in England, siding more and more with the Pope, who was to him the embodiment of law and right in a world of tyranny and wrong.

In 1098 Anselm was at Rome, waiting the results of his appeal to Pope Urban II. against William Rufus. But the air of Rome was unwholesome to one, who, though Piedmontese by birth, was accustomed to a northern climate. He therefore visited Abbot John of St. Salvator, a former monk of Bec, now the ruler of a monastery at Telesia, between Benevento and Capua. On the higher slopes of the neighbouring mountains was a village called Schlavia, to which the monks resorted in the summer months. To this beautiful spot Anselm was taken. On the hill-top, in the crisp mountain air, respited from his cares, surrounded by the simplicities of life and the charms of nature, the old man's heart leaped within him. " This," he broke forth, like Gall, in the words of a psalm (cxxxii., verse 15), " shall be my rest for ever; here will I dwell, for I have a delight therein." It was at Schlavia that he thought out and composed his famous treatise, *Cur Deus Homo ?* in which he discussed the rational ground of the Atonement, and expounded his profound and original view of the Incarnation.

In the protracted struggle between Henry II. and Thomas à Becket, the same issue was involved. But the sacrilege of Becket's murder at Canterbury (Tuesday, December 29th, 1170) gave the temporary victory to the Church over the State.

At five o'clock on a winter's evening, the monks were singing vespers in the dimly-lighted cathedral. Suddenly came the news that soldiers were forcing their way into the cloisters on the north side of the building. Becket had mounted the fourth step of the staircase, which led from the Chapel of St. Benedict to the choir of the church, when the four knights, in full armour, their mail hiding their faces, burst into the building. At the summons of Fitzurse, he descended into the transept, and in his white rochet, a cloak and hood thrown over his shoulders, faced the murderers. A blow on the head from Tracy drew blood. As the archbishop wiped the stain from his face, he said the familiar words, " Into Thy hands I commend my spirit " (Ps. xxxi., verse 6). The deed was soon accomplished. But misfortunes crowded on the king. At Avranches, in May 1172, Henry had done penance for the crime of his adherents. Yet troubles seemed only to increase, and at Canterbury he made a further and final expiation. On July 12th, 1174, he entered the streets of the city, walking barefoot,—naked, except for a shirt and cloak. In the cathedral, he kissed the stone where Becket had fallen, recited the penitential psalm against wrath (Ps. vi.), prostrated himself before the tomb of the archbishop, and then, placing his head and shoulders upon it, was scourged by the bishops, abbots, and each of the eighty monks who were present. His humiliation was so profound, that the chroniclers appeal to the language of the Psalms to describe the impression it produced—" The mountains trembled at the presence of the Lord," " the mountain of Canterbury smoked before Him who touches the hills and they smoke."

Yet another scene in the struggle between Church and State is illustrated by the Psalms. In July 1177, the long conflict between Pope Alexander III. and the Emperor Frederick Barbarossa drew to its close. The hand of God,

The Middle Ages 59

so it seemed to pious minds, struck down the German Emperor in his hour of triumph. Master of Rome, he had forced his creature into the chair of St. Peter. But pestilence destroyed his army. Disguised, and almost alone, Barbarossa made his way by an unfrequented pass to Germany. The Lombard League supported Alexander III. against his rival and the emperor; the battle of Legnano (May 29th, 1176) broke Barbarossa's power, and compelled him to make terms with the Pope. At Venice, in the summer of 1177, Pope and emperor were reconciled. Himself a Sienese, it was at Siena that Alexander commemorated his triumph in the frescoes with which Spinello has adorned the Sala di Balia. But in the porch of St. Mark's at Venice is another record of the scene. Three marble slabs mark the spot where Barbarossa humbled himself before his enemy. Legend is at least true to the spirit of the conflict, when it represents the Pope as placing his foot on the neck of the kneeling emperor, and quoting the words of Ps. xci., verse 13, " Thou shalt go upon the lion and adder; the young lion and the dragon shalt thou tread under thy feet." In this case the Sienese frescoes may have bred the legend, which Rogers uses in his *Italy* (" St. Mark's Place "):

> " In that temple porch
> (The brass is gone, the porphyry remains),
> Did Barbarossa fling his mantle off,
> And, kneeling, on his neck receive the foot
> Of the proud Pontiff—thus at length consoled
> For flight, disguise, and many an aguish shake
> On his stone pillow."

It is to the same legend that Wordsworth refers in his *Ecclesiastical Sonnets* (No. xxxviii.):

> " Black Demons hovering o'er his mitred head,
> To Cæsar's Successor the Pontiff spake;
> ' Ere I absolve thee, stoop! that on thy neck
> Levelled with earth this foot of mine may tread.'
> Then he, who to the altar had been led,
> He, whose strong arm the Orient could not check,
> He who had held the Soldan at his beck,
> Stooped, of all glory disinherited,
> And even the common dignity of man!"

Among mediæval agencies which, like the unity of the Church, fostered the intercourse of nations, bridged the distances between class and class, and promoted the growth of the idea of an universal empire, pilgrimages and the crusades were powerful instruments. In both, European Christendom, rich and poor, united for common objects. In both, the Psalms were at work.

Pilgrimages to Palestine practically began with the journey of the Empress Helena, mother of Constantine the Great, and her " invention " of the true Cross at Jerusalem (326). A few years later, the Bordeaux Pilgrim wrote the first Christian guide-book to the Holy Land; and during the lifetime of Jerome, pilgrims, fired by his example, or attracted by his fame, greatly increased in number. Between 385 and 388, Silvia of Aquitaine visited the Holy Land, and even passed beyond the bounds of the Roman Empire. As they journeyed towards their goal, pilgrims sang together three psalms at the canonical hours, and, on reaching Jerusalem, their first act was to ascend the tower of David, and recite the whole Psalter. Saturated, as they were, with the language of the Psalms, the early pilgrims brought back strange reports of the miracles which were worked in Palestine, even as the Psalmist had foretold. After the sun was up, a cloud rose from the Hill of Hermon, and stood over the church at Jerusalem, as David had sung of the dew of Hermon which fell upon the Hill of Sion. So says Antoninus of Placentia, surnamed the Martyr, who visited Palestine in the days of Justinian. He also relates how, during the Epiphany festival, at the baptism of catechumens on the banks of the Jordan, when the waters were blessed, the river returned upon itself with a roar; the upper part stood still until the ceremony was completed, the lower part running away to the sea. Thus, as David had said, " Jordan was driven back." His contemporary Theodosius, in his work *De Situ Terræ Sanctæ*, tells how " a vine which the Lord had planted," close to the field where He had Himself ploughed a furrow, regularly provided the wine for the Pentecostal communion; how the " little hills " had walked exulting before the Lord, when He descended to Baptism, even as David had said, " The mountains skipped like rams, and the little hills like young sheep "; and how, to the pious eye of the traveller, " even to this day they seemed in the act of

The Middle Ages 61

jumping." With the lapse of years, religious fervour cooled. Mixed motives influenced the motley crowds, who, with knobbed iron-shod staves in their hands, a scrip for provisions slung at their sides, their hats and clothes studded with leaden medals and pewter brooches, journeyed to Walsingham or Canterbury, to Rocamadour or Compostella, and even to Rome or Jerusalem. Some travelled barefoot, or naked but for their shirts, to expiate their sins; others toiled wearily in the hope of miraculous healing; others fulfilled a vow made in sickness; some protested against the government by visiting the shrine of a canonised rebel; others became pilgrims by profession, from laziness, for the pleasures of the journey, from love of adventure. But however great may have been the abuses which were satirised by Langland and Wyclif, by the author of *Reynard the Fox* and Erasmus, there never failed to be numbers of simple devout pilgrims, who, as they travelled singly or in companies, chanted the Psalms on the way in the spirit of an earlier faith, and returned strengthened and consoled by beholding the mysterious object of their pious veneration.

The Crusades, like the struggle between the temporal and spiritual powers, and like mediæval pilgrimages, were necessarily permeated by religious influences. If they do not exclusively belong to the domain of Church History, they move in that broad belt of twilight, where things secular and things ecclesiastical are as closely associated as the beginnings of night or day.

There were but few of the battlefields against the Saracens which had not resounded with the *Venite* (Ps. xcv.), the battle-cry of the Templars, as, in after ages, the Psalms supplied the war-shout of John Sobieski, the motto of the Great Armada, the watch-words of Gustavus Adolphus and of Cromwell, the *Marseillaise* of the Huguenots and the Cevenols. From the Psalms the Crusade was preached by St. Bernard, who made special use of Ps. cxliv. (" Blessed be the Lord my strength," etc.), and Ps. cxvi., verse 13 (" Right dear in the sight of the Lord is the death of His saints.") When, on October 3rd, 1187, Jerusalem was again taken by Saladin, it was once more from the Psalms that Pope Clement III. urged the bishops to preach another Holy War (Ps.

cxxvii., " Except the Lord build the house," etc.) Baldwin, Archbishop of Canterbury, responded to the appeal, donned the White Cross of England, raised the banner of St. Thomas, and preached the Crusade in Wales, chanting the Psalms as the war-song of his recruits. At the head of his troop, he left England, March 6th, 1190, eager to win back " the sepulchre of Christ," and

> " To chase these Pagans, in those holy fields,
> Over whose acres walked those blessed feet,
> Which fourteen hundred years ago were nail'd
> For our advantage on the bitter cross." [1]

From the first he was doomed to disappointment. In the language of the Psalms, his chaplain sums up the archbishop's horror at the licentiousness of the Crusaders' host. " God," he says, " is not in the camp. There is none that doeth good, no not one " (Ps. xiv., verse 2). In his despair, the archbishop prayed for death, in words that plainly allude to another Psalm (cxviii., verse 18), " O Lord, my God! such need is there for chastening and correcting with Thy holy grace, that, if it please Thy mercy, I pray to be removed from the turmoil of this life. I have tarried long enough with this army." Fifteen days later (19th November 1190), he died at Acre. In the words of a psalm, Richard I. poured out his indignation, when he found himself deserted by his followers, and knew that the crusade had failed, " My God, why hast Thou forsaken me? " (Ps. xxii., verse 1). After the battle of Agincourt (1415) the English army, fresh from victory, sang on bended knees the first verse of Psalm cxv. (" Not unto us, O Lord, not unto us, but unto Thy Name give the praise "), which Henry IV. had given to his son as a motto when he called him to a share in the government of his kingdom. It was a psalm that reminded the victor of his life-long ambition. As Psalm li. was read to Henry V. on his deathbed, verse 18, " O be favourable and gracious unto Sion; build Thou the walls of Jerusalem," reminded the dying king of his cherished hope of rescuing the Holy City from the hands of the Mussulman.

More strongly political than the Holy War in Palestine,

[1] *Henry IV.*, Part I., Act 1, scene i.

were the struggles by which Spain was wrested from the Moors, or Russia from its Mongol oppressors, and from each may be quoted instances of the use of the Psalms.

Adelme, Abbot of the Benedictine House of Chaise-Dieu, accompanied the army of Alphonso the Valiant, first King of Castile, who in 1085 had driven the Moors from Toledo. At the passage of the Tagus, the Christian soldiers recoiled from entering the swollen flood. But Adelme, mounted on his ass, rode into the stream, singing the 7th verse of Ps. xx., " Some put their trust in chariots, and some in horses; but we will remember the Name of the Lord our God." His courage shamed the hesitating soldiers; they plunged into the stream, and the whole Christian army crossed the river. The final stage of the struggle was reached in 1510, when Cardinal Ximenes in full pontificals led the Spanish troops against the Moors at Oran. The town was captured, and the victorious cardinal rode through the streets, chanting Ps. cxv., " Not unto us, O Lord, not unto us, but unto Thy Name give the praise."

In the latter half of the fourteenth century, the young Demetrius, as a child of twelve, became Grand Prince of Russia, with Moscow for his capital (1363). Two centuries were yet to elapse before Ivan the Terrible was crowned and anointed first Czar of Muscovy. But it was under the youthful Demetrius, known from his victory by the title of " the Don," that Russia made her first great step towards national independence and national unity. In 1380, the Tartar hordes, leaving blackened solitudes in their rear, were advancing upon Moscow. For Russia, enervated by Mongol domination, torn by civil discord, hard pressed on her western borders, and menaced by invasion from the east, the crisis was supreme. The issue seemed inevitable. But it was as a Holy War that resistance was preached. Blessed by Sergius, the hermit of the Holy Trinity, Demetrius, advanced to meet Mamaï and the Mongol invaders on the banks of the Don (September 8th, 1380). If his heart quailed at the numbers of the enemy, it was with a psalm that he renewed his courage. After reading aloud Ps. xlvi., " God is our refuge and strength," he plunged into the fight, which ended in the total defeat of the Tartars at Koulikoff. The memory of the victory lives in contemporary literature, in pictures and sculptures, in the Donskoi and Simonoff monasteries, and in the legends with which national gratitude has surrounded the names of Sergius and of Demetrius of the Don.

In their devotional aspect the Crusades, like pilgrimages, had developed a reverential love for the scenes of our Lord's life on earth. In theory at least, the Pope represented the moral grandeur of mankind, and, in the struggle between the Papacy and the empire, was asserted the claim of the spirit to supremacy over the flesh. Meanwhile the millennium had come and gone, and, with its passing, hopes of the future of humanity were revived. On these and other sides, men's minds were disposed to religious revivals and religious reforms, like those associated with the Cistercian or Franciscan Orders. With the need came the men. St. Bernard, by his character and genius, exemplified in practice the principles which he maintained, and embodied them in a personality at once winning and commanding. Free, in its simplicity and purity, from religious or secular politics, the Cistercian reform was, in its early stages, the spiritual movement which the Christian world was demanding. In the establishment of the Cistercians in England may be traced, broadly and strongly, the influence of the Psalms.

The Founder of the Order was Stephen Harding (1066–1134), a monk of the Benedictine house of Sherborne. It is significant that, as he made his pilgrim's journey to Rome through city, forest, or mountain pass, he daily recited the whole Psalter. On his return, as he passed through the diocese of Langres in Burgundy, he came on a cluster of huts, surrounding a wooden oratory on the slope of a hill above the river Leignes. It was the newly founded (1075) Benedictine monastery of Molesme. Fascinated by the solitude of the spot, attracted by the poverty and strictness of the brethren, he entered the community. Time passed. The monastery grew wealthy, and relaxed its discipline. In vain Abbot Robert, Prior Alberic, and Stephen Harding struggled to revive the ancient spirit. At last they determined to leave Molesme, and with twenty-one brethren, the three leaders settled (1098) at Citeaux, in the marshy glade

The Middle Ages 65

of a wild forest. Here, on the death of Alberic (1109), Stephen was chosen the third Abbot of Citeaux, and here he framed the Rule of the Cistercian Order.

Poverty, solitude, and simplicity were the essence of the reform which the Order initiated. The brethren were thus members of a militant community, in warfare with worldliness, luxury, and insincerity, both in Church and State. Unlike the Benedictines, they were compactly organised. They were not isolated monastic homes, which might relapse unnoticed from their high ideals. Careful provision was made for the periodical visitation and inspection of all the dependencies of Citeaux, as well as of Citeaux itself. The dress was of the simplest; but, as the black scapular fell over the white tunic, it seemed to the brethren that they bore in daily life the Cross of Christ. Their life was to be passed in sequestered villages, in hard manual toil among vineyards or cornfields, or in that meditation which "gathers itself from earthly things to contemplate God." Their scanty food—a daily portion of bread and two messes of vegetables—was earned by the sweat of the brow. They possessed no property which had ever belonged to the parochial clergy. Their churches were severely simple, but filled with the austere perfection of form and outline. Their music was the Gregorian chant, sung in unison by grave masculine voices. Instead of crucifixes of gold or silver, a crucifix of painted wood was alone allowed. Sculptures, pictures, gorgeous vestments were banished. As in the church, so in the scriptorium. Illuminated figures, elaborate capitals, marginal arabesques, were alike forbidden.

In the bareness, severity, and simplicity of their religious life, the Cistercians made no appeal to imagination. For fifteen years no novices were attracted to the marshy solitude of Citeaux. It seemed as though the new community would perish with the deaths of its first founders. But Stephen Harding persevered in his resolution. If any novices came, they would be men of the right stamp. At last his confidence was rewarded. In 1113, thirty men, headed by Bernard, and belonging to the noblest families of Burgundy, entered Citeaux as novices. The "barren woman" was made "to keep house, and to be a joyful mother of children." In 1115 had been established the daughter houses of La Ferté, Pontigny, Morimond, and Clairvaux, with Bernard as its first abbot. From each there sprang a whole line of monasteries.

In the Cistercian cloisters was thus planted a vine, which spread its branches far and wide, and bore fruit in many lands. A new life was breathed into the monasteries of Europe. In 1128, the first Cistercians settled in England, at Waverley, in Surrey. A little later, another body of monks, sent by Bernard himself, found a home on the banks of the Rye in Yorkshire, where now stand the ruins of the Abbey of Rievaux. A third was established at Fountains; and the story of the foundation, as told by the Monk Serlo and Hugh of Kirkstall, is almost clothed in the language of the Psalms.

The fame of the Cistercians spread abroad through the cloisters of Northern England. It penetrated within the precincts of the Benedictine Abbey of St. Mary at York, where lived many men who walked honestly in the traditions of their predecessors, but fell short of the Cistercian discipline. The piety of the new-comers woke the Benedictines from their lethargy; it stirred their dormant energies. They chafed at their sojourning " in the tents of Kedar," sickened of the flesh-pots of Egypt, wearied of the fret and fever of men and cities, sighed for " the wings of the dove," that they " might flee away, and be at rest." They longed to wander " far off, and remain in the wilderness." (Ps. lv., verses 6, 7).

Chief of the men who were thus moved by the example of the Cistercians was Richard, the sacrist of the house. He and six of his brethren, like-minded with himself, entered into a bond that they would seek a stricter life, and atone for past remissness by a severer discipline. But they dared not reveal their purpose to the prior, let he should bring their design to nothing. Their fears were without cause. Prior Richard had felt the same stirring, and formed the same purpose. He gladly associated himself with the others, whose numbers presently rose to thirteen men of but " one heart and one soul." They longed to depart from the convent, and to be grafted on the fruitful vine of the Cistercian Order.

But their design became known to other members of the

house, and reached the ears of the aged Abbot Godfrey. He charged them to give up an undertaking that cast a slur upon their Order. He even threatened punishment, if they persisted. Within the convent they were treated as traitors and as rebels, and it was only by taking refuge within the church and by appealing to Turstin, Archbishop of York, that they escaped violence. In 1132, the thirteen associates passed through the gates of the abbey in the train of Turstin, who begged the Archbishop of Canterbury to protect them, as Legate of the Apostolic See. Their only desire, he urged, was to follow, in their fullest meaning, the vows of their profession. The spirit of God, he says, speaks by the mouth of the Psalmist. "Promise unto the Lord your God, and keep it; pay thy vows unto the most Highest; I will pay thee my vows which I promised with my lips." The luxury of their surroundings had choked their spiritual aspirations. They longed to flee from the fate of the Israelites in the desert, who " did eat and were filled, for He gave them their own desire; they were not disappointed of their lust." If these men felt that they could not live uprightly so long as they stayed where they were, it was wrong to compel them to remain. "God," he continues, "who is our hope and strength, a very present help in trouble," was making them a way to escape. Was not their longing to withdraw from the world like that of David, when he yearned to escape from the clash of arms and the tumult of the people: "Lo, then would I get me away far off, and remain in the wilderness " (Ps. lv., verse 7)?

Whether the legate intervened, or not, is uncertain. But, in December 1132, Turstin himself took the brethren with him to celebrate the Nativity on his great manorial domains at Ripon. The next day, he led them along the valley of the Skell to a narrow glen, in a tangled thicket of thorns and brushwood, overhung by the hill of Herles-how. Here he left them, after giving them his blessing, and confirming their election of Prior Richard as their first abbot.

The new abbot had monks, but no monastery. He had "nowhere to lay his head," no hiding-place in which to escape the "stormy wind and tempest " (Ps. lv., verse 8). Beneath an elm, which at the time of the dissolution of the monasteries was still standing, the brethren thatched a shelter to serve as church and home, and betook themselves to their labours, plaiting mats, gathering sticks, cutting stakes, and enclosing a garden. So the winter passed. The new community had had time to consider their future mode of life and form of discipline. They determined to send to Bernard himself, narrating their simple history, and telling him that they had adopted the Cistercian Rule, had chosen him as their spiritual father and Clairvaux as their nursing mother. When Bernard heard the story of the two brethren, who were sent to him, he exclaimed, " It is the finger of God. Would that I myself could come over, and behold this exalted spectacle, which makes ' glad ' the whole ' City of God ' " (Ps. xlvi., verse 4). His letter was carried to the monks of Fountains by a monk of Clairvaux, who was charged to instruct them in the Cistercian Rule. Thus was founded the great house of Fountains.

Years passed, and as the Benedictine fervour had cooled from its early glow, so the Cistercian discipline lost its pristine simplicity. Even at their highest, the ideal of both had been the withdrawal from the world. Cloisters were the realisation of the *beata solitudo* and the *sola beatitudo*. To timid anxious souls, the inviolable sanctuaries of monastic life seemed the only refuge from the pillage and pestilence which wasted the fields, the only barrier against the stagnant mass of squalor, famine, and disease that festered in the towns. The times were evil. In the tearful passion of the *Stabat Mater*, as in the austere grandeur of the *Dies Iræ*, were expressed the fears and forebodings of the age. But hope was mingled with terror. Europe seemed to be thrilled by a common movement, and Gioacchino di Fiore, the Calabrian seer, expressed the popular instinct, that the dawn was whitening with the glory of a day which should usher in the " age of the spirit," the " age of love," the " age of lilies."

Such were the thoughts with which the air of Italy was charged, when St. Francis of Assisi grew to manhood (1182-1226). Artless, almost infantine, in the simplicity of his nature, he was the gentlest and most blameless of mankind—the saint and the poet of a poetic people. From the moment that he took Poverty for his bride, and consecrated his life to Christ, no temptation ever allured him from his inviolate fidelity. Active love, not contemplative piety, was the soul of his religion; practical life, not the seclusion of the cloister, was the sphere of its exercise. The father of the poor, the nurse of the leper, he had the faith to see the Divine image, and the charity to love it, even in its most neglected and repulsive tenements. Though his Brothers Minor developed into an Order, it was as a protest against the monastic spirit that they were originally founded, and it was only so long as the Lady Poverty walked among the sunburned hills of Umbria with a free step by the side of Chastity, and carolled hymns with Obedience, that the institution exemplified the idea of its founder.

The call of Francis came to him in the words of the Gospel. But if, as is recorded of him in Brother Leo's Legend of the Saint, Francis refused to allow a novice the use of a Psalter, the same biographer again and again illustrates his love of the Psalms. Thus he ever walked upon stones " with great trembling and reverence " for the love of Him that is called " the Rock," repeating the words " Thou didst set my feet upon the rock " (Ps. xl., verse 2). On Psalm cxlviii. is modelled his Canticle of the Sun, in which he sums up his love towards all created things, and especially towards those in which he saw a figure of anything pertaining to God or religion.

" Most high, almighty, and excellent Lord, to Thee be praise and glory and honour, and all blessing! To Thee alone, Most High, do they belong, and no man is worthy to name Thy name.

" Praised be Thou, my Lord, with all Thy creatures, and, above all, our Brother the Sun, who brings to us the light and the day. Beautiful is he, and radiant in his glorious splendour; and to us, Most High, he beareth witness of Thee.

" Praised be Thou, my Lord, for our Sister the Moon, and for all the Stars. In the heavens Thou hast set them, bright and precious and beautiful.

" Praised be Thou, my Lord, for our Brother the Wind, for the air, the cloud, the calm, and all weather, whereby Thou sustainest life in all Thy creatures.

" Praised be Thou, my Lord, for our Sister the Water, for

manifold are her services, and she is humble, precious, and pure.

"Praised be Thou, my Lord, for our Brother the Fire. By him Thou dost lighten our darkness. Beautiful is he, joyful, very mighty, and strong.

"Praised be Thou, my Lord, for our Sister, mother Earth, who doth sustain and nourish us, and bringeth forth in abundance divers fruits, flowers of many colours, and grass.

"Praised be Thou, my Lord, for those who for love of Thee, forgive their enemies, and endure weakness and tribulation. Yea, blessed are those who shall continue in peace, for by Thee, Most High, shall they be crowned.

"Praised be Thou, my Lord, for our Sister, the Death of the body, from whom no living man can escape. Woe to those who die in mortal sin! Blessed are they who are conformed to Thy most holy will, for the second death shall have no power to hurt them.

"Praise and bless my Lord! give thanks to Him and serve Him with all humbleness of heart." [1]

This was the song that the brethren chanted to the dying man, while, above the house where he lay, multitudes of crested larks, circling round the thatch, "by their sweet singing did seem to be praising the Lord along with him." As he had lived, so he died—in the arms of his Lady Poverty, stripped of his clothing, and laid on the bare ground. Psalms were sung to him, and from time to time he added his voice to the voices of his brethren, returning with special fondness to Psalm cxlii.: "I cried unto the Lord with my voice; yea, even unto the Lord did I make my supplication," etc. At nightfall, on October 3rd, 1226, he passed away.

Hitherto the influence of the Psalms has been illustrated from religious or semi-ecclesiastical history; but examples are not wanting in the more purely secular history of the Middle Ages. They moulded public opinion, and created a

[1] The text will be found in Sabatier's *Life of St. Francis of Assisi* (tr. L. S. Houghton, 1896, adopting M. Arnold's version), pp. 304-5:

"Altissimu, omnipotente, bon signore,
tue so le laude la gloria e l'onore," etc.

An English verse translation is given in *A Vision of Saints*, by Lewis Morris, "Saint Francis of Assisi."

The Middle Ages 71

standard of civil government. With them are associated scenes in the lives or deaths of William the Conqueror, Vladimir Monomachus, David I. of Scotland, Abelard and Heloïse, St. Louis of France, and William Wallace.

William the Conqueror died in September 1087, in circumstances which moved the historian, Ordericus Vitalis, to moralise in the language of the Psalms. The aggressions of Philip of France, and, as the story runs, the jest which he had aimed at the unwieldy size of the English king, aroused the latter's wrath. Claiming as his own the borderland of France and Normandy, William swore by the resurrection and splendour of God, that he would light a hundred thousand candles at the expense of Philip. He kept his word. Cornfields, vineyards, and orchards blazed up to the gates of Mantes, and the border fortress itself lay a heap of burning ashes. In his hour of triumph, William received his deathwound. His horse, stumbling among the embers, threw the king upon the iron pommel of his saddle with such force that he received a fatal injury. Carried to Rouen to die, he caused himself to be conveyed from the noise of the city to the Abbey of St. Gervais. In the early morning of September 9th, the great bell of the cathedral went for prime. The king asked what it meant. When he received the answer, he stretched forth his arms, raised his eyes to heaven, commended himself to his Lady Mary, the Holy Mother of God, that, by her intercession, she would reconcile him to her dear Son, Jesus Christ, and so breathed his last. His attendants hastily mounted their horses, and rode at speed to secure their houses and lands. His servants, after stripping the body of the dead king, made off, " like kites with their prey." " In a house not his own, foully stripped by his servants, there lay on the bare floor, from the first to the third hour of the day, the body of the mighty king, whom, but now, a hundred thousand warriors had eagerly served, and before whom many nations had trembled in fear." " Put not your trust in princes," moralises the chronicler, Ordericus Vitalis, whose pages teem with passages from the Psalms, " which are nought, O ye sons of men; but in God, the Living and the True, who is the Maker of all. If riches increase, set not your heart upon them. For all flesh is grass, and all the glory of it as the flower of grass. The grass withereth, and the flower thereof fadeth away; but the word of the Lord endureth for ever."

With the baptism of St. Vladimir at Cherson, and that of his whole people, in the waters of the Dnieper at Kieff, in 988, had begun the history of Russia. A century later, in Vladimir Monomachus, who is said to have married, as his first wife, Gytha, the daughter of Harold of England, Russia came into contact with the remotest power of Western Europe. When, in 1113, Vladimir became the Great Prince at Kieff, he was instructed by the Patriarch Nicephorus in his duties as a ruler. The lesson was a comment on Ps. ci., with an exhortation to get it by heart, to recite it often, to meditate upon it, and by it to fashion his government. "My song," so begins the letter, "shall be of the duties of my station; of mercy and judgment; first, of mercy, that is, of tender fatherly care for the welfare, spiritual, moral, and temporal, of all my subjects; and then, also, of judgment, that is, of doing true justice between man and man, of the restraint of wickedness and vice, and of the punishment of wrongdoers, both for their own chastisement and for the good of their fellows. Unto Thee, O Lord, will I sing. Unto Thee will I lift up my heart in meditation. I will not follow any other guide in my rule. I will not look to the tempter, though he offer me all the kingdoms of the world; nor to the idols of ambition, glory, praise of men, love of country, civilisation, knowledge, progress; nor yet to any selfish motives of pleasure, passion, ease. But, with fear and love, will I offer my thoughts, my motives, my designs, my deeds, my meditations, my prayers unto Thee, O Lord; for Thou art my King and my God, and I am Thy servant. For Thy sake only, and because it is Thy will, I will strive, with Thy help, to rule my fellow-men my brethren, whom otherwise I would choose to serve. So shall I have understanding in the way of godliness."

In the spirit of the psalm Vladimir ruled his subjects. With all his faults, there burned within him a spark of manly goodness, which lights up his dying injunctions to his son, and draws its heat from the Psalter. After describing the wonders of creation and the goodness of the Creator, in the words of David, Vladimir thus proceeds: " Praise God and love men. Neither fasting, nor solitude, nor monastic life will bring you life eternal; but doing good alone. Forget not the poor; feed them. Remember that all riches come from God, and are given you but for a while. . . . Be fathers to the fatherless; judge the cause of widows; suffer not the strong to oppress the weak. . . . My brethren said to me, ' Help us to drive out the sons of Rostislaf, or else give up our alliance.' But, I said, ' I cannot forget that I have kissed the Cross.' Then I opened the Book of Psalms, and read there with deep stirring of the heart, ' Why art thou so vexed, O my soul, and why art thou so disquieted within me? Put thy trust in God. I will confess my faults, and He is gracious.' "

Peter Abelard, in 1114, was the most famous teacher in Paris, then the most renowned school in Europe. The idol of the city, he had reached the pinnacle of worldly success. Then began his fatal passion for Heloïse. The lovers were separated; on Abelard a barbarous vengeance was taken, and Heloïse was immured in a convent. It is doubtful whether they ever met again.

On the banks of the Ardusson, in a quiet side-valley, twelve miles from Troyes, Abelard built the oratory of the Paraclete. There he passed several years, till, in 1125, he was invited to be abbot of the ancient Abbey of St. Gildas de Rhuys, near Vannes. He accepted the offer, moved, perhaps, by memories of his boyish studies at the dependent monastery of Locmenach. Meanwhile Heloïse and her nuns had been driven from Argenteuil. When Abelard heard that she was a wanderer once more, he made over to her and her nuns his deserted hermitage of Paraclete. There, by " Paraclete's white walls and silver springs," the love of Heloïse for Abelard once more broke silence. Pope was right in thinking that her life could never have been

" The blameless vestal's lot,
The world forgetting, by the world forgot ";

that Abelard's image may have often stolen between her and her God; that she may have heard his voice in every psalm, or dropped with every bead too " soft a tear." But be this as it may, Abelard's mournful autobiography, the *Historia*

Calamitatum, fell into her hands. The grave of her past was reopened by the story of his sufferings, and Heloïse wrote to " her lord, yea, her father; to her husband, yea, her brother; from his handmaid, yea, daughter; from his wife, yea, his sister; to Abelard from Heloïse." Abelard answers her tender words, if the letters are genuine, in the language of a man to whom all earthly things had grown cold and colourless. To her second letter he replies by sending, at her request, rules for her convent. At the close of his answer, he exhorts her to patience and resignation, concluding with a prayer, in which he betrays the depth of his own feeling, and definitely quotes from the Psalter:

" Forgive, O most Merciful! forgive, O Mercy itself! our sins, great as they are; and may the multitude of our offences know the height and breadth of Thy unspeakable clemency. Chastise the guilty here, that Thou mayest spare them hereafter. Punish them for a time, that Thou mayest spare them for eternity. Use against Thy servants the rod of correction, not the sword of wrath. Afflict the body, that Thou mayest save the soul. Cleanse, avenge not; be gentle rather than just; a merciful Father, rather than an austere Lord. ' Examine us, O Lord, and prove us,' as the prophet asked for himself (Ps. xxvi. 2). It is as if he said, ' Examine the strength there is, and suit the burden of temptation to it.' . . . Thou hast joined us, O Lord, and hast set us apart, when it pleased Thee, and as it pleased Thee. Now, O Lord, that which Thou hast begun in mercy, do Thou in mercy perfect, and those whom Thou hast severed in the world, join for ever unto Thyself in Heaven. O Lord, our hope, our portion, our expectation, our consolation, who art blessed for ever. Amen.

" Farewell in Christ, thou Spouse of Light, in Christ farewell, in Christ live! Amen."

Contemporary with Vladimir Monomachus and with Abelard, was David I., the just and merciful ruler of Scotland, who died May 24th, 1153. As Ailred of Rievaulx tells the story of his death, the king received the *viaticum*, venerated the famous black cross, and spent his last hours of conscious existence in repeating verses from the Psalms: " I deal with the thing that is lawful and right: O give me

The Middle Ages

not over unto mine oppressors " (Ps. cxix., verse 121), and " In the time of my trouble I will call upon Thee, for Thou hearest me " (Ps. lxxxvi., verse 7).

By a psalm St. Louis of France regulated his life. Before taking the seat of judgment, he was wont to repeat the words: " Blessed are they that alway keep judgment, and do righteousness " (Ps. cvi., verse 3). The Mass for the first Sunday in Advent began with the words, " Unto Thee, O Lord, will I lift up my soul. My God, I have put my trust in Thee " (Ps. xxv., verse 1). On that day Louis was crowned (1226). Joinville, who notes the fact, observes that even in his death the king had perfect trust in God. It was with a psalm on his lips that Louis died. In July 1270, he had taken the Cross, and embarked at Aigues Mortes for Africa. Before the walls of Tunis, the climate and the plague did their deadly work. At last Louis IX. himself was struck down by sickness. Three weeks he lingered. On August 25th, 1270, laid on a bed of ashes, he died, murmuring the words of Ps. v., verse 7, " But as for me, I will come into Thine house, even upon the multitude of Thy mercy; and in Thy fear will I worship toward Thy holy temple."

At the execution of William Wallace, the dying patriot found comfort in the Psalter, which had been the companion of his adventurous wanderings. Betrayed to the English by the " fause Menteith," tried for treason in Westminster Hall, he was executed at West Smithfield (August 23rd, 1305) with all the barbarities of the age. As he stood on the scaffold, in the midst of the instruments for his torture, he begged Lord Clifford to restore to him the Psalter, which had been taken from him at his capture. The prayer was granted. Unable to hold the book in his chained hands, he asked a priest to keep it open for him, and, as he hung from the gallows, he continued to look on it with love and devotion. After he was taken down and, still alive and sensible, disembowelled, his eyes remained fixed upon the Psalter, until they closed in death.

Nor was it only in mediæval action that the influence of the Psalms may be traced. Mediæval thought also fell under their spell. The science and the literature as well as the history of the Middle Ages felt their sway.

By the Psalms the science of the Middle Ages was to a great extent governed. The earth, argued mediæval cosmogonists, cannot be in motion, or suspended in mid-air; rather, it is firmly fixed, for " He hath made the round world so fast that it cannot be moved " (Ps. xciii., verse 2), and " He laid the foundations of the earth that it never should move at any time " (Ps. civ., verse 5.) And its centre is Jerusalem. The column in the Holy City, at midday, casts no shadow, and " God is in the midst of her, therefore shall she not be removed " (Ps. xlvi., verse 5). On the text, " Praise him, all ye heavens; and ye waters that are above the heavens " (Ps. cxlviii., verse 4), were built strange theories. Heaven was divided into two by the firmament, which lay between our atmosphere and the Paradise of God. Below the firmament lived the angels; above it were the waters. Jerome held that the waters were frozen; Ambrose believed that the outside firmament was a hard shell, on the outer edge of which were stored the waters; some thought that the terrestrial universe was surrounded by huge walls, on which were supported the firmament and the waters they contained. The purpose for which the waters were collected, was disputed. It was believed that they were gathered for another deluge, or to moderate the fervent heat of the heavenly bodies, or to lubricate the axis on which the heavens moved round the earth. In the air exhaled from the earth were lightning and hail, snow and vapours, wind and storm (Ps. cxlviii., verse 8). Earthquakes were explained from Psalm cxxxv., verse 7, by the winds being drawn from God's secret treasuries, or by the motions of Leviathan (Ps. civ., verse 26), who, when his tail is scorched by the sun, seeks to seize it, and labours so powerfully that the earth is shaken by his efforts. The rise and fall of tides was explained by his drinking in and spewing out vast volumes of water. With a strange mixture of Pagan with Christian thought, it was supposed that the powers of the air could produce thunder, lightning, and rain, and against their baneful influences the favourite exorcism was Psalm civ.

Of the monastic spirit in literature, the *De Imitatione Christi* is the finest product. The writer, according to some of the best authorities, was Thomas Hæmmerlein, called, as was the custom of the day, à Kempis, from the small town of Kempen, near Dusseldorf. A little, fresh-coloured man, simple in worldly affairs, shy and retiring in his habits, too absent-minded to be long entrusted with any practical part of the government of the convent of Mount St. Agnes, Thomas à Kempis was given, as a biographer says of him, " to the interior life and devotion." In solitude, silence, and humility, he bowed himself before his Saviour, that so he might catch the faintest whisper of His voice, and conform himself, without hindrance of earthly barriers, to its slightest command. The fruit of that close personal communion is the wonderful book, in which throbs the spiritual heart of mediæval Christianity. From the nature of its subject, the *Imitation* might be expected to rely mainly on the New Testament. But in thought, feeling, and language, it is largely based on the Psalter. " I will hearken what the Lord God will say concerning me; for He shall speak peace unto His people, and to His saints, that they turn not again " (Psalm lxxxv., verse 8) supplies the keynote to the third book, which treats of internal consolation; and throughout the whole work, the Psalms are more largely cited than the Gospels, and the illustrations from the Psalter outnumber all the passages which are quoted from the four records of our Lord's life upon earth.

The religious calm, which, together with the most ardent love, characterises the *Imitation*, was not lightly won. In his *Soliloquy of the Soul*, Thomas à Kempis gives the history of his inner life, and chronicles the perplexities through which his soul gained its absolute peace. The book is in great part an impassioned expansion of texts drawn from the Psalms, such as :˙ " Blessed be the name of His Majesty for ever " (Ps. lxxii., verse 19) : " All my bones shall say, Lord, who is like unto Thee ? " (Ps. xxxv., verse 10) : " Say unto my soul, I am thy salvation " (Ps. xxxv., verse 3) : " My soul hangeth upon Thee " (Ps. lxiii., verse 9): " Praised be God, who hath not . . . turned His mercy from me " (Ps. lxvi., verse 18).

Yet another illustration of the influence of the Psalms upon devotional literature may be taken from Thomas's " Little Alphabet of the Monks in the School of Christ," a series of short precepts, drawn up for those who wished to adopt the Rule of the brotherhood of the Canons Regular. In form it is modelled on the 119th Psalm, the initial letters of the precepts running consecutively through the alphabet:

> "Aspire to be unknown, and to be accounted nothing; for this is more healthful and profitable for thee than the praise of men.
>
> "Be benevolent to all thy fellows, alike to the good and to the evil; and be burdensome to none.
>
> "Care for it that thy heart be kept from wandering thoughts, thy mouth from vain speech, thy senses under discipline.
>
> "Dwell in solitude and silence, and therein shalt thou find great peace and a good conscience; for in a multitude are much noise and many distractions of the heart.
>
> "Elect poverty and simplicity and be content with a few things, and thou wilt not be quick to complain.
>
> "Flee the conversation of worldly men; for with both God and man, with things both transitory and eternal, thou canst not be satisfied."

The last precept runs thus:

> "Zaccheus, my brother, come down from the tree-tops of knowledge. Come thou and learn in the school of God the way of humility, of meekness, and of patience; so, by the teaching of Christ, wilt thou at length be able to attain to the glory of eternal blessedness."

In the sphere of devotional literature, the *De Imitatione* is, as has been said, the finest fruit of monasticism. Compared with the *Divina Commedia* of Dante, it marks the vivid contrast between religious life in the world and in the cloister. Both books are, as it were, studies of the human soul in its passage from darkness to light. In both, Christian theology strikes the keynote. But the one is as harmonious in its whole as the other is incongruous in its details. With his vision, Dante has interwoven elements which the *De Imitatione* seeks to exclude, or feelings that it hopes to crush. In the *Divina Commedia*, passionate scorn and holy mysteries of faith, coarse satire and hymns of the blessed, contemporary scandal and lofty idealism, the most ardent faith in the Divine government of the world and the politics of the day, the personal bitterness of private wrongs and the keenest perception of the issues of good and ill doing, are inextricably mingled.

Dante's admiration of the Psalms is not only shown by the version of the Seven Penitential Psalms, which is attributed to him. It is also again and again illustrated from his great Christian poem, which ushers in the literature of Europe. In some passages he refers to David himself; in others he quotes from the Book of Psalms. Thus, after he had passed the threshold of the gate of Purgatory (*Purgatorio*, canto x., l. 1, and following), Dante and his guide climb upwards by a rocky ascent to the lowest circle, where those are purified who have sinned through pride. On one side of the path rises a precipitous cliff of white marble, curiously adorned with sculptures commemorating humility. There in the marble were carved the car and oxen, drawing the sacred ark, and (ll. 64-6)

> " Preceding the blest vessel, onward came
> With light dance leaping, girt in humble guise,
> Sweet Israel's harper; in that hap he seemed
> Less, and yet more, than kingly."

Ruth, on her throne in Paradise (*Paradiso*, canto xxxii., ll. 10-12), is described as

> " The gleaner-maid,
> Meek ancestress of him, who sang the songs
> Of sore repentance in his sorrowful mood."

In the planet Jupiter, which is the sixth heaven, the souls of those who have rightly administered justice on the earth are disposed in the figure of an eagle. Those that glitter in the eagle's eye are the chief and greatest (*Paradiso*, canto xx., ll. 37-42), and here David is placed:

> " This that shines
> Midmost for pupil, was the same who sang
> The Holy Spirit's song, and bare about
> The ark from town to town; now doth he know
> The merit of his soul-impassion'd strains
> By their well-fitted guerdon."

In other passages the Psalms are quoted. Cheered by St. James, Dante lifts his eyes, heretofore bent on the ground with their over-heavy burden, " To the hills from whence cometh my help " (*Paradiso*, canto xxv., ll. 37-39, and

Ps. cxxi., verse 1). Hope had first come to him, as he tells St. James (*ibid.*, ll. 71-5, and Ps. ix., verse 10):

> " From him who sang
> The songs of the Supreme, himself supreme
> Among his tuneful brethren. ' Let all hope
> In Thee,' so spake his anthem, ' who have known
> Thy name.' "

At an earlier stage in his journey, as he lingered by the shores of the Island of Purgatory (*Purgatorio*, canto ii., ll. 40-8), Dante sees at early dawn a light bark, without oars or sails, driven swiftly to land by the wings of the angel who stands on the poop. Within are a hundred spirits and more, who sing with one voice together Ps. cxiv., " When Israel came out of Egypt." So also in the fifth circle (*Purgatorio*, canto xix., ll. 70-5, and Ps. cxix., verse 25), those who had sinned from avarice and prodigality, lay with their faces downwards, prone upon the ground, weeping sore:

> " ' My soul hath cleaved to the dust,' I heard,
> With sighs so deep, they well-nigh choked the words."

Such illustrations might be multiplied; but as an example of the use which Dante makes of the Psalms, directly or symbolically, those stanzas of the *Purgatorio* may be taken, in which Beatrice appears. Dante has passed through the fire, climbed the mountain, and, followed by Virgil and Statius, traverses a wood, bright with the fresh flowers of May. Through it floats a light breeze, ruffling the leaves as it passes, scented with sweet odours, and mingling with the songs of birds. He is stopped by a stream, three paces across. In a meadow on the opposite side walks Matilda, singing as she gathers the flowers that paint her way. Dante wonders at the brightness of her smile, till she tells him that she is gladdened by the verse of Ps. xcii., beginning " Delectasti " (Ps. xcii., verse 4.), " Thou, Lord, hast made me glad through Thy works," etc. (" Quia delectasti me, Domine, in facturâ tuâ, et in operibus manuum Tuarum exsultabo.") It is this delight in God's work, and labour in His service, that make the perfect happiness of active life on earth. All other bliss is but a dream that closes with death. This alone is the waking vision, for it is the pathway and vestibule of Heaven.

The Middle Ages

She further explains to him that the spot is the earthly Paradise, and that the stream by which he stands is called Lethe and Eunoe, because its twofold properties are to take away the memory of sin, and to restore the recollection of every good deed. Then she returns, like an enamoured dame, to her song (*Purgatorio*, canto xxix., ll. 1-3, and Ps. xxxii., verse 1), " Blessed is he whose unrighteousness is forgiven, and whose sin is covered." As Matilda, alone on the one bank, and the three poets on the other, move upwards against the stream, a great brightness flushes, and then suddenly floods, the forest; sweet melody floats through the luminous air; a procession of figures comes into view; and a triumphal car, drawn by a gryphon, halts over against the spot where Dante stood. The poet has seen the vision of the perfect active life, which delights, not in its own labour, but in God's work. Now he beholds the perfect contemplative life, which may be lived on earth if only it has for its object, not its own beauty, but God's person and love in Christ. On the car appears Beatrice, white-veiled, olive-crowned, strewn with flowers, and clad in the mystic colours of Love, Faith, and Hope (*Purgatorio*, canto xxx., ll. 82-5, and Ps. xxxi., verses 1-9). In her eyes are reflected the twofold nature of Christ, and she bids him mark her well; but his gaze shrinks from her stern pity:

> " And, suddenly, the angels sang,
> ' In Thee, O gracious Lord! my hope hath been,'
> But went no further than ' Thou, Lord, hast set
> My feet in ample room.' "

Chaucer quotes but little from the Psalms. It may be taken as a slight proof of his dramatic insight that he is careful to make "Dame Abstinence Streyned" (*Romaunt of the Rose*, l. 7366), remember "hir Sawter" as part of her disguise of a Beguine; and, when he cites the Psalms, he places his quotations in the mouths of persons like the Prioress, who begins the prologue of her tale with Ps. viii., verses 1, 2 :

> " ' O Lord, our Lord, Thy name how marveillous
> Is in this large world y-sprad,'—quod she,"

or like the Parson, the Summoner, and the " Frere." But

in William Langland fourteenth-century England had her people's Dante. Clad in hermit's garb, and sleeping heavily from weariness of wandering, Langland saw on the Malvern Hills the *Vision of Piers Plowman*. Far inferior to the great Italian in grandeur of conception and nobility of execution, the English poet was Dante's rival in realistic power. He paints with a wire brush, and a force that is almost fierce; but his tender sympathy with human suffering redeems the harshness of his rugged lines, and gives to his racy vigour and homely language something of spiritual intensity.

That Langland should clothe much of his *Vision* in the language of the Psalms, is not surprising. Bred in a monastery, he lived by singing. "The tools," he says, "wherewith I labour and earn my bread are *Paternoster*, and my primer *Placebo* and *Dirige*, and sometimes my *Psalter* and my *Seven Psalms*." As the whole world of men, busy with their varied occupations, pass before the dreamer's vision, he sees that Bribery is all-powerful, in spite of what David had said of those who take bribes : " Lord, who shall dwell in Thy tabernacle? He that hath not taken reward against the innocent " (Ps. xv., verses 1 and 6). He sees also that Justice and Favour are bestowed on men " in whose hands is wickedness," provided that " their right hand is full of gifts " (Ps. xxvi., verse 10). Yet, evil though the world is, Scripture bids men not despair; no offence is beyond God's pardon, for " His mercy is over all His works " (Ps. cxlv., verse 9).

In sect. v., the dreamer sees again the " field full of folk," where the sinners are induced to confess and repent. The Deadly Sins make their penitential confession. Repentance prays for the penitents, and Hope seizing a horn, blows upon it (Ps. xxxii., verse 1), " Blessed is he whose unrighteousness is forgiven; and whose sin is covered." Then all together, saints in glory and men on earth, cry upward " to Crist and to his moder " with the Psalmist David, " Thou, Lord, shalt save both man and beast; how excellent is Thy mercy, O God " (Ps. xxxvi., verse 7).

In sect. xv., Langland describes Charity. Riches, as the dreamer reflects, hinder men in their way towards heaven; but Poverty is the gift of God, and sweet to the human soul.

The dreamer has not found Charity in London, for there all are covetous. Where then is he to be found? and the answer of the Soul is given, that Charity seldom comes to Court. He wears russet and fur, sometimes ragged clothes, and once—long ago—the frock of a friar. Proud of a penny as of a pound of gold, he is full of gladness, trusts his fellows, finds in sickness a solace, fears neither death nor dearth. Who provides for him? asks the dreamer. He cares nothing for rent or riches. He neither craves nor covets. In the Lord he lays him down, and takes his rest (Ps. iv., verse 9). He has a friend, who never fails: " When thou openest thy hand, they are filled with good " (Ps. civ., verse 28). He visits the poor and the prisoner; he feeds, clothes, and comforts them, telling them of Christ's sufferings. He purgeth men of pride, cleansing them in the Laundry, with groans and tears (Ps. vi., verse 6). With the warm water from his eyes, he washes them whiter than snow (Ps. li., verse 7), singing with his work, and sometimes weeping, for he knows that " a broken and contrite heart, O God, shalt Thou not despise " (Ps. li., verse 17).

In sect. xviii. is told in part the Resurrection Legend, based on Psalm xxiv. (verses 7-10), " Lift up your heads, O ye gates," etc. Christ had died on the Cross, and in Hell the devils saw a soul " hitherward sailing—with glory and with great light," and knew the coming of the King of Glory. Then the " Dukes " of that " dymme place " are bidden to undo the gates,

> " That Crist may come in
> The Kynges sone of hevene."

With the breath of that command Hell breaks. The hundreds of angels strike their harps, and Peace pipes—

> " After sharpe showres
> Most shene is the sonne;
> Is no weder warmer
> Than after watry cloudes."

Truth makes her covenant with Peace, and Righteousness kisses her reverently (Psalm lxxxv., verse 10). Finally Truth takes the lute, and to it sings, " Behold how good and joyful a thing it is, brethren, to dwell together in unity" (Ps. cxxxiii., verse 1).

All over South-Western France has spread the popular legend, that on Easter day, when the words "Lift up your heads, O ye gates" (Ps. xxiv.) are being sung in church, the treasure-houses marked by dolmens, cromlechs, and menhirs, or concealed, as at Boussac, in the walls of castles, spring open, and men may, for a brief space, enter and enrich themselves unharmed by their infernal guardians. It is the recurring moment of which Drummond of Hawthornden sings:

> "Bright portals of the sky,
>   Emboss'd with sparkling stars;
> Doors of Eternity,
>   With diamantine bars,
> Your arras rich uphold,
>   Loose all your bolts and springs,
> Ope wide your leaves of gold,
>   That in your roofs may come the King of Kings."

But the prevalence of the legend in France, and elsewhere, is probably due to the popularity of the *Golden Legend* in devotional literature. In that book is enshrined the religious heart of the Middle Ages, with its fears and fancies, its longings, its child-like yet soaring faith. In it is revealed the soul of those cathedrals which still stand in our midst, like beings of another world. In it, too, are unlocked the secrets of the intuitive glories and imaginative mysteries of mediæval painting and architecture. As Caxton says of it: "In like wise as gold is most noble above all other metals, in like wise is this Legend holden most noble above all other works." The following is the story of Our Lord's visit to Hell, condensed from the version of the *Golden Legend*:—

The news of the Resurrection struck Jerusalem with consternation. While the priests and princes of the people were holding counsel, there were brought into the assembly two sons of the aged Simeon, Leucius and Carinus, who had risen with Jesus and returned from death to life. Each asks that tablets should be given them, and each wrote thereon his tale. We were, they wrote, in the dim place of Shadow with our fathers the Patriarchs, when suddenly a great light of gold and crimson, as it had been the sun in his glory, shone round about us. Then, straightway, Adam, the father of the human race, rejoiced and said, "This light is that of the Author of all light, who has promised to send us His eternal day." And Isaiah cried aloud, "This light is that of God, of whom I foretold that the people which walked in darkness should see a great light." Then came to us the aged Simeon, and with him John the Baptist, and they both bore witness to the Saviour—the one, that he had carried Him in his arms; the other, that he had baptised Him, and that His coming was nigh. And all the Patriarchs were filled with joy unspeakable.

Then Satan, the prince of Death, said unto Hell, "make ready to receive Jesus, who boasted Himself to be the Son of God, but who is only a man in fear of death, for He hath said, 'My soul is exceeding sorrowful even unto death.' Behold how I have tempted Him! I have stirred up the people against Him! I have sharpened the lance; I have mingled the gall and vinegar; I have made ready the tree of the cross. The time is at hand, when I shall bring Him hither a captive."

Then Hell asked, "Is it this same Jesus who raised up Lazarus?" And Satan made answer, "It is He." Then Hell cried, "I adjure thee, by thy power and by mine, that thou bring Him not hither; for when I heard the command of His word, I trembled, and I could not hold Lazarus, but he, wresting himself from me, took flight like an angel and escaped out of my hands."

Now, while Hell was thus speaking, there came a voice, like the crash of thunder, which said, "Open your gates, ye Princes, lift up your everlasting doors, and the King of Glory shall come in." At the sound of this mighty voice, the devils hastened to close the brazen gates with bars of iron. But when he saw what they did, the prophet David said, "Have I not prophesied that He would break the gates of brass, and smite in sunder the bars of iron?" Again the voice sounded, "Open ye your gates, and the King of Glory shall come in." Then Hell, hearing that the voice had thus twice spoken, asked, "Who then is this King of Glory?" And the prophet David made answer; "It is the Lord Strong and Mighty, even the Lord mighty in battle; He is the King of Glory."

Even as David spake, the King of Glory appeared, His splendour shining through all the halls of shadows, and he stretched forth His right hand and took the right hand of Adam, saying, " Peace be with thee, and with all thy sons that have been just." And so the Lord passed forth from the gates of Hell, and in His train followed all the just.

Leucius and Carinus ceased to write, and, becoming white as snow, disappeared.

CHAPTER V

THE REFORMATION ERA

The influence of the Psalms among pioneers of the Reformation—Wyclif, John Hus, Jerome of Prague; among mediæval reformers—Savonarola; among Protestant leaders—Luther and Melancthon; among champions of the Papacy—the Emperor Charles V.; among discoverers of New Worlds—Christopher Columbus; among men of the New Learning—Erasmus, Pico della Mirandola, Sir Thomas More; John Fisher; John Houghton; among leaders of the Catholic Reaction—Xavier, and St. Teresa; among Protestant and Catholic Martyrs—Hooper, Ridley, and Southwell.

ON St. Sylvester's day, 1384, John Wyclif lay dying at Lutterworth. The friars, so runs the story, crowded round him, urging him to confess the wrongs that he had done to their Order. But the indomitable old man caused his servant to raise him from the pillow, and, gathering all his remaining strength, exclaimed with a loud voice, " I shall not die, but live; and declare—the evil deeds of the Friars " (Ps. cxviii., verse 17).

Before Wyclif's day, devout men had assailed the corruption of the Church, or disputed her doctrines of the Sacraments. Some had protested against the claims of the Papacy, or upheld the rights of national churches. Others had demanded the preaching of the true Gospel. Others had deplored the worldliness of the clergy, denounced the wealth of the Monastic Orders, or preached the blessings of poverty. But all had remained loyal to the Pope; none had looked beyond existing agencies for the reform of the Church and of society. Wyclif's attitude marks an advance so distinct as to proclaim a new epoch. He not only attacked practical abuses, but aimed at erecting an ecclesiastical fabric which should differ from the old in doctrine as well as in organisation. In the last years of his life, he urged complete separation from the Papacy as Antichrist, established his " Poor

Priests," aspired to reform England by the translation of the Bible into the vulgar tongue, and, in religion, politics, and society, insisted on the freedom of the human conscience from every restraint except Christ's written law. His importance as the centre of all pre-Reformation history was instinctively recognised. When the Bishop of Lincoln ordered his body to be exhumed and burned, and its ashes thrown into the river Swift—or when Walsingham, the Chronicler, calls him "that weapon of the Devil, that enemy of the Church, that sower of confusion among unlearned people, that idol of heresy, that mirror of hypocrisy, that father of schism, that son of hatred, that father of lies "—the one by his action, the other by his language, expresses his sense of the fact that Wyclif was not a reformer of the mediæval monastic type, but had introduced a new era.

Wyclif's attitude was, in part, produced by changed circumstances. Traditions of universal empire were obscured by the rise of separate nations, one in race, language, and religion; the temporal claims of the Pope had increased as his spiritual hold on the world relaxed, and both became intolerable, when claimants of the papal throne excommunicated their opponents or doomed their rivals to eternal damnation. In part, it expressed profound discontent with the corruptions of religious life, intensified by the horrors of the plague. Even the most vicious were terrified into paying that vicarious homage to virtue which demands from the clergy an elevated moral standard. In part, it resulted from political or social conditions. The English nation was at war with France; the Pope was the puppet of the French king, and papal tributes fed the French treasury with English money. The nobles desired to oust the clergy from public affairs, the commons to lighten their own burdens by taxing ecclesiastical property, the people to relieve their poverty by appropriating the wealth of the Church. But the peculiar position which Wyclif adopted was even more the effect of his own temperament. To his austere piety, logical intellect, unimaginative nature, the faith of the Middle Ages made but weak appeal. Blind to its beauties, he saw with exaggerated clearness only its deformities. He chafed against the fetters it imposed upon his mental inde-

The Reformation Era

pendence, and failed to appreciate its spiritual insight, mystical ardour, religious rapture, intense realisation of the mysteries of the unseen. When once a man of this temperament was startled into opposition by intellectual difficulties or moral shortcomings, he could not stop short at reform, but was irresistibly impelled towards revolution. He was the precursor, not of the Anglican reformer, but of the Puritan iconoclast.

Without Wyclif, there would have been no Hus and no Jerome of Prague. Both men were accused of sympathy with the English Reformer. At Prague, a portion of Wyclif's tomb was worshipped as a relic: numerous manuscripts of his writings exist in foreign libraries, especially at Vienna; and Hus's work on the Church (*De Ecclesiâ*) is derived, sometimes verbally, from the English Reformer. Like Wyclif, both Hus and Jerome died repeating the words of a psalm.

On July 6th, 1415, the Council of Constance held its fifteenth general session in the cathedral. Sigismund, King of the Romans, presided; before his throne, nobles and princes of the empire bore the insignia of the imperial dignity; the cardinals and prelates were assembled in their nations. After Mass had been said, John Hus, a pale, thin man, in mean attire, was brought into the presence of his judges, and placed on a small raised platform. In vain he protested that he had come to Constance under a safe-conduct from Sigismund himself. He was condemned as a heretic, and handed over to the secular arm for execution. The sentence was carried out without delay. On the road from Constance to Gottlieben the stake was prepared. When Hus reached the spot, wearing a paper cap of blasphemy, adorned with "three devils of wonderfully ugly shape," and inscribed with the word "Heresiarcha," he fell on his knees, and prayed, chanting Psalm xxxi. He died, choked by the flames, but repeating with "a merry and cheerful countenance," the words, "Into Thy hands I commend my spirit" (Ps. xxxi., verse 6).

On the same spot, on May 30th, 1416, died Jerome of Prague. Tall, powerfully built, graceful of speech, one of the most brilliant laymen of the day, he had come to the

Council to plead the cause of Hus. Panic-stricken at his friend's fate, he fled, only to be captured and brought back to Constance. His courage revived when escape was hopeless. An imprisonment of six months did not induce him to acknowledge the justice of the sentence passed upon Hus. Like his friend, he perished at the stake, dwelling with his latest breath on the same words, " Into Thy hands I commend my spirit."

The Council of Constance healed the papal schism. But it accomplished little more. With its dissolution, and that of the Council of Basle, faded the hope of any complete or universal reform of the Church from within. It was a time, not of transition only, but also of sifting. Men like Luther, Erasmus, or Fisher, who were of one mind in condemning abuses, passed into opposite camps, impelled by the differences in their own temperaments. Vast efforts were indeed made for internal reform; but they were too narrow, too local, or too late. The pent-up stream of intellectual life and classic culture had burst its barriers, shattering the old channels of thinking, believing, and acting, which centuries of habit had grooved. Fed from innumerable sources, the Protestant Reformation had swelled into a headlong torrent. In the sea of human faith and thought, both currents met the flowing tide of the Catholic reaction. It was a time of fierce shock and collision. But among the " green pastures " of the Psalms, and beside their " waters of comfort," men, who, in all else, were at bitter strife, refresh their weariness, renew their aspirations, recover their strength and courage. From the same pages, side by side, read mediæval reformers like Savonarola, heroes of the Protestant Reformation like Luther and Melancthon, imperial champions of the Papacy like Charles V., discoverers of new worlds like Christopher Columbus, lights of the new learning like Sir Thomas More, leaders of the Roman Catholic reaction like St. Teresa or St. Francis Xavier.

Savonarola (1452-98), the great Dominican preacher, who for five years held within the hollow of his hand the destinies of Florence, is one of the most fascinating figures in history. His worn face, as it is presented to us in the best known of his portraits, is harsh and even ugly, yet full of concentrated

The Reformation Era 91

force, both intellectual and moral. His blue-grey eyes burn like live coals under thick black eyebrows, and light up the yellow, wax-like complexion; his nose is long, and highly arched; his large mouth is quick to compress into resolve or to relax into a smile; the projecting lower lip gives an air of pugnacity to the whole face; his cheeks are hollowed by anxieties and abstinence; his low yet massive forehead is furrowed by the deep wrinkles of thought. His delicate transparent hands, with their long tapering fingers, tell the story of his enthusiastic, imaginative temperament.

Long had the hard-featured stripling pondered over the sin and misery of the world, praying, as he tells his father, in the words of the Psalm (cxliii., verse 8), " Shew Thou me the way that I should walk in, for I lift up my soul unto Thee." To escape the stifling atmosphere of wickedness by which he was surrounded, he fled to the cloister. Seven years later (1482), he was transferred from the Dominican convent of Bologna to that of San Marco at Florence, and began his career as preacher, reformer, and prophet. His indignation burned into flame as he watched the Church plundered by false friends, and saw spiritual death stealing over her pulseless form, like some quiet flowing tide. But his ideals were not those of a Wyclif or a Luther. He looked to a General Council to purify the vices of the Church: a rebel against an individual Pope, he was loyal to the Papacy: a stern reprover of practice, he advocated no change in doctrine. Throughout the struggle that followed, the contrast between the personal characters of the opponents heightens the tragic interest. On one side stands Roderigo Borgia, Pope Alexander VI., whose name has passed into a byword as a monster of iniquity; on the other, Savonarola, whose pure enthusiasm, unsullied morality, and religious zeal, can neither be denied nor disputed.

On April 7th, 1498, occurred a crisis in Savonarola's fate. It was the Friday before Palm Sunday. A Franciscan friar had challenged him to prove the truth of his preaching by the ordeal of fire. The challenge was accepted by one of his devoted adherents, Fra Domenico. Through the crowded streets of Florence passed the long procession of the Dominicans from San Marco to the great square in front of the

Palazzo Vecchio, where the ordeal was prepared. Their enthusiastic supporters heard the very buildings take up their chant, when the friars thundered forth the words of Psalm lxviii., "Let God arise, and let His enemies be scattered." All day the populace waited; but the challenger did not appear. The blind adoration of the fickle Florentines turned to fury. Savonarola's power was at an end. He was at the mercy of his enemies. On Palm Sunday, the 9th of the month, he was dragged from San Marco and thrown into prison. There he suffered repeated tortures, inflicted in the hope of wringing from him the confession that his revelations of the future were impostures. To a man of his highstrung sensitive temperament the physical agony was intense, and to it were added the mental pain of desertion, the pang of lost confidence, the bodily weakness of frequent fasts. With subtle refinement of cruelty, his torturers, who had broken his left arm and crunched the shoulder bone out of its socket, had left his right arm whole in order that he might sign his so-called confessions. He used it to write his meditations on the 51st and the 31st Psalms. The last was unfinished. Whether ink and paper were taken from the prisoner, or whether the arrival of the Papal Commissioners on May 19th, and his execution on the 22nd, cut short his task, is uncertain. Only three verses were completed:

"Sorrow," he begins, "hath pitched her camp against me. She hath hemmed me in on every side. Her men of war are strong and many. She hath filled my heart with the shout of battle and the din of arms. Day and night she ceaseth not to strive with me. My friends have become my foes, and fight under her standard.

"Unhappy being that I am! who will free me from the hands of the ungodly? Who will shield me? Who will come to my succour? Whither shall I flee? How can I escape? I know what I will do. I will turn to heavenly things, and they shall do battle with the things of the earth. Hope shall lead the forces of Heaven; Hope shall march against Sorrow, and overcome her. Hear what the prophet hath said: 'For Thou, Lord, art my hope; Thou hast set thine house of defence very high' (Ps. xci., verse 9). I will call unto the Lord, and He will hasten to come to me, and

The Reformation Era

will not suffer me to be put to confusion. Lo! He hath come already. ' Cry aloud,' He saith, ' Cry aloud always.' And what, Lord, shall I cry? ' Cry in full assurance, and with all thy heart.' In Thee, O Lord, have I put my trust; let me never be put to confusion; deliver me in Thy righteousness!

" Bowed at the feet of the Lord, my eyes bathed with tears, I cried, ' The Lord is my light and my salvation; whom then shall I fear; the Lord is the strength of my life; of whom then shall I be afraid? ' Though a host of men were set against me, yet shall not my heart be afraid; and though there rose up war against me, yet will I put my trust in Him."

Here the Commentary, of which only the beginning and the end are given, closes abruptly. But in the peace which the Psalms brought him, Savonarola slept soundly on the night before his execution, and, as the morning light struggled through the bars of the prison, a Penitent of the Temple, watching at his side, saw a smile play over his face while he slept, as soft and gentle as the smile of a little child. With the strength which the Psalm gave him he met his death, in silence and with unflinching courage, on the open space before the Palazzo Vecchio. It is from the Psalms (Ps. li., verse 13), "Then shall I teach Thy ways unto the wicked; and sinners shall be converted unto Thee," that the motto is taken for Michel Angelo's picture of Savonarola.

Savonarola was in no sense of the word a Protestant. But his Commentaries on Pss. xxxi. and li. were published by Luther, with a preface, in 1523. With Wyclif and his immediate followers neither Luther nor Melancthon was in full sympathy. The first censured the English Reformer for his sacramental views, the second thought him mad on the subject of Church property. Yet the same text from the Psalms, which Wyclif adapted on his deathbed, was inscribed on the walls of Luther's study, " I shall not die, but live, and declare the works of the Lord " (Ps. cxviii., verse 17), and both the German Reformers died (Luther, February 18th, 1546; Melancthon, April 19th, 1560) committing their souls to God in the same words of the Psalm which Hus and Jerome of Prague had repeated, with their latest breath, " Into Thy hands I commend my spirit " (Ps. xxxi., verse 6).

Luther's love of the Psalms might be fully illustrated by

the lectures on them with which he began his public career, as a teacher at Wittenberg (1512), by his Commentaries on the Seven Penitential Psalms (1517), by his hymns, by his life and conversation. He clung to his "old and ragged" Psalter as a tried and trusty friend. With an exposition of Ps. cxviii. he busied himself in his solitude at Coburg. "This," he says, in the dedication of his translation, "is my psalm, my chosen psalm. I love them all; I love all Holy Scripture, which is my consolation and my life. But this psalm is nearest my heart, and I have a familiar right to call it mine. It has saved me from many a pressing danger, from which nor emperor, nor kings, nor sages, nor saints could have saved me. It is my friend; dearer to me than all the honours and power of the earth."

Mention has been already made of Luther's love for Psalm iv., and his wish to hear sung in his last moments the soothing words, "I will lay me down in peace, and take my rest" (Ps. iv., verse 9). Another of his favourites was Psalm cx. "The 110th," he says, "is very fine. It describes the kingdom and priesthood of Jesus Christ, and declares Him to be the King of all things and the intercessor for all men; to Whom all things have been remitted by His Father, and Who has compassion on us all. 'Tis a noble psalm; if I were well, I would endeavour to make a commentary upon it." Another favourite was Psalm ii., and his remarks upon it bring out salient features in the character of a man whose very words were "half-battles": "The 2nd Psalm is one of the best psalms. I love that psalm with all my heart. It strikes and flashes valiantly among kings, princes, counsellors, judges, etc. If what this psalm says be true, then are the allegations and aims of the papists stark lies and folly. If I were as our Lord God, and had committed the government to my son, as He to His Son, and these vile people were as disobedient as now they be, I would knock the world in pieces."

But if his comment on Psalm ii. illustrates the violence of Luther's character, his use of Psalm xlvi. exemplifies his magnificent courage, and suggests the source from which it sprang. There were moments when even he felt something akin to despair, and he asked with the Psalmist, "Why art

The Reformation Era 95

thou cast down, O my soul?" In such hours he would say to Melancthon, "Come, Philip, let us sing the 46th Psalm," and the two friends sang it in Luther's version, "Ein' feste Burg ist unser Gott." The version is characteristic of the man. It has his heartiness, his sincere piety, his joyful confidence, his simplicity and strength, his impetuosity and ruggedness. Harmony, delicacy, spiritual tenderness, are not there. But the words of his hymn breathe the same undaunted spirit which flamed out in his answer to the warning of his friends, "Were there as many devils in Worms as there are roof-tiles, I would on." They also reveal the secret of the confidence which inspired his memorable words before the Council: "I cannot and will not retract anything. It is neither wise nor right to do aught against conscience. Here stand I; I cannot otherwise. God help me. Amen."

From Carlyle's rugged translation of "Ein' feste Burg ist unser Gott," the first and the last of the four stanzas of Luther's version of Psalm xlvi. are quoted:

> " A safe stronghold our God is still,
> A trusty shield and weapon;
> He'll help us clear from all the ill
> That hath us now o'ertaken.
> The ancient Prince of Hell
> Hath risen with purpose fell;
> Strong mail of Craft and Power
> He weareth in this hour,
> On earth is not his fellow.

> " God's Word, for all their craft and force,
> One moment will not linger,
> But, spite of Hell, shall have its course,
> 'Tis written by his finger.
> And though they take our life,
> Goods, honour, children, wife,
> Yet is their profit small;
> These things shall vanish all,
> The City of God remaineth."

The Diet of Worms (January 1521), by which Luther was condemned and placed under the ban of the empire, was opened by Charles V., the champion of the Pope against the Protestants. Yet, in love of the Psalms, emperor and reformer were not divided. Charles presented Marot with 200 gold doubloons for his metrical version of thirty psalms, and asked him to translate his own special favourite, Psalm cxviii.[1] His delight in the Psalter increased in later life, especially in the period of ill-health which ended his long rule (1550–6), when he sang them with his friend, William von Male. During those years his cherished plan of abdication took definite shape.

In November 1556, Charles crossed the pass of Puertonuevo and descended into the valley of the Vera in Estramadura, where he intended to pass the closing years of his life. The beetling crags at the topmost crest of the Sierra closed, as it were, the gates of the world behind him; " 'Tis the last pass," he said, " that I shall ever go through." The Jeromite Convent of Yuste was the scene of the emperor's retirement. He entered it on February 3rd, 1557, bringing with him two illuminated Psalters, and the commentary of Tomas de Puertocarrero on the Psalm, *In te, Domine, speravi*. From the windows of his cabinet he looked over a cluster of rounded knolls, clad in walnut and chestnut, varied with the massive foliage of the fig, and the feathery sprays of the almond. Here he lived, transacting business of the State, punctilious in his devotions, delighting in the music of the choir, giving to his garden or his pets much of the leisure which he enjoyed. In September 1558, he lay on his death-bed. Portents heralded his approaching end. The bell of Vililla in Arragon, which, ringing of itself, had foretold the death of Ferdinand the Catholic, and the sack of Rome by the army of Bourbon, sent out its mysterious warnings over the plains of the Ebro. A comet blazed in the sky during his illness, and disappeared on the day of his death. A lily bud, which had remained a bud all the summer, burst into bloom on September 20th, as a token, it was believed, of the whiteness of the departing spirit, and as a pledge of its reception into the mansions of bliss. On Monday the 19th, he had received the longer or ecclesiastical form of extreme unction, which consisted in the recitation of the seven Penitential Psalms, a litany, and several portions of Scripture. Throughout the 20th of September, passages were read aloud to him by his confessor, from the Bible, but especially from the Psalms,

[1] Bovet (*Histoire du Psautier*, p. 6, note 3) thinks the Psalm was cxviii. It might, however, have been Psalm cvii.

his favourite being Psalm xc., "Lord, Thou hast been our refuge." On the same evening he received the Sacrament, at his urgent request. "It may not," he said, "be necessary; but it is good company on so long a journey." In spite of his extreme weakness, he followed all the responses, and repeated with the utmost fervour the whole verse, "Into Thy hands I commend my spirit: for Thou hast redeemed me, O Lord, Thou God of truth" (Ps. xxxi., verse 6). On St. Matthew's day (September 21st), at two o'clock the next morning, the Emperor Charles V. was dead.

To men of Luther's temper, leaders of the New Learning were cowardly palterers with truth. He denounced Erasmus as "a very Caiaphas," and whenever he prayed, prayed "for a curse upon Erasmus"; to him also Sir Thomas More (1478–1535) appeared "a cruel tyrant." Yet here again the Psalms were common ground.

Many of the Renaissance scholars, in their eagerness to conquer the new worlds of thought and knowledge which opened out before them, doubtless relaxed, lost, or abandoned their earlier faith. It was not so with Christopher Columbus, the man of action. The young Genoese wool-comber, who discovered the New World of America, was essentially a man of the Middle Ages, and died clad in the habit of St. Francis. His imaginative, enthusiastic mind was imbued with the firm conviction that, in devoting all his energies to his great idea, he was the chosen instrument for the fulfilment of a Divine design. The impulse to the work of the greatest maritime genius of the century was essentially religious. His habitual signature was an invocation to Jesus, Mary, and Joseph, placed above his own name of Christopher, or the Christ-bearer. In the constancy of his faith at least, if in no other respect, his death was worthy of his life and work. In a wretched hired lodging at Valladolid, dressed in the Franciscan habit, fortified by the rites of the Church, he died on the eve of Ascension Day, May 20th, 1506, repeating, like John Hus, or Luther, or More, or like Tasso, who sang the swan-song of Italian chivalry, the familiar words, "Into Thy hands I commend my spirit."

Nor were the men of the New Learning, who explored new worlds of knowledge, or re-discovered lost continents of thought and literature, necessarily hostile to the older faith. Erasmus, himself a commentator on the Psalms, writing from Louvain (May 30th, 1519), praises Luther's commentaries on the Psalms, which pleased him "prodigiously," and should be "widely read." Pico della Mirandola, one of the most brilliant scholars of the Italian Renaissance, was the friend and apologist of Savonarola, without whom he could not live, and in whose church of San Marco he lies buried. His life and works were translated by More. "Let no day pass," writes Pico, "but thou once, at the least-wise, present thyself to God by prayer, and falling down before Him flat to the ground . . . not from the extremity of thy lips, but from the inwardness of thine heart, cry these words of the prophet, 'O remember not the sins and offences of my youth; but according to Thy mercy think upon me, O Lord, for Thy goodness'" (Ps. xxv., verse 6). The advice was daily practised by More himself, even when he was surrounded by the splendours of the court of Henry VIII., and in the midst of the active life of a diplomatist and statesman, man of letters, Chancellor, and Treasurer. The Psalms formed part of his morning and evening prayers, and he had made a small collection of special psalms for frequent use. In the days of his disgrace, a prisoner in the upper ward of the Beauchamp Tower because he would not swear an oath against his conscience, he composed many works, chiefly meditations on the Christian faith, by the dim light that flickered through the bars of his prison.

Whatever view may be taken of the course of the Protestant Reformation in England, at the different stages of its progress, it is difficult to justify the public farce of Queen Catherine's divorce and Anne Boleyn's coronation. With or without the Pope's sanction, Henry VIII. was resolved to go all lengths in order to obtain his will. "He was," says Bishop Stubbs, "the King, the whole King, and nothing but the King: he wished to be . . . the Pope, the whole Pope, and something more than Pope." The question of the marriage was still before the Pope when Anne was crowned (June 1st, 1533), and when the Princess Elizabeth, in the following September, was born. In March 1534, an Act of Parliament (25 Henry VIII., c. 22), declared Catherine's

The Reformation Era

marriage illegal, the divorce pronounced by Cranmer valid, the marriage of Anne Boleyn lawful, and her children rightful heirs to the throne. On March 23rd, 1534, Pope Clement pronounced the marriage of Henry and Catherine to be valid. A plain issue was thus raised. Armed rebellion, aided by foreign intervention, was in the air. An oath of allegiance was framed, the actual terms of which seemed to be doubtful; a commission sat at Lambeth to tender it, and foremost among those who refused to accept the oath, in whole or in part, stood Sir Thomas More, and John Fisher, Bishop of Rochester, bell-wethers of the flock which adhered to the older faith. Both were committed to the Tower of London in April 1534. Both found in the Psalms their strength and solace.

Twelve years before his imprisonment began, More was writing an English treatise on the words of Ecclesiasticus, " In all thy works remember thy last end, and thou shalt never sin." In the fragment on Death, he says: " Mark this well, for of this thing we be very sure, that old and young, man and woman, rich and poor, prince and page, all the while we live in this world, we be but prisoners, and be within a sure prison, out of which there can no man escape. The prison is large, and many prisoners in it, but the Jailer can lose none: He is so present in every place, that we can creep into no corner out of His sight. For as holy David saith to this Jailer, ' Whither shall I go from Thy Spirit, and whither shall I flee from Thy face?' (Ps. cxxxix., verse 6), as who saith—no whither." To such thoughts his mind now naturally reverted. Scantily fed, and " besides his old disease of the breast, grieved in the reins by reason of gravel and stone, and with the cramp that divers nights seized him," he yet maintained his cheerful temper. By her own earnest suit, Margaret Roper was allowed to visit him in his cell. On one occasion, " after the Seven Psalms and Litany said (which whensoever she came unto him, ere he fell into talk of any worldly matter, he used accustomably to say with her)," he even made light of the rigour of his confinement. " I find," he says, " no cause, I thank God, Meg, to reckon myself in worse case here than at home: for methinketh God maketh me a wanton " (*i.e.*, a spoiled child), " and setteth me on His lap and dandleth me."

But fifteen months' confinement in " a close, filthy prison, shut up among mice and rats," told upon More's strength. When, on July 1st, 1535, he was sentenced to death, he was aged by suffering, his head white, his " weak and broken body leaning on a staff, and even so, scarcely able to stand." Five days later (July 6th), he was executed on Tower Hill. The scaffold was unsteady, and, as he put his foot on the ladder, he said to the lieutenant, " I pray thee see me safe up, and for my coming down let me shift for myself." After kneeling down on the scaffold, and repeating the Psalm, " Have mercy upon me, O God " (Ps. li.), which had always been his favourite prayer, he placed his head on the low log that served as a block, and received the fatal stroke.

Another victim, scarcely less illustrious than the Chancellor, was John Fisher, Cardinal of the Holy Roman Church, and Bishop of Rochester (1459-1535), whose worn face, with its " anxiously conscientious expression," lives for us in the powerful sketch of Holbein. His public services, his reputation at home and abroad, his pure and simple life, his charities, his great but unostentatious learning, made his refusal to take the oaths of succession and supremacy a matter of extreme importance. A collector of books, the owner of the best private library in England, an early master of English prose, he was a friend of Erasmus, who wrote of him in 1510: " Either I am much mistaken, or Fisher is a man with whom none of our contemporaries can be compared, for holiness of life or greatness of soul." In his sermons on the Penitential Psalms, preached in English, early in the sixteenth century, at the " sterynge " of the Lady Margaret, Countess of Richmond, occurs a passage, which unconsciously foreshadows the part that, thirty years later, he was himself to play. He is commenting on Psalm cii., verse 13, " Thou shalt arise, and have mercy upon Sion: for it is time that Thou have mercy upon her, yea, the time is come." He shows that when the Church was first built, the soft slipper earth in which the foundation was set was hardened into stone by the fire of Love. Peter, who denied his Master, became a rock. So now he prays that God may " chaunge and make the softe and slypper erth into harde stones," and " set in Thy chirche stronge and myghty pyllers

The Reformation Era

that may suffre and endure grete labours, watchynge, pouerte, thurst, hungre, colde, and hete, whiche also shall not fere the thretnynges of prynces, persecucyon neyther deth . . . for *the* glory and laude of Thy holy name." For the glory of God, as he in his conscience believed, Fisher braved threats, persecution, and death.

Fourteen months of imprisonment in the Bell Tower of the Tower of London were passed by Fisher, partly in writing two devotional treatises for the use of his sister. Possibly the action of Paul III., who, May 20th, 1535, created the bishop a cardinal, hastened his execution. On Thursday, June 17th, he was sentenced: on the following Tuesday, June 22nd, he was beheaded on Tower Hill, so weak and emaciated that he could scarcely stand. At the foot of the scaffold to which he had been carried, his strength seemed to revive. As he mounted the steps alone, the south-east sun shone full in his face. Lifting his hands, he murmured the words of Psalm xxxiv., verse 5, " They had an eye unto him, and were lightened; and their faces were not ashamed." On the scaffold, after a few words to the spectators, he knelt down upon his knees in prayer, repeating Psalm xxxi., " In Thee, O Lord, have I put my trust." Then, with the joyful mien of a man who receives the boon for which he craves, he received the blow of the axe upon his slender and feeble neck, and so passed to his rest.

Many monastic houses, as well as individuals, refused the oath of supremacy, and suffered the penalty in loss of life, or of home and possessions. Comparatively few yielded to the temptation of accepting it. Conspicuous among the sufferers were the Franciscans of the Regular Observance at Greenwich, headed by their warden, John Forest, confessor to Queen Catherine, who was herself a tertiary of the Franciscan Order. The story of their sufferings strikingly illustrates the power of the Psalms. But, as Forest's life, for some unknown reason, was spared till 1538, an earlier victim may be chosen from another Order, John Haughton, prior of the London Charterhouse, a zealous servant of God, governing his community by example rather than by precept. He had been twenty years a monk, before the reign of Henry VIII. disturbed the peace of his cloistered life.

Neither he nor his monks had meddled in the question of the king's marriage; but when, in 1533, the Commissioners asked his opinion on the divorce of Catherine of Arragon, he boldly said that he could not understand how a marriage, ratified by the Church and so long unquestioned, could now be undone. In 1535, Henry assumed the title of Supreme Head, and the prior prepared for the end which he saw approaching. From the text, "O God, Thou hast cast us out, and scattered us abroad" (Ps. lx., verse 1), he preached a sermon in the chapel, ending with the words, "It is better that we should suffer here a short penance for our faults, than be reserved for the eternal pains of Hell hereafter." Then he and the brethren, each from each, implored pardon for any offence they might have committed by thought, word, or deed, against one another, and, thus prepared, awaited their fate. Haughton, and the priors of two daughter houses, refused to acknowledge the new title, were tried for treason, condemned, and, on May 4th, 1535, executed at Tyburn, with all the horrible barbarities of the time. Haughton suffered first. "Pray for me," he said, "and have mercy on my brethren, of whom I have been the unworthy prior." Then, kneeling down, and reciting a few verses of Psalm xxxi., he calmly resigned himself into the hands of the executioner. All died with the same calm, unflinching courage.

In the case of England, whatever might have been the personal wishes of Henry VIII., there could be no turning back. Directly attacked by the Protestant Reformers, threatened from various directions by the New Learning, the Roman Catholic Church roused herself from her torpor. The assault was not only checked, but for the time driven back; lost ground was recovered; new spheres of work were conquered. Among all the adherents who rallied to the defence of the Church, none were more zealous, none more self-devoted, none, in two different senses of the word, more successful, than St. Francis Xavier or St. Teresa.

On December 2nd, 1552, Francis Xavier lay dying on the island of San Chan, half a day's sail from Canton. Winged by pity, armed by faith, and fired by love, he had travelled seas and explored lands that were only known to Europe by vague report. He had braved dangers and endured privations which might well be thought superhuman, and literally compassed sea and land to win a single human soul to Christianity. The spirit of love which is breathed in the well-known hymn attributed to his pen (" O Deus, ego amo Te "),[1] was the consuming passion of his life:

> " My God! I love Thee, not to gain
> The bliss of Thy eternal Reign,
> Nor to escape the fiery Lot
> Reserved for those that love Thee not.
>   Thou, Thou, my Jesu, on the Tree
>   Didst in Thine Arms encompass me.
>
> " Thou didst endure the Nails, the Lance,
> Disgraces manifold, the Trance
> Of Bloody Sweat, and boundless Seas
> Of Bitterness and Anguishes,
> Nay even Death's last Agony—
> And this for me—for sinful me!
>   Most loving Jesu, shall this move
>   No like return of Love for Love?
>
> " Above all things I love Thee best,
> Yet not with Thought of Interest:
> Not thus to win Thy promised Land,
> Not thus to ward Thy threat'ning Hand;
> But as Thou lov'st me, so do I
> Love, and shall ever love—and why?
>   Because Thou art my God and King,
>   The Source and End of Everything."

It had been Xavier's ambition to carry the Gospel message to China. But for weeks he could find no one who dared to brave the penal laws of that country. It was death for foreigners to enter the empire; it was death to anyone who conveyed them within its borders. At last he bribed a merchant to land him on the coast. Fever struck him down while awaiting the arrival of his agent, " tendentemque manus ripæ ulterioris amore." For a fortnight he lay in his cabin: then he was put on shore, and a shelter was hastily erected of brushwood and coarse grass. Feeling that his end was near, he desired that his attendants should leave the hut. Far from his native land, without a friend at his side, racked with pain, his death is enviable even by the happiest of mankind. To mortal eyes he was alone. But

[1] The version given above enters into no vain competition with Caswall's beautiful rendering of the hymn; but it may be thought to preserve more faithfully the mediæval quaintness of the original.

to his unclouded vision there floated round him bright forms ready to bear him to his heavenly home, and, as the wings of the approaching angel of death winnowed the mists from before his eyes, he saw the blessed figure of his Master standing with outstretched arms to welcome His faithful servant. As he entered the dark valley, the glow upon his face was of sunrise, not of sunset; and it was a ray from the Divine Presence itself which lit up his face, as with an expiring effort he fixed his eyes upon his crucifix, and, gathering all his strength to utter the words, " In Thee, O Lord, have I put my trust: let me never be put to confusion " (Ps. xxxi., verse 1), breathed his last.

Xavier has been called the canonised saint of Europe. It is not, on the other hand, everyone who sympathises with the mysticism of Teresa, or gives credence to her visions. Yet few can withhold their admiration from the solitary, sickly woman, who restored the austerities of Spanish conventual life, and replanted in Spain the great monastic ideals of poverty, humility, and self-sacrifice.

Born in 1515, at Avila, she began in early childhood to show the bent of her mind. The lives of saints were her nursery tales; her doll's house was a nunnery; at the age of seven, she set out with her little brother to walk to Africa, and win from the Moors the crown of martyrdom. Such a childhood prepares us for a life of ascetic zeal: it gives no hint of the calm, self-reliant, tranquil nature, which, combined with ready wit, charm of manner, and an eloquent tongue, enthralled the greatest of Spanish grandees. Her enthusiasm, her patience, her adroitness triumphed over difficulties which others would have found insuperable. Though continually harassed by intrigues and opposition, she established sixteen nunneries of the Reformed Carmelites and fourteen foundations of friars belonging to the same Rule. In worldly matters shrewd, energetic, and a keen judge of character, Teresa seemed a different being from the enraptured mystic who in her autobiography—a favourite book of the Duke of Alva—sets down her visions and illuminations. Nowhere, and by no man or woman, was a stronger resistance offered to the new ideas that warred against mediæval opinions than was made in Spain by Teresa. At

The Reformation Era

her voice the dying aspirations of a previous age revived, as she travelled through the country, attracting to her austere, ascetic Rule many of the best and most conscientious men and women of the day. The little inns where she stopped in her ceaseless wanderings are still, after the lapse of three centuries, hallowed spots to the inhabitants of rural Spain.

About Teresa hangs the pathos of a lost cause, though she herself was spared the pain of disillusion. She did not live to see the edifice, on which she had lavished the labours of a lifetime, crumbling to decay. Death came to the worn-out woman at Alba, October 4th, 1582. On her lips were the words (Ps. li., verses 10-11, 17), " Make me a clean heart, O God, and renew a right spirit within me. Cast me not away from Thy presence, and take not Thy holy Spirit from me. The sacrifice of God is a troubled spirit; a broken and contrite heart, O God, shalt Thou not despise."

First from one side, then from the other, as the fierce struggle between Roman Catholic and Protestant swayed backwards and forwards, the note of encouragement, comfort, or deliverance sounds clear and high for combatants on either side, in the verses of the Psalms. As More, Fisher, and Haughton, or as Xavier and Teresa, had drawn strength from the Psalter, so, in their day of trial, Protestants like Bishop Hooper, or Bishop Ridley, and at a later stage in the struggle, Jesuits like Robert Southwell, faced the terrors of the stake and the torment of the rack with words from the same book upon their lips, and, as they spoke them, seemed possessed by a heavenly ecstasy.

John Hooper, at the close of the reign of Henry VIII., had fled for his life to Strasburg; had married, and, March 1547, settled at Zurich. Two years later, he determined to return to England, in order to help those who were contending for the religious principles which he himself zealously advocated. He knew his danger. Taking leave of his friend Bullinger in March 1549, he used words prophetic of his fate. He promised to write to those who had shown him so much kindness; " but," he added, " the last news of all, I shall not be able to write: for there, where I shall take most pains, there shall you hear of me to be burnt to ashes." In 1551, he was consecrated Bishop of Gloucester. No man ever entered upon his work with a stricter sense of duty. If he erred, it was in the severity of the discipline which he exacted from himself as well as from others. On the accession of Queen Mary, he was a marked man. He might have escaped, but he refused. "I am," he said, "thoroughly persuaded to tarry, and to live and die with my sheep." In September 1553, he was committed to the Fleet prison, to a "vile and stinking chamber," with nothing for his bed but a "little pad of straw" and "a rotten covering." In his prison he wrote an "Exposition" of Psalms xxiii., lxii., lxxiii., lxxvii. "All men and women," he says, "have this life and this world appointed unto them for their winter and season of storms. The summer draweth near, and then shall we be fresh, orient, sweet, amiable, pleasant, acceptable, immortal, and blessed, for ever and ever; and no man shall take us from it. We must, therefore, in the meantime learn out of this verse to say unto God, whether it be winter or summer, pleasure or pain, liberty or imprisonment, life or death, 'Truly God is loving unto Israel, even unto such as be of a clean heart'" (Ps. lxxiii., verse 1). To his wife, Anne Hooper, who had escaped to the continent, he wrote a letter (October 13th, 1553), bidding her read Psalm lxxvii. ("I will cry unto God with my voice," etc.), because of the "great consolation" which it contains for those who are "in anguish of mind"; and Psalm lxxxvii., "wherein is contained the prayer of a man that was brought into extreme anguish and misery, and, being vexed with adversaries and persecutions, saw nothing but death and hell." Also he recommends Psalms vi., xxii., xxx., xxxi., xxxviii., lxix., for their lessons of "patience and consolation" at times "when the mind can take no understanding, nor the heart any joy of God's promises."

It was not till February 9th, 1555, that, by his death, Hooper passed from the winter of imprisonment into the summer of eternal life. The bishop had been sent to Gloucester for execution. If his enemies hoped that his demeanour at the stake would weaken his hold upon his people, they were disappointed. With unflinching courage, he met the tortures of the fire—needlessly protracted for three-quarters of an hour by the greenness and

The Reformation Era 107

insufficiency of the materials, resigning himself to his fate with the words, which More, Fisher, and, it may be added, Thomas Cromwell had used, " Into Thy handes I commend my spirite; Thou haste redeemed me, O God of truthe " (Ps. xxxi., verse 6).

Psalm ci. was the favourite psalm of Nicholas Ridley (1500–55), Bishop of London. He often, as Fox relates, read and expounded it to his household at Fulham, " being marvellous careful over his family, that they might be a spectacle of all virtue and honesty to others." On the night preceding his execution, his brother offered to pass his last hours in his company. But the bishop refused, saying that he meant to go to bed and sleep as quietly as he ever did in his life:—" I will lay me down in peace, and take my rest; for it is Thou, Lord, only, that makest me dwell in safety " (Psalm iv., verse 9). The next morning he was chained to the stake in the town ditch, opposite the south front of Balliol College, Oxford. As the flames rose round him, he exclaimed, " with a wonderful loud voice, In manus tuas, Domine, commendo spiritum meum (Ps. xxxi., verse 6): Domine, recipe spiritum meum " and then in English, " Lord, Lord, receive my spirit."

Equally courageous, equally firm in their religious convictions, were those, who, as the tide of victory ebbed and flowed, suffered a violent death on the other side. The dungeons in the Tower still record the power of the Psalms to soothe the " sorrowful sighing " of Roman Catholics who suffered for their faith. Here, for example, are the words of Ps. cxi., verse 10 (" The fear of the Lord is the beginning of wisdom "), inscribed by Charles Bailly on the walls of his cell in the Beauchamp or Cobham Tower : " Principium sapientie timor Domini, I.H.S.X.P.S. Be frend to one. Be ennemye to none. Anno D. 1571, 10 Sept." Here, again, is the inscription carved by Philip Howard, Earl of Arundel, in 1587: " Gloriâ et honore eum coronasti Domine " (" Thou madest him lower than the angels; to crown him with glory and worship," Ps. viii., verse 5). Here, lastly, is another, hidden for three centuries under the whitewash in St. Martin's Tower, and only brought to light in 1902. Beneath an emblem of the Trinity appear the sacred letters " I.H.S.," and then the name, "George Beisley, Priest." On the left is a shield containing the *fleur de lis*, the word "Maria," and the date "1590." A mutilated Latin inscription follows, in which words are illegible or wanting; but it seems to be from Ps. xlii., verse 1: " Like as the hart desireth the waterbrooks; so longeth my soul after Thee, O God." But in the history of Robert Southwell, a Jesuit and an Elizabethan poet, the power of the Psalms is illustrated in fullest detail. Born in 1560, he came to England twenty-six years later, knowing well the peril that he ran. To be a Roman Catholic was a crime; to be a priest, high treason; to be a Jesuit was to be a wild beast and hunted down as vermin. In a letter, written in January 1590, he describes the fate of two priests and other brethren in Bridewell, a fate which at any moment might be his own. "Some," he says, "are there hung up, for whole days, by the hands, in such manner that they can but just touch the ground with the tips of their toes. In fine, they that are kept in that prison truly live in the horrible pit, in the mire and clay (Ps. xl., verse 2). This purgatory we hourly look for, in which Topcliffe and Young . . . exercise all manners of torments. But come what pleaseth God, we hope that we shall be able to bear all in Him that strengthens us. In the meantime, we pray that they may be put to confusion that work iniquity; and that the Lord may speak peace to His people, that, as the royal prophet says, ' His glory may dwell in our land ' " (Ps. lxxxv., verse 9).

In a later letter he alludes to the martyrdoms of Bayles and Horner, and the effect which their holy ends had produced upon the people, "With such dews as these the Church is watered, *ut in stillicidiis hujusmodi lætetur germinans* (Ps. lxv., verse 11). We also look for the time (if we are not unworthy of so great a glory) when our day (like that of the hired servant) shall come."

He had not long to wait. In 1592 he was betrayed by a woman, Anne Bellamy, into the hands of Topcliffe, who boasted that " he never did take so weighty a man, if he be rightly considered." Thirteen times tortured, no word was wrung from him. Not even would he confess the colour of the horse on which he had ridden, lest his enemies should gain a clue to his companion. Thus, to quote his own words, with "murd'red life" he couched in "Death's abode," sighing for the kindly touch of death to end his misery :

> "O Life! what letts thee from a quicke decease?
> O Death! what drawes thee from a present praye?
> My feast is done, my soule would be at ease,
> My grace is said; O death! come take away.
>
> "I live, but such a life as ever dyes;
> I dye, but such a death as never endes;
> My death to end my dying life denyes,
> And life my living death no whitt amends."

In his lonely misery, he compares himself like David to the sparrow and the pelican (Ps. cii., verses 6, 7) :

> "In eaves sole sparrowe sitts not more alone,
> Nor mourning pelican in desert wilde,
> Than sely I, that solitary mone,
> From highest hopes to hardest happ exil'd:
> Sometyme, O blisfull tyme! was Vertue's meede
> Ayme to my thoughtes, guide to my word and deede.
> But feares are now my pheares,[1] greife my delight,
> My teares my drinke, my famisht thoughtes my bredd;
> Day full of dumpes, nurse of unrest the nighte,
> My garmentes gives,[2] a bloody feilde my bedd;
> My sleape is rather death than deathe's allye,
> Yet kill'd with murd'ring pangues I cannot dye."

Three years he lingered in prison, first in a filthy dungeon in the Tower, and then in a better cell, where he was allowed the books for which he asked—the Bible and the Works of St. Bernard. At last his end came. On February 21st, 1595, he was drawn on a sledge from Newgate through the streets to Tyburn. Rising up in the cart, with pinioned hands, and with the rope round his neck, he made a short address to the people who had flocked to see his execution. Then, looking for the cart to be drawn away, he blessed himself as well as his bonds allowed, and " with his eyes rais'd up to heaven, repeated, with great calmness of mind and countenance, these words of the Psalmist, 'Into Thy hands, O Lord, I commend my spirit ' " (Ps. xxxi., verse 6). Such was the effect produced by his courage, that the bystanders interfered to prevent the executioner from cutting the rope till he was dead, in order that the ghastly formalities of disembowelling and quartering might not be carried out on his living body.

[1] *I.e.*, companions or bedfellows. [2] *I.e.*, fetters.

CHAPTER VI

THE STRUGGLE BETWEEN PROTESTANT ENGLAND AND ROMAN CATHOLIC SPAIN

The Psalms in the vulgar tongue, the English Prayer-book version; metrical translations, Germany, France, England, Scotland; growth of the influence of the Psalms in the sixteenth and seventeenth centuries; Lady Jane Grey; the Duke of Suffolk; Counts Egmont and Horn; accession of Queen Elizabeth; the murder of Darnley; execution of Mary Queen of Scots; the Spanish Armada; the Turkey merchantmen; the wreck of the *Tobie*; the Earl of Essex; Burghley; Lord Bacon; Shakespeare; Richard Hooker; Bishop Jewel; George Herbert; Hooker on the Psalms.

THROUGHOUT the Middle Ages, the Bible as a whole was, except to the clergy, a sealed book. But the Psalms were permitted to be in the hands of laymen; the Council of Toulouse (1220) excepted them from the general prohibition which forbade the use of the Old Testament to the laity. Versions in Anglo-Saxon, Anglo-Norman, or Old English, are among the earliest specimens of our vernacular literature. The translation and commentary of Richard Rolle of Hampole (*circ*. 1325) illustrate, on its spiritual side, one of the movements which led up to the Reformation. Mediæval Primers contained a selection of the Psalms, sundry prayers, and a Kalendar in which were sometimes entered the births and deaths of families, or the dates of events like the battles in the Wars of the Roses. Our Prayer-book version of the Psalter in prose, originally made by Tyndall and Coverdale, subsequently corrected by Cranmer and his colleagues, was put forth in the Bishops' Bible of 1541. Its rhythmic movement preserves something of the cadenced and sonorous roll of the Latin version, and thus, by wedding English words to mediæval harmonies, it links together old and new forms of divine worship. Translated into the vulgar tongue, the Psalms seemed to gather fresh youth and vigour. They gained their full power, answering every need, adapting themselves to all spiritual conditions. Now the stream of historical association, already broad and deep, becomes a flood, whose force and volume are swollen by metrical translations set to music, and sung by congregations at public worship.

The Psalms in Latin, as well as hymns and sequences in the same tongue, had been consecrated by centuries of use in public worship. But they were chanted by priests or choristers, and to the people they were for the most part unintelligible. Church hymns to be sung by the whole congregation in the vulgar tongue were the special creation of the Lutherans. To Luther the German people owed not only the catechism, and the Bible, translated into forcible, racy, idiomatic language, but also a hymn-book. Three of his best known hymns, " Ach Gott vom Himmel, sieh darein " (Ps. xii.: " Ah God, from heav'n look down, and see "), " Ein' feste Burg " (Ps. xlvi.), " Aus tiefer Noth schrei ich zu dir " (Ps. cxxx.: " Out of the depths I cry to Thee "), are founded on psalms. Burkhard Waldis of Hesse (1485-1557) versified the whole Psalter, and other Lutherans like Justus Jonas (" Wo Gott der Herr nicht bei uns hält," Ps. cxxiv.: " If God were not upon our side "), or Philip Nicolai (" Wie schön leuchtet der Morgenstern," Ps. xlv.: ' O Morning Star! how fair and bright "), or Paul Gerhardt (" Ich, der ich oft in tiefes Leid," Ps. cxlv.: " I who so oft in deep distress "), followed Luther in basing their hymns on psalms. But their special contributions to divine worship were rather original hymns than metrical versions of the Psalter. The French Lutheran Church held the same views as their German brethren. But with other Reformed bodies, and especially with the followers of Calvin or Zwingli, it was different. Separating more entirely from the past, revolting from the human intervention of the priesthood in prayer or praise, worshipping the Bible as a new-found book, venerating its text with almost superstitious reverence, they rejected original hymns, treated the Hebrew Psalter as the only inspired manual of devotional praise, and concentrated their efforts on adapting its language to congregational singing. The Psalms, in metrical versions, thus gained new dignity, authority, and popularity, by their exclusive use in the public worship of the Reformed Churches. The more completely the Reformers severed themselves from the Middle Ages, the more absolutely they swept away the venerable liturgies, and beautiful hymns of the Fathers and Doctors of the Church, the greater was their reverence for the Psalms, which were the daily bread of the Roman Catholic clergy.

Early in the sixteenth century (1533), Clement Marot,[1] the favourite of Marguerite de Valois, and *valet de chambre* to Francis I., began to translate the Psalms into French verse, and his translations were circulated in manuscript throughout the King's Court. His *sanctes chansonettes*, set to simple ballad tunes, drove from the field the love-songs of gallants, and Marot's verses were sung by the princes and princesses, the royal mistresses, and the lords and ladies of the luxurious Courts of Francis I. and Henry II. The translation, completed partly by Marot, partly by Beza and others, passed into the hands of the people. In 1558, in the Pré aux Clercs at Paris, thousands of persons assembled every evening to chant the Psalms to the music of Louis Bourgeois, Guillaume Franc, and Claude Goudimel, and among the singers might be heard the King of Navarre, and the greatest nobles of France.

In England, in the reign of Henry VIII., Thomas Sternhold, "groome of ye Kynges Majesties roobes," began to translate the Psalms "for his own godly solace." As a boy of twelve, so the story runs, Edward VI. heard the "groome" singing the Psalms to the organ, and expressed his delight at the words and the music. The first edition of Sternhold's Psalms, perhaps published in 1548, included nineteen translations. The third edition (1551) contained forty-four psalms, thirty-seven by Sternhold and seven by Hopkins. In dedicating the book to Edward VI., Sternhold says: "Seeing that your tender and godlie zeale doth more delight in the holie songs of veritie than in any faymed rymes of vanytie, I am encouraged to travayle further in the said

---

[1] Marot's version of Psalm vi. appeared in 1533, at the end of the first part of *Le Miroir de treschrestienne Princesse Marguerite de France, Royne de Navarre . . . auquel elle voit et son neant et son tout*. Paris, 1533, 18mo. He did not continue the work till 1537, and it was not till 1542 that his *Trente Pseaulmes de David, mis en francoys par Clement Marot, valet de chambre du Roy* were published.

booke of Psalms." To the versions of Sternhold and Hopkins, seven Psalms, translated by Whittingham, making fifty-one in all, were added in the Genevan edition of 1556. But the first complete version of the Psalter was published by Daye in 1562, and the renderings were the work of many hands. Another complete translation into verse was made by Matthew Parker, afterwards Archbishop of Canterbury. During the Marian persecutions, close search was made for him, and he only saved himself by flight. In one of his escapes, a fall from his horse probably laid the seeds of the disease from which he subsequently died. Yet he seems to have passed his time in contentment, cheered by the work on which he was engaged. On his birthday, August 6th, 1557, he wrote in his Diary: "I persist in the same constancy, upholden by the grace and goodness of my Lord and Saviour, Jesus Christ, by whose inspiration I have finished the *Book of Psalms* turned into vulgar verse." It was, however, the composite work of Sternhold, Hopkins, Whittingham, Wisedome, William Kethe, John Craig, and others, which remained in general use from 1563 till 1698, when the old version was superseded in the Established Church by that of Tate and Brady.

To scholars and to critics the metrical translation often seems to be sheer doggerel; yet its popularity and its influence in extending a knowledge of the Psalms can hardly be exaggerated. Fuller speaks of the versifiers as having drunk more of Jordan than of Helicon, and adds that two hammerers on a smith's anvil would have made better music. Queen Elizabeth condemned the new "Geneva jigs." Edward Phillips, the Cavalier poet, describes some one, singing "with woful noise,"

> "Like a crack'd saints' bell jarring in the steeple,
> Tom Sternhold's wretched prick-song for the people."

The sound of psalm-singing, as he heard it issuing from a church, moved the Earl of Rochester to write the lines:

> "Sternhold and Hopkins had great qualms,
>   When they translated David's Psalms,
>   To make the heart right glad:
>   But had it been King David's fate
>   To hear thee sing and them translate,
>   By God! 'twould set him mad!"

Yet, in spite of the judgment of fastidious taste, the version was so popular that, after the regular services, as Bishop Jewel notes, six thousand persons, old and young of both sexes, might be heard chanting the Psalms in metre at Paul's Cross. Mrs. Ford [1] imagined that the 100th Psalm would not agree with the tune of " Green sleeves." But the " grand old Puritan anthem," [2] " All people that on earth do dwell," composed by William Kethe, a friend of John Knox, and set to the music of Louis Bourgeois, survives all the changes of thought or fashion that the progress of four centuries has witnessed.

In Scotland it had been the ambition of James I. to reunite once more the offices of king and psalmist. But though his version, to which he is said to have contributed thirty psalms, was sanctioned by Charles I. in 1634, it was never accepted by the Scottish people. They clung to the book introduced by Knox from Geneva, in which renderings by Kethe, Craig, and others, were substituted for some of those contained in Sternhold's Psalter. Printed in 1564, it had been the psalm-book of the Scottish Reformers. But in 1650 the General Assembly adopted, with many variations, the version of Francis Rous, an English Puritan, M.P. for Truro, ultimately Speaker of the Barebones Parliament, and Provost of Eton College. In no other country, except France, have metrical paraphrases of the Psalms exercised a greater influence than in Scotland. The Lutherans and the Anglicans had their hymns; but it was many years before any religious music was sung by Calvinist or Presbyterian except the Psalms of David.

From the treasure-house of the Psalter, whether in the ancient Latin version, or in vernacular prose, or in rough rhyme wedded to simple music, Roman Catholics and Protestants alike drew inspiration. The Psalms clave to the memories, and rooted themselves in the hearts of the people. But the application of their language to the conduct and actions of individuals of every shade of religious opinion, does not exhaust the value of the Psalter. There remains its collective influence when employed in common worship.

[1] " *Merry Wives of Windsor*," Act II., scene 1.
[2] Longfellow: " Courtship of Miles Standish," Canto iii., l. 40.

Struggle between England and Spain

Whatever changes were made in forms of services, the Psalms retained their place. The general use of the same book united men who, in character and feeling, time and place, race and language, were widely separated. It is to this aspect of the subject that Hooker refers, in commenting upon the words, " We took sweet counsel together; and walked in the house of God as friends " (Ps. lv., verse 15). If, he argues, community of worship forges the chains of human love, then assuredly, true religious feeling is fostered and strengthened in all those between whom, in the hearing of God Himself, and in the presence of His holy angels, are interchanged " songs of comfort, psalms of praise and thanksgiving."

Apart from the extension of printing, or vernacular versions, or congregational use, there were circumstances in the sixteenth and seventeenth centuries which specially favoured the growth of the influence of the Psalms. The proscribed Protestant Reformer, the tortured Roman Catholic, the hunted Huguenot or Covenanter, the persecuted Cévénol, beheld himself in David fleeing to the mountains as a bird to the hills, betrayed by his own familiar friend, or plunged in the mire and clay of a prison from which death was his release. In the strength of the Psalms, martyrs went to the stake, mounted the scaffold, or endured the rack. Men, women, and children, dragged to gaol, sang psalms along the road, and, as in the days of Paul and Silas, dungeons resounded with earnest praise of God, clothed in the sublime yet familiar language of the Psalmist. Or, again, for the evil was ever blended with the good, it was with the words of the Psalmist that fanatics denounced their foes, cursed them with the awful imprecations pronounced on the divine enemies, excused their own barbarities, and appropriated to themselves, in the presumption of personal election, the promises made, and the mission given, to the chosen people of God. It was, for example, with Ps. cxlix. that Thomas Müntzer stirred up the German peasants to revolt, and that Caspar Schopp, whose *Classicum Belli Sacri* is written in blood, incited the Roman Catholic princes to embark in the war that for thirty years convulsed Europe. In the struggle between Catholics and Protestants, were linked the destinies of nations, the fate of dynasties, the fortunes of illustrious statesmen and famous captains. When men of obscure birth and humble station gave up their lives for conscience' sake, their sacrifice derives pathos and effectiveness from their weakness in the presence of temporal power. But, on the other hand, in dramatic impressiveness the historical grandeur of such a spectacle is often enhanced by the fame of the actors, the importance of the issue, or the magnificence of the stage.

The long struggle between Protestant England and Catholic Spain practically opened with Monday, July 10th, 1553. On that day, at three o'clock in the afternoon, Lady Jane Dudley was brought in state from Richmond to the Tower. In the midst of a " shot of gunnes and chamburs," such as was rarely heard before, she landed at the broad stairs, a great company of nobles and gentry with her, and her mother, the Duchess of Suffolk, bearing her train. The same evening, between six and seven o'clock, from the " Crosse in Chepe " to " Fletstreet," three heralds and a trumpeter proclaimed the Lady Jane Queen of England.

But the friends of the House of Grey were few, and the loyal supporters of the legitimate heir were many. Even at Jane's proclamation " few or none sayd God save hare." Nine days later, for she was barely even a " twelfth-day queen," her father entered her room at the Tower, and with his own hands tore down the canopy under which she sat. Her brief reign was over. Suffolk himself had that day proclaimed Mary Queen of England at the gates of the Tower. Lady Jane received with simple pleasure the news that the crown was no longer hers, only asking, in the innocence of her heart, if she might not now go home. Her palace had become her prison.

Prisoner though she was, and in November formally arraigned for treason and condemned to death, her life was saved for a time. All the arguments of Renard, the ambassador of Charles V., failed to shake Mary's resolution to spare her fallen rival and cousin. The dangerous insurrection of Sir Thomas Wyatt, in which the Duke of Suffolk had joined, sealed Jane's fate. On Ash-Wednesday, February 7th, 1554, the rebellion was quelled. On Thursday, while the *Te Deum*

Struggle between England and Spain 117

for the Queen's victory was sung in every church, and the bells rang from every steeple in London, Feckenham, a gentle, pious old man, afterwards the last Abbot of Westminster, was sent to tell Lady Jane that she must die the following day, and to prepare her for her end by bringing her, if possible, to the Roman faith. A brief reprieve was afterwards granted, in order that Feckenham might have more time to effect her conversion. On Monday, February 12th, 1554, she was to go to the scaffold.

Lady Jane's time on earth was too short for theological discussion. Out of courtesy to Feckenham, she defended her Protestant opinions. But her few remaining hours were chiefly spent in writing to her father, bidding him not to reproach himself for her death, and exhorting him to remain firm in his religion. To "Master Harding," formerly chaplain to the Duke of Suffolk, "but now fallen from the truth of God's most Holy Word," she wrote an appeal, couched in vehement language of reproach for his apostasy. She urged him to lay to heart " the saying of David, in his hundred and fourth Psalm (Ps. civ., verses 29, 30), where he saith thus: 'When Thou takest away Thy Spirit, O Lord, from men, they die, and are turned again to their dust; but when Thou lettest Thy breath go forth, they shall be made, and Thou shalt renew the face of the earth.' ' Viriliter age,' she adds, ' confortetur cor tuum, sustine Dominum ' (Ps. xxvii., verse 16). Fight manfully, come life, come death: the quarrel is God's, and undoubtedly the victory is ours." To her sister, Lady Katharine, she sent her New Testament, urging her to " desire with David to understand the law of the Lord God."

Her husband was condemned to die on the same day. He begged for a last interview and a last embrace. Jane refused. The meeting could only increase their trial, and disturb their preparation for death. In the other world they would meet soon enough. Yet she saw her husband twice. Her place of imprisonment was in " Partrige's house," traditionally the Brick Tower, on the north-east side of the fortress. Lord Guildford Dudley was taken out of the Tower, " about ten of the clocke, to the scaffolde on Tower Hill." The procession passed under her window, from which she thus once more saw him alive. She saw him yet again. His body was thrown into a cart, the head being wrapped in a cloth, and carried back to "the chappell within the Tower, wher the Lady Jane dyd see his dead carcase taken out of the cart, as well as she dyd see him before on lyve going to his deathe—a sight to hir no lesse than death."

But the sight did not shake her own firm resolution. The scaffold on which she was to die, was prepared "upon the grene over against the White Tower." She was led forth from the prison by the Lieutenant of the Tower, Sir John Brydges, wearing the same dress in which she had been, in the previous November, conducted on foot, the axe borne before her, to be arraigned for treason at the Guildhall. In her hand she carried a book, from which she prayed until she came to the foot of the scaffold. Her countenance was steadfast, her eyes not even "moistened with teares, although her ij gentlewomen, Mistress Elizabeth Tylney and Mistress Eleyn, wonderfully wept." At the foot of the scaffold, she dismissed Feckenham with kindly words. Mounting the steps, she spoke to the people, acknowledging that her acts had been unlawful; "but touching the procurement and desyre thereof by me or on my behalfe, I doo 'wash my handes thereof in innocencie,' before God, and the face of you, good Christian people, this day;" and therewith, "she wrong her handes, in which she had hir boke."

Then, kneeling down, she turned to Feckenham, who had followed her to the scaffold, saying, "Shall I say this psalm?" He answered, "Yea." So she said the *Miserere* (Ps. li.) in English to the end. The psalm ended, she stood up, and gave her gloves and handkerchief to her maiden, Mistress Tylney, and her book to Master Brydges, brother to the Lieutenant of the Tower. The book is the small manual of prayers on vellum which is preserved in the British Museum.

With the help of her two gentlewomen, she untied and put off her gown, laid aside her head-dress and neckerchief, and took from them "a fayre handkercher to knytte about her eyes. Then the hangman kneeled downe, and asked her forgivenesse, whome she forgave most willingly. Then he willed her to stand upon the strawe; which doing, she sawe the block. Then she sayd, 'I pray you dispatch me quickly.' Then she kneeled down, saying, 'Will you take it off before I

Struggle between England and Spain

lay me downe?' and the hangman answered her, 'No, madame.' She tied the kercher about her eyes: then feeling for the blocke, saide, 'What shall I do? Where is it?' One of the standers-by guyding her therunto, she layde her heade down upon the block, and stretched forth her body, and said, 'Lorde, into Thy hands I commende my spirite!' And so she ended."

In the short time between her sentence and her death, Lady Jane Dudley had been haunted by the fear that her father might fall from the Protestant faith. Her dread proved groundless. The Duke of Suffolk was beheaded at Tower Hill, on February 23rd, 1554, resisting all efforts to turn him from his religion. That reparation, at least, he could make to the daughter whom his ambition had destroyed. His own remorse, her appeal, her constancy, and her example gave him a courage which scarcely belonged to the weakness of his character. He died with the same psalms upon his lips. "Then the Duke," says Fox, " kneeled down upon his knees, and said the Psalm ' Miserere mei, Deus ' unto the end, holding up his hands and looking up to heaven. And when he had ended the psalm, he said ' In manus tuas, Domine, commendo spiritum meum,' " etc. His head fell at the first blow of the axe.

The execution of Lady Jane Dudley established for the time the triumph of Spain, and, with it, the victory of authority over freedom. So long as Queen Mary lived, and Philip was at her side, no effort should be spared to win back England to the Roman Catholic faith. At her death, the same policy was to be pursued by different means, but with the same resolution. Another scene brings before us, on another stage, the working of the same policy, directed by the same hand and will.

Slow in the execution of his purpose, but inflexibly tenacious of his end, Philip set himself to crush the Netherlands and extirpate the pestilent heresy. The Duke of Alva was his instrument. In 1567, the duke as governor-general, entered on his task, at the head of a Spanish army. The Reign of Terror began. Within the space of three months, the Council of Troubles, better known as the Council of Blood, had put to death eighteen hundred human beings.

Among its later victims were Lamoral, Count of Egmont and Prince of Gavre, and his friend, Count Horn.

On the 22nd of August 1567, Egmont rode out from Brussels to meet the governor-general. Passing his arm lovingly round his neck, Alva talked with him in friendly fashion, as he was escorted to the house of Madame de Jasse, where the governor was lodged. In spite of friendly warnings, again and again reiterated, Egmont believed in the duke's honour. His confidence inspired Horn with a sense of the same security, and he joined Egmont at Brussels to show respect to the king's representative. On September 9th, the blow fell. Egmont and Horn were arrested, and under a strong guard conveyed to Ghent. They scarcely had even the mockery of a trial. On June 2nd, 1568, the sentence of death was passed upon the two nobles by the Council of Blood. The same day, the prisoners, in separate carriages, guarded by hundreds of soldiers, were conveyed to the Brod-huys in the great square at Brussels.

Late on the evening of the 4th of June, Alva sent for the Bishop of Ypres, and charged him to prepare the prisoners for death on the following day. The bishop implored for mercy, or at least delay. The only answer he received was the rebuke, that he had been summoned to confess the criminals, not to advise the governor. The rumour of the sentence quickly spread. The Countess of Egmont heard it, and hurried to the presence of the duke. On her knees she begged for her husband's life. " On the morrow," was the ironical reply, " your husband is certain to be released."

It was not till eleven o'clock at night, that the bishop reached the chamber on the second storey of the Brod-huys, where Egmont was confined. The count heard his sentence with surprise rather than with flinching. " Since," he said, " my death is the will of God and His Majesty, I will try to meet it with patience." He had but a few hours to live. The bishop exhorted him to withdraw himself from all earthly interests, and turn his thoughts only to God. Kneeling at his feet, Egmont confessed, and received the Sacrament. Then nature reasserted itself, as he thought on his wife and children. " Alas! " he exclaimed, " how weak and frail is our human nature. When we would think only of

God, the images of wife and children come between." His loss of self-control was but momentary. Recovering his calmness, he sat down and wrote to the king, as the day began to dawn on which he was to die. "Although," he wrote, "I have never had a thought, and believe myself never to have done a deed, which could tend to the prejudice of Your Majesty's person or service, or to the detriment of our true, ancient, and Catholic religion, nevertheless I take patience to bear that which it has pleased the good God to send." "I pray Your Majesty," he concluded, "to forgive me, and to have compassion on my poor wife, my children, and my servants, having regard to my past services. In which hope I now commend myself to the mercy of God.

"*Ready to die*, this 5th June 1568. Your Majesty's very humble and loyal vassal and servant,
                                                "LAMORAL D'EGMONT."

Then, with his own hands, he cut the collar from his doublet and his shirt, that the hangman might not defile him with his touch. The rest of the twilight hours were spent in prayer and meditation.

The scaffold was raised in the centre of the famous Grande Place of Brussels, the scene of many a brilliant tournament and cruel execution. Opposite to the Brod-huys stands the magnificent Town Hall, and on either side of the space rise the picturesque mediæval guild-houses of the butchers, brewers, archers, tailors, and carpenters. On the morning of the 5th of June 1568, the bells tolled from the churches; gloom hung over the city, as though, to use the language of a contemporary, "the day of judgment were at hand." The roofs, the balconies, the windows, that looked upon the square, were thronged with spectators. Strong bodies of arquebusiers guarded the avenues that led to the Place. Three thousand Spanish troops, some of whom had doubtless followed Egmont in his brilliant feats of arms at St. Quentin and Gravelines, were massed round a scaffold, draped with black cloth. In its folds was concealed the executioner. Upon the scaffold itself, were placed two velvet cushions, and a small table bearing a crucifix. At the corners rose two poles, spiked with steel points. Immediately below the scaffold, motionless on his horse, sat the Provost Marshal, holding in his hand his red wand of office.

At eleven o'clock, Egmont, with the bishop at his side, walked with steady step along the platform which led from the balcony of the Brod-huys to the scaffold. As he made his way to the block, he repeated aloud portions of the 51st Psalm. With one vain wish that he had been allowed to die in the service of king and country, he knelt down on one of the cushions, and prayed aloud. Then, after repeatedly kissing the crucifix, and receiving absolution at the hands of the bishop, he rose to his feet. Stripping off his mantle and robe, he again knelt down, drew a silk cap over his eyes, and, repeating the words, " Lord, into Thy hands I commend my spirit " (Ps. xxxi. verse 6), awaited the stroke of the executioner. His head, which was severed from the body at a single blow, was set on one of the spikes, and a cloak thrown over the mutilated trunk.

A few minutes later, Count Horn was led to the scaffold. He died with the same courage, and with the same words on his lips. On the pole opposite that of Egmont, his head was fixed. With these executions began the Revolt of the Netherlands.

In England, the struggle of Protestantism against Spain and Roman Catholicism centred round the rivalry of two women. On the death of Queen Mary, Queen Elizabeth, relieved from constant dread of execution, had expressed her gratitude in the words of Ps. cxviii., verse 23, " This is the Lord's doing; and it is marvellous in our eyes." The Latin text was the stamp of her gold, as another quotation adapted from the Psalms—*Posui Deum adjutorem meum* (" Thou art my helper . . . O my God," Ps. xl., verse 21), was the stamp of her silver. Her love of the Psalter is further shown by her version of Ps. xiv., beginning—

> " Fooles, that true fayth yet never had,
> Sayth in their hartes, there is no God!
> Fylthy they are in their practyse,
> Of them not one is godly wyse."

But though she ruled as few have ever done in the hearts of

her people, her throne, and all that was implied in its stability, were insecure so long as Mary, Queen of Scots, was her heir and the pivot of religious and political intrigues. On the character of Mary, Queen of Scots, historians will never cease to dispute, and her share in the murder of Darnley is a subject on which they are still divided.

On Saturday, March 9th, 1566, Riccio, Mary's Italian secretary, was murdered, almost before the Queen's eyes, in the Palace of Holyrood. In this brutal crime, Henry Stuart, Earl of Darnley, had borne a part, which might well have turned to hatred Mary's love for the handsome, but dissolute husband on whom she had conferred the title of king. Even the birth of their son, three months later, could scarcely restore an affection thus outraged, especially as Darnley ostentatiously absented himself from the child's baptism. Nor was his subsequent conduct, sullen and wayward as it was, likely to heal the breach. Yet, though the circumstances create suspicion, Mary's connivance at Darnley's assassination is not absolutely proved. His insolence and caprice had made him many enemies among the haughty nobles who attended the Scottish Court.

In the winter of 1566-7, Darnley lay sick at Glasgow, from some mysterious and apparently infectious malady. When he was slowly recovering, Mary visited him, and husband and wife were outwardly reconciled. At the end of January 1567, though still suffering from the disease, he was removed in a litter to Edinburgh, and lodged, not in the Palace of Holyrood, but in a house which stood on a space of ground called Kirk-o'-Field.

The Kirk-o'-Field, situated where now stands the northeastern corner of the old University buildings, lay close to the town-wall, which was built after the battle of Flodden to protect the Cowgate. Through this wall, on the south side of the open space, led a postern gate. To the north ran a row of mean cottages, called Thief Row. On the east stood the ruined, roofless Church of Our Lady-in-the-Field, wrecked by the English invaders. On the west was a quadrangular building, also partially in ruins, which had belonged to the Dominican Friars. It was in the western wing of this convent that Darnley was lodged.

The rooms in this wing were not many; but they were occupied as a dwelling-house, and were detached from the rest of the building, having a separate staircase and door which gave access from without. The wing contained a hall, and a bedroom, on the ground floor; above these were another bedroom, a wardrobe, a cabinet, and a corridor. There was also a cellar below the hall. These rooms had been prepared for Darnley's reception, and furnished with a touch of regal splendour. The hall was hung with tapestry, and fitted with a chair of state, and a dais of black velvet fringed with silk. Darnley's bedchamber on the first floor was hung with tapestry, and carpeted with the rare and costly luxury of a little Turkey carpet. A chair of purple velvet, two or three cushions of red velvet, a small table covered with a green velvet cover, a bed, hung with brown velvet, "pasmented with cloth of silver and gold," and embroidered with cypress and flowers, formed the furniture. The bed had belonged to Mary's mother. The cabinet was of "yellow shot taffeta, fringed with red and yellow silk." The wardrobe was hung with tapestry, figuring, by a grim irony, a rabbit hunt. Never was wild animal more helplessly trapped and at the mercy of his pursuers, than was Darnley in the hands of his enemies. In the bedroom on the ground floor, immediately beneath Darnley's chamber, was a bed of red and yellow damask, with a coverlet of marten's fur. Here the queen slept on Wednesday, February 5th, and on Friday, February 7th. Here, also, she was to have slept the following Sunday.

About ten o'clock, on the night of Sunday, the queen with her attendants was seen passing along the Blackfriars Wynd, lighted by torch-bearers, on her way from Holyrood to visit Darnley at Kirk-o'-Field. Arrived at the house, she went straight to her husband's room, without entering her own chamber. There she sat for two hours, talking with the sick man. At midnight she rose, placed a ring on Darnley's finger, kissed him, bade him good-night, and left him. That afternoon, Sebastian Paiges, one of the Court musicians, had been married to one of Mary's waiting-women, and, in honour of the event, there was given at the Palace a masked ball, which Mary had promised to attend. At the door of the king's chamber, she turned, and said to Darnley, "It is eleven months to-day since Riccio was slain." So Mary departed, returning as she came, by the light of torches to Holyrood. On her way, she sent back her page to fetch the furred coverlet from her room.

Darnley, still a mere boy, only twenty years old, was left alone with his page, Taylor, who slept in his room, and two servants, Nelson and Symonds, who slept in a corridor outside his chamber. Two grooms also slept somewhere in the house. When Mary had gone, Darnley turned to Nelson, and said, "She was very kind; but why did she speak of Davie's slaughter?" Her parting words sounded ominously in his ears. The place was a solitary one, among the ruins of churches, the graves of dead men, and the lurking corners of thieves. "It is very lonely," he said. Restless and wakeful, weak with his long illness, chilled by a sense of his loneliness and a vague foreboding of evil, he opened the Book of Psalms. Perhaps the wayward boy, who, in the days of his short-lived power, had made so many enemies by his imperious insolence, had learned to turn to them for comfort as he lay on his bed of sickness. He opened the pages at the 55th Psalm, which was one of the portions appropriated in the English Prayer-book for the day that was dawning. They were the last words that he read on earth. With what force must their words have struck into his heart, if he suspected his impending doom, and his wife's complicity in the crime!—

"My heart is disquieted within me; and the fear of death is fallen upon me.

"Fearfulness and trembling are come upon me; and an horrible dread hath overwhelmed me.

"And I said, O that I had wings like a dove! for then would I flee away, and be at rest.

"For it is not an open enemy that hath done me this dishonour; for then I could have borne it.

"But it was even thou, my companion, my guide, and mine own familiar friend.

"The words of his mouth were softer than butter, having war in his heart; his words were smoother than oil, and yet be they very swords."

An hour later he went to bed, with his page at his side. All that follows is shrouded in mystery. At two o'clock on Monday morning, a terrific explosion startled the sleeping citizens from their beds. Nelson, alone of those who slept in the house, escaped alive. The bodies of Darnley and his page were found, side by side, many yards away, with no sign of fire upon them. Near the king, who was in his nightgown, lay his fur pelisse and slippers. The probability is that he and his page, aroused by the noise which the murderers made in arranging the powder, escaped from the house into the garden, and were there seized and strangled. So sudden and wide-spread was the alarm created by the explosion, that the murderers had no time to place the bodies near the ruins, but fled for their lives.

Twenty years later, Mary, Queen of Scots, was herself executed at Fotheringay. Even her bitterest enemies could not deny that she met her fate with dignity. At daybreak, on the morning of February 8th, 1587, she desired Jane Kennedy to read aloud to her from her favourite book, *The Lives of the Saints*. After dressing with unusual care, she retired to her oratory. There she remained till the appointed hour, when, with tranquil composure, she took her seat upon the scaffold. The commission for her execution was read by the Clerk to the Council, to which she briefly replied, declaring her innocence. Throughout the long harangue of Dr. Fletcher, the Protestant Dean of Peterborough, who exhorted her to abandon her religion, she remained silent, absorbed in her own thoughts or devotions. It was only by the intervention of the Earl of Shrewsbury, that she was relieved from the divine's ill-timed pertinacity, and allowed to pray according to the forms of her own faith.

Her prayers ended, she put off her black satin robe and long white veil of lawn, and appeared in a bodice and petticoat of crimson velvet. The executioner, on his knees, begged her forgiveness. "I forgive all," she replied. Then, with a handkerchief bound over her eyes, she " kneeled downe upon the cushion resolutely, and, without any token of feare of deathe, sayde allowde in Lattin the Psalme, *In te Domine, confido* (Ps. xi.). Then groaping for the block, shee layde downe hir heade." Another authority states that she said

aloud several times, " Into Thy hands I commend my spirit."
The Latin lines, which she is supposed to have written before
her execution, seem to be based on the Psalms, and especially on Psalm lxxi.:

> " O Domine Deus, speravi in te:
> O care mi Jesu, nunc libera me:
> In durâ catenâ, in miserâ poenâ
> Desidero te!
> Languendo, gemendo, et genuflectendo,
> Adoro, imploro, ut liberes me! "

Meanwhile Spain was preparing the expedition which was designed to crush Protestant England. The Invincible Armada lay off Lisbon ready to sail. One hundred and thirty galleons, carrying 30,000 men, covered the broad waters of the Tagus. No crusade against the Saracens had ever excited greater enthusiasm than did this Holy War against the heretic, this final effort of authority against freedom. Treasure had been lavished like water; high and low had given their money, according to their means. For three years prayers had been said daily for success. Each noble family in Spain sent a son to fight for Christ and Our Lady. The ships were named after apostles and saints; the crews were to abstain from vice and evil-speaking; at sunrise the Buenos Dias, at sunset the Ave Maria, were to be sung on board. The standard, which flew from the flag-ship, as the *San Martin* led the way to sea in May 1588, unrolled the motto, " Exsurge, Deus, et vindica causam tuam "—" Awake, and stand up to judge my quarrel; avenge Thou my cause, my God, and my Lord " (Ps. xxxv., verse 23).

In the space of a few weeks, the great fleet was scattered and destroyed. Victor Hugo, in his *Légende des Siècles*, imagines the little Infanta of Spain standing by a fountain in the gardens of the Escurial. In her tiny hand the child holds a rose in which her laughing face is buried, till the damask of cheek and flower can scarcely be distinguished. Suddenly an evening breeze sweeps the petals into the basin of the fountain, and dashes the smooth waters into miniature waves, on which the scattered leaves toss like disabled hulks. " What does it mean? " asks the wondering, half-frightened child, in whose hand only the bare stalk is left. " Madame," replies the Duenna, " to princes belong all that is on earth, save only the wind."

It was in a psalm (Psalm iii., " Lord, how are they increased that trouble me ") that the English nation expressed their fears of impending invasion, as, five centuries before, they had, with the same words, invoked divine aid against the Norsemen. In a psalm (Ps. lxxvi., " In Jewry is God known "), they gave voice to their gratitude; with the same words the citizens, led by the great preacher, Robert Bruce, celebrated the triumph at the Market Cross of Edinburgh; and from a third psalm (Ps. cxlvii., verse 18), is taken the motto which was engraved upon the coins struck to commemorate the victory: *Afflavit Deus*.

The defeat of the Invincible Armada saved England from the horrors of invasion; but it did not end the war. The victory was only an episode in that religious struggle which gave to Great Britain the sceptre of the sea, and laid the foundations of her colonial empire. In those " spacious times," when men were endowed with a variety of gifts and qualities, any one of which, in later days, would distinguish its possessor, Sir Walter Raleigh and Sir Philip Sidney were conspicuous figures as gallant knights, courtiers, and scholars. On Raleigh, in the midst of his adventurous career by sea and land, the Psalms had laid their spell. From Jerome's cave at Bethlehem to Raleigh's dungeon in the Tower their influence passes without breach of continuity, although, in the lapse of twelve centuries, scarcely any aspect of human life remained unchanged—except that human nature to which they remain eternally true. In his *History of the World*, the bold explorer and learned student writes:

" For his internal gifts and graces, David so far exceeded all other men, and, putting his human frailty apart, he was said by God Himself to be a man according to His own heart. The Psalms which he wrote instance his piety and excellent learning, of whom Jerome to Paulina : ' David,' saith he, ' our Simonides, Pindarus, and Alcæus, Horatius, Catullus, and Serenus, playeth Christ on his harp, and on a ten-stringed lute raiseth Him up rising from the dead. And being both king and prophet, he foretelleth Christ more lightsomely and lively than all the rest."

Spenser's version of the Penitential Psalms has perished. But the metrical translation of the "Psalmes of David," 'begun by that noble and learned gentleman, Sir Philip Sidney, Knight, and finished by The Right Honourable the Countess of Pembroke," has been preserved. It was printed in 1823, and a portion was edited by Ruskin in his *Bibliotheca Pastorum* (1877). The fact that Sidney should have set himself the task, is itself significant; but his version is specially noteworthy in its mingled familiarity and dignity. It has the energy of the times, the fixed effort to reach the heart of the meaning and make it unmistakably clear. As Ruskin says, "Sir Philip Sidney will use any cowboy's or tinker's words, if only they help him to say precisely in English what David said in Hebrew; impressed the while himself so vividly by the majesty of the thought itself, that no tinker's language can lower it or vulgarise it in his mind."

Nor was it only to courtiers and learned scholars that the Psalms appealed. To them also, even simple mariners turned for strength in peril from enemies or shipwreck.

In 1586, five Turkey merchantmen, equipped for trade and not for war, encountered on the high seas eleven Spanish galleys and two frigates. The English ships were summoned by the Spaniards to surrender. On their refusal, a fight began, which is thus described by Philip Jones. "Although," he says, "our men performed their parts with singular valure according to their strength, insomuch that the enemie is amased therewith would oftentimes pause and stay, and consult what was best to be done, yet they ceased not in the midst of their businesse to make prayer to Almighty God, the revenger of al evils, and the giver of victories, that it would please him to assist in that good quarell of theirs, in defending themselves against so proud a tyrant, to teache their hands to warre and their fingers to fight (Ps. cxliv., verse 1), that the glory of the victory might redound to his Name, and to the honor of true Religion, which the insolent enemie sought so much to overthrowe." At the end of four hours, the Spaniards drew off, and the English merchantmen pursued their voyage unmolested.

On the 16th day of August 1593, "the *Tobie* of London,

a ship of 250 tunnes, manned with fiftie men, set sayle from Blackwall." She was cast ashore on the Barbary coast, and broke up so fast that there was no time to make a raft. Climbing up into the shrouds, the crew hung there for a time. " But seeing nothing but present death approch, we committed our selves unto the Lord, and beganne with doleful tune and heavy hearts to sing the 12 Psalme: ' Helpe, Lord, for good and godly men,' etc. Howbeit, before we had finished foure verses, the waves of the sea had stopped the breathes of most of our men . . . and only twelve, by God's providence, partly by swimming and other meanes of chests, gote on shoare, which was about a quarter of a mile from the wracke of the ship."

Yet another incident connects the Psalms with the progress of the same war. In 1598 the question of peace with Spain was hotly debated in Elizabeth's Council. The Earl of Essex, supported by the envoys from the States-General of Holland, warmly urged the continuance of the war. Burghley as strongly pleaded for peace. In the midst of the debate, he drew from his pocket a Prayer-book, and read to Essex the verse, " The bloodthirsty and deceitful men shall not live out half their days " (Ps. lv., verse 25). Three years later, on Wednesday, February 25th, 1601, Essex was led to the high court above Cæsar's Tower, in the precincts of the Tower of London, and there beheaded.

Like the queen herself, and like her first archbishop, her greatest statesman was a lover of the Psalter. All his life Burghley had been a diligent student of the Psalms. In his declining days, as a friend and contemporary writes of the great minister, " there was no earthly thing wherein he took comfort but in . . . reading, or hearing the Scriptures, Psalmes, and Praieres." His will, dated October 20th, 1579, disposes of his lands and goods in a manner that he hopes " shall not offend God, the giver of them all to me; considering, as it is in the Psalm, ' Cœlum cœli Domino, terram dedit filiis hominum ' " (Ps. cxv., verse 16, " All the whole heavens are the Lord's; the earth hath he give to the children of men ").

The genius of Bacon is one of the glories of the Elizabethan age. He also studied and quoted the Psalms. In his essay

Struggle between England and Spain

" On Atheism," he comments on the 1st verse of Ps. xiv., that the fool who said in his heart, " there is no God," " saith it rather by rote to himself, as that he would have then that he can throughly believe it or be persuaded of it." Another verse quoted in Bacon's *Essays* (" Nature in Men ") is Ps. cxx., verse 5, " My soul hath long dwelt among them that are enemies unto peace." Like Sir Thomas Wyatt, Surrey, Spenser, Sir Philip Sidney, Queen Elizabeth, James I., and Phinehas Fletcher, Bacon was himself a versifier of the Psalms. His *Certaine Psalmes written in sickness*, published in 1624, and dedicated to George Herbert, are so unmelodious, that it is difficult to imagine that he could ever have been a poet. It was on a psalm (Ps. ci.), known as the " Mirror for Magistrates," that he founded his advice to George Villiers, Duke of Buckingham. He bade him take that psalm for his guide in promoting courtiers. " In these the choice had need be of honest faithful servants, as well as of comely outsides who can bow the knee and kiss the hand. . . . King David (Ps. ci., verses 6, 7) propounded a rule to himself for the choice of his courtiers. He was a wise and good king, and a wise and good king shall do well to follow such a good example; and if he find any to be faulty, which perhaps cannot suddenly be discovered, let him take on him this resolution as King David did, ' There shall no deceitful person dwell in my house ' " (Ps. ci., verse 10).

In stormy scenes of violence or peril, in dramatic incidents on which great events have turned, in episodes in the lives of rulers of the earth, the power of the Psalms has been noted by historians. On masterpieces of Elizabethan literature the same power may be traced. Whether Shakespeare, for example, was indeed " untutored in the lore of Greece and Rome," may be open to dispute; but none can doubt his familiarity with the Psalms. " Death, as the Psalmist saith, is certain to all: all shall die." So says Justice Shallow to Silence, alluding to Psalm lxxxix. 47, " What man is he that liveth and shall not see death ? " When Queen Margaret asks, in the Second Part of " Henry the Sixth,"

> " What! Art thou, like the adder, waxen deaf?
> Be poisonous too, and kill their forlorn Queen ";

or when Hector tells Paris, in "Troilus and Cressida,"

> "Pleasure and revenge
> Have ears more deaf than adders to the voice
> Of any true decision,"

the allusion is to Psalm lviii. 4.

Buckingham's words in "King Henry the Eighth" refer to Psalm cxli. 2, "Let the lifting up of my hands be an evening sacrifice":

> "And, as the long divorce of steel falls on me,
> Make of your prayers one sweet sacrifice,
> And lift my soul to Heaven."

Antony's prayer in "Antony and Cleopatra"—

> "Oh, that I were
> Upon the hill of Basan, to outroar
> The horned herd! for I have savage cause"—

plainly refers to the Psalmist's "hill of Basan" (Psalm lxviii. 15) and the "fat bulls of Basan" (Psalm xxii. 12). The prayer of Adam in "As You Like it"—

> "He that doth the ravens feed,
> Yea, providently caters for the sparrow,
> Be comfort to my age!"—

is partly founded on Psalm cxlvii. 9, "He feedeth the young ravens that call upon Him." In "King Henry the Fifth," where the king sings his "Non nobis, Domine!" in thanksgiving for his victory at Agincourt,—

> "O God, Thy arm was here;
> And not to us, but to Thy arm alone
> Ascribe we all,"—

he only paraphrases the "Not unto us, O Lord, not unto us, but unto Thy Name, give the praise," of Psalm cxv. 1. So the description of God, in "Richard II.," as the "widow's champion and defence" is taken from the Psalmist's "Father of the fatherless, and defendeth the cause of the widow" (Psalm lxviii. 5). When the king in "Hamlet" asks,

> "What if this cursed hand
> Were thicker than itself with brother's blood,
> Is there not rain enough in the sweet heavens
> To wash it white as snow?"

he refers to Psalm li. 7, "Thou shalt wash me, and I shall be whiter than snow." The description of the approach of Alcibiades in " Timon of Athens "—

> " Who, like a boar too savage, doth root up
> His country's peace "—

suggests Psalm lxxx. 13, " The wild boar out of the wood doth root it up." The address of Romeo to Juliet, where he compares her to " a winged messenger of Heaven,"—

> " When he bestrides the lazy-pacing clouds
> And sails upon the bosom of the air,"—

recalls such sentences in the Psalms as " Magnify Him that rideth upon the Heavens, as it were upon an horse " (Ps. lxviii. 4), or, " Who maketh the clouds His chariot, and walketh upon the wings of the wind " (Ps. civ. 3), or, " He came flying upon the wings of the wind " (Ps. xviii. 10).

> " See how the morning opes her golden gates,
> And takes her farewell of the glorious sun!
> How well resembles it the pride of youth,
> Trimmed like a younker, prancing to his love,"

is a reminiscence of Psalm xix., verse 5, where the sun rejoices " as a giant to run his course." Finally, in the speech from the Second Part of " King Henry the Sixth," addressed by the king to Humphrey, Duke of Gloster,—

> " Stay, Humphrey, Duke of Gloster; ere thou go
> Give up thy staff; Henry will to himself
> Protector be: and God shall be my hope,
> My stay, my guide, and lantern to my feet;
> And go in peace, Humphrey,"—

Shakespeare makes use of such passages as, " truly my hope is even in Thee " (Ps. xxxix. 8); " but the Lord was my stay " (Ps. xviii. 18); " our guide unto death " (Ps. xlviii. 13); and, " a lantern unto my feet, and a light unto my paths " (Ps. cxix. 105).

On the quieter influence of the Psalms over daily conduct, or by peaceful deathbeds, history is comparatively silent. Yet three instances may be quoted to illustrate this aspect of the subject. In his dying moments, the thoughts of Richard Hooker, the pride of English theologians, dwelt on Psalm cxxx., the *De Profundis*, on which Luther has founded one of his best known hymns, and Phinehas Fletcher has meditated in the lines:

> " As a watchman waits for day,
>   And looks for light and looks again,
> When the night grows old and gray,
>   To be relieved he calls amain;
> So look, so wait, so long my eyes
>   To see my Lord, my Sun arise."

Hooker's *Ecclesiastical Polity* by its massive dignity still retains its place in theological literature. But Bishop Jewel's *Apology for the Church of England* (1562), as a vindication of the doctrine and discipline of the Reformed Church, was in its day equally famous, and circulated throughout Europe when the Council of Trent was still sitting. Jewel himself died a peaceful death, at Monkton Farleigh in Wiltshire, on September 23rd, 1571. On his deathbed, he desired that the 71st Psalm might be sung. At the words, " Thou, O Lord, art my hope and my trust, from my youth up," he cried out: " Thou, O Lord, hast been my *only* hope." When they reached the passage, " Cast me not off in time of age," etc., he exclaimed: " Every one who is dying is, in truth, old and grey-headed, and failing in strength." The Psalm ended, he broke forth into frequent ejaculations: " Lord, now lettest Thou Thy servant depart in peace "—" Lord, suffer Thy servant to come to Thee "—" Lord, receive my spirit "—and so died.

Great though Hooker and Jewel were as theologians and apologists, George Herbert (1593-1632) was, in temperament and character, more typical of the Elizabethan age in which he was born. A man of saintly piety, at once an ascetic and a mystic, he had also the courtly grace and refined instincts of the high-bred gentleman. Men of his type, who both venerated the Church of the Fathers and inherited the culture of the Renaissance, were unintelligible to the Puritans.

Retiring from Court, and taking holy orders, Herbert spent his closing years as a parish priest among the green meadows of Bemerton, in view of the tapering spire of Salisbury Cathedral. It was in something of the Psalmist's spirit that he poured out his soul in verse, adorning his poetry with the quaint conceits and fancies of the Elizabethan age. To him, as has been already mentioned, Bacon dedicated his *Certaine Psalms*. His hymn, "The God of Love my Shepherd is," is one of the most popular versions of Psalm xxiii. The motto of his *Sacred Poems and Private Ejaculations*, published at Cambridge in 1633, is, "In his temple doth every man speak of his honour" (Ps. xxix., verse 8), and the same verse suggested for his book the title of *The Temple*. "Thou shalt answer for me, O Lord my God" (Ps. xxxviii., verse 15), is the burden of his admirable poem, "The Quip." The poet, flouted by all that this world holds dear—Beauty, Money, brave Glory, quick Wit and Conversation—takes refuge in the comfort ministered by the words of the Psalm:

> "Yet when the houre of Thy design
>   To answer these fine things shall come,
> Speak not at large; say, I am Thine,
>   And then they have their answer home."

In 1632, he died at Bemerton, dwelling, like Jewel, with his latest breath, on the text, "Forsake me not when my strength faileth" (Ps. lxxi., verse 8), and committing his soul to God in the familiar words, "Into Thy hands I commend my spirit" (Ps. xxxi., verse 6).

Instances of the influence of the Psalter on uneventful lives, or on everyday actions, are, perhaps, uninteresting to note. But the point needs no labouring. The power of the Psalms has been instinctively felt in the conduct of countless men and women whose careers were obscure, unpicturesque, unknown. It is here, though unrecorded, that their teaching, their encouragement, their warning, their consolation have been most widely felt. Here their sway has been so general as to be almost universal; here, also, it has been so enduring as to be practically everlasting. From age to age, from hand to hand, across the centuries, has passed their torch of truth, the flame burning bright and steady, ever pointing the way through the darkness, ever exploring the mysteries of the Divine dealings with mankind, always lighting up the recesses of the human heart. It was the sense of this continuous influence of the Psalms that roused Richard Hooker from his absorbing studies to a noble outburst of feeling. Yet, here again, not only by his eloquence but by its source, the universality of the Psalms, and their superiority to religious differences, are strikingly illustrated. Hooker's words are little more than a paraphrase from the exposition of Torquemada, the Dominican Inquisitor. The passage is familiar enough: "What is there necessary for man to know, which the Psalms are not able to teach? They are to beginners an easy and familiar introduction: a mighty augmentation of all virtue and knowledge in such as are entered before, a strong confirmation to the most perfect amongst others. Heroical magnanimity, exquisite justice, grave moderation, exact wisdom, repentance unfeigned, unwearied patience, the mysteries of God, the sufferings of Christ, the terrors of wrath, the comforts of grace, the works of Providence over this world, and the promised joys of that world which is to come, all good necessarily to be either known or done or had, this one celestial fountain yieldeth. Let there be any grief or disease incident into the soul of man, any wound or sickness named, for which there is not in this treasure-house a present comfortable remedy at all times ready to be found. Hereof it is that we covet to make the Psalms especially familiar unto us all. This is the very cause why we iterate the Psalms oftener than any other part of Scripture besides; the cause wherefore we inure the people together with their minister, and not the minister alone, to read them as other parts of Scripture he doth."

CHAPTER VII

THE HUGUENOTS, 1524-98

Marot's *Psalms* at Court; the distinctive heritage of the Huguenots; the power of the Psalms in the public and private lives of the Huguenots—Palissy the potter, Calvin, Theodore de Beza, Robert Estienne, Casaubon, Jean Rousseau; traces in modern France of the struggle between Roman Catholics and Huguenots; beginning of the persecution of Protestants—Jean Leclerc (1524), Wolfgang Schuch (1525); indecision of Francis I.; the Huguenot martyrs of Meaux—Jean Rabec, massacre of Vassy; commencement of the Wars of Religion (1562); Coligny at Noyers and Moncontour; Massacre of St. Bartholomew (1572); Henry of Navarre, flight from Paris to Alençon, battles of Courtras and Château d'Arques; Edict of Nantes (1598).

WHEN Marot's *Psalms* first appeared, they were sung to popular airs alike by Roman Catholics and Calvinists. No one delighted in the *sanctes chansonnettes* more passionately than the Dauphin, afterwards Henry II. He sang them himself, set them to music, and surrounded himself with musicians who accompanied his voice on the viol or the lute. To win his favour, the gentlemen of the Court begged him to choose for each a psalm. Courtiers adopted their special psalms, just as they adopted their particular arms, mottoes, or liveries. Henry, as yet without an heir, sang to his own music Ps. cxxviii., which promises to the God-fearing man a wife " as the fruitful vine," and children " like the olive-branches." Catherine de Medicis, then a childless wife, repeated Ps. vi. (" O Lord, rebuke me not in Thine indignation "). Anthony, King of Navarre, chose Ps. xliii. (" Give sentence with me, O God "). Diane de Poitiers sang the *De Profundis* (Ps. cxxx.) to the tune of a dance. In after years, when Catherine had borne her husband ten children, Henry carolled Ps. xlii. (" Like as the hart desireth the water-brooks ") as he hunted the stag in the Forest of Fontainebleau, riding by the side of Diane, for the motto of whose portrait as a huntress he chose the first verse of his favourite psalm.

But with the Huguenot, love of the Psalms was more than a passing fashion; they became in a peculiar sense his special inheritance. "When the Catholics," says Florimond de Rémond, " saw simple women seek torments in order to manifest their faith, and meet death, crying only on Christ their Saviour, or singing a psalm; when they saw young virgins go to the scaffold as gaily as they would go to the bridal couch; when they saw the men rejoice at the sight of the horrible preparations and instruments of death, and, half-burned and roasted, contemplate from the stake their impending tortures, standing firm as rocks among the billows of grief—in a word, dying with a smile—their hearts wept as well as their eyes."

With the Psalms is bound up the history of French Protestantism. Their translation into verse and their setting to music were, says Strada, among the chief causes of the Reformation in the Low Countries. So in France the metrical version of the Psalter, in the vulgar tongue, set to popular music, was one of the principal instruments in the success of the Reformed Church. The Psalms were identified with the everyday life of the Huguenots. Children were taught to learn them by heart; they were sung at every meal in households like that of Coligny; to chant psalms meant, in popular language, to turn Protestant. On the battlefield, and in the discipline of the camp, the Psalms held their place. A psalm, as has been already mentioned, was the war-cry of the Britons at Mold, of the Knights Templars, of Demetrius of the Don; a verse from the Psalms had floated on the banner of the Spanish Armada; the battle-song of John Sobieski at Choczin in 1663, when the tide of Mahomedan invasion was finally checked, was Ps. cxv. So now, in the French Wars of Religion, the Psalms became the Huguenot *Marseillaise*. With a psalm they repelled the charge or delivered the assault. In Condé's army, so La Noue has recorded, the sentries were posted and relieved to the chant of psalms. Ps. iii. (" Lord, how are they increased that trouble me ") gave the signal of danger. Day after day, the hymn of thanksgiving for victory was raised in Ps. cxxii. ("I was glad when they said unto me," etc.) from the walls of Huguenot strongholds, like Montauban or La Rochelle, as the soldiers of the League drew off their beaten forces.

Nor was it only in the shock of battle, or the glow of victory, that the power of the Psalms was exercised. Other songs, from the days of Tyrtæus to those of Körner, have warmed the blood and fired enthusiasm. But the Psalms alone have been equally powerful in defeat, disaster, or humiliation. In vain was the chanting of the Psalms proscribed. Equally in vain was it to burn the books by the hands of executioners, or to thrust the pages into the gaping wounds of the dying. *Colporteurs* risked their lives in carrying to the remotest corners of Protestant France copies of Marot's version of the Psalms, printed so small that they could be readily concealed in the clothes of refugees. Thus it was that the Psalms sustained the courage of the martyrs in the midst of torture, and of the *Forçats de la Foi* who were condemned to the living death of the galleys. The meetings of the proscribed and persecuted Huguenots were summoned by the singing of a psalm; in woods and caverns, in dungeons, in exile in America, the Psalms still sounded from the lips of the sturdy Protestants. In the language of psalms was commemorated the escape of those who fled from the country; and an old seal is in existence, once the property of a Huguenot refugee, which bears as its device a net below; and above, a bird soaring upwards; and, as its motto, the words, "My soul is escaped even as a bird out of the snare of the fowler" (Ps. cxxiv., verse 6). To sing the Psalms of David, men left their native land, and sought remote recesses of the earth. François Leguat and six companions made their home on the Island of Rodrigues in the Indian Ocean, in order that there, without hindrance, they might indulge in the consolation of singing praise to God. The spectacle of these seven fugitives gathered together to chant the Psalms of David, in an otherwise uninhabited island, is at once a strange scene to conjure up with the imagination, and a striking commentary on the enduring power of the Hebrew hymns.

Scarcely less impressive, perhaps, are the more peaceful

associations which made the Psalms not only the banner and the symbol, but also the synonym of the Reformed Churches, and connect them with the industries, the private lives, the learning, or the arts of the Huguenots.

"Palissy ware," with its lustrous glaze and lifelike reproductions of natural objects, was the invention of Bernard Palissy, the Huguenot potter, "ouvrier en terre et inventeur de rustiques figures." In his indomitable efforts to solve the mystery of enamel, he had stripped his dwelling bare of furniture, and had beggared himself, his wife, and his children. Worn out with watching his furnace, shrunk to a skeleton, mocked by his neighbours, bitterly reproached by his family, he found consolation in the Psalms. As he wandered through the fields round Saintes, observing the beauty and variety of that nature, which he learned to imitate with such marvellous skill, he compared the infinite power and wisdom and goodness of God with his own petty cares and trials. "I have fallen on my face," he says, "and adoring God, cried unto Him in spirit, ' What is man that Thou art mindful of him ' (Ps. viii., verse 4); and, ' Not unto us, O Lord, not unto us, but to Thy Name give the praise ' " (Ps. cxv., verse 1).

To John Calvin, the theologian of the French Protestants, belongs the honour of editing the first printed edition of metrical psalms for church worship. Marot's translation of thirty Psalms had received the royal licence on November 30th, 1541. Three years before, Calvin had become the pastor of the French Protestant Church at Strasburg. There, in 1539, he had caused to be printed one Psalm in prose (cxiii.), and seventeen in verse, set to music. Of these metrical translations, twelve were by Marot; the remaining five were by Calvin himself, in whom the genius of philosophy had not destroyed the natural taste for poetry. At Geneva, it was one of Calvin's first acts to introduce the chanting of psalms into the public worship of the Reformed Church (Nov. 1541). In his preface to the Genevan edition of Marot's Fifty Psalms, together with a liturgy and a catechism, June 10th, 1543, he says that, for the worship of God, " Nous ne trouverons meilleures chansons ne plus propres pour ce faire, que les pseaumes de David, lesquels le sainct

The Huguenots, 1524-98

Esprit luy a dictez et faits." It was to the Psalms that he himself turned in mental troubles, as well as in the throes of pain and death. In any anxiety of mind, he repeated the words of Psalm vi., verse 3, " My soul is sore troubled: but, Lord, how long wilt Thou punish me? " In the agony of mortal pain, he groaned out, " I became dumb, and opened not my mouth; for it was Thy doing " (Ps. xxxix., verse 10). It was fully enough, for him, he said, to know that it was God's hand. Almost his last words were a fragment from the Psalms, " How long, O Lord? " (Ps. xiii., verse 1); but even the cry of weariness rather expressed his lament for the calamities of the Huguenots, than his own impatience of spirit.

In his later years, Calvin's colleague at Geneva was Theodore de Beza (1519-1605), the writer of the metrical version of Psalm lxviii., which was the battle-song of the Huguenots. Taste for the culture of the Renaissance, passion for poetry, worldly success and fame, had weakened the impression of the religious training of his youth. A dangerous illness revived his former feelings. Escaping from the bondage of Egypt, as he called his previous life, he took refuge with Calvin at Geneva. In 1548, when he, for the first time, attended the service of the Reformed Assembly, the congregation was singing Psalm xci., " Whoso dwelleth under the defence of the Most High, shall abide under the shadow of the Almighty." He never forgot the effect of the words. They supported him in all the difficulties of his subsequent life; they conquered his fears, and gave him courage to meet every danger. To the work of translating the Psalms into French verse, and into Latin prose and Latin verse, Beza devoted the best years of his life. His translation into French verse, completing that of Marot, was published at Lyons in 1562. During sleepless nights, Beza used to repeat to himself the morning hymn of eastern Christians, the favourite psalm of St. Chrysostom, " O God, Thou art my God; early will I seek Thee," etc. (Ps. lxiii.). When this veteran of the Reformation died (Oct. 13th, 1605), it was with a text from the Psalms upon his lips, " If Thou, Lord, wilt be extreme to mark what is done amiss, O Lord, who may abide it? " (Ps. cxxx., verse 3).

By a text from the Psalms, Robert Estienne, the famous printer, was sustained throughout his long struggle with the theologians of the Sorbonne, who proscribed his editions of the Bible in the vulgar tongue. "Whenever," he said, "I recall to mind the war that I have waged with the Sorbonne, these twenty years and more, I have been astonished that so small and frail a person as myself could have had strength to continue the struggle. Yet every time that memory reminds me of my deliverance, that voice which in Psalm cxxvi. celebrates the redemption of the Church, strikes an echo in my heart: 'When the Lord turned again the captivity of Sion, then were we like unto them that dream'" (verse 1).

On August 20th, 1608, the great scholar, Casaubon, was going with his wife to the Huguenot worship at Charenton in an open boat on the Seine, singing psalms as they went. They had finished Psalm xci., and had reached verse 7 of Psalm xcii., when a heavy barge struck the stern of his boat and threw his wife into the river. Casaubon saved her, after almost losing his own life in the effort. But, in doing so, he dropped into the river his Book of Psalms, given to him by his wife as a wedding-present, and for twenty-two years the constant companion of his travels. They reached the Temple, and were present at the services. When the chant of the Psalms began, Casaubon put his hand into his pocket for his book, and for the first time discovered his loss. He did not recover himself till the congregation had finished more than half the 86th Psalm. The verse at which he was able to join in the singing was the end of the 13th: "and thou hast delivered my soul from the nethermost hell." "I could not but remember," says Casaubon in his journal, "that place of Ambrose where he says, 'This is the peculiarity of the Psalter, that every one can use its words as if they were completely and individually his own."

A story which illustrates his love of the Psalms, is told of Jean Rousseau, the Huguenot painter (1630–93), who, for his religious opinions, was shut out from the Royal Academy of painting, and died an exile in London. The Duchess of Orleans, who had been compelled to leave her home in the Palatinate, to abjure the Protestant faith, and to marry the

The Huguenots, 1524-98

brother of Louis XIV., wrote to her sister: "You must not think that I never sing the Psalms or Lutheran hymns. I sing them constantly, and find in them the greatest comfort. I must tell you what happened to me in connection with them. I did not know that M. Rousseau, who has painted the Orangery at Versailles, belonged to the Reformed Religion; he was at work on a scaffolding, and I, thinking myself alone in the gallery, began to sing the 16th Psalm. I had hardly finished the first verse, when I saw some one come hurriedly down from the scaffolding and fall at my feet. It was Rousseau. I thought he had gone mad. 'Good God! Rousseau,' said I, 'what is the matter?' 'Is it possible, Madame,' he answered, 'that you still remember your Psalms and sing them? May God bless you, and confirm you in these good feelings!' His eyes were full of tears."

Upon France of to-day the history of the Reformed Churches has left its lasting mark. Memories of this struggle for existence linger round the ruins of castles, churches, and towns. They are preserved in caves, like those of Lozère, which were the refuges and the storehouses of the Huguenots. New cathedrals, like those of Orleans or Uzés, are monuments of the religious bigotry which destroyed the older edifices; new towns, such as Privas, record the atrocities of a religious war which did not hesitate to turn cities into deserts. Places, like the Place du Mûrier at Angoulême, or the bridge of Orthez, are traditionally associated with deeds of atrocity, when the Huguenots, goaded to desperation by persecution and massacre, turned, with the Psalms on their lips, to destroy their oppressors. The poetry of the Huguenots, partly religious, partly polemical, partly warlike, is still sung in country districts, where it enshrines the hopes of the Protestants, long since dispelled, as in the stanza:

> " Nostre Dieu renversera
> Vous et vostre loy romaine,
> Et du tout se moquera
> De vostre entreprise vaine.
> Han, Han, Papegots!
> Faites place aux Huguenots."

In the Angoumois, to this day, covered utensils of earthenware are called *Huguenotes*, because they were used by the

Protestants to cook meat on *jours maigres*. Inscriptions over the doors of houses still indicate the homes of the Huguenots; at Xainton (Dept. des Deux Sèvres), for example, is the motto from Psalm cxxvii., verse 1:

" On a beau sa maison bâtir,
Si le Seigneur n'y met la main,
Cela n'est que bâtir en vain."

The *Rue du Renard*, no uncommon name in street nomenclature, commemorates the times when Protestants hunted Catholic priests with cries of " Renard." " *Le Roi Hugon*," with whose midnight depredations children are frightened at Tours, is wrongly supposed to have given his name to the Huguenots, who glided through the city in the shelter of the darkness to attend their places of worship. In Bas-Poitou wolves were popularly called *Soubises*, in memory of the terrible leader of the Protestants; and many of the Druidic stones, which are scattered over the country, are indifferently known as *Pierres du Diable* and *Pierres de Soubise*. Even the nicknames of the Huguenots suggest the desperate character of the strife. Soubise was called *le roi des Parpaillaux* (the patois for *papillons*), because he and his followers fluttered round the fire and the stake. The word *mouchard* is supposed to be derived from Antoine de Mouchy, the most zealous ferreter-out of heretics. Proverbs like *riche comme un Huguenot*, or *honnête comme un Huguenot*, recall the envy which was roused by the virtues and wealth of the Protestants. Deepest of all is the mark which the suppression of French Protestantism has left on the political, industrial, and intellectual life of the nation. It paved the way for the absolute despotism of the Crown and the consequent reaction of the Revolution. It robbed France of the hands and brains, arts and industries, of the best educated, the most laborious, frugal, and conscientious of her sons. It encouraged, by its repression of liberty of thought, the scepticism of the eighteenth century and the anti-clerical feeling of the late Republic.

From the martyrology of Crespin, and other writers, might be cited almost innumerable instances, in which the Psalms sustained the courage of French Protestants in the midst of mortal agony. In 1524, when the Psalter had not been versified, and was hardly known in the prose translation of Lefèvre d'Etaples, Jean Leclerc, the wool-comber of Meaux, was burned alive at Metz. Before the fires were lighted, he was subjected to horrible tortures; but his constancy never wavered as he repeated the same words which had encouraged the martyrs of the early Christian era: "Their idols are silver and gold: even the work of men's hands. . . . They that make them are like unto them; and so are all such as put their trust in them" (Ps. cxv., verses 4-8). A year later, in the same year (1525) in which the Inquisition was established in France, Wolfgang Schuch, the Lutheran preacher in Lorraine, was burned alive at Nancy, repeating at the stake the words of Psalm li.

The persecution of the Protestants had begun while Francis I. was engaged in war with Charles V., or detained a prisoner in Spain, and while Louise of Savoy was Regent of France. Taken captive at the battle of Pavia (1525), Francis had been brought under a guard to the Church of the Certosa. When he entered the building, the monks were singing Psalm cxix., verses 65-70. At verse 71 the king recovered himself sufficiently to join in the words, "It is good for me that I have been in trouble, that I may learn Thy statutes." Strong hopes were entertained that Francis, for love of his sister Marguerite, from political rivalry, or from personal sympathy, might place himself at the head of the Reformed movement. The policy of the Crown was indeed, for a time, more tolerant. Francis had delayed to execute the decree of the Sorbonne against Marot's versions. Though he ultimately forbade their publication, he was often heard humming the airs, and, on his deathbed, he ordered the book to be read aloud for his consolation. "Knowing that his last hour was come, he set the affairs of his house in order, commanded that the Psalms of Clement Marot should be brought to him, caused some to be read aloud to him, and, commending his people and his servants to the Dauphin," died March 31st, 1547. But the general policy was not reversed, and Leclerc and Schuch head the long list of Protestant martyrs, who, from 1542 onwards, chanted the Psalms in Marot's version as they were led to the scaffold or the stake. Their song was taken up by the bystanders in the street. It was thus that at Meaux, in 1546, the fifty-seven prisoners, and their friends in the crowd, joined in Psalm lxxix. as they were led to prison; and it was the same Psalm which the fourteen who were condemned to death sang on their way to the scaffold:—

> " Les gens entrez sont en ton heritage,
> Ils ont pollu, seigneur, par leur outrage,
> Ton temple sainct, Jerusalem destruite,
> Si qu'en monceaux de pierres l'ont reduite.
> Ils ont baille les corps
> De tes seruiteurs morts
> Aux corbeaux pour les paistre,
> Le chair des bien-viuans
> Aux animaux suyuans
> Bois et pleine champestre."

This is the Psalm which was used by the Jews every Friday, in lamentation over the ruins of Jerusalem. The same Psalm was applied alike to the zealous excesses of the Huguenots or the Puritans, and to the profane outrages of the French Revolution. It was used by the Carthusians of Woburn Abbey at the time of the dissolution of the monasteries, when Abbot Hobbs called the brethren together, and bade them, " for the reverence of God," to pray devoutly, and recite the Psalm *Deus venerunt gentes*. Verse 2 of the same Psalm was the motto chosen by the Jesuit Parsons for his book, *De persecutione Anglicana* (1581). The same words were suggested to Luisa de Carvajal by the sight of those Roman Catholics who were executed in London in 1608. " We can hardly go out to walk without seeing the heads and limbs of our dear and holy ones stuck up on the gates that divide the streets, and the birds of the air perching on them; which makes me think of the verse in the Psalms, ' The dead bodies of thy servants have they given to be meat unto the fowls of the air ' " (Psalm lxxix., verse 2).

In vain the Catholic priests, attending at the executions of the Huguenots, tried to drown the thunder of Marot's Psalms with their Latin chants. The words lacked the savage energy of the vernacular French; the unknown tongue awakened no response from the crowd. Many victims were gagged before being burned: but the fire severed the cords which held the instruments in their place,

The Huguenots, 1524-98

and, with charred lips, the sufferers raised the Psalms. Others, whose tongues had been cut out, uttered sounds in which, though barely articulate, bystanders recognised the familiar words. So it was at Angers, in 1556, that Jean Rabec at the stake, while he was being alternately raised and lowered into the flames, continued to sing Psalm lxxix., half choked with blood, till his end arrived. It was while a Protestant congregation was singing psalms in the grange at Vassy, in 1562, that Guise gave the signal for the massacres of the Huguenots which finally provoked the Wars of Religion. When once the sword was drawn, the Psalms became the war-songs of the Huguenots. On the battlefields of Coligny or Henry of Navarre were heard such chants as Psalms lxxvi. or cxviii., or, above all, Beza's version of Psalm lxviii.:

> "Que Dieu se monstre seulement,
> Et on verra soudainement
> Abandonner la place
> Le camp des ennemis espars,
> Et ses haineux, de toutes pars,
> Fuir deuant sa face."

In the early periods of the civil wars of the sixteenth century, the Huguenots moved as one man; their union was their strength. The central figure is Gaspard de Coligny, as Henry IV. is the leader of their later stages. Throughout the struggle, the royal family gave chieftains to Roman Catholics and Protestants alike; both sides fought under princes of the blood. On both sides were arrayed the heads of powerful families, who led their feudal levies to the field. Politics and religion were mingled; the Roman Catholics represented the influence of Spain: the Protestants raised the cry of "France for the French." Though the Roman Catholics showed but little religious enthusiasm, and all the zeal was to be found among the Huguenots, yet the ultimate triumph of toleration was effected by the triumph of a political party, which placed its chief upon the throne in the person of Henry of Navarre.

In March 1568, the Treaty of Longjumeau gave the Huguenots a breathing space. Their leaders retired to their homes in the country; their followers were disbanded, their mercenaries dismissed. Gaspard de Coligny, Admiral of France, returned to his gardens on the terraced slopes of

Chatillon-sur-Loing, and, clad in farmer's dress, pruned his fruit trees. But the treacherous calm only half concealed the coming storm. Catherine de Medicis merely sought to gain time. The peace was unreal. No effort was made to restrain the violence of the Roman Catholics. Coligny's treasures had been seized, and he could obtain no redress. Shots were fired at him; he was ordered to reduce his retinue; one of his gentlemen was murdered. He retired to the castle of his brother Andelot, at Tanlay, near Tonnerre, so that he might be close to Condé at Noyers. There the stern, reserved Coligny, whose thoughtful, serious face, with its square, high forehead, firm mouth and melancholy grey eyes, looks down from among the portraits of the Grands Amiraux of France, held frequent counsel with his colleague. No two men could be more different from each other than the two leaders of the Huguenot cause. The one was the Washington, the other the Rupert, of the Huguenots. Coligny, cold in manner, severe in demeanour, slow in the expression of his opinions, pitiless towards himself, inflexible in his judgment towards others, was most formidable in defeat, and won his greatest successes in retrieving disasters. Upon this distinctive feature in the Admiral's greatness Voltaire has seized, in the *Henriade*:

> " Savant dans les combats, savant dans les retraites,
> Plus grand, plus glorieux, plus craint dans ses défaites,
> Que Dunois ni Gaston ne l'ont jamais été
> Dans le cours triomphant de leur prospérité."

Condé was a dashing cavalry officer, whose charge was irresistible. Chivalrously courageous, fond of pleasure, with nothing of the Puritan in his nature; loving other people's wives, so Brantôme says, as much as his own; excelling, in spite of his slight figure and round shoulders, in all manly exercises; he was the darling of the people of Paris, and disputed their favour with the Duc de Guise. On these two men, each so different, depended the fortune of the Huguenot cause. To destroy them was the aim of Catherine. Had not the Duke of Alva said, that the head of one salmon was worth a thousand frogs?

In the summer months of 1568 the royal troops were collected in the neighbourhood of Tanlay and Noyers. Royal

The Huguenots, 1524-98

guards held the gatehouses, fords, and bridges. A warning reached Condé and Coligny. A horseman galloped past Noyers, sounding his horn, and crying out, " The stag is in the snare! The hunt is up! " Instant flight was necessary. At midnight, on August 25th, 1568, the Huguenot leaders, with their families and fifty followers, left Noyers to run the gauntlet of their enemies, and traverse the many hundred miles which lay between them and their refuge at Rochelle. The pursuit was hot. Led by a huntsman who knew the fords and forest paths, they reached the Loire at a spot above Cosne, near Sancerre. They crossed the river, their horses wading only to their girths. As day broke, the river rose in flood. The fugitives were saved. They had placed a barrier between themselves and their pursuers. Rochelle could yet be reached in safety. They fell on their knees on the farther bank, and gave thanks, singing the 114th Psalm, " What ailed thee, O thou sea," etc.

The war was renewed. At Jarnac (1569) the Roman Catholics gained a victory, in which Condé was killed. At Moncontour, in the same year, Coligny himself was disastrously defeated. Wounded in three places, he was carried from the field in a litter. As Lestrange, one of his old companions in arms, also severely wounded, was being carried past him, he thrust his head into the Admiral's litter, and without strength for more, whispered, " Si est-ce que Dieu est tres doux." (" Truly God is loving unto Israel, even unto such as are of a clean heart," Ps. lxxiii., verse 1.) The words, as Coligny told a friend, revived his failing courage. His firmness returned, and he set himself to restore the fortunes of his cause. From all the mountain districts of the Vivarais, the Cevennes, and the Forez, the Huguenots flocked to his standard. A new spirit animated his followers. They sang, as they passed through a hostile country and deserted villages,

> " Le prince de Condé
> Il a esté tué,
> Mais monsieur l'Amiral
> Est encore à cheval
> Pour chasser les papaux, papaux."

Coligny's name overshadowed that of the king. " De

l'Amiral de France," says Brantôme, " il etait plus parlé
que du roi de France." At the head of his army he had,
within a year, extorted from Catherine de Medicis, and the
unhappy red-haired youth, who bears the sinister title of
Charles IX., the Treaty of St. Germain-en-Laye (1570).

Coligny was the chief victim of the Massacre of St. Bartholomew, August 24th, 1572. The same event introduces the
hero of the second period of the Civil Wars. A prisoner at
the court of Charles IX., surrounded in Paris by the murderers of his friends, tempted by all the sensual allurements
which Catherine de Medicis had thrown in his way, Henry of
Navarre seemed to have forgotten ambition, and to welcome
inaction. Only two of his former attendants remained
faithful to the young king—his squire, d'Aubigné, and his
valet, Armagnac. Even they were weary of the task, and on
the eve of quitting so unworthy a master. But one evening,
when Henry was in bed, ill, feverish and depressed, they
heard him singing softly to himself the words of Psalm
lxxxviii. (verses 7-10, 18), " Thou hast put mine acquaintance far from me, and made me to be abhorred of them. I
am so fast in prison that I cannot get forth. . . . Dost Thou
shew wonders among the dead; or shall the dead rise up
again and praise Thee? . . . My lovers and friends hast
Thou put away from me, and hid mine acquaintance out of
my sight." The squire felt that the young king's chivalrous
spirit was not wholly extinct. He urged him to throw in his
lot with the faithful adherents who were fighting that enemy
whom Henry himself was serving. A few months later, the
king escaped from Paris, crossed the Seine at Poissy, traversed a country held by the forces of the Guises, and at
Alençon placed himself at the head of the Huguenots. The
next morning when he attended service, the psalm which
was appointed to be sung was Psalm xxi., " The king shall
rejoice in thy strength, O Lord," etc. The omen seemed so
propitious that Henry asked whether the psalm had been
selected to welcome him to the camp. But it had come in
its natural course. Henry remembered, so d'Aubigné tells
the story, that this was the same psalm which the companion
of his passage across the Seine at Poissy had sung, as, with
their bridles on their arms, they walked the horses to and

fro by the side of the river, waiting for the rest of the party.

Already Rochelle had repulsed the triumphant Roman Catholics. The town had preserved its municipal independence since it was surrendered by the English at the Peace of Bretigny. Taxing itself, electing its own magistrates, protected on the land by impregnable walls, opening or closing its port at its own pleasure, sweeping the seas with its own powerful navies, Rochelle was the Venice or Amsterdam of France. It was also its Geneva, the city of refuge to which fled Protestants from all parts of the country. But for the moment its fate trembled in the balance. Outside the walls of the Huguenot stronghold were encamped the royal armies, in which Brantôme held a command. Within the city were crowded the citizens and refugees. After five weeks of battering and skirmishes, a general assault was delivered. Four times the besiegers were driven back, and, as they recoiled, the battle-song of the Huguenots, *Que Dieu se monstre seulement* (Ps. lxviii.), rose in triumph from the ramparts. The siege was raised (1573), and thus the claim of the citizens was vindicated that Rochelle was founded on an impregnable rock.

In the years that followed, the interest of the Wars of Religion centres round Henry of Navarre. With two at least of his victories, the Psalms are strikingly associated. At the battle of Courtras, October 20th, 1587, before the fight began, the Huguenots knelt in prayer, and chanted Ps. cxviii., verses 24, 25:

" La voici l'heureuse iournee
Que Dieu a faite a plein desir,
Par nous soit ioye demenee
Et prenons en elle plaisir.
O Dieu eternel, ie te prie,
Ie te prie, ton Roy maintien:
O Dieu, ie te prie et reprie,
Sauue ton Roy et l'entretien."

" 'Sdeath," cried a young courtier to the Duc de Joyeuse, who commanded the Roman Catholics, " the cowards are afraid; they are confessing themselves." " Sire," said a scarred veteran, " when the Huguenots behave thus, they are ready to fight to the death." The battle ended in the triumph of Henry. The Duc de Joyeuse was killed, and his army utterly routed. More than forty years afterwards (1630), d'Aubigné lay on his deathbed. Perhaps the memory of the victory returned at his last moments to the dying man. "Two hours before his death," so wrote his widow, "with a glad countenance, and with a peaceful contented mind," he repeated the Psalm, "La voici l'heureuse iournee," etc., and so passed to his rest.

In 1589 Henry gained another victory under the walls of the Château d'Arques, the picturesque ruins of which are still standing in the neighbourhood of Dieppe. There the king and his Huguenot followers were threatened with destruction by the Duc de Mayenne and the army of the League. His forces were but few compared with the number of those arrayed against them; his reinforcements had failed him; the courage of his men was crushed by the weight of superior numbers. "Come, M. le Ministre," cried the king to Pastor Damour, "lift the psalm. It is full time." Then, above the din of the marching armies, rose the austere melody of the 68th Psalm, set to the words of Beza, and swinging with the march of the Huguenot companies. Pressing onwards, the men of Dieppe forced themselves like an iron wedge through the lines of the League, and split them asunder. The sea fog cleared away; Henry's artillery-men in the castle could see to take aim; the roll of cannon marked the time of the psalm; and the Leaguers were scattered.

The triumph of Henry IV. in 1598 restored the Psalter to the Court of France. Once more the Psalms, which Francis I. had hummed so gaily, were sung at the Louvre. By the Edict of Nantes, peace was for a time imposed upon France. It was the Magna Charta of the Reformed churches, guaranteeing to the Huguenots freedom of worship in specified places, admitting them to civil rights, offices, and dignities, providing for the trial of Protestant causes by mixed benches of judges, and securing enjoyment of these privileges by the possession of fortified towns. During the life of Henry IV., the son of Jeanne d'Albret, pupil of Coligny, and hero of a hundred fights against the Catholic League, the king's personal influence maintained the compact. Yet, at the best, the Edict of Nantes proclaimed a truce rather than a lasting peace.

CHAPTER VIII

THE HUGUENOTS, 1600-1762 (*continued*)

The Roman Catholic Reaction—Vincent de Paul, François de Sales: changed conditions of the Huguenot cause; their effect on the character of the Wars of Religion 1621-29—Henri de Rohan, sieges of Montauban and la Rochelle; The Roman Catholic triumph and maintenance of the strictest orthodoxy—Port Royal, Pascal, Madame Guyon: Edicts against the Huguenots and the use of the Psalter: the Vaudois and Henri Arnaud; Revocation of the Edict of Nantes (1685); persecution of the French Huguenots; the rising in the Cevennes—murder of François du Chayla, Cavalier and the Camisards, Bellot, Martignargues (1704), Salindres (1709); the Pastors of the Desert—Rang, Roger, Benezet, Rochette; effect of the Psalms on the virtues and defects of the Huguenots.

THE French Wars of Religion, waged in the seventeenth century by the Duc de Rohan and Cardinal Richelieu, differed materially from those led by the Guises on the one side, and by Coligny or Henry of Navarre on the other. The Huguenots were now confronted by a Roman Catholic reaction. The austerities of monastic life were revived, and to these was added the cultivation of learning. Benedictines, Dominicans, Franciscans, set their houses in order; Clairvaux, Citeaux, and Cluny underwent a reformation. Jesuits laboured in the world for the advancement of the Roman faith, and multiplied their schools and seminaries. New religious orders supplied preachers and made proselytes. Missions were conducted among country people by the new congregation of St. Vincent de Paul. Women shared the same movements. Montmartre, Val de Grace, Port Royal, became models of conventual piety. The Feuillantines and Jesuitines rivalled the zeal of the Jesuits and the Feuillants. The work of educating young girls was taken up by the Port-Royalists. Sisters of Charity found cells in the sick-room, and lived in the world unscathed, with the fear of God for their *grilles*, and pure modesty for their veils. Religious communities breathed the new life which the spirit of St. François de Sales, St. Vincent de Paul, or Madame de Chantal inspired. The ranks of the secular clergy were recruited by men of ardent faith and irreproachable conduct. Bishops, for the most part men of unstained reputation, reformed their dioceses, rebuilt churches, reorganised parishes, revived ecclesiastical discipline, or headed philanthropic movements, such as those for the erection of charitable hospitals. Lay society felt the influence of the movement. Missioners rekindled the Roman faith among the poorer classes. Provincial magistrates, who had been attracted to the Reformed doctrines by their logical consistency or by jealousy of the Papacy, returned to the older faith. Even at Court, men and women, for whom Fénelon wrote his Counsels, found it possible to live pure lives without renouncing the business or pleasures of the world.

The power of the Roman Catholics was growing, that of the Protestants was decaying. As their hold on France relaxed, the Reformed churches grew more tenacious of their privileges, while the Gallican clergy demanded changes in the Edict of Nantes. The balance of parties, on which the Edict was founded, was disturbed by gains on the one side and losses on the other. Was the Edict to remain untouched?

In this religious reaction the Psalms played their part. They were not the exclusive possession of the Huguenots. Men of the type of Montaigne might condemn "the promiscuous, rash, and indiscreet use of the holy and divine songs which the Holy Spirit inspired in David," or deprecate placing them in the hands of "shop-boys." But their power was recognised. The Abbé Desportes, the effeminate Petrarch of the Court of Henry III., translated the whole Psalter into French verse. Courtiers and state officials, like Jean Metezeau, or Michel de Marillac, versified the Psalter in the hope of rivalling the work of Marot and of Beza. The preface to the version of Metezeau, which is dedicated to Henry IV., is a strange production. "David," he says, "was somewhat prone to love women, and that love of women is the only charge which Your enemies can make against Your Majesty; but Your Majesty has one advantage over the wise King, that You have not on this account drawn down the wrath of God neither upon Yourself nor upon Your people." Corneille and Racine translated portions of the Psalter. But of the numerous translations that were made as pious or literary exercises, the only successful version was that of Godeau, Bishop of Grasse and Vence. His paraphrases were set to music, and four of the airs were composed by Louis XIII. himself. In his preface, Godeau explains the object of his work. " To know the Psalms by heart," he says, " is among Protestants a sign of their communion. To our shame it must be said, that, in towns or districts where Protestants are numerous, the Psalms are ever on the lips of artisans and labourers, while Catholics are either dumb or sing obscene songs." Godeau's success was greatest in a direction which he scarcely anticipated, or desired. Forbidden by edicts to sing psalms at home, in the version of Marot and Beza, the Huguenots sang them in that of the Roman Catholic bishop. So widespread became the practice, that fresh edicts were issued in general terms, altogether prohibiting the singing of Psalms in French.

But, apart from the multiplication of versions of the Psalms, their universal influence may be illustrated from the lives of leaders of the Roman Catholic reaction. Such men as St. Vincent de Paul or St. François de Sales may be taken as examples.

From Cadiz to Patras the Mediterranean and its coasts were scoured by the corsairs of Barbary. Their light galliots and brigantines swept down on their prey with the swiftness and precision of the osprey, overbearing resistance and baffling pursuit. Nor was it only the seaman, the merchant, or the traveller, who ran the risk of slavery. Landing on the shore, the corsairs swept off whole villages into captivity. The peasant of Provence, returning home at nightfall from pruning his vines or his olives, might find himself in the morning chained to the oar. The friar, who told his beads on the outskirts of Valencia, might, before the week was out, be hoeing the rice-fields of Tripoli. In 1605, Vincent de Paul was making his way from Toulouse by Narbonne to Marseilles. The ship in which he was crossing the Gulf of

Lyons was seized by Barbary pirates, and both passengers and crew carried to Tunis. Sold as a slave to a fisherman, he passed after a time into the hands of an apostate Christian from Nice, who carried him away to labour on an inland farm. As he dug in the fields under a burning sun, he excited the interest of one of the Turkish wives of his master. "One day," as Vincent writes in his letter to M. De Commet, "she asked me to sing to her some of the praises of my God." The remembrance of the captive Israelites, "How shall we sing the Lord's song in a strange land?" filled his heart, and he sang, "By the waters of Babylon" (Ps. cxxxvii.). The woman told her husband that he had done wrong to change his faith, and she warmly praised the religion that Vincent had expounded to her. Her words sank into the renegade's heart, and woke his slumbering conscience. He determined to escape and take Vincent with him. In 1607, they landed together at Aigues Mortes, and the captive was once more free.

The same words have often expressed the sorrows of prisoners or exiles. They rose to the lips of John II., King of France, a prisoner in England after the Battle of Poictiers, and a guest at a tournament. He looked on the brilliant scene with sorrowful eyes, and, when urged to enjoy the splendour of the pageant, answered mournfully, "How shall we sing the Lord's song in a strange land?" (Ps. cxxxvii., verse 4). So also the same psalm had appealed with peculiar force to Luiz de Camoens, the epic poet of Portugal. In March 1553, he had been released from prison on condition that he sailed for India. As in the twilight the ship dropped down the "golden-sanded" Tagus, he exclaimed, like Scipio Africanus, "Ungrateful country! thou shalt not possess my bones." Even at Goa he found no rest. His satires on the vices of the inhabitants caused, it is said, his banishment to Macao. There much of the *Lusiad* was written; there also he made a modest fortune. Embarking on board ship, he set sail for Goa. But, on the voyage, he was wrecked off the Mekong river, on the coast of Cochin China. All that he had was lost; he had only preserved the manuscript of his poem, when, friendless, ruined, and alone, he landed on the "gentle Mecon's friendly shore."

" Now blest with all the wealth fond hope could crave,
Soon I beheld that wealth beneath the wave
For ever lost; myself escaped alone,
On the wild shore, all friendless, hopeless, thrown;
My life, like Judah's heaven-doomed King of yore,
By miracle prolonged." [1]

As he sat by the banks of the Mekong, waiting for means of returning to Goa, his heart by the Tagus, his eyes searching the ocean for a sail, he wrote the paraphrase of Psalm cxxxvii., which is the finest metrical version of the poem. By the same words Heine was inspired to begin a metrical version of a psalm, which, in another mood, he parodied. How often, and with what pathetic force, must the words of the exiles' lament have appealed to the Puritans in New England, or to the Huguenots in Canada! What memories of silent tragedies must they have stirred in the hearts of the Covenanters, toiling among the slaves in the sugar plantations or the rice-fields of the West Indies and America!

This digression on the use of a particular psalm may be allowed, in view of its peculiar appropriateness to the lot of the exiled Huguenots. But, here, Psalm cxxxvii. was referred to as an illustration of the influence of the Psalter on the lives of leaders in the Roman reaction. A psalm had freed St. Vincent de Paul to labour for the Catholic faith in his native land. By the Psalms was inspired the life of St. François de Sales, Bishop of Geneva (1567–1622).

Few men have been more widely revered for the sanctity of their characters and the active beauty of their careers. To some he is most widely known as the friend of Madame de Chantal, whom he placed over his Order of the Visitation; others know him best from the reminiscences which Bishop Camus gathered in his *Esprit de St. François de Sales* : others revere his name for the charm which he gave to personal holiness. Nobly-born, brilliant in intellect, he added to his mental and spiritual gifts the fascination of a singularly attractive appearance. From his birth near Annecy, among the beautiful mountain scenery of Savoy, his mother, whose first child he was, looked upon him as " lent to the Lord," and, at an early age, the bent of his character was clearly shown. His mind was so steeped in the Psalter, that his

[1] *Lusiad*, Book vii.

thoughts naturally clothed themselves in the words of the Psalms. The rule of life which he laid down for himself in his twentieth year, is founded on their language. He promises to hear Mass with all the earnestness of his soul, crying out, "O come hither and behold the works of the Lord." If in the night he wakes, he will pray the Lord to "lighten his darkness"; he "will water his couch with tears" for his indifference to sin. If midnight terrors beset him, he will remember that "He that keepeth Israel shall neither slumber nor sleep" (Ps. cxxi., verse 4), and that he will be "safe under his feathers" (Ps. xci., verse 4). "The Lord is my light and my salvation, . . . of whom, then, shall I be afraid?" (Psalm xxvii., verse 1).

While studying law at Padua in 1591, he was seized with rheumatic fever. His life was despaired of. Ready for death, he received the last Sacrament, and awaited his end with resignation, repeating such verses as, "O how amiable are Thy dwellings, Thou Lord of Hosts: my soul hath a desire and longing to enter into the courts of the Lord" (Ps. lxxxiv., verses 1, 2); and again, "The Lord is my light and my salvation; . . . of whom, then, shall I be afraid?" or again, "Blessed is he whose hope is in the Lord his God." But he recovered, and, two years later, was ordained, sorely against the will of his father, who desired him, as his eldest son and heir, to take his place in the world. His life at Chablais as a missionary among the Calvinists (1593–1603), or at Geneva as the administrator of a diocese (1603–22), was a psalm in action. It was to the Psalms that in death he turned for the expression of his confidence and hope.

On the feast of St. John, 1622, he was struck down by a paralytic seizure, which left his mind unclouded. A friendly visitor expressed regret at his condition; "Father," he replied, "I am waiting on God's mercy: Expectans, expectavi Dominum et intendit mihi." (I waited patiently for the Lord, and He inclined unto me, and heard my calling, Ps. xl., verse 1.) "If it were God's will, ye would gladly depart now?" continued his friend. "If God wills it, I will it too," answered the bishop: "now, or a little while hence—what matters it?" As other friends came to see the dying man, the words of the Psalms seemed ever on his lips.

Often he was heard to murmur: " My soul hath a desire and longing to enter into the courts of the Lord: my heart and my flesh rejoice in the living God " (Ps. lxxxiv., verse 2). " My song shall be alway of the loving-kindness of the Lord " (Ps. lxxxix., verse 1). " When I am in heaviness, I will think upon God " (Ps. lxxvii., verse 3). " When shall I come to appear before the presence of God? " (Ps. xlii., verse 2). " Did he," asked one of the watchers by his bedside, " fear the last struggle? " " Mine eyes are ever looking unto the Lord, for He shall pluck my feet out of the net " (Ps. xxv., verse 14), was the reply. He died in the evening of the Holy Innocents' Day, 1622.

Men like St. Vincent de Paul, or St. François de Sales, had turned the tide of religious enthusiasm. It was now on the side of Roman Catholics. The change brought into clear relief the position occupied by the Huguenots, who formed a State within a State, a smaller France within the arms of the larger, a separate people protected by fortified cities, organised by distinct political institutions, defended, if need be, by its own armies, maintaining its own ambassadors, supported by foreign alliances. The strangeness of the position was further illustrated by the political condition of France during the years which intervened between the death of Henry IV. and the ascendency of Richelieu. The queen, the ministers, the princes of the blood, the nobility, each fought for their own hand. No leader and no party espoused any great cause; personal ambitions over-rode public policy; individual interests supplanted patriotism. The Crown had been respected; it was now despised. State affairs had been guided towards definite ends; now they drifted to and fro in confusion. Favourites without services, ministers without ideas, marshals without armies, successively wielded an authority of which they knew not the use. Before many years had passed, absolute power proved the only cure for anarchy; from a want of government, France passed to its excess. For the next few years, however, two forces— the nobility and the Reformed churches—now allied, now divided, opposed the Crown and convulsed the country. Internal peace and external strength seemed to be lost to France, till Richelieu had restored and aggrandised the power of the monarchy. Thus the Reformed churches were fighting against the needs and spirit of the age. In the sixteenth century, the struggle for religious and political independence was not in conflict with the general tendencies of a period which had barely emerged from feudal chaos. But in the seventeenth century they were contending against the new force of centralisation. They fought for existence as a State within a State, when the State itself was to be merged in the Crown; for liberty, when liberty itself was on the eve of extinction; for walled cities of security, when feudal castles were razed to the ground on every side; for municipal independence, when all but the shadow of civic freedom was approaching annihilation; for representative assemblies, when the voice of the States-General was to be silenced for a century and a half.

In the character of the religious wars of the seventeenth century the changed conditions, within and without, were clearly marked. The Psalms had not indeed lost their power. Henri de Rohan, the soul of the Protestant cause in France, still relied on their support. Threatened with assassination, he had no fear, for, as he wrote to his mother, April 30th, 1628, " Whoso dwelleth under the defence of the Most High, shall abide under the shadow of the Almighty " (Ps. xci., verse 1). But the Huguenots no longer counted allies in the royal family: the nobility, with the exception of Rohan and Soubise, sided with the Crown. The Reformed churches had ceased to move as one man: their faith was chilled; their religious differences were revealed; they disputed the policy of armed resistance. North of the Loire, no Protestant stirred hand or foot. The struggle was confined to the Cevennes, the burghers of Rochelle, and the cities of the south. Even in the latter there was division, for the civic aristocracy dreaded the republican teaching of Huguenot pastors. The three short wars of 1621-2, 1625-6, and 1627-9, were wars of sieges, within a contracted area: pitched battles were not, as in the previous century, fought in every part of the country. With two of those sieges, that of Montauban in 1621, and of Rochelle in 1627, the Psalms are associated.

On August 21st, 1621, the royal army, consisting of

The Huguenots, 1600-1762

20,000 men, began the siege of Montauban, on the defence of which Rohan had concentrated all his energies. The king himself was in the camp: the Duc de Mayenne, Luynes, five Marshals of France, and a crowd of the most distinguished of the French nobility, were among the officers. By day, on the ramparts of the Huguenot stronghold, men and women fought side by side; by night, they repaired together the breaches made by the cannonade of the preceding day. Six weeks passed. Winter was approaching. The royalists made no progress; the Duc de Mayenne was killed, losses in officers and men were heavy, and, at the end of September, Rohan threw 700 men and a convoy of provisions into the town. At nightfall, on October 17th, a Protestant soldier, serving in the king's army, played under the battlements of the town the familiar tune of Psalm lxviii., " Let God arise, and let his enemies be scattered." It was a signal that the siege was raised. The next day the camp was struck, and the royalists retired.

The siege of Rochelle, in 1627-8, was the central point of interest in the third and last of the civil wars. On November 6th, 1627, the French drove Buckingham from the island of Rhé. The English fleet sailed away, and Richelieu drew round the doomed city his iron girdle of famine. Within the walls provisions ran short. Every unclean animal was eaten. Bones, parchment, plaster, leather gloves, shoulder belts, and saddles were devoured. Then the starving people fed on the corpses of the dead. One woman died gnawing her own arms. As the siege progressed, it is said that the daily death-roll was 400. On October 27th, 1628, the town surrendered, and with its fall ended both the war and the independence of the Reformed churches.

During the blockade, when her neighbours were starving, a widow named Prosni generously supported many of the poor from her present surplus. Her sister-in-law, Madame de la Goute, remonstrated with her, asking what she would do when her store was expended. " The Lord will provide," was her reply. " Behold," she said, " the eye of the Lord is upon them that fear him, and upon them that trust in His mercy; to deliver their soul from death, and to feed them in the time of dearth " (Ps. xxxiii., verses 17, 18). The siege continued, and Madame Prosni with her four children was in sore straits. Her sister-in-law taunted her with her faith and its fruits, and refused all help. In her dejection she returned home, resolving that she would at least meet death with patience. At the door she was welcomed by her children, dancing with joy. A stranger, during her absence, had knocked at the door, and, on its being opened, had thrown in a sack of wheat and departed. She never discovered the name of her benefactor, whose timely aid enabled her to support herself and her family till the siege was ended.

The Peace of Alais (June 1629) guaranteed to the Huguenots a full measure of civil equality, as well as freedom of religious exercises. Had the spirit of the compact been observed, it might have healed the breach. But the triumph of the Roman Catholic reaction was too complete. The extreme men, who assumed the lead, demanded uniformity of faith; heresy, both within and without the Church, was to be extinguished; and the strife was renewed.

In the general reform of conventual and monastic life, the Abbey of Port Royal had set a striking example. Behind its cloistered walls, almost within sight and hearing of Versailles and Paris, yet in a valley so sequestered as to terrify Madame de Sévigné by its solitude, were gathered some of the purest and most devoted women of France, under the strict rule of Mère Angélique Arnauld. The spiritual directions of St. François de Sales, who loved the Port-Royalists, had tempered firmness with gentleness, and given a charm to the pursuit of personal holiness; the *Petites Ecoles* of the abbey rivalled the educational establishments of the Jesuits. But St. Cyran, who succeeded François de Sales as spiritual director, was suspected of heresy, and Port Royal was involved in the charge. Persecution fell upon the community. It was to a psalm that they appealed. "The sisters of Port Royal," says Blaise Pascal (and his own sister was one of the first victims of the persecution), "astonished to hear it said that they were in the way of perdition, that their confessors were leading them to Geneva by teaching them that Jesus Christ was neither in the Eucharist nor at the right hand of God, and knowing that the charge was false, committed themselves to God, saying with the Psalmist, ' Look well if there

be any way of wickedness in me ' " (Ps. cxxxix., verse 24).
Mère Angélique died August 6th, 1661, with the same words
of the Psalms upon her lips which Xavier had used at the end
of his toilsome career, " In Thee, O Lord, have I put my
trust; let me never be put to confusion " (Ps. xxxi., verse 1).
Her brother Antoine, an exile, or in hiding for fear of the
Bastille, had learned the Psalms by heart lest his eyesight
should grow too dim to read them daily. It is a psalm that
strikes the keynote of the *Pensées* of Pascal, the glory
and the champion of the Port Royal community. His
" Thoughts," in which the Psalms are repeatedly quoted,
are jotted down, with a failing hand, on loose fragments of
paper, in his brief respites from the agony of mortal sickness.
They show us his passionate heart in the midst of strife and
perplexity. They reveal, with the unsparing severity of
scientific detachment, the depths of mystery that surround
the narrow ledge on which men stand. Yet, through all the
gloom and shadow, there ever burns the sacred flame of
personal conviction, that in God, and in God alone, is light.
Reason had, he thought, attained its highest point when it
realised that an infinite number of things lie beyond its reach.
Men ought to know when to doubt, when to be certain, when
to submit. " Feel no surprise," he says, " that plain,
unlettered men believe the Christian faith without exer-
cising their reason. They are inspired by God with a love
of holiness and a hatred of themselves. God inclines their
hearts to faith. If God does not so incline the heart, no man
will believe with a true, effectual faith. But if the heart be
so inclined by God, none can refuse belief. Of this truth
David was well aware when he wrote, ' Incline my heart unto
Thy testimonies ' " (Ps. cxix., verse 36).

Like the Port-Royalists, Madame Guyon suffered persecution from the leaders of the Catholic reaction. In her
prison at Vincennes, she wrote those spiritual songs, many
of which were translated into English verse by William
Cowper. Yet into whatever mazes of speculation she was
tempted, her own words, expressed in the language of the
Psalms, reveal the starting-point of her spiritual fancies,
disclose the object of her quietism, and justify the defence of
Fénelon. She learnt, by frequent yieldings to temptation,

her entire dependence on the Divine aid. " I became," she says, " deeply assured of what the prophet hath said, ' Except the Lord keep the city, the watchman waketh but in vain ' (Ps. cxxvii., verse 2). When I looked to Thee, O my Lord, Thou wast my faithful keeper; Thou didst continually defend my heart against all kinds of enemies. But, alas! when left to myself, I was all weakness. How easily did my enemies prevail over me!"

When slight deviations from strict orthodoxy were punished with exile or imprisonment, it was not likely that open revolt would be spared. The Treaty of Alais was torn up; the Edict of Nantes revoked (1685). Under Louis XIII. and Louis XIV. successive edicts were directed against the Huguenots, and especially against their use of the Psalter. The singing of psalms was prohibited in streets or shops, forbidden in private houses, restricted even in Protestant temples. As the seventeenth century closed, legislation grew more severe under the austere piety of Madame de Maintenon and the religious zeal of Père la Chaise. Penal laws banished Protestant pastors. Death was the penalty for those who returned, or for any who sheltered them: possession of the heretic's property rewarded those who betrayed them. Protestant meetings were proscribed; possessors of a Protestant Bible or Psalter were liable to imprisonment and confiscation. The *dragonnades* inflicted untold horrors. A brutal soldiery, quartered in the houses of the Huguenots, was encouraged to pillage, torture, and outrage. Nor were the victims suffered to escape. Guards were doubled on the frontiers, and the peasants were armed to assist in arresting fugitives. But the Huguenot buried his books under a tree, hoped for better times, and continued his psalmody in cave or forest, careless that the sound might betray him to his persecutors or consign him to the galleys.

Even among the Alps, liberty of singing psalms was denied. The Protestants of the Vaud were driven from their homes, and dispossessed of their property. The exiles, diminished in number by the hardships of a winter journey across the Alps, with voices choked by exhaustion and misery, sang Psalm lxxiv. (" O God, wherefore art Thou absent from us so long? why is Thy wrath so hot against the sheep of Thy

The Huguenots, 1600-1762   165

pasture?") as they streamed into Geneva, and the words were re-echoed by the crowds who thronged the streets of the City of Refuge. Three years later (1689), it was the same psalm which was chanted in triumph by seven hundred of the exiles, who, led by their pastor, Henri Arnaud, had fought their way back to their homes. "The gallant patriots took an oath of fidelity to each other, and celebrated Divine service in one of their own churches for the first time since their banishment. The enthusiasm of the moment was inexpressible: they chanted the 74th Psalm to the clash of arms, and Henri Arnaud, mounting the pulpit with a sword in one hand and a Bible in the other, preached from the 129th Psalm, and once more declared in the face of heaven, that he would never resume his pastoral office in patience and peace, until he should witness the restoration of his brethren to their ancient and rightful settlements."

On the 22nd of October 1685, Michel le Tellier, as Chancellor of France, set the seal, almost with his dying hand, to the Revocation of the Edict of Nantes. The towns and villages and houses of the Protestants were pillaged and set on fire; their fields and vineyards were laid waste; they were burned alive, broken on the wheel, hung from the gibbet, or cut to pieces by the dragoons. Their midnight assemblies were again and again surprised, and the most venerated of their pastors were executed. The victims who died by sudden death were to be envied. More terrible still was the fate of the men who were chained to the oar at the galleys under the lash of barbarous officers, or of the women who were doomed to perpetual imprisonment in the loathsome dens of mediæval cruelty, such as the Tour Constance in the Castle of Aigues Mortes, where the prisoners, herded together in dark and stifling dungeons, were left a prey to the melancholy thoughts that harmonised with the monotonous cadence of the waves, or the wind moaning over the marshes.

Among the rocky savage fastnesses of the Cevennes, the simple religion of the Protestant mountaineers assumed a stern and gloomy cast. Fervour easily passed into fanaticism, and ecstasies of faith readily lent themselves to self-deception. The *enfants de Dieu*, possessed by hysterical hallucinations, claimed for their wild words a prophetic inspiration. Goaded to desperation by their sufferings, seeing at every cross-road the corpses of friends swinging in the air, the peasants were carried away by the fiery appeals of prophets and prophetesses, who urged them to arm against the enemies of God, and fight to the death for the true Church. Upon their excited minds the Psalms exercised an almost supernatural power. "As soon," says Durand Fage, "as we began to sing the chant of the Divine Canticles, we felt within us a consuming fire, an ecstatic desire which no words can express. However great our fatigue, we thought of it no more. The moment the chant of the Psalms struck our ears, we grew light as air."

With such temperaments, it needed but a spark to kindle the smouldering fury of the people into a flame which should spread through the mountains with the devastating rapidity of lightning. That spark was lighted by François du Chayla, Prior of Laval, and Inspector of Protestant Missions in the district of Gévaudan.

This man was the chief agent in the persecution of the Protestants of the Cevennes. His house at Pont de Montvert, close to the bridge over the Tarn, was at once a prison and a torture-chamber, in which neither sex nor age was spared, and where children and young girls received no mercy. In 1702 the Abbé du Chayla held as prisoners a number of Protestants who had been captured in an attempted escape to Geneva. On the evening of July 23rd, 1702, a party of resolute men, numbering fifty in all, goaded by the appeals of their prophets, determined to rescue the prisoners. As night fell, they met under three gigantic beeches on the slope of the mountain of Bougés, called in the patois of the country "Alte fage." Some were armed with swords, some with scythes, some with halberds of ancient make; only a few carried guns or pistols. Before they set out on their enterprise, they prayed together, and then, chanting the Psalms of Marot as they went, marched on Pont de Montvert. They reached the village about nine in the evening, and, still singing the Psalms, surrounded the house of the abbé.

The abbé was dining in company with his fellow-labourers, when the rude chant of the Psalms reached his ears. Supposing that the Protestants had ventured to hold a conven-

The Huguenots, 1600-1762

ticle within earshot of his house, he ordered his guard to seize the rash worshippers. But the house was surrounded so that none could pass out. On all sides the cry was heard, "Bring out the prisoners." The abbé, a determined man, showed that he would yield only to force. At his command the soldiers fired upon his assailants, and one of the prophets was killed and others of the party wounded. The infuriated Protestants, seizing the trunk of a tree, beat down the door, swarmed into the house, and rushed to the dungeons. A second discharge proved fatal to another of the rescuing party. Exasperated by the sight of their tortured brethren, and provoked by resistance, the Cévénols piled together the furniture of the house, raked up the straw on which the soldiers slept, threw on the heap the seats from the chapel, and set the building on fire. Then the abbé and his friends endeavoured to escape from the windows at the back of the house. Tying the sheets of their bedding together, they attempted to reach the garden. The abbé fell and broke his thigh, but, crawling into the bushes, hid himself. Others, more fortunate, came to the ground safely, and, plunging into the Tarn, escaped.

As the fire gathered fierceness and caught hold of the timber of the house, the glare of the flames revealed the lurking-place of the abbé. His cry for mercy was mocked. Dragged into the open, he was killed. Each successive assailant as he delivered his blow, cried out that it was in vengeance. "Take that," cried one, "for my father's sake, whom you broke on the wheel." "Take that," cried another, "for my brother, whom you sent to the galleys." "And that," shouted a third, "for my mother, whom you killed with grief." Fifty-two wounds were found on his body, of which twenty-five were mortal. Only two persons discovered in the house were spared. All the livelong night, amid the crash of falling timbers, and the roar and hiss of flames, which drowned the murmur of the Tarn, the deliverers chanted their psalms in wild ecstasy of vengeance, and as the day dawned, it was with a psalm of triumph that they withdrew with their rescued brethren to their mountain fastnesses.

With this ferocious act of vengeance began the war of the

Cevennes, in which, with the Psalms for their battle-cry, a handful of peasants defied the armies of Louis XIV., defeated his most skilful marshals, and negotiated on equal terms with the Grand Monarque himself.

On Sunday, December 24th, 1702, Jean Cavalier had assembled eighty of his followers for worship on Christmas Eve. The service had barely begun, when his sentinels, posted on the hills, gave the alarm. The commandant of Alais, with six hundred foot-soldiers and fifty mounted gentry, was upon them. It was with a psalm that the Camisards attacked their assailants, routed them, and pursued the fugitives up to the gates of Alais.

Four months later, April 1703, Cavalier and his band bivouacked in a deserted farm-house called Bellot, near Alais. Built on the ruins of a feudal castle, the house was surmounted by a tower, and surrounded by a wall and deep ditch. At midnight a traitor led the soldiers to the spot. Four thousand royalists surprised four hundred sleeping Camisards. Cavalier escaped along the moat, and, after a vain attempt to rescue those who were hemmed in within the enclosure, drew off a portion of his men under the cover of darkness. From midnight till eight the next morning the defenders of Bellot held their own. Their ammunition was spent; but, refusing to yield, they perished to a man in the blazing ruins, still raising with their latest breath the words of their beloved psalms.

The Psalms were again the battle-cry of the Huguenots at Les Devois de Martignargues, where, in March 1704, Cavalier won a brilliant victory. The royalist general, La Jonquière, with a considerable number of foot-soldiers, dragoons, and grenadiers, had pursued the Camisards from Moussac to Brignon, and thence higher up the mountains to the bleak uninhabited spot which was the final scene of the conflict. There Cavalier determined to make his stand. After praying with his men, he took up a strong position, posting an ambuscade to his left and right. La Jonquière led his men to the attack. The Camisards lay down till the royalists had discharged their pieces. Then, springing to their feet, and thundering out the Psalms, they charged the enemy, while at the same moment the men in ambush attacked on both flanks. The royalists broke and fled, the victorious Camisards in hot and merciless pursuit.

It was with the Psalms that Roland, another of the Camisard leaders, routed the royalists at the Bridge of Salindres, in the spring of 1709. In pursuit of Cavalier, the Marquis de Lalande, one of the greatest coxcombs of the day, but an experienced soldier, had reached Anduze. There two peasants were introduced into his presence to tell him that Roland was about to seize the Bridge of Salindres, over the river Gardon. The men were in truth emissaries of the Camisard chief. Lalande fell into the trap. Acting on their information, he determined to seize the Bridge. To reach it, he had to penetrate a narrow, winding pass. On one side rose bare precipitous cliffs; on the other ran a deep ravine, at the bottom of which seethed the mountain torrent of the Gardon. At the entrance of the gorge, Roland had concealed a body of his troops; on the rocks above, he had stationed another band; he himself, with a third company, held the Bridge of Salindres. Lalande, suspecting nothing, entered the ravine. When he had entangled himself in its narrow windings, a signal was given, and he found himself attacked in front and rear, while enormous rocks, hurled from the cliffs above, swept his men by files at a time into the river. Above the rattle of the musketry, the crash of the falling rocks, and the confused cries of the soldiers, was heard the triumphant psalm of the Camisards. The whole army seemed doomed to perish. One path alone had not been occupied by the mountaineers; it descended the side of the ravine, and crossed the Gardon by a mill-dam. Down this path of safety rushed Lalande with a few of his followers, so hotly pursued that he left his plumed hat behind him, and escaped with his wig in flames. As evening fell, the din of battle ceased. In the quiet valley, whose silence was only broken by the roar of the Gardon, rose the 48th Psalm:

> " Dieu aux palais d'elle est cognu
> Et pour sa defense tenu," etc.

As the unequal war dragged on,—as, time after time, at unequal odds, the king's troops were defeated,—as the mountaineers held their own against trained soldiers and experienced generals, they grew strong in the conviction that

God was on their side. "Our enemy," says Mazel, one of the Camisard historians, "were as the sand on the seashore in number, and we were but a little company. They had horses, and chariots, and gold, and weapons, and castles. We had no such aid, but the Lord God of Hosts was our strength."

The same serene confidence which had nerved the arms of the Camisards, inspired the quiet heroism of the Protestant "Pastors of the Desert," who, in the first half of the eighteenth century, braved danger and death to carry on their proscribed ministrations. In the long list of executions, there are but few victims who were not sustained in their last hours by the words of the Psalms.

In 1745, Louis Rang, the brother of a minister who only saved himself from the scaffold by flight, a young man of twenty-five years of age, and himself a minister of the Protestant religion, was arrested at Livron. He was thrown into prison at Valence, and condemned to die at Grenoble, March 2nd, 1745. In vain the President of the Court had offered him his life if he would abjure his faith. He rejected all offers. His sentence was that he should be hung in the market place at Dié, and that his head should be severed from his body and exposed on a gibbet opposite the little inn at Livron, where he had been arrested. On his way to the scaffold, he sang verse 24 of Psalm cxviii.:

> "La voici l'heureuse journee
> Qui repond a notre desir;
> Louons Dieu, qui nous l'a donnee;
> Faisons en tout notre plaisir."

His voice was drowned by the roll of drums. With his eyes raised to heaven, he reached the foot of the scaffold, fell on his knees in prayer, then mounted the ladder and met his death.

A few weeks later, Jacques Roger, a venerable man of seventy years of age, forty of which he had spent as a Protestant pastor, was betrayed to the government and arrested. Ordained at Würtemburg, and therefore one of the few regularly ordained ministers, he had braved the law which made it a capital offence to return to France. For forty years he had escaped, often by a hair's breadth, the pursuit of the soldiers, who had tracked him like a wild beast. The officer in command asked him who he was. "I am he," he replied, "whom you have sought for thirty-nine years; it was time that you should find me." Condemned to death at Grenoble, he spent his last hours in encouraging some Protestant prisoners to be true to their faith. When the executioner and his assistants arrived to take him to the place of execution, he received the summons cheerfully, quoting the same verse which Louis Rang had sung on the scaffold (Ps. cxviii., verse 24). From prison he went to his death chanting Psalm li.

The same Psalm (li.) was sung, on his way to execution, by François Benezet, a young man who was studying for Holy Orders. He was executed in January 1752, on the esplanade at Montpellier. His youth, his courage, and the fact that he left a widow and child, created a profound impression among his co-religionists. His fate is commemorated in one of the rude songs which, through their uncouth stanzas, breathe the fervent piety and indomitable resolution of the Protestants.

The last of the martyred pastors of the desert, was François Rochette, who, in 1760, had been consecrated pastor at the provincial synod of Haut Languedoc. In the district of Querçy he spent some laborious months, preaching, administering the Communion, visiting the sick, teaching the young, celebrating marriages, baptisms, and funerals, for the twenty-five Reformed churches which fell to his charge. His health being injured by his incessant labours, he left Montauban, in September 1761, to drink the waters at Saint Antonin. On his way through Caussade, he was asked to baptise a child. It was midnight, and, not knowing his way, he sent his guides into the town to find a native of the place who would take him to the house where his services were required. As the guides were returning to the pastor, they endeavoured to evade observation by leaving the main road. Some passers-by, catching sight of them, mistook them for robbers who infested the neighbourhood, and sent the town-guard in pursuit of them. They were seized by the patrol, and with them Rochette. Taken before the magistrates, Rochette boldly avowed his calling, and was committed to prison.

The excitable populace of the South were aroused. Believing that a plot was on foot among the Protestants to pillage the town, they rang the tocsin, donned the white cockades of St. Bartholomew's Day, and attacked the heretics. The Protestants, on their side, armed themselves, and a bloody conflict seemed imminent. Though the outbreak was prevented, the affair sealed the fate of Rochette and his companions. Petitions were presented to the Duc de Richelieu, and to Marie Adelaide, Princess of France, the daughter of Louis XV., who had shown herself inclined to mercy. All was in vain. Rochette was tried at Toulouse in November 1761; in the following February the sentence of death was pronounced. He was offered his life if he would abjure his faith. He refused, and, on February 20th, 1762, the sentence was executed. To the last, Rochette encouraged his companions. Through the crowded streets, thronged with spectators, the car was drawn to the place of execution in the Place du Salin. Rochette mounted the scaffold with a firm step, chanting as he went, " La voici l'heureuse journee," etc. (Ps. cxviii., verse 24).

It was fitting that the last words of the last Protestant martyr should be taken from that Book of Psalms which, through two centuries of conflict and persecution, had meant so much to the Huguenots. "It was," said Florimond de Rémond, "the Book of Psalms which fostered the austere morals of the Huguenots, and cultivated those masculine virtues that made them the pick of the nation. It was that book which supported fainting courage, uplifted downcast souls, inspired heroic devotion. Their affirmations were *certes* or *en verité*; they were enemies of luxury and worldly follies; they loved the Bible or the singing of spiritual songs and psalms better than dances and hautboys. Their women wore sober colours, and in public appeared as mourning Eves or penitent Magdalens; their men, habitually denying themselves, seemed struck by the Holy Spirit." Nor was it only their virtues which the Psalms had fostered. From the same book they justified their ferocity. To them Rome was Babylon, and the Reformed Church was Sion. Their enemies were God's enemies. They were His appointed instruments of vengeance, and they made war in the spirit of Calvin's commentary on Psalm cxxxvii., verses 8, 9, and of his defence of its imprecations on the women and children of their foes.

CHAPTER IX

THE PURITANS, 1600–1660

The Pilgrim Fathers and Benjamin Franklin: the Psalms among the royalists—Jeremy Taylor, Bishop Sanderson, Strafford, and Laud: the Civil War—Marston Moor, John Hampden, Charles I. at Newark: Puritanism as a poetical, religious, and political force in Milton, Bunyan, and Cromwell.

To the Puritans of the seventeenth century, the Psalter was the book of books. Psalms were sung at Lord Mayor's feasts, at City banquets. If the clown in the "Winter's Tale" (Act iv., sc. 2) be accepted as a witness, they were sung to "hornpipes" at rustic festivals. Soldiers sang them on the march, by the camp fire, on parade, in the storm of battle. The ploughman carolled them over his furrow; the carter hummed them by the side of his waggon. They were the songbook of ladies and their lovers, and, under the Commonwealth, the strains of the Psalms floated from windows in every street of Puritan strongholds.

To gain liberty of worship and of psalm-singing, men and women crossed the seas, seeking in the New World the freedom that was denied them in the Old. With this object the little congregation of Separatists, which gathered at Scrooby in Nottinghamshire, made their way in 1608 to the East Coast, and thence to the Low Countries. For twelve years they made the "goodly and pleasant city" of Leyden their "resting-place." But in July 1620, the *Speedwell*, a vessel of sixty tons burden, lay at Delft Haven equipped for their transport to the New World. "When," says Winslow, 'the ship was ready to carry us away, the brethren that stayed having again solemnly sought the Lord with us and for us, they that stayed at Leyden feasted us that were to go, at our pastor's house, being large, where we refreshed ourselves, after tears, with singing of psalms, making joyful melody in our hearts as well as with the voice, there being many of the congregation very expert in music. And indeed it was the sweetest melody that ever mine ears heard."

To the singing of psalms the sails of the *Mayflower* were set to catch the winds that wafted the Pilgrim Fathers to the white sandbanks of Cape Cod; to their music were laid the foundations of the United States of America. "At Salem is his tabernacle" (Ps. lxxvi., verse 2), were the words which suggested to John Endicott's company the name of their first settlement. The denial of the liberty of "singing psalms and praying without a book," drove Francis Higginson, the first appointed teacher at Salem, to exchange the Old World for the New. At the Sabbath services, both in Salem and in Plymouth, the Psalms were sung without music, from the version of Henry Ainsworth of Amsterdam. But it was not long before the Puritan divines had prepared their own version, and the third book printed in America was the Bay Psalm Book (1639–40). Till the end of the eighteenth century, the Psalms were exclusively sung in the churches and chapels of America. In the language of the Psalms the early progress of the first colony is recorded. "The Lord," says Johnson in his *Wonder-Working Providence*, "whose promises are large to His Sion, hath blest His people's provision, and satisfied her poor with bread, in a very little space." The Psalms were the chief instrument of Eliot in his missionary enterprises among the Red Indians. From the Psalms, Eliot's successor, David Brainerd, drew the language in which he clothed his daily thoughts. In versifying the Psalms, the early poets of the young Republic, such as Barlow, Dwight, or Bryant, exercised their powers. In the same task, Cotton Mather had previously found respite from his dark musings on the mysteries of the unseen world. In the Psalms was laid the coping-stone of American independence. In 1787, it was to the 1st verse of Psalm cxxvii. that Benjamin Franklin appealed, when speaking before the Convention assembled to frame a Constitution for the United States of America:—

"In the beginning of the contest with Britain, when we were sensible of danger, we had daily prayers in this room for the Divine protection. Our prayers, Sir, were heard, and they were graciously answered. All of us who were engaged in the struggle must have observed frequent instances of a superintending Providence. To that kind Providence we owe this opportunity of consulting in peace on the means of establishing our future national felicity. And have we now forgotten this powerful Friend? or do we imagine that we no longer need His assistance? I have lived for a long time (81 years), and the longer I live the more convincing proof I see of this truth, that God governs in the affairs of men. And if a sparrow cannot fall to the ground without His notice, is it probable that an empire can rise without His aid? We have been assured, Sir, in the sacred writings, that ' Except the Lord build the house, they labour in vain that build it.' I firmly believe this, and I also believe that without His concurring aid we shall proceed in this political building no better than the builders of Babel. I therefore beg leave to move that, henceforth, prayers, imploring the assistance of Heaven and its blessing on our deliberations, be held in this assembly every morning before we proceed to business, and that one or more of the clergy of this city be requested to officiate in that service."

In the spirit of the Psalms, as they interpreted them, the brethren of the Pilgrim Fathers, the Puritans who remained behind in England, fought out their quarrel with Charles I. But the Psalter was not the peculiar property of the Parliamentary party. Charles I. himself caused his father's version of the Psalms to be printed. From Psalm lxxxii., verse 1 ("God standeth in the congregation of princes; He is a Judge among gods"), Bishop Andrewes had silently protested against the intrusion of churchmen into secular affairs. From another Psalm (Psalm lx., verse 2, "Thou hast moved the land, and divided it: heal the sores thereof, for it shaketh"), Bishop Hall appealed for peace, in the Lent sermon which he preached in 1641 before Charles I. at Whitehall. To Anglican divines, as well as to Puritan preachers, the Psalter was as " the balm of Gilead." Jeremy Taylor (1613–67), who acted as chaplain in the army of Charles I., suffered both in person and in purse for his loyalty to Church and King. Of " liberty of prophesying " he was an assailant, of the Church's Liturgy a champion.

But, in the midst of his persecution and troubles, it is in the Psalms that he finds consolation. "When I came," he writes, "to look upon the Psalter with a nearer observation, . . . I found so many admirable promises, so rare variety of the expressions of the mercy of God, so many consolatory hymns, the commemoration of so many deliverances from dangers and deaths and enemies, so many miracles of mercy and salvation, that I began to be so confident as to believe there would come no affliction great enough to spend so great a stock of comfort as was laid up in the treasury of the Psalter." In the *Rule and Exercises of Holy Living* and *of Holy Dying*, he teaches from experience. His gorgeous, richly-tinted prose differs absolutely from the homely English of Bunyan. It winds its devious way along like some Roman triumph, laden with the captives and the spoils of other languages and literatures. Yet, when Taylor comes to the practical aids of holy life or death, it is on the Psalms that he almost exclusively relies. From the Psalter are drawn his prayers, ejaculations, and devotional forms of preparation, alike in health or old age, by day or at night, in sickness or at the moment of death.

Another peaceful yet shining light of the Church during the Civil Wars, was Robert Sanderson (1587–1662), who at the Restoration was consecrated Bishop of Lincoln, and has left his mark on the history of the Common Prayer Book. By the Parliamentarians he was ejected from his professorship at Oxford, and imprisoned. But his sorrows deepened and enlarged his love of the Psalter—"the treasury," as he told Izaak Walton, "of Christian comfort, fitted for all persons and all necessities; able to raise the soul from dejection by the frequent mention of God's mercies to repentant sinners: to stir up holy desires; to increase joy; to moderate sorrow; to nourish hope, and teach us patience, by waiting God's leisure; to beget a trust in the mercy, power, and providence of our Creator; and to cause a resignation of ourselves to his will: and then, and not till then, to believe ourselves happy." He added, that, by the frequent use of the Psalms, "they would not only prove to be our souls' comfort, but would become so habitual, as to transform them into the image of his soul that composed them." He himself

used them constantly. " As the holy Psalmist said," writes
Walton, " that *his eyes should prevent both the dawning of the
day and the night watches, by meditating on God's Word* (Psalm
cxix., verse 148), so it was Dr. Sanderson's constant practice
every morning to entertain his first waking thoughts with
a repetition of those very psalms that the Church hath
appointed to be constantly read in the daily morning service;
and having at night laid him in his bed, he as constantly
closed his eyes with a repetition of those appointed for the
service of the evening, remembering and repeating the very
psalms appointed for every day." On the day before his
death, he desired his chaplain to give him absolution.
' After this desire of his was satisfied, his body seemed to be
more at ease, and his mind more cheerful; and he said,
Lord, forsake me not now my strength faileth me (Ps. lxxi.,
verse 8); *but continue thy mercy, and let my mouth be filled·
with thy praise.* He continued the remaining night and day
very patient, and to himself during that time did often say
the 103rd Psalm, and very often these words, *My heart is
fixed, O God; my heart is fixed where true joy is to be found* "
(Ps. lvii., verse 8). " Thus," continues Walton, in the con-
clusion of one of the most charming of his biographies, " this
pattern of meekness and primitive innocence changed this
for a better life. It is now too late to wish that my life may
be like his; for I am in the eighty-fifth year of my age; but
I humbly beseech Almighty God, that my death may; and
do as earnestly beg . . . any reader . . . to say Amen.
Blessed is the man in whose spirit there is no guile " (Ps. xxxii.,
verse 2).

In love of the Psalter, Anglican and Independent, Cavalier
and Roundhead, might be united. In all else they were
bitterly opposed. Even before the execution of the Earl
of Strafford and of Laud, men recognised that an appeal to
arms was almost inevitable. Yet it was to the Psalms
that those two ministers, whom the people held directly
responsible for the king's most oppressive acts, appealed in
the moment of their death.

In November 1640, Thomas Wentworth, Earl of Strafford,
had been committed to the Tower. It was not till five
months later that his trial began. During that interval,

the feeling against him grew every day more bitter. "Black Tom Tyrant" was hated by his former colleagues in the House of Commons as an apostate from the popular cause. Stronger than desire for vengeance or personal dislike was the fear with which his commanding ability and indomitable will inspired his opponents. Vague forebodings of violence, rumours of popish plots, suspicion of the king's purpose, were whispered in the House of Commons. Nothing is more cruel than a panic; as long as Strafford lived, men felt their own lives and liberties to be in peril. "Stone dead hath no fellow," and his punishment was demanded as a protection against a public enemy. Strafford knew his danger, when he obeyed Charles's summons, and came from Yorkshire to London. But he had the king's assurance that he should suffer neither in his person, nor in his honour, nor in his estate. On this explicit promise he relied. Even after his committal to the Tower, he had written to his wife, bidding her keep up her heart. "I am," he said, "in great inward quietness and a strong belief that God will deliver me out of all these troubles."

On March 22nd, 1641, the trial had begun. In the centre of Westminster Hall was raised a stage, taking up the whole breadth of the building from wall to wall, and about a third part of the length. At the north end was set a throne of state for the king, and a chair for the prince. These stood empty; but on either side of the throne was a gallery, on one side of which sat the King and Queen, Princess Mary, the Prince Elector, and some ladies of the Court, and on the other side various French nobles. In front of the throne sat the Earl of Arundel, who acted as Speaker. Below him were seats for the Judges, and a little table at which were the black-gowned clerks of the House. On forms, covered with red cloth, sat the Peers, in their red and ermine robes. On either side of the Hall, along its east and west walls, and at its southern end, were ranged stages of forms, on which sat the members of the House of Commons and spectators. Above the highest stage of forms, were boxes crowded with ladies.

At eight o'clock on the morning of March 22nd, the Earl of Strafford, dressed in a black habit, and wearing his

The Puritans, 1600-1660

George, was brought in, in custody of the Lieutenant of the Tower. His crisp dark hair was turning grey, and his figure stooped slightly from recent illness. He took his place at the bar, with his secretaries behind him, and on a level with him were the eight managers who conducted the case for the House of Commons. Hour after hour, he stood at bay. Every morning those who wished for seats were in the Hall by five; the king arrived at half-past seven; the Lords took their seats, with heads covered, at eight, and continued sitting till four in the afternoon. When Strafford was preparing his replies to special points in the indictment, the Lords rose from their seats, talked and clattered about; the members of the House of Commons discussed the progress of the trial; " bread and flesh " were eaten, " bottles of beer and wine going thick from mouth to mouth without cups." Sometimes the speeches were hissed; at other times a deep hum marked the approval of the audience; and Strafford, as Baillie, his enemy, remarked, daily gained the affections of the ladies by his eloquence and address.

On April 13th, he made his defence against the whole charge of treason. It was evident that he was likely to escape. The Commons therefore determined to proceed by a Bill of Attainder, and to vote him a traitor. The Bill was read a third time in the Lower House on April 21st, and in the Upper House on May 8th. Would the king accept or reject it? Four days before the third reading, Strafford wrote a letter to Charles, " to set " the king's " conscience at liberty." " My consent," he says, " shall more acquit you herein to God than all the world can do besides. To a willing man there is no injury done; and as, by God's grace, I forgive all the world, with calmness and meekness of infinite contentment to my dislodging soul, so, Sir, I can give to you the life of this world with all the cheerfulness imaginable, in the just acknowledgment of your exceeding favours."

The king delayed his assent to the attainder. All Sunday, May 9th, an armed mob paraded the streets and threatened an attack on Whitehall. At length, late in the evening, Charles yielded. " My lord of Strafford's condition," he said, as he signed his name to a commission charged to give his assent, " is more happy than mine." On Tuesday morning, he made a final appeal to the Lords to commute Strafford's sentence to one of imprisonment. "But if," he adds, "no less than his life can satisfy my people, I must say *Fiat justitia*." Then follows the postscript, " If he must die, it were a charity to reprieve him to Saturday."

His weak appeal was made in vain. The next day, May 12th, 1641, Strafford met his death courageously on Tower Hill. The news that Charles had deserted him had come to him with the shock of surprise. Perhaps he may have relied to the last on the king's promise. It is thus that a poet has represented him turning to the messenger of his fate:

> " See this paper, warm—feel—warm
> With lying next my heart! Whose hand is there?
> Whose promise? Read, and loud for God to hear!
> ' Strafford shall take no hurt '—read it, I say!
> ' In person, honour, nor estate.' "

But if such thoughts were in his mind, it was to the Psalms that, in bitterness of spirit, he turned for their expression: " O put not your trust in princes, nor in any child of man; for there is no help in them " (Ps. cxlvi., verse 2). Strafford's quotation recalls the words which Shakespeare places in the mouth of the fallen Wolsey:

> " O, how wretched
> Is that poor man that hangs on princes' favours!
> There is, betwixt that smile we would aspire to,
> That sweet aspect of princes, and their ruin,
> More pangs or fears than wars or women have;
> And when he falls, he falls like Lucifer,
> Never to hope again."

With Strafford, in all the high-handed acts of Charles's Government, was associated Laud. Against the archbishop were, in addition, arrayed the bitterness of religious feeling and the desire for vengeance on a persecutor. It was partly the error of his time, partly the bias of his legal mind, which led him to depreciate the value of diversities and to exaggerate that of uniformity, in matters of belief and opinion. But adversity revealed in him virtues which official severity had too often concealed. " Prejudged by foes determined not to spare," imprisoned in the Tower, old and failing in health, stricken with ague, subjected to unworthy insults, threatened with violent death, he never lost his courage, his

The Puritans, 1600-1660

patience, or his dignity. Libels against him flowed from the pens of his opponents; slanders ran from mouth to mouth; abusive ballads were sung in streets and taverns. Laud comforted himself with the thought that he was "in the same case as the Prophet David." "They that sit in the gate speak against me; and the drunkards make songs upon me" (Ps. lxix., verse 12). Placed in confinement in December 1640, committed to the Tower in the following March, he waited for his trial till the spring of 1644. The proceedings against him were conducted with as little respect to law as the most arbitrary act with which he himself was charged. On 10th January 1645, he suffered death on Tower Hill in the seventy-second year of his age, his face showing so little fear of death that his disappointed enemies accused him of having painted his ruddy cheeks. In his speech from the scaffold he quoted Psalm ix., verse 12, "For, when he maketh inquisition for blood, he remembereth them; and forgetteth not the complaint of the poor." It was the Psalms that had sustained his courage during his long imprisonment. His prayers, of which the following may be quoted, are cast in the mould of their thoughts, and echo their language.

"O Lord, blessed is the man that hath Thee for His help, and whose hope is in Thee. O Lord, help me and all them to right that suffer wrong. Thou art the Lord, which looseth men out of prison, which helpest them that are fallen. O Lord, help and deliver me, when and as it shall seem best to Thee; even for Jesus Christ His sake. Amen."

"O Lord, Thine indignation lies hard upon me; and though Thou hast not (for Thy mercy is great) vexed me with all Thy storms, yet Thou hast put my acquaintance far from me, and I am so fast in prison that I cannot get forth. Lord, I call daily upon Thee, hear and have mercy; for Jesus Christ His sake. Amen."

"Lord, turn Thee unto me, and have mercy upon me, for I am desolate and in misery. The sorrows of my heart are enlarged; O bring Thou me out of my troubles. Look upon mine adversity and misery, and forgive me all my sins; through Jesus Christ our Lord. Amen."

"Hear my crying, O God, give ear unto my prayer; from the ends of the earth, whithersoever Thou shalt cast me, I will call upon Thee when my heart is in heaviness. O set me upon the rock that is higher than I, to be my hope and a strong tower against my oppressors. Amen."

"Save me, O God, for the waters are entered into my soul. I stick fast in the deep mire, where no stay is; I am come into deep waters, and the streams run over me. They that hate me without a cause are more than the hairs of my head, and they which would destroy me causeless are mighty. O let not these water-floods drown me, neither let the deep swallow me up, and let not the pit shut her mouth upon me. Hear me, O Lord, for Thy loving-kindness is great; turn unto me according to the multitude of Thy tender mercies. Hide not Thy face from Thy servant, for I am in trouble, but draw near unto my soul, and redeem it; for Jesus Christ His sake. Amen."

When once the Civil War had begun, it was with the Psalms that the shock of battle was often heralded. So was it at the battle of Marston Moor. About two o'clock in the afternoon of July 2nd, 1644, the armies of the King and Parliament faced each other. The great ordnance began to play. "The first shot killed a son of Sir Gilbert Haughton that was a captain in the Prince's army; but this was only a showing their teeth; for after a few shots made, they gave over, and in Marston corn-fields fell to singing psalms." With a psalm also is associated the death of distinguished leaders like John Hampden. On Saturday, June 17th, 1643, about four in the afternoon, Prince Rupert rode out from Oxford at the head of his men, clattering over Magdalen Bridge, and crossing the Thame at Chislehampton. They encountered Hampden and his troop at Chalgrove Field. Early on Sunday morning, 18th June, Hampden was seen riding out of the fight before it was ended, his head bent, his hands resting on his horse's neck. It was a thing, says Lord Clarendon, "he never used to do, and from which it was concluded he ·was hurt." He was indeed mortally wounded. It is supposed that he first tried to reach Pyrton, where he had wooed and won his first wife, and where he would fain have died. But he was cut off by Rupert's horsemen, and forced to turn back and ride to Thame. There, in the house of Ezekiel Browne, after six days' agony,

The Puritans, 1600-1660

he died. His troopers, as they bore his body to the grave through the beech-woods of Buckinghamshire, chanted Psalm xc., which, since 1662, has had its place in the burial service of our Prayer-book.

His power broken at Marston Moor, Charles I. was a hostage or a prisoner in the Scottish camp at Newark. The triumphant ministers insulted their captive by ordering Psalm lii. to be sung: "Why boastest thou thyself, thou tyrant, that thou canst do mischief; whereas the goodness of God endureth yet daily?" It was by an appeal to the Psalms that Charles robbed the insult of its sting. His only reply was to ask for Psalm lvi.: "Be merciful unto me, O God, for man goeth about to devour me; he is daily fighting, and troubling me. Mine enemies are daily in hand to swallow me up; for they be many that fight against me, O Thou Most Highest."

Instances of the use of the Psalms by one side or other might be multiplied. But their influence upon a movement, which is still a living force in our midst, may be best illustrated in the lives or writings of Milton, Bunyan, and Cromwell—the finest products of Puritanism as a literary, spiritual, or political force.

Over Milton the Psalms threw their spell in early life. At the age of fifteen, already an undergraduate at Christ's College, Cambridge, he translated into verse Psalms cxiv. and cxxxvi. Of the latter, his version is the well known:

"Let us with a gladsome mind
Praise the Lord for he is kind,
For his mercies aye endure
Ever faithful, ever sure."

In 1648, he translated from the original "into meter" nine Psalms (lxxx.-lxxxviii.), and in 1653, eight more Psalms (i.-viii.) were "done into verse." Throughout his poems are scattered allusions, more or less direct, to the Psalms. There is an echo of Psalm xxiv., verses 7-10, in his lines in *Paradise Lost* (Book vii., ll. 205-9, and ll. 565-9):

"Heav'n open'd wide
Her ever-during gates, harmonious sound
On golden hinges moving, to let forth
The King of Glory in His powerful Word
And Spirit coming to create new worlds."

and, as God returns heavenward, his creative work accomplished:

> "Open, ye everlasting Gates, they sung,
> Open, ye Heav'ns, your living doors; let in
> The great Creator, from his work return'd
> Magnificent, his six days' work, a World."

In the same Book (ll. 370-4), the picture of the Sun rejoicing " as a giant to run his course " (Ps. xix., verse 5) is in his mind, when he writes:

> "First in his East the glorious lamp was seen,
> Regent of day, and all th' horizon round
> Invested with bright rays, jocund to run
> His longitude through Heav'n's high road."

Portions of the speech of Adam (*Paradise Lost*, Book xii., ll. 561-6) seem a paraphrase of Psalm cxlv.:

> "Henceforth I learn, that to obey is best,
> And love with fear the only God, to walk
> As in his presence, ever to observe
> His providence, and on him sole depend,
> Merciful over all his works, with good
> Still overcoming evil, and by small
> Accomplishing great things, by things deem'd weak
> Subverting worldly strong, and worldly wise
> By simply meek."

So also in "Samson Agonistes" (ll. 932-7), when the blind Samson rejects the appeal of Delilah, he refers to the "deaf adder" of Psalm lviii., verse 4:

> "I know thy trains,
> Though dearly to my cost, thy gins, and toils;
> Thy fair enchanted cup, and warbling charms
> No more on me have power; their force is null'd;
> So much of adder's wisdom I have learn'd,
> To fence my ear against thy sorceries."

Finally, when, in *Paradise Regained*, Satan tempts Christ with the wisdom of the ancient Greeks, it is with praise of the Psalms, couched in the true spirit of the Puritan, that the Saviour repels the temptation:

> "All our Law and Story strow'd
> With hymns, our Psalms with artful terms inscrib'd,
> Our Hebrew songs and harps, in Babylon
> That pleas'd so well our victor's ear, declare
> That rather Greece from us these arts deriv'd—
> Ill imitated, while they loudest sing
> The vices of their deities . . .

> Remove their swelling epithets thick laid
> As varnish on a harlot's cheek, the rest,
> Thin sown with aught of profit or delight,
> Will far be found unworthy to compare
> With Sion's songs, to all true tastes excelling,
> Where God is prais'd aright and god-like men,
> The Holiest of Holies, and his Saints," etc.
>
> (Book iv., ll. 334-49.)

Paradise Lost enshrines in stately verse the general scheme of Puritan theology: *The Pilgrim's Progress* applies that system in allegorical form to the sphere of individual life. Milton's sonorous grandeur suits the theme of God's dealing with the world and with mankind; equally well is Bunyan's language, homely yet never vulgar, simple but always adequate, racy without irreverence, adapted to his dramatic presentation of the moral warfare waged by a human soul against the powers of evil.

One secret of the undying charm of the great Puritan allegory, is its truth to Bunyan's own nature. He describes his own experience: he paints, with vivid realism, the picture of his own inner self; the struggle of Christian is a transcript of his own spiritual conflict. He has himself been plunged into the Slough of Despond, himself fought hand-to-hand with Apollyon, himself passed through the Valley of the Shadow of Death, himself reached the Heavenly landing-place. In his *Grace abounding to the Chief of Sinners*, which bears the motto, " Come and hear all ye that fear God, and I will declare what he hath done for my soul " (Ps. lxvi., verse 14), he has recorded, with a pen of iron and in letters of fire, his own passage from death to life. His religious autobiography traces his steps towards the attainment of that inward peace, which passes all human understanding because it is the Peace of God. It chronicles every fluctuation of hope and despair; it arrests and examines, with strange ingenuity of self-torture, every secret thought, every passing doubt, every momentary fear. His vivid imagination makes his feelings actors in a real drama. As a boy, he had felt the devil's claws strike into his flesh, till he all but screamed with pain. As a man, he holds soundless colloquies with Satan, whose words seem to be spoken so loudly in his ear that he almost turns round, expecting to find the tempter in bodily shape at his elbow.

The "loose, ungodly wretch" had become a "brisk talker" about religious matters, well spoken of by his neighbours before his face and even behind his back. The struggle began when he realised that he was but a "poor, painted hypocrite," ignorant of the meaning of true personal religion. Had he faith? he asked himself, and he was tempted to put his possession of the gift to the test by bidding " the puddles in the horse-pads be dry." In a vision, he saw himself shivering on the dark, frozen, snow-clad side of a high mountain, while on the other side all was bright and bathed in sunshine. At first he could find no passage in the wall which divided the two sides of the mountain; but at length he found a gap, through which, with much " sideling striving," he squeezed first his head, then his shoulders, then his whole body. The mountain was God's Church—the sunshine, His merciful face—the wall, the world—the gap, Jesus Christ. In his vehement desire to be of the number of those who sat in the sun, he would often sing Psalm li. But new fears disquieted him. Was he elected? Was the day of grace past and gone? Would Christ call him? His heart a-flame to be converted, he yet found that his unbelief set its shoulder to the door to keep out his Lord. Then, with many a bitter sigh, he would cry, " Good Lord, break it open: Lord, break these gates of brass, and cut these bars of iron asunder." (Ps. cvii., verse 16). So convinced was he of his own inward pollution, that he was, in his own sight, loathsome as a toad. Sin and corruption seemed to bubble from his heart as from a fountain. Yet at times the sense of God's love cheered him. The words, " Thou art my love, thou art my love," burned within his heart till they kindled a cheerful blaze. In his joy he could hardly refrain from telling his gladness to the crows that fed on the freshly turned plough-lands.

Once again the comfort was dashed from his lips by the thoughts—are the words true?—had he committed the unpardonable sin against the Holy Ghost?—was he beyond the pale of God's mercy? He would gladly have changed his condition for that of any other living creature. A horse or a dog were happier. He prayed. But in his prayers Satan was ever at his side, chilling the warmth of his aspirations, or distracting his thoughts with wandering fancies. Though "his soul was much in prayer," he failed to pray to be kept from the temptations and the evil that were to come. Of his error, he was, he says, "made deeply sensible by the prayer of holy David, who when he was under present mercy yet prayed that God would hold him back from sin and temptation to come: 'So shall I be undefiled, and innocent from the great offence'" (Ps. xix., verse 13). Even when he was consoled by the conviction of God's continued love towards him, and by the sense of his own earnest love for Christ, the struggle was renewed. He was assailed by a "yet more grievous and dreadful temptation than before," which never left him for a day. The tempter bade him exchange Christ for the things of this world. "Sell Him for this," whispered Satan, as he put a morsel of food in his mouth. "Sell Him for this," as he chopped a stick, or stooped to pick up a pin. At last he thought that he had yielded to the temptation, and had committed the "great offence" of Psalm xix., verse 13. He compared himself to Esau, who could not ransom his bartered birthright by an eternity of repentance. Like Judas, he felt his breast-bone splitting asunder. At moments the words of Psalm lxviii., verse 18 ("Thou hast received gifts for men, yea, even for Thine enemies"), consoled him. If God had gifts for His enemies, why not for him? Yet so despondent was he, that he thought the sun grudged him his light, and the very roof-tiles and paving-stones were banded together against him. Again happiness returned to him, as he pondered over the words, "If Thou, Lord, wilt be extreme to mark what is done amiss; O Lord, who may abide it? For there is mercy with Thee; therefore shalt Thou be feared" (Ps. cxxx., verses 3, 4). But once more he felt that his own transgressions had left him neither foot-hold nor hand-hold "among all the stays and props in the precious word of life." For two years and a half the discouragement continued. As he was vehemently desiring to know whether there was indeed hope for him, these words came rolling into his mind: "Will the Lord absent Himself for ever; and will He be no more intreated? Is His mercy clean gone for ever; and is His promise come utterly to an end for evermore? Hath God forgotten to be gracious, and will He shut up His loving-kindness in displeasure? " (Ps. lxxvii., verses 7-9). He was not far from the end of his struggle. " One day," he says, " as I was passing into the field, and that too with some dashes on my conscience, fearing lest yet all was not right, suddenly this sentence fell upon my soul, ' Thy righteousness is in heaven.' And methought withal, I saw with the eyes of my soul, Jesus Christ at God's right-hand; there, I say, was my righteousness; so that wherever I was, or whatever I was doing, God could not say of me, ' He wants my righteousness,' for that was just before Him. I also saw, moreover, that it was not my good frame of heart that made my righteousness better, nor yet my bad frame that made my righteousness worse; for my righteousness was Jesus Christ Himself, ' the same yesterday, to-day, and for ever,' Heb. xiii., verse 8." He returned home rejoicing; his temptations fled away: the " dreadful Scriptures of God " ceased to trouble him; he " lived very sweetly at peace with God through Christ." He penetrated " the mystery of union with the Son of God "; realised that he was joined to Him, flesh of His flesh, bone of His bone.

A man who had gained his peace at such a cost, was not likely to surrender his convictions lightly. Yet the thought of the misery that might befall his family, and especially his blind child, made him shrink from imprisonment. The irresolution was momentary. " If I should," he says, " venture all for God, I engaged God to take care of my concernments; but if I forsook Him and His ways, for fear of any trouble that should come to me or mine, then I should not only falsify my profession, but should count also that my concernments were not so sure, if left at God's feet while I stood to and for His name, as they would be if they were under my own tuition, though with the denial of the way of God. This was a smarting consideration, and was as spurs unto my flesh. That Scripture (Ps. cix., verses 6-20) also greatly helped it to fasten the more upon me, where Christ prays against Judas, that God would disappoint him in his selfish thoughts, which moved him to sell his Master; pray read it soberly, Psalm cix., verses 6, 7, 8," etc.

The personal grip with which Bunyan had laid hold of his religion, gave him powers as a preacher which were envied by the most learned of his contemporaries. " In my preaching," he writes, " I have really been in pain, and have, as it were, travailed to bring forth children to God; neither could I be satisfied unless some fruits did appear in my work: if I were fruitless, it mattered not who commended me; but if I were fruitful, I cared not who did condemn. I have thought of that, ' Lo, children and the fruit of the womb are an heritage and gift that cometh of the Lord. Like as the arrows in the hand of the giant, even so are the young children. Happy is the man that hath his quiver full of them; they shall not be ashamed when they speak with their enemies in the gate ' " (Ps. cxxvii., verses 4-6).

In the poetry of Milton, in the mental history of Bunyan, the power of the Psalms is strongly marked. Their influence is still more clearly seen in the career of Oliver Cromwell, the foremost figure in the stirring times of the Puritan revolution, the strongest type of the stern religion which raised him to the summit of fame and fortune. The spirit that he read into the Psalms governed his actions at each supreme crisis of his stormy life; the most striking stages in his career are marked by quotations from the Psalms; in his private letters, his public despatches, his addresses to Parliament, the imagery, metaphors, and language of the Psalms drop from his lips, or from his pen, as if by constant meditation he had made their phraseology a part of his very life.

In January 1636, Cromwell had moved his home to Ely from St. Ives, where, as a farmer, a grazier, and a notable man in parochial business, he had left his mark. At Ely, as the heir of his uncle, Sir Thomas Stewart, Knight, he lived close to St. Mary's Churchyard, at the corner of the great Tithe Barn. From that house he wrote one of his first extant letters, addressed to his cousin, Mrs. St. John, the wife of the celebrated ship-money lawyer. In it he speaks of himself and his lot in life.

" Truly, then," he says, " this I find; that He giveth springs in a dry, barren wilderness where no water is. I live, you know where,—in Meshec, which they say signifies *prolonging*; in Kedar, which signifies *blackness*; yet the Lord forsaketh me not. Though He do prolong, yet He will, I trust, bring me to His tabernacle, to His resting-place " (Ps. cxx.).

Twenty years later, after prolonged and bitter strife, Oliver Cromwell had become Lord Protector. On the 16th of September 1656, as he sat in his Palace of Whitehall, he was reading and pondering the 85th Psalm. The following day he rode in state from Whitehall to the Abbey Church of Westminster to open the second Parliament of the Protectorate. Before his coach went " hundreds of gentlemen and officers, bareheaded, the Life Guards, and his pages and lacqueys richly clothed." The service ended, he returned to Whitehall with the same pomp and ceremony, and, entering the Painted Chamber, delivered a speech to the newly assembled members, which in part is an exposition of the 85th and 46th Psalms.

Within those twenty years had passed some of the most stirring scenes of English history. In all of them Cromwell was a principal actor, and in all, the Book of Psalms—sometimes misread, sometimes grimly travestied, rarely if ever interpreted by the tender light of the New Testament—was his constant companion and guide.

Throughout the war he never ceases to speak the language of the Psalms. He relies not on men and visible helps, though no practical detail which can give success to his arms escapes his keen eye. It is God's cause in which he fights. In God is his strength. It is God who says, " Up and be doing, and I will stand by you and help you." It is God who makes the Royalists as " stubble " before the swords of the Puritans. In him and in his troopers burns the spirit of young Walton, who died at Marston Moor with one thing only lying heavy on his soul—that " God had not suffered him to be any more the executioner of His enemies."

At Naseby fight, Cromwell had seen " the enemy draw up and march in gallant order towards us, and we, a company of poor, ignorant men, at pains to order our battle." Yet " he smiled out to God in praises, in assurance of victory, because God would, by things that are not, bring to naught things that are. Of which I had great assurance; and God did it. Oh that men would therefore praise the Lord, and declare the wonders that He doeth for the children of men! " (Ps. cvii., verse 8).

As the victory at Naseby is the " hand of God," and " to

Him alone belongs the glory," so in the storming of Bristol he " must be a very atheist who doth not acknowledge God's work." The same spirit is manifested at Basing House. Old and New Basing, each fitted to make " an emperor's court," stood, as Hugh Peters described it, " in its full pride, and the enemy was persuaded that it would be the last piece of ground that would be taken by the Parliament." It had stood siege after siege, till the Royalists called it Basting House; and truly, so long as it was held for the king, no Parliament man could travel the western roads in safety. The Marquis of Winchester, to whom it belonged, was a zealous Roman Catholic; and to Cromwell it was a nest, not only of malignants, but of papists, a stronghold of darkness, a place of idols.

On the 8th of October 1645, Cromwell arrived before Basing with a train of heavy artillery. On the 11th his batteries were in position, and the garrison was summoned to surrender. If they refused quarter now, on their heads be it. No mercy would be shown. The summons was lightly set aside. Lord Winchester would hold " Loyalty House " to the uttermost.

At midnight on the 13th, two wide breaches were effected, and it was resolved to storm the place before sunrise on the morning of the 14th. The assault was delivered. The defenders were too few to resist the storming parties. No quarter was asked, and none given. " Our muskets and swords," says a contemporary newspaper, " showed little compassion." Great was the plunder of plate and jewels, of gold and silver, tapestry and rich attire. When Cromwell's army moved away, the defenders had been put to the sword, the altars thrown to the ground, the priests killed or reserved for the knife and the gallows, and Basing House was a heap of blackened ashes. A grim comment on the power of the Psalms follows. Lieutenant-General Cromwell, Hugh Peters tells us, " had spent much time with God in prayer the night before the storm; and seldom fights without some text of Scripture to support him. This time he rested upon that blessed Word of God, written in the 115th Psalm, verse 8, *They that make them are like unto them ; so is every one that trusteth in them.* Which, with some verses going before, was now accomplished."

When the war was ended, it is still in the same strain that Cromwell speaks. Thus, in November 1648, he writes to Colonel Robert Hammond:

" We have not been without our share of beholding some remarkable providences and appearances of the Lord. His presence hath been amongst us, and by the light of His countenance we have prevailed."

It was, again, in the spirit of the sternest of the Psalms that Cromwell entered on the Irish War. He is an armed soldier of God, executing His judgments upon His enemies, terrible as death, relentless as doom. With the sword in one hand and his Acts of Parliament in the other, he offers the choice of disobedience and death, or obedience and life. And, as Drogheda and Wexford testified, his words represented deeds.

In July 1650, the war with Scotland began. Charles II. accepted the Covenant, and with Buckingham and Wilmot at his side—strange instruments for such a task—had crossed the seas from Breda to be the earthly representative of that theocracy which the Scottish Kirk desired to see established. Cromwell, returning from Ireland, was made Commander-in-Chief, and sent to the front to check the threatened Scottish invasion. It was with a psalm in his mind that he set out on his mission. A few days before his departure, he had a strange interview with Colonel Edmund Ludlow, one of the sternest of Republicans. Calling Ludlow aside into a private room at Whitehall, he charged him with a changed countenance towards him, and with suspicions of his objects. He professed his readiness to sacrifice his life in the service of the people; he declared that he desired nothing better than a " free and equal Commonwealth "; he spoke at length of the " great providences of God now abroad upon the earth." Then he " spent at least an hour in the exposition of 110th Psalm," saying that he looked upon the design of the Lord in that day to be the freeing of His people from every burden, and that he himself was the chosen instrument for the accomplishment of the events foretold in that psalm.

So Cromwell set out, assured that the Lord would make His enemies His footstool that " in the day of His wrath He would wound even kings," and that He would " judge among the heathen," and "fill the places with the dead bodies." At the end of July he had crossed the Border, and reached Musselburgh. Between him and Edinburgh lay General David Leslie, entrenched behind strong lines, and protected by the guns of Edinburgh and Leith. It was a crisis on which were centred mighty interests. Two hosts, each claiming to be the Lord's chosen people, were about to put their claims to the test. To which should victory be given? All Cromwell's efforts to induce the Scots to risk a battle were vain. Affairs of outposts and skirmishes took place: but day after day Leslie lay steady within his lines, while Cromwell's provisions were failing, and his numbers dwindling through sickness. Equally futile were Cromwell's attempts to persuade the Kirk Commissioners that their cause was unrighteous, and that Charles Stewart was unfit to rule over a godly people. He received but a curt answer to his appeal, backed though it was by the confident assertion that "before it be long, the Lord will manifest His good pleasure so that all shall see Him, and His people shall say, 'This is the Lord's work, and it is marvellous in our eyes; this is the day that the Lord hath made; we will rejoice and be glad in it.'"

Days passed; Cromwell's provisions ran short; the weather was wet and stormy, so that his stores could not be landed, and at the end of August he fired his huts and marched towards Dunbar, Leslie hanging on his rear and keeping on the higher ground. Taking full advantage of his superior knowledge of the country, the Scottish commander occupied the Doon Hill, a spur of the Lammermoor Hills, standing forward from the range like a watch-tower, and, seizing the Cockburnspath, the wild river chasm eastward of Dunbar, which forms the approach to Berwick, thrust in his army between Cromwell and the English Border. Here then was Cromwell with a force of 11,000 opposed to 23,000, hemmed in between the hills and the sea, with Scotland in his rear and Leslie's army in his front.

Cromwell knew that he was in desperate case. "Our condition," he says, "was made very sad." On the 2nd of September he wrote a letter, hastily folded before the ink was dry, to Sir Arthur Haslerigg, the Governor of Newcastle, asking for aid, and bidding him prepare for the worst. On the same day on which this letter was written, Leslie began to move his army down from the Doon Hill to lower ground, from which he proposed the next morning to attack the English army.

The moment that Cromwell saw this movement he recognised the advantage which it gave him. "The Lord hath delivered them into our hands" is the traditional exclamation that burst from his lips as he saw his antagonist "shogging" down the hill. He determined that he would himself be the assailant at sunrise on the next morning. Throughout the wet and cold night of Monday the 2nd, in the storms of rain and sleet, he made his dispositions. When at four o'clock, the moon shone out through the hail-clouds, all was not yet ready. An hour later, the trumpets pealed, the cannon roared along the line, and Cromwell's horse and foot, shouting their watchword, "The Lord of Hosts," burst upon the Scottish troops, who, stiffened by the cold and with unlighted matches, were beginning to stir themselves as the twilight crept among the shocks of corn where they had bivouacked. Here and there the fight was stubborn; Leslie's horse boldly answered back the English challenge with their shout of "The Covenant." But the position was such that the Scottish general could make no use of his superior numbers, and when, over St. Abb's Head and the German Ocean, burst the rising sun, the gleam drew from Cromwell's lips the triumphant cry, "Let God arise, and let His enemies be scattered." The horse broke and fled, trampling down the undisciplined masses behind them; the rout was complete. The "chase and execution" of the fugitives lasted for eight miles, till the Lord General made a halt in his pursuit, and sang the 117th Psalm. It was but a brief respite. Practical in his religion as in all else, Cromwell chose the shortest Psalm in the book.

A year later, on the same day of the month, September 3rd, 1651, came the "crowning mercy" of the battle of Worcester. On the enemy, writes Cromwell to Mr. Cotton, of Boston, New England, the Lord "rained snares," so that "of the whole army of the Scottish King and the Malignant

The Puritans, 1600-1660

party, not five men were returned. Surely," he adds, " the Lord is greatly to be feared, and to be praised."

In 1653 the Rump had been expelled, and in their place were assembled " divers persons, fearing God, and of approved fidelity and honesty," who constituted the " Barebones " Parliament. On July 4th, Cromwell, standing by the window opposite the middle of the table in the centre of the Council Chamber of Whitehall, the officers of the army ranged on his right and left, addressed that strange assembly, every member of which was a man in whom Cromwell hoped to find " faith in Jesus Christ, and love to all people and saints." His speech is loaded with references to the Psalms, especially Psalm cx. and Psalm lxviii. He hints that their meeting may be " the door to usher in the things that God has promised, which He has set the hearts of His people to wait for and expect." They are " at the edge of the promises and prophecies "; and then he expounds Psalm lxviii. God is bringing His people out of deep waters; He is setting up the glory of His Gospel Church. Kings of armies had fled, and the spoil had been divided.

" And indeed the triumph of that psalm is exceeding high and great; and God is accomplishing it. And the close of it —that closeth with my heart, and I do not doubt with yours —' The Lord shaketh the hills and mountains, and they reel.' And God hath a hill too; an high hill as the Hill of Bashan; and the chariots of God are twenty thousand, even thousands of angels; and God will dwell upon this hill for ever!"

On Monday, September 4th, in the following year (1654), the Lord Protector had returned in state to Whitehall from Westminster Abbey. Entering the Painted Chamber, in all the plenitude of his power, he delivered a speech to the assembly. In it he enlarged on the stupendous providences of God.

" As David," he continues, " said in the like case (Ps. xl., verse 6), ' Many, O Lord my God, are Thy wonderful works which Thou hast done, and Thy thoughts which are to usward; they cannot be reckoned up in order unto Thee; if I would declare and speak of them, they are more than can be numbered.' "

Once more. On Tuesday, September 16th, 1656, Cromwell was reading the 85th Psalm in Whitehall. It was the day before the meeting of the second Parliament of the Protectorate. The next day, with the usual ceremonies, Parliament was opened, and the Lord Protector addressed a speech to the members. "Yesterday," he said, "I did read a psalm, which truly may not unbecome both me to tell you of, and you to observe. It is the 85th Psalm; it is very instructive and significant; thought I do but a little touch upon it, I desire your perusal and pleasure." Then he expounded to them his vision of hope—God's will done on earth, and England an emblem of heaven where God's will reigns supreme. To this work he exhorted his Parliament to set their hearts.

"And," he says, "if you set your hearts to it, then you will sing Luther's Psalm (xlvi.). That is a rare psalm for a Christian! and if he set his heart open, and can approve it to God, we *shall* hear him say, ' God is our refuge and strength, a very present help in trouble.' . . . If Pope and Spaniard, and devil and all, set themselves against us—yet in the name of the Lord we should destroy them! 'The Lord of Hosts is with us; the God of Jacob is our refuge.'"

Two years later, on Thursday, September 2nd, 1658, Cromwell lay dying. "He was very restless most part of the night, speaking often to himself," using "towards morning divers holy expressions, implying much inward consolation and peace." When the morrow's sun rose, he was speechless. By three or four in the afternoon he lay dead. Did he strengthen himself with the Psalms for the last battle of his militant life? Were the words which he spoke to himself such as these?—" Though I walk through the valley of the shadow of death, I will fear no evil; for thou art with me; thy rod and thy staff comfort me."

CHAPTER X

THE SCOTTISH COVENANTERS AND THE REVOLUTION OF 1688

Progress of the Reformation in Scotland—George Wishart, John Knox, James Melville; the Solemn League and Covenant (1638); the restoration of Episcopacy (1661-4); popular discontent—the Pentland Rising, Hugh M'Kail, Drumclog and Bothwell Bridge, Cameron, Donald Cargill, Baillie of Jerviswood, Alexander Peden, James Renwick, the Wigtown Martyrs; the Revolution of 1688; siege of Derry (1689).

IN words of vehement hatred, Patrick Walker described prelacy as "That old strumpet mother and eldest beautiful daughter of Antichrist, with which the blinded nations have been and are sadly bewitched: but vile, vile, loathsome and hateful in the eyes of all zealous serious godly in Scotland, ever since the Lord made light to arise to see her abominations." The passage expressed, with little exaggeration of language, the feelings of the majority of the Scottish people in the seventeenth century. The hatred of prelacy was not indeed shared by the aristocracy, nor had it extended to the north of Scotland. But in the Lowlands, and among the middle and lower classes, it was as bitter as the love of Presbyterian forms was deep and strong.

"In the year of God 1544 . . . came to Scotland that Blessed Martyr of God, Master George Wishart." So John Knox began his story of the beloved master, of whom he speaks with a reverent tenderness that rarely comes to the surface of his independent, self-reliant character. Not a few martyrs had already suffered in Scotland for conscience' sake. Even so illustrious a scholar as George Buchanan had narrowly escaped the clutch of Cardinal Beaton, though the archbishop's wrath was less stirred by Buchanan's Latin version of the Psalms than by his satires on clerical vices.

What Buchanan did in the language of scholars, Sir David Lindsay did in homely Scotch. But the true vernacular poetry of the day was enshrined in the collections of " Spiritual Sangis," including " the Psalmes of David, with uther new plesand Ballatis." No edition of the collected verses, which are mainly the work of three brothers, James, John, and Robert Wedderburn, is known till 1568. But the Songs and Psalms, printed on separate sheets, or sung by wandering minstrels, had already circulated among the people and filtered into common knowledge.

The way was paved for the Reformed doctrines before Wishart's arrival in Scotland. But there was about him that personal fascination, which made him the leader of the movement, and won him the devotion of his disciple, John Knox. His tall figure and bearded face, with his round French hat, long frieze mantle, black doublet and hose, white falling bands and cuffs, soon became familiar, as he preached by market crosses, at the dyke-side of Mauchline, in private houses, or, more rarely, in parish kirks. He was preaching in Kyle when " word was brought that the plague of pestilence was risen in Dundee . . . and the pest was so vehement, that it almost passed credibility, to hear what number departed every four-and-twenty hours." Hastening to the plague-stricken city, Wishart took his station at the East Port; those that were " whole sat or stood within, and the sick and suspected without the Port." Standing, as it were, between life and death, he preached to the people from Psalm cvii., verse 20, " He sent His word, and healed them," and by his words " so raised up the hearts of all that heard him, that they regarded not death, but judged them more happy that should depart, than such as should remain behind."

Wishart, already inhibited from preaching, knew that he would not long remain unmolested. In December 1545, he had left Haddington, bidding Knox return to his pupils, and causing the two-handed sword which he carried to be taken from him. " One is sufficient for one sacrifice," he said. He spent the night at Ormiston with the laird and other friends. Supper ended, the company sang together Psalm li. in Wedderburn's version:

> " Have mercy on me now, good Lord,
> After Thy great mercie;
> My sinful life does me remord,
> Which sore has grieved me."

Then he passed to his bed-chamber, with the words, " God grant quiet rest." That night he was seized by Earl Bothwell, and eventually carried to the " Sea-Tower of St. Andrews." Convicted of heresy, he was burned, March 1st, 1546, at the foot of the Castle Wynd, opposite the castle gate. Almost his last words were taken from a psalm. " When he came to the fire," says Knox, " he sat down upon his knees, and rose up again, and thrice he said these words: ' O Thou Saviour of the world, have mercy upon me! Father of Heaven, I commend my spirit into Thy holy hands '" (Ps. xxxi., verse 6). As a sign of forgiveness he kissed the executioner on the cheek, saying, " Lo, here is a token that I forgive thee. My harte, do thy office." So died George Wishart.

But for Wishart's personal influence and tragic death, it seems possible that John Knox, already forty years of age, and still unknown, might never have taken part in public affairs. A quarter of a century later, in November 1572, the reformer of a kingdom was dying in his house at the Netherbow Port of Edinburgh. As he lay, to all appearance asleep, he was often heard repeating to himself the words, " Come, Lord Jesus; sweet Jesus, into Thy hands I commend my spirit." The text from the Psalms was that used by Wishart. But, in all external circumstances, the deaths of the two men were widely different. The cause for which Wishart suffered had triumphed. Knox's iron will, passionate eloquence, and grim self-reliance had swept aside the leadership of the sovereign and the nobility. He had carried the people with him, and Scotland had for ever broken with Rome.

One side of Knox's work remained incomplete. Episcopacy was not abolished; for political reasons it was revived. The complete organisation of the Scottish Church was perfected on the Presbyterian model by Andrew Melville (*Second Book of Discipline*, 1581–92). At Knox's death, indeed, the final triumph of the Presbyterian cause still seemed distant and uncertain. It was the year of St. Bartholomew, and it was to the Psalms that men turned for the expression of their sorrow. James Melville, a nephew of the Presbyterian leader, and at that time passing through his course of philosophy at the University of St. Andrews, notes in his Diary, that "The primarius (James Wilkie) a guid, peaceable, sweit auld man, wha luiffed me weill, . . . causit sing, commownlie the 44 and 79 Psalmes, quhilk I lernit *par cœur*, for that was the yeir of the bludie massacres in France, and grait troubles in this countrey." Already the singing of psalms, the only part of ordinary worship in which the people directly joined, was becoming popular. Melville has recorded their introduction in 1570 at Montrose. "The Lard of Done," he says, "of his charitie interteined a blind man, wha haid a singular guid voice; him he causit the doctor of our scholl teatche the wholl Psalmes in miter, with the tones thairof, and sing tham in the Kirk; be heiring of whome I was sa delyted, that I lernit manie of the Psalmes and tones thairof in miter quhilk I haiff thought ever sen syne a grait blessing and comfort."

In many of the vicissitudes of the struggle, in which James Melville took a leading part, he found in the Psalms the best expression of his emotions. The eight texts with which his Diary begins, are all taken from the Psalms, and in his pages are recorded two notable instances of their use. Among the staunchest champions of the Presbyterian cause was John Durie, Minister first at Leith, then in Edinburgh. He had been suspended for his plain speaking against the Duke of Lennox. But in 1582 he returned to his "awin flok of Edinbruche." The whole town gathered to meet him at the Netherbow Port, and "goeing upe the streit, with bear heads and laud voices, sang to the praise of God, and testifeing of grait joy and consolation, the 124th Psalm, 'Now Israel may say, and that trewlie,' etc., till heavin and erthe resonndit." So determined was the attitude of the vast concourse of people, that the duke, when he heard the noise and saw the crowd, tore his beard for anger, and hastened out of the city. Two years later, Melville himself was a fugitive, flying for his life. By yet another change in the struggle, he was, in 1585, enabled to return to Scotland. As he and his fellow-

Covenanters and the Revolution 201

exiles reached Alnwick on their homeward journey, rejoicing that the " bountifull and gratius hand of our God was with us," they were many times constrained to sing Psalm cxxvi., " When the Lord turned again the captivity of Sion," and other psalms of the same character.

Neither of the Melvilles died in Scotland. Andrew Melville died at Sedan, James at Berwick. But, as, during his troubled life, James Melville had found in the Psalms the expression of his sorrow, his gratitude, or his triumph, so, at the moment of death, they brought him their message of strength and courage. The pain of his disease was " wonderfull vehement "; yet he was content, thinking " of the sight of the face of God in glorie; rehearsing that verse of the 16th Psalm (verse 12), ' Thow wilt schaw me the pathe of lyffe; in thy sicht are fulness of all joyes, at thy right hand is the plentie of pleasures for evir.' " As the pain and weakness increased, he " comforteth himselff with sundrie speeches out of the Psalmes, quhilk he rehearsit in Hebrew; as, nameli ane speich out of Psalm 4th (verse 7), ' Lord lift up the lyght of thy countenance upon me.' Psalm 27th, verse 1, ' The Lord is my light and my salvatione, quhat can I fear?' Psalm 23rd (verse 4), ' Albeit I walkit through the valley of the shadow of death, yet will I fear none evill, because God is with me.' The candell being behind his bak, he desyred that it should be brought before him, that he might sie to die. Be occasionne quhairof that pairt of the Scripture wes rememberit, ' Light aryses to the righteous in the middes of darknes ' (Psalm cxii., verse 4); and Psalm xviii., verse 28, ' The Lord will lighten my candell; He will inlighten my darknes.' "

In spite, and partly in consequence, of the effort of James I. to re-establish Episcopacy, and to assimilate the Church in Scotland with that in England, the Presbyterian Kirk, with its General Assembly, had become the organ of the Scottish people, its Parliament, its press, its platform, and something more. It was their " Mount Zion in Jerusalem," the " joy of the whole earth," the " city of the great King." When, therefore, in 1637, Charles I. attempted to introduce a book of Canons and a Liturgy framed on the English model, he outraged some of the deepest feelings of the nation. A wave of excitement swept over Scotland. Thrilled with solemn enthusiasm, the people had witnessed the signature of the National Covenant on the last day of February 1638, in the Greyfriars Church of Edinburgh. Rallying to the cry of " Christ's Crown and Covenant," disciplined by the genius of Alexander Leslie, and obeying the " old little crooked soldier," as if he were " the Great Soleyman " himself, the Covenanters easily wrung from Charles I. the concession of all their demands. The " blue banner " had triumphed. But Scottish liberties were still in peril, if the king prevailed against the English Parliament. In 1643, the Solemn League and Covenant bound the Presbyterians of the North and the Puritans of the South in a firm alliance to root out popery and prelacy from the three kingdoms.

The House of Stuart was slow to take warning from experience. On May 29th, 1660, Charles II. was restored to the throne, and the dark times swept over Scotland with one giant stride. While the guns roared from the castle of Edinburgh, to celebrate the national thanksgiving, Donald Cargill foretold Charles's future from the pulpit. " Whoever of the Lord's people," he said, " are this day rejoicing, their joy will be like the crackling of thorns under a pot; he will be the woefullest sight that ever the poor Church of Scotland saw. Wo, wo, wo to him; his name shall stink while the world stands, for treachery, tyranny, and leachery." Thus began, in mingled joy and foreboding, " that never to be forgotten unheard-of twenty-eight years of reigning tyrants, and raging tyranny of Prelatical Protestants upon Presbyterian Protestants."

Cargill's predictions were soon verified. The " Drunken Parliament " of 1661 imposed a new oath of allegiance to the sovereign as supreme over all persons and in all causes, exacted it from all ministers presented to benefices, pronounced assemblies to be unlawful, prohibited the renewal of the Solemn League and Covenant, and, by an " Act Rescissory," repealed the whole legislation of Scotland for the past twenty years. In the following year Episcopacy was established in Scotland, and James Sharp, who was acting in London as agent for the Presbyterian ministers, was ordained, and consecrated Archbishop of St. Andrews. The ballad-mongers of the day expressed the popular detestation of the new primate's treachery:

> " Most viper-like, I in the Kirk
> My mother's bowels rent;
> And did cast out those zealous men
> Whose money I had spent."

Nor were Sharp's colleagues men of high reputation; with the single exception of Leighton, who was wont to say that the Psalter should lie like myrrh in the human heart. From these bishops, all ministers who had entered on their livings since 1649 were to receive collation; those who refused to do so were to be ejected. Rather than submit to episcopal rule and the revival of patronage, nearly four hundred ministers gave up their churches and houses. Their places were filled by curates, " mostly young men from the northern parts, raw, and without any stock of reading or gifts." Most of the " outed " ministers had endeared themselves to their flocks by years of faithful service. The parting of Welsh, for instance, from the people of Irongray, described by Blackader, himself an eye-witness of the scene, shows the hold which men of his character had gained on the hearts of their congregations. "There was," he says, " great sorrowing and outcrying of the poor multitude beside the water of Cluden, when he (Welsh) was to take horse. It was with great difficulty he got from among them, who were almost distracted, and cried most ruefully, with tears. But he being resolute, would not be detained; and after two or three of the ministers had knelt down and prayed, he got to horse, the people still holding him. The ministers and he rode quickly through the water, to win from among them;—many, both men and women, brak in on foot after him, and followed on the road a good space, with bitter weeping and lamentation."

The example quoted does not stand alone. Congregations, as a rule, remained faithful to their former pastors. Dispossessed ministers, though banished from their parishes, held their services in the neighbourhood: the field-meetings were thronged, the churches deserted. Determined to effect their object, the Government framed another Act (1663), familiarly known as the " Bishops' Drag Net." Ministers who preached without episcopal sanction, parishioners who were absent from " the ordinary meetings of divine worship, in their own parish church on the Lord's Day," were guilty of seditious acts, punishable by fines and imprisonment. Soldiers, drafted into the south and west of Scotland to compel attendance at public worship according to Episcopalian forms, quartered themselves upon the recusants, and were encouraged in every violence and licence. To enforce the legislation " for the peace and order of the Church, and in behalf of the Government thereof by archbishops and bishops," a Court of High Commission was appointed (1664). Before this tribunal were summoned hundreds of persons, scarcely one of whom escaped punishment, whether by fines, branding, scourging, imprisonment, or exile. The Court called before it whom it chose, heard no arguments, asked few questions, and almost always condemned. It was compared to the lion's den, into which led many tracks, but from which none returned.

Throughout the Lowlands, discontent deepened and widened, till, goaded to desperation, the people rose in arms. Their open resistance in the field was short-lived. But, for twenty-five years, they maintained an unequal struggle against overwhelming odds, defending their convictions with a constancy which has been rarely equalled in history. Whatever were the faults of the " Hill Folk," the " Wild Whigs," the " Remnant," or the " Cameronians," their tenacity of purpose in suffering, danger, and death, commands the admiration of those who most strongly condemn them as narrow and exclusive. The Lowland peasant is justly proud of

"The tales
Of persecution and the Covenant
Whose echo rings through Scotland to this hour."

As with the Cevenols, so with the Covenanters. The Psalms were the inspiration of a popular movement. To the strained senses of the peasantry were manifested signs of the future. Mysterious apparitions disturbed the solitude of the moors; unearthly chantings of the Psalms broke their silence. On " Clyde side, east of Glasgow," a shadowy throng of men and women seemed to gather round a tent, and

Psalm xciii. was chanted with such celestial sweetness that all who heard the strains stood motionless till they were ended. Thus were revealed the future triumphs of field-conventicles. "At Craigmad, between Falkhill and Moranside," the hills were crowded with ghostly worshippers, who were singing Psalm cxxi., and among them appeared a milk-white horse, with a blood-red saddle on its back. Thus were portended the preaching of the Gospel and the persecution that was to follow. When the crisis came, it was with a psalm that the Covenanters faced General Dalzell at Rullion Green. With a psalm, they routed Claverhouse at Drumclog. Supported by a psalm, Hugh M'Kail, Donald Cargill, James Renwick, Isabel Alison, Marion Harvie, Margaret Wilson, and a host of other heroes and heroines of the Covenant, met torture or a violent death. The Psalms were the daily support of the charmed life of Alexander Peden. They cheered the captives on the Bass Rock or in the dungeons of Dunottar, and solaced their weary imprisonment. It was the Psalms, again, that encouraged others to endure a still harder fate, as they toiled in exile and slavery among the rice-fields and sugar plantations of the New World. True to the spirit of the Covenanters, Scott has embodied in his novels the influence of the Psalms. It was a psalm that nerved Mause Headrigg to leap her horse over the wall (Ps. xviii., verse 29): it was a psalm (xxxvii., verses 16, 25) that the daughter of a Covenanter, Jeanie Deans, marked with her "kylevine pen" for her lover, Reuben Butler, on the eve of her adventurous journey to plead for her sister's life: it was a psalm (xlii., verses 14, 15; and xliii., verses 5, 6) that she repeated in her hour of peril, when she was at the mercy of desperate ruffians on Gunnerby Hill.

Armed resistance began with the Pentland Rising in November 1666. The "honest zealous handful," as Patrick Walker calls them, involved in an accidental scuffle with the soldiers at Dalry, near Dumfries, drifted, without plan or leaders, into insurrection. At Lanark, as they marched towards Edinburgh, they were 1500 strong. But only a few were armed with swords, pistols, or muskets; scythes, forks, staves, were the weapons of the rest. Closely followed by Dalzell at the head of 3000 well-appointed troops, struggling through snow-drifts, spent with hunger and fatigue, disappointed of help from the Lothians, they staggered back from Edinburgh into the Pentland Hills. Their numbers had dwindled to 900 men. At Rullion Green they were attacked by Dalzell's troops. Hopelessly overmatched, they yet made a gallant fight. Chanting their despairing appeal to God in the words of Psalm lxxiv.,

> " O God, why hast Thou cast us off?
> Is it for evermore?
> Against Thy pasture-sheep why doth
> Thine anger smoke so sore? "

they met and defeated a charge of the enemy's horse. It was not till dusk that they were finally dispersed. Of the prisoners, some were executed, some imprisoned, some shipped to the plantations. The grave of those who were killed in the fight is marked by a stone, inscribed with rugged lines beginning thus:

> " A cloud of witnesses lie here
> Who for Christ's interest did appear," etc., etc.

Among the victims of the vengeance which the Government executed upon the insurgents was Hugh M'Kail, a young man of twenty-six, the prototype of Scott's MacBriar. Well connected and well educated, he is supposed to have incurred the personal hatred of the primate, to whom he had given the name of Judas. Appeals to save his life were made in vain. Tortured in the boot—yet forgetting his shattered leg, as he jestingly said, in fear for his neck—he solaced his imprisonment by writing Latin elegiacs. Under sentence of death, it was in the Psalms that he found strength. On the evening before his execution in the Grassmarket, he read Psalm xvi., " Preserve me, O God, for in Thee have I put my trust." The next day, December 22nd, 1666, at two o'clock in the afternoon, he was carried to the scaffold. There he sang part of Psalm xxxi., including the sixth verse, using the old metrical rendering:

> " Into Thy hands I do commit
> My spirit; for Thou art He,
> O Thou, Jehovah, God of truth,
> Who hast redeemed me."

Inspired by the same words which in the moment of death had sustained generations of the hated " Papists and Prelatists," he broke into the impassioned anthem of triumph, often repeated or imitated by his fellow-sufferers. "Now I leave off to speak any more to creatures, and turn my speech to Thee, O Lord! Now I begin my intercourse with God, which shall never be broken off. Farewell father and mother, friends and relations! farewell the world and all delights! farewell meat and drink! farewell sun, and moon, and stars! Welcome God and Father! Welcome sweet Jesus Christ, the Mediator of the New Covenant! Welcome blessed Spirit of grace, God of all consolation! Welcome glory! Welcome eternal life! Welcome death!"

With the execution of Hugh M'Kail, the Government seemed satisfied. For some months after the suppression of the Rising, moderate counsels prevailed. But gradually, as the necessity of crushing field-conventicles seemed more urgent, the persecution grew hotter. The country was devastated. "It was better," said Lauderdale, "that the West bore nothing but windle-straws and laverocks than that it should bear rebels to the king." Preachers and hearers alike were dogged by spies. Death was the penalty for preaching; fines, imprisonment, transportation, slavery, were the punishments inflicted upon hearers. The remotest caves and dens of the upland districts of Galloway, Nithsdale, Ayr, and Clydesdale, were tenanted by hunted ministers. There lurked gaunt "Wanderers," in whose eyes gleamed the grey light which flickers on the borders of enthusiasm and madness—with one hand gripping the hilts of their shabbles, with the other clasping their Bibles to their bosoms. Their surrender of their souls into God's keeping was absolute, their realisation of His Presence vivid and intense, their conviction of the justice of their cause so absorbing as to foster, not the serenity, but the fatalism of religion. As they pored over the Scriptures, alone in the wild solitudes of nature, stung by memories of wrong, in daily expectation of torture and death, confronted by dispensations of Heaven which hourly seemed more frowning and mysterious, their faith grew savage in its earnestness, vindictive in its zeal, dark with gloomy superstition. Their preaching soared into ecstatic utterance, and all the surroundings of field-worship heightened its effect. By day the gathering mist, by night the fall of darkness or the solemn starry skies, the monotonous solitude of the moors running up into labyrinths of rolling hills, the silence broken only by the melancholy cry of the plover, the armed sentries posted on the hills, the imminence of ever-present danger—attuned the minds of their hearers to rhapsodies of faith, calls to penitence, experiences of Satanic agency, bursts of prophecy, fierce denunciations of vengeance.

In his " Night-hymn of the Cameronians," Moir lays stress on the characteristic confidence in God's protection, which field-conventicles held under such conditions naturally encouraged:

> " Ho! plaided watcher of the hill,
> What of the night? what of the night?
> The winds are lown, the woods are still,
> The countless stars are sparkling bright;
> From out this heathery moorland glen,
> By the shy wild-fowl only trod,
> We raise our hymn, unheard of men,
> To Thee—an omnipresent God.
>
> " Jehovah! though no sign appear,
> Through earth an aimless path to lead,
> We know, we feel, Thee ever near,
> A present help in time of need—
> Near, as when, pointing out the way,
> For ever in the people's sight,
> A pillared wreath of smoke by day,
> Which turned to fiery flame at night."
> Etc., etc.

The murder of Archbishop Sharp on Magus Moor (May 3rd, 1679) gave the signal for a renewal of the open struggle between the Covenanters and the Government. Fresh enactments were directed against Conventicles. But " the Whigs," says Wandering Willie, " were as *doure* as the Cavaliers were fierce." At Drumclog, on June 1st, 1679, a field-conventicle was surprised by the approach of Claverhouse himself. The sentry gave the alarm by the discharge of his musket; the armed men drew out from the congregation of hearers, and, as they moved down the hill to meet the dragoons, raised their challenge to the foe in the words of Psalm lxxvi.:

> " In Judah's land God is well known,
> His name's in Israel great;
> In Salem is his tabernacle;
> In Zion is his seat.

> There arrows of the bow he brake,
> The shield, the sword, the war,
> More glorious thou than hills of prey,
> More excellent art far."

The struggle was soon over. The dragoons broke and fled. Claverhouse himself, " proof against lead," was saved by his gallant roan, which carried him off the field, though its " guts hung out half an ell," from a pitchfork thrust in its belly. The Covenanters spared the lives of their prisoners. But this mercy was condemned by Sir Robert Hamilton, who urged them to give no quarter to Babel's brats, and supported his advice, like Calvin, by quoting Psalm cxxxvii., verses 8, 9. In this same leniency, Patrick Walker finds a reason for the ultimate failure of the Covenanting cause:

" After the Lord," so he writes, " gave us the victory over Clavers and his party at Drumclog, anno 1679, we behaved not as persons that were fighting the Lord's battles: but, instead of pursuing the victory that God wonderfully put in our hands, and sanctifying the Lord of Hosts in our hearts and before the people by giving Him the praise, did greedily run upon the spoil, and took some of the enemy prisoners, and gave them quarter, tho' guilty of death, and so brought ourselves under the curse of doing the work of the Lord deceitfully, by withholding our sword from shedding of their blood; and yet we refused to be convinced that our sparing of the lives of these, whom God has appointed to utter destruction, is one of the causes why our lives go for theirs."

The insurrection which had flamed up so suddenly was extinguished at Bothwell Bridge, June 22nd, 1679. The battle was fought on Sunday, and, forty miles distant, Peden's hearers waited for a sermon. " Let the people," he said, " go to their prayers; for me, I neither can nor will preach any this day; for our friends are fallen and fled before the enemy at Hamiltown; and they are hagging and hashing them down, and their blood is running like water." No effort was again made by the Covenanters to put an armed force into the field. But their spirit remained unbroken. Their resistance, indeed, assumed a more determined form. A year to the day after Bothwell Bridge, twenty armed horsemen rode into Sanquhar, formed a circle round the market cross, and two of their number, Richard and Michael Cameron, dismounted. A psalm was sung, a prayer offered, and a " Declaration " read disowning Charles II. as a tyrant and usurper, and, " under the standard of our Lord Jesus Christ, Captain of our salvation, declaring war upon the king." Henceforward there could be no turning back, either for the Government or for the " Remnant " who approved *the Declaration*, which renounced allegiance to the king, defied his laws, and proclaimed the forfeiture of his throne.

Richard Cameron did not long survive his audacious act. On July 18th, 1680, he preached his last sermon, " upon the Kype-ridge in Clidsdale," choosing for his text Psalm xlvi., verse 10, " Be still, then, and know that I am God." Four days later, Thursday, July 22nd, he and his companions were hiding " in the east end of Airs-moss, a very desert place," when they were surprised by Bruce of Earlshall, with 120 men, well-armed and mounted. The Covenanters resisted stoutly. Richard Cameron was killed. His head and hands, " hagged off with a dirk," and thrown into a sack, were carried to Edinburgh to be fixed upon the City Port. They were first shown to Cameron's father, then a prisoner at the Tolbooth, and he was asked if he knew to whom they belonged. The old man, kissing the brow of his fair-haired son, said, " I know them, I know them: they are my son's, my dear son's." Then, with the same submission to God's judgment which, nine centuries earlier, was shown by the Emperor Maurice, and in words which recall Psalm xxiii., verse 6, he added, " It is the Lord; good is the will of the Lord, who cannot wrong me nor mine, but has made goodness and mercy to follow us all our days."

Cameron's successor in the leadership of the stricter Covenanters, or Cameronians, was Donald Cargill, according to Wodrow, the only remaining preacher at field-conventicles. He had taken part in the Sanquhar Declaration. Now, in September, 1680, at Torwood, he had publicly excommunicated the king, the Duke of York, the Duke of Monmouth, and others. He was a marked man. A reward of 5000 marks was set on his head as a " most seditious preacher," and a " villainous and fanatical conspirator." His escapes were narrow, both on foot and on horseback. But one of

Covenanters and the Revolution 211

his hearers remarked to him that when his danger was sorest, then he preached and prayed his best. He replied by saying, half to himself, as was his habit, "The Lord is my strength and song, and is become my salvation" (Ps. cxviii., verse 14). At last, July 11th, 1681, he was captured, and hurried, his legs tied hard under his horse's belly, to Glasgow, and thence to Edinburgh. While in prison he wrote a letter to James Skene, the closing sentence of which contains a metaphor now familiar to the world through Tennyson's lines. 'The God of mercies," he writes, " grant you a full gale and a fair entry into His kingdom, which may carry sweetly and swiftly over the bar, that you find not the rub of death." He was executed at the Cross of Edinburgh, July 27th, 1681. On the scaffold he sang his favourite psalm, Psalm cxviii., from the 16th verse to the end; and his last words were, "Welcome Father, Son, and Holy Ghost! Into Thy hands I commend my spirit."

As, one by one, his companions were killed or captured, Alexander Peden (1626-86) alone seemed to bear a charmed life. He is the Prophet of the Covenant, and, in some respects, its most romantic figure. Ejected in 1663 from his Galloway parish, outlawed for his complicity in the Pentland Rising, imprisoned on the Bass Rock (1673-7), banished to Virginia, and conveyed on the outward voyage to London, where he was for some unknown reason liberated, he spent his remaining years in Ireland or Scotland, "going," as he says, "from the one bloody land to the other bloody land." Dogged by spies, and hunted by dragoons, he yet died in his bed. A man of great personal strength and activity, his escapes were so hairbreadth as to seem miraculous. Peden himself would have been at no loss for an explanation. So long as God had work for him, no harm could befall him. Dogs snuffed at the entrance of the cave in which he was hiding, and still he was not discovered. Soldiers stabbed the beds or heaps of unthreshed corn under which he lay concealed; yet they touched him not. Through bogs, in which his pursuers were drowned, he knew and found the path of safety. Once, as he lay under a bank, a dragoon's horse grazed his head with his hoof, pinning his bonnet deep into the clay, and leaving him uninjured. In his mind the words, " Snow and vapours, wind and storm, fulfilling His word " (Ps. cxlviii., verse 8), were ever present; and, again and again, the Lord heard his prayer, and answered him in the day of his distress. Escaping to Scotland from Carrickfergus with a number of fellow-sufferers, his boat was becalmed and in danger of capture. " Waving his hand to the west, from whence he desired the wind, he said, ' Lord, give us a loof-full of wind; fill the sails, Lord, and give us a fresh gale, and let us have a swift and safe passage over to the bloody land, come of us what will.' " Before he ended his prayer, the flapping sails filled like blown bladders, and he and his comrades were saved. More than once a mist, gathering at his prayer, hid him from pursuit. On one occasion, horse and foot chased him so closely that escape seemed hopeless. If God saved them not, he and his companions were dead men. " Then he began and said, ' Lord, it is Thy enemies' day, hour, and power; twine them about the hill, Lord, and cast the lap of Thy cloak o'er old Sandy and thir (these) poor things, and save us this one time; and we'll keep it in remembrance, and tell it to the commendation of Thy goodness, pity, and compassion, what Thou didst for us at such a time.' " And, as he prayed, the mist covered the hills and the fugitives.

In all his wanderings and escapes, the Psalms were to him a perennial source of strength. Patrick Walker relates that he had " preached in a shield or sheep-house in a desert place," upon a Sabbath night. " When ended, he and those that were with him lay down in the sheep-house, and got some sleep: he rose early, and went up to the burn-side and stayed long: when he came in to them, he did sing the 32nd Psalm, from the 7th verse to the end; when ended, he repeated the 8th verse:

> ' Thou art my hiding-place, thou shalt
> From trouble keep me free;
> Thou with songs of deliverance
> About shalt compass me ';

" saying, ' These and the following are sweet lines, which I got at the burn-side this morning, and we'll get mo tomorrow, and so we'll get daily provision: He was never behind with any that put their trust in Him, and He will not

Covenanters and the Revolution

be in our common, nor none who needily depends on Him; and so we will go on in His strength, making mention of His righteousness and of His only.'"

A deep vein of melancholy traversed Peden's mind. Yet his sympathy, tenderness, and racy humour light up, like glints of sunshine, the gloom of his forebodings of judgment. His pithy sayings bear his own hall-mark; his keen insight into human nature made his nicknames stick like burrs. His intense realisation of God's abiding presence and fatherly care bred in him a filial familiarity; yet never, in its simplest or homeliest expressions, does his language lose a natural dignity. Men so constituted by nature, so moulded by the circumstances of their times, so fashioned by their own manner of life, have not only the temperament, but the training of the seer. The visions of Peden's fervent faith, painted with all the force of his picture-making imagination, were received with awe by his hearers, who trembled at the strange verification of his predictions.

Two specimens of his preaching, both given by Walker, may be quoted. In both, the text is taken from the Psalms. The first illustration is from the year 1682, when Peden " was in Kyle, and preaching upon that text, ' The plowers plowed upon my back, and drew long their furrows ' (Ps. cxxix., verse 3); where he said, ' Would you know who first yoked this plough? It was cursed Cain, when he drew his furrows so long and so deep, that he let out the heart-blood of his brother Abel . . . and that plough has and will gang summer and winter, frost and fresh-weather, till the world's end; and at the sound of the last trumpet, when all are in a flame, their theats (traces) will burn, and their swingle-trees will fall to the ground; the plow-men will lose their grips of the plough, and the gade-men will throw away their gades; and then, O the yelling and skreeching that will be among all his cursed seed, clapping their hands, and crying to hills and mountains to cover them from the face of the Lamb and of Him that sits upon the throne, for their hatred of Him and malice at His people!' "

The second illustration belongs to the year 1685, when he was " preaching in the night-time, in a barn at Carrack, upon that text, Psalm lxviii., 1, 2, ' Let God arise, and let His enemies be scattered; let them also that hate Him flee before Him. As smoke is driven, so drive thou them '; so insisting how the enemies and haters of God and godliness were tossed and driven as smoke or chaff, by the wind of God's vengeance while on earth, and that wind would blow and drive them all to hell in the end; stooping down, there being chaff among his feet, he took a handful of it, and said, ' The Duke of York, the Duke of York, and now King of Britain, a known enemy of God and godliness; it was by the vengeance of God that he ever got that name; but as ye see me throw away that chaff, so that the wind of vengeance shall blow and drive him off that throne; and he, nor no other of that name shall ever come on it again.' "

Throughout the last few years of Peden's life the severity of the Government towards the Cameronians increased, till it culminated in the " Killing Times " of 1684-5. Their bold repudiation of the king's authority, coupled with their declaration that his throne was forfeited, was a political danger which could not be ignored. Revolution was in the air. A popular party was forming both in England and Scotland, and the Government, making the Rye House Plot their plea, struck hard against its leaders, as well as against the Cameronians.

On the purely political side, Baillie of Jerviswood, the " Algernon Sydney of Scotland," was one of the first and most important victims. Condemned to death on December 24th, 1684, he was hanged the same afternoon at the market cross of Edinburgh, with all the attendant barbarities of an execution for high treason. His property was confiscated and forfeited to the Crown. Yet even in his last hours, oppressed by mortal sickness, hourly expecting his sentence, he felt, as he told his son, that God's promises were sure, and that the " testimony of David " would, in his case also, be verified. " I have been young, and now am old, and yet saw I never the righteous forsaken, nor his seed begging their bread " (Ps. xxxvii., verse 25).

The last of the Cameronians who suffered on the scaffold was James Renwick, though his sentence was due rather to his political tenets than to his religious opinions.

Among the crowd who had witnessed Cargill's execution

Covenanters and the Revolution 215

in the Grassmarket of Edinburgh, was a lad of nineteen, the son of a Nithsdale weaver. The lad was James Renwick. So stirred was he by the scene, that he cast in his lot with the persecuted remnant of the Cameronians. Ordained to the ministry after six months' study at Groningen, he returned to Scotland, and began to preach in October 1683. On his shoulders, young though he was, rested the burden of the struggle. The spirit which he threw into his work is revealed by a passage from one of his letters from Holland. " Courage yet ! " he writes, " for all that is come and gone. The loss of men is not the loss of the cause. What is the matter though we all fall ? The cause shall not fall." Thus inspired, Renwick speedily became the soul of the movement among the Cameronian Societies, who disowned the king, and declared war against him as the subverter of the religion and liberty of the nation.

During the " Killing Times " vigorous search was made for Renwick. But he evaded capture, and it was not till January 1688 that he was taken. On him were found the notes of his last two sermons, one of which was on Psalm xlvi., verse 10, " Be still, then, and know that I am God: I will be exalted among the heathen, and I will be exalted in the earth." He was charged with denying the authority of King James VII., teaching the unlawfulness of paying the tax called " cess," and exhorting the people to carry arms at field-meetings. The charges were admitted, and he was sentenced to death. On February 17th, 1688, he was executed at the Grassmarket in Edinburgh. More than once his words were drowned by drums. But he sang a part of Psalm ciii., the psalm which was always chanted by " the Saints " at the celebration of the Sacrament; and, as he was turned over the ladder, his last words were " Lord, into Thy hands I commend my spirit; for Thou hast redeemed me, O Lord, Thou God of truth " (Ps. xxxi., verse 6). The same text, in whole or in part, was quoted by more than half of the great army of " witnesses " who suffered on the scaffold, between Hugh M'Kail in 1666 and James Renwick in 1688. Nearly all of them, like John Nisbet, died " protesting against and disowning Popery in all its superstitions and bloody bigotry, and Prelacy the mother of Popery "; and yet, in the moment of their death, they committed their souls to God in the same words which were consecrated by their use on the lips of hundreds of Roman Catholic and Anglican martyrs.

Nor was it only on the scaffold that men died. There were many murders which were not even judicial. On January 1st, 1685, for example, Daniel McMichael was led out into the fields to be shot, and died singing part of Psalm xlii. In the following February, Alexander McRobin was hanged upon an oak tree near the Kirk of Irongray. At the tree-foot, a friend asked him if he had any word to send to his wife. "I leave her and the two babes upon the Lord," answered McRobin, "and to His promise: a father to the fatherless, and a husband to the widow, is the Lord in His holy habitation" (Ps. lxviii., verse 5). And so he died, as Wodrow records, "in much composure and cheerfulness." In the parish of Ingliston was a cave, which had been a place of safety to not a few of the Covenanters. On April 29th, 1685, guided by a traitor, the soldiers were brought to the mouth of the cave, where they seized five of the wanderers who had found refuge in its shelter. John Gibson, who alone was permitted to pray before he was shot, sang part of Psalm xvii., telling his mother and sister that it was the joyfullest day of his life. The rest were shot, "without being allowed to pray separately."

Nor were the women spared. In January 1681, two "honest, worthy lasses," as Peden calls them, Isabel Alison and Marion Harvie, were hanged at Edinburgh. On the scaffold they sang together, to the tune of "Martyrs," Psalm lxxxiv. "Marion," said Bishop Paterson, "you would never hear a curate; now you shall hear one," and he called upon one of his clergy to pray. "Come, Isabel," was the girl's answer—she was but twenty years of age—"let us sing the 23rd Psalm," and thus they drowned the voice of the curate.

No execution of the time was more universally condemned than that of these two women. A roughly-drawn picture of the scene, with the title "Women hanged," is prefixed to the first edition of the *Hind Let Loose* (1687). By its side is another engraving, which represents "The Wigtown Martyrs, drowned at stakes at sea."

Covenanters and the Revolution 217

In 1684, the Cameronian Societies had answered the renewed violence of the Government by their *Apologetical Declaration*. In this document, posted on the doors of parish churches and on market crosses, they declared war on the Government and its supporters, " disowned the authority of Charles Stewart and all authority depending upon his," and warned their assailants that they would meet force by force. In reply, the authorities devised an oath of abjuration, which was framed as a test, and imposed on all who were suspected of belonging to the Societies or of hostility to the Government. In April 1685, a commission, sitting at Wigtown, condemned Margaret Maclachlan or McLauchlison, an elderly widow of sixty, and Margaret Wilson, a girl of eighteen, who refused to abjure the *Apologetical Declaration*. They were sentenced to be " tied to stakes fixed within the flood-mark in the Water of Blednoch, near Wigtown, where the sea flows at high water, there to be drowned." The sentence was carried out, probably not with the sanction of the Government, on May 11th, 1685.

Twice a day, up the deep channel of the sluggish Blednoch, fringed by steep and sloping mudbanks, sweeps the yellow tide of the sea. Stakes were set in the ooze of the tideway, to which the two women were bound. The elder woman, Margaret Maclachlan, was set lower down the river, that the younger sufferer might see her struggles, and her course finished, before she herself was reached by the rising sea. Pitying her youth, the executioners tried to save Margaret Wilson. As the water swirled about her body, she was drawn to the edge of the bank, and offered her life, if she would say, " God save the king," and take the test. She was ready to say, " May God save the king, if He will," for she desired, she said, the salvation of all men: but she would not forswear her faith, or take the test. So she was once more secured to the stake, and left to her fate. With her fresh young voice, as the salt waves curled above her breast and all but touched her lips, she sang the 25th Psalm:

> " My sins and faults of youth
> Do Thou, O Lord, forget;
> After Thy mercies, think on me,
> And for Thy goodness great ";

and so continued singing till her voice was choked in the rising tide.

The political principle, on which the Cameronians founded their resistance to the king, was, that the throne had been forfeited, and was vacant. It was not long before that principle became a corner-stone of the Constitution. On November 5th, 1688, William of Orange cast anchor at Torbay, pledged to support the Protestant faith. He landed exactly a century after the Spanish Armada, and on the anniversary of the Gunpowder Plot. As a sign of his mission, the debarkation of the troops was treated as a religious solemnity. No sooner were the soldiers on shore, than divine service was conducted by William Carstares; and before they encamped, the troops, standing along the beach, sang Psalm cxviii., " O give thanks unto the Lord, for He is gracious; because His mercy endureth for ever."

But the success of the Revolution was not assured so long as Ireland was held for King James. " Oh secure Ireland!" cried Alexander Peden in 1685, " a dreadful day is coming upon thee within a few years, so that they shall ride many miles and not see a reeking house in thee: Oh hunger! Hunger in Derry! Many a black and pale face shall be in thee." The defence of Derry became one of the turning-points in the struggle. It saved Ireland for King William; and it was the prelude to his victory at the Boyne (July 1st, 1690).

The importance of the city as a military and naval stronghold was clearly recognised. In December 1688, Antrim's regiment, described by a contemporary as " a pack of ruffians," many of " whose captains were well known to the citizens, having lain in their jails for thefts and robberies," was sent to garrison Londonderry for King James. On the 7th of the month, the soldiers were seen crossing the river and approaching the Ferry Gate of Londonderry. Acting on the impulse of the moment, a number of young men ran to the main guard, sword in hand, seized the keys, drew up the bridge, and locked the gate in the face of the soldiers. When news of this revolt, as it was called, reached Dublin, Lord Mountjoy was sent to reduce the citizens to submission. Without arms, ammunition, or provisions, Londonderry made the best terms it could. Two companies of Protestant soldiers, commanded by Colonel Lundy, himself a Protestant, were admitted as a garrison for King James. So matters rested for some three months. But on March 20th, 1689, William and Mary were proclaimed king and queen at Londonderry with great joy and solemnity. The city had thrown in its fortunes with the Revolution and the Protestants against James and the Roman Catholics.

Vigorous efforts were at once made by Lord Tyrconnel, the Lord Lieutenant, to regain possession of the city for his master. As James's army approached, the Protestants of the North of Ireland fled to Londonderry for refuge. Within the walls, cowardice and treachery were at work. Lundy and his officers escaped to the ships in Lough Foyle, and left the city to its fate.

Deserted by their leaders, the garrison chose the Rev. George Walker and Major Baker to be their governors, and prepared to hold the city against the forces of King James. Surrounded by a numerous army, with no leaders experienced in war, imperfectly armed, without engineers to instruct them in their defence, without trenching tools, " without Fire Works, not so much as a Hand Granado to annoy the Enemy," with but few guns well mounted in the town, with 30,000 mouths to feed, and, as was estimated, with only ten days' provision for them, the position seemed desperate. There was truth in the comparison which Walker makes in his Diary, when he likens the lot of the citizens of Derry to that of " the *Israelites* at the *Red Sea*." But the first care of the defenders was, to quote again his words, " to recommend ourselves and the Cause we undertook to the Protection and Care of the Almighty; for we might then truly say, with the Church in the Liturgy, ' There is none other that fighteth for us, but only Thou, O God.' "

The siege lasted from April 17th, to July 31st. Closely pressed by the besiegers, harassed by their continuous fire, threatened by their mines which were pushed close to the walls, the citizens held their ground with singular courage and resolution. Women played their part in the defence by the side of the men. Not only did they bring up the match and ammunition, and serve out bread and drink to the soldiers on the walls, but they beat back an attack of the enemy with the stones which had been torn up from the streets to deaden the effect of the bombs. Treachery and mutiny were Walker's daily dread. His honesty, as matters grew more and more desperate, was called in question. Deserters every day passed into the camp of the enemy, carrying intelligence of the straits to which the garrison was reduced. Provisions ran short. Horses, dogs, cats, rats, and mice were eaten. Except the men, women, and children, hardly a living thing was to be found within the walls. They had no fuel left with which to cook. Their food was tallow, meal, and salted hides, herbs and weeds. Water was their drink, and that was scarce, and only obtained with difficulty and danger. A wet season added to the misery of the citizens, who in their half-starved condition fell easy victims to the diseases that it fostered. As though to mock their hopes with disappointment, a fleet of thirty sail was discovered in the Lough on June 14th. It was the force sent for the relief of the garrison. But across the channel the besiegers had thrown a boom. Major-General Kirke did not attempt to force the passage, but sailed away, sending a messenger to Walker in the beleaguered city, promising succour, and bidding the citizens "Be good husbands of your Victuals."

Yet the resolution of Walker, whose colleague was dead, and of the mass of the citizens, remained firm. When the enemy delivered an assault, the starving soldier, who had fallen under the weight of his musket as he went to the walls, stood gallantly to his post, though his face was blackened with hunger, till the attack was repelled. "I am sure," writes Hunter in his Diary, " it was the Lord that kept the city, and none else, for there were many of us that could hardly stand on our feet before the enemy attacked the walls, who, when they were assaulting the out-trenches, ran out against them most nimbly and with great courage. Indeed, it was never the poor starved men that were in Derry that kept it out, but the mighty God of Jacob, to whom be praise for ever and ever, Amen."

On the 28th of July, the fighting force of the garrison had dwindled from 7361 men to 4300, and of these fully a quarter were unfit for service owing to sickness, famine, or wounds.

Still Walker and his officers clung to their post with the tenacity of despair. "The Governor, finding in himself," says Walker in his Diary, " still that confidence, that God would not (after so long and miraculous a Preservation) suffer them to be a Prey to their Enemies, preaches in the Cathedral, and encourages their Constancy, and endeavours to establish them in it, by reminding them of several Instances of Providence given them since they first came into that Place, and of what consideration it was to the Protestant Religion at this time; and that they need not doubt, but that God would at last deliver them from the Difficulties they were under."

The sermon is still in existence. Never were words spoken to people in sorer need of consolation and encouragement, and it is from the Psalms that they are chiefly drawn. With strange power must the verses have come home to the crowd of starving men and women who listened to the preaching of their governor. "Let but the Lord arise," says holy David, " and His enemies shall be scattered." (And again), " God is our refuge and strength, a very present help in trouble. Therefore will we not fear though the earth be moved, and though the mountains be carried into the midst of the sea; though the waters thereof roar and be troubled " (Ps. xlvi., verses 1, 2, 3). . . . " Considering the deliverance wrought for the besieged city of Samaria, as for Jerusalem by the destruction of Sennacherib's host, holy David says, to comfort himself and his people, viz., ' The Lord of hosts is with us; the God of Jacob is our refuge. Come, behold the works of the Lord, what desolation He hath made upon the earth. He maketh wars to cease unto the end of the earth: He breaketh the bow, and knappeth the spear in sunder, and burneth the chariot in the fire. Be still, and know that I am God: I will be exalted among the heathen, I will be exalted in the earth. The Lord of Hosts is with us; the God of Jacob is our refuge ' " (Ps. xlvi., verses 7-11). Gideon, Deborah, and Barach were instruments in the hand of God. " So that we see," continues the preacher, " that God confounds strength with weakness; for when men presume too much on the arm of flesh, they frequently deceive themselves, and in the midst of their security are overthrown. Therefore let a good Christian consider that his strength is in the Lord. And if God hear his side, he need not be afraid though danger beset him round about, but be comforted and made valiant by the words of the kingly prophet, ' The Lord is my light and my salvation; whom then shall I fear? The Lord is the strength of my life; of whom then shall I be afraid? When the wicked, even mine enemies and my foes, came upon me to eat up my flesh, they stumbled and fell. Though a host should encamp against me, my heart shall not fear; though war shall arise against me, in this will I be confident ' " (Ps. xxvii.).

"It was always well," he says, " with the seed of Jacob when they clave fast to the Rock of their Salvation. But when they grew regardless, He gave them up to the oppressing nations, who grieved His chosen Heritage, for it is said (Ps. xviii.), ' With the merciful Thou wilt show Thyself merciful. And with an upright man, Thou shalt show Thyself upright; with the pure Thou shalt show Thyself pure; with the forward Thou shalt show Thyself forward. For Thou wilt save the afflicted people, but wilt bring down high looks.' "

" There is nothing," he concludes, " too hard for the Lord, when He designs to bring about His purposes. ' I called upon the Lord in my distress (says holy David). The Lord answered me, and set me in a large place. The Lord is on my side. I will not fear what man can do unto me. The Lord taketh my part with them that help me, therefore shall I see my desire upon them that hate me. It is better to trust in the Lord, than to put any confidence in princes. All nations compassed me round about, but in the name of the Lord will I destroy them ' (Ps. cxviii.). . . . Let us take courage, then, and faint not, but acquit yourselves like men."

Sunday, July 28th, 1689, was a memorable day. "It was," says Ash, " a day to be remembered with thanksgiving by the besieged of Derry as long as they live, for on this day we were delivered from famine and slavery. With the former they were threatened if they staid here, and the latter if they went away or surrendered the garrison."

Ships were seen in the Lough, and were recognised as the vessels which Kirke had promised to send to their relief. A

Covenanters and the Revolution

favourable wind blew from the north-east; the Protestant wind, as the Dutch sailors called it, which had wafted William to the English coast and blew in the teeth of James. The flag on the cathedral tower was twice struck, and eight guns were fired, in order that the ships might know that the garrison were at their last gasp, and that " if they came not now, they might stay away for ever." The fleet answered with six guns, which the besieged understood to mean that an attempt would be made that day.

About five o'clock in the afternoon, the wind and tide serving, three ships hoisted sail, and entered the river. The *Dartmouth*, a frigate commanded by Captain Leake, acted as convoy to the *Mountjoy* of Derry, Captain Micaiah Browning, commander, and the *Phœnix* of Coleraine, Captain Andrew Douglas, master, both laden with provisions. From each side of the river the besiegers opened a brisk fire upon the advancing vessels. Off Culmore Point, a musket-shot from the fort, the *Dartmouth* anchored, and cannonaded the castle, diverting its fire from the merchant ships. The *Mountjoy*, followed by the *Phœnix*, sailed past the fort, and, proceeding up the river, reached the boom. She struck it with such force as to break it, but the recoil drove her aground, for the wind had dropped, and she had not way enough to carry her past the obstruction. The smoke from the guns was so thick that the garrison, watching anxiously from the walls of Derry, could not see what had happened. But the triumphant shouts of the enemy, " the most dreadful to the besieged that ever we heard," the increased firing, and the preparations to board the grounded vessel, told to the starving citizens the misfortune of the *Mountjoy*. " Our trouble is not to be expressed at this dismal prospect," says Walker. It " struck," writes Mackenzie, another of the garrison, " such a sudden *terror* into our hearts, as appeared in the blackness of our countenances." Succour was at their doors, yet could not enter.

But the commander of the *Mountjoy*, himself a native of Derry, and carrying help to his fellow-townsmen, was not disheartened. " He stood upon the deck with his sword drawn, encouraging his men with great cheerfulness." Loading his guns with " partridge shot," he fired a broadside which scattered his assailants. It did more. The shock loosened his vessel; the rising tide floated her, and carried her past the boom. At the very moment of his triumph, he was shot through the head. But Derry was saved. By ten o'clock, both ships were at the quay, " to the inexpressible joy and transport of our distressed garrison, for we only reckoned upon two days' life, and had only nine lean horses left, and among us all one pint of meal to each man." The siege was practically over. On the 31st of July 1689, the enemy decamped, and the cause of the Revolution was saved in Ireland.

CHAPTER XI

1688-1900

Changed character of the romance of religion: the Psalms in the lives of religious leaders—Baxter, Law, John Wesley, Charles Wesley, William Wilberforce, Keble, Manning, Newman, Thomas Arnold, Julius Hare, Neander, Charles Kingsley, Stanley, Chalmers, Irving; the Psalms in the lives of men of science—Locke, Humboldt, Maine de Biran, Sir W. Hamilton, Sir James Simpson, Romanes; the Psalms in literature—Addison, Cowper, Boswell, Scott, Byron, Hogg, Wordsworth, Tennyson, Matthew Arnold, Robert Browning, Elizabeth Barrett Browning, Fitzgerald, Ruskin, Carlyle.

THE first seventy years of the eighteenth century lie like a plain between two ranges of hills. Behind it rise the picturesque highlands, in which the theology of the Middle Ages had fought every inch of ground with Protestantism, and where the voluptuous sensibility of the Cavalier had crossed swords with the stern morality of the Puritan. Before it loom the volcanic heights of the French revolutionary era, destined to be the scene of new conflicts, where once more, without thought of compromise or acquiescence, opposing principles contended for absolute victory. Between the mountain ranges extends the plain of the eighteenth century, rich and fertile, but deficient in many of the virtues which flourish best on more barren soils and in more bracing air.

England under the last two Stuarts had retained the heat of a life-and-death struggle, though the fire was already burning low. Men acted, thought, spoke, and wrote with something of the romance and passion of their ancestors. At least they preserved the grand manner, if they had lost the high-toned sentiment which was its impulse. But in the age of Anne, and still more under the House of Hanover, the temperature was chilled. Society banished enthusiasm from politics, philosophy, literature, religion, and took its ease. In politics—loyalty gave place to expediency, divine right to constitutional monarchy. In philosophy—reason and experience dethroned faith and tradition; the thought of Locke, clear, sensible, and practical, reigned supreme. In literature—passion, spontaneity, imagination were succeeded by the finish, taste, restraint, and intellectual fancy of an impulse which had lost the fervour of youth.

In religion, the change was equally conspicuous. Alarmed at the results of Catholic zeal or Puritan fervour, society invoked the aid of the established religion to control extravagance, to restrain vehemence, and strengthen order. Never was the Church, in a sense, more popular. Never was Christianity more ably defended; but it was on the ground of human reasonableness alone. Its most powerful champions fought with the weapons of their assailants, and rejected the aid of all that was miraculous, mysterious, supernatural. Cold and rational, they endeavoured to argue men into goodness, appealed to a system of rewards and punishments, ignored the power of the heart or the imagination. The result was disastrous. Religion grew formal, full of propriety, drowsy, prosperous. Its authority was put forward with cautious regard to the probability of its acceptance. Seeming to distrust itself, it was regarded as something which could be ignored, not as something which imperatively demanded to be either obeyed or condemned. The devotional cast of mind, the enthusiasm, the mystery, the prophetic vision, the martyr's passion, were left behind in the natural sanctuaries of the mountains. Nothing remained but a religion of the plains—low-lying, level, utilitarian, prosaic.

During the last half of the eighteenth century, the dying embers of religious fervour were fanned into flame by the Methodists and the Evangelicals. Meanwhile new forces were coming into play which gave fresh impulse and direction to every form of national life. Industrial development was advancing with rapidity. Science shook off its dilettantism, and became a power. As the nineteenth century advanced, the mental attitude of inquirers grew to be scientific. The supremacy of theology was challenged; the claim of authority sifted or denied. Out of the shock of the collision emerged the religious parties in the Church as we know them to-day. Bitterly opposed as they were, and are, in love of the Psalter they were united. Under new impulses, the romance of religion revived, though in an altered form. It has not disappeared, nor even diminished; but it has changed in character. It has passed from without to within, from action to thought, from deeds to emotions. It has become, for that reason, less adapted for pictorial treatment. The Psalms, as of old, still nerve men and women to suffer, to dare, to endure. But, on the stage of history, the opportunity of witnessing for the faith grows rarer as the world becomes more tolerant or more indifferent to diversity of opinion. Religious tragedies are still played on every side of us, and in our midst. If they could be revealed, they would have the special interest of familiar conditions and contemporary circumstances. They would come closer to us than scenes of martyrdom. But modern tragedies of religion are, for the most part, withdrawn from observation, enacted in the privacy of home rather than on the public stage. Their scene is the human heart, or the human brain. The rack, the dungeon, the scaffold, are all there. But the torture is the chill agony of doubt, the iron grip of remorseless logic, the keen analysis of searching introspection, the desperate effort to hold or regain cherished beliefs, to shake off the gradual deadening of senses once susceptible to holy impressions, to resist the creeping numbness of nerves formerly responsive to sacred influences. To the vanquished, come the solitude, the void, the darkness of lost creeds; to the victors, belong the peace and triumph of a faith that has withstood the test. The scene is less dramatic, less picturesque. But the trial is not less fiery than the stake. Who can say that the drawn-out agony of those who have succumbed does not exceed the pains of those who, upheld by triumphant confidence in their cause, have endured the most exquisite tortures of the body? Who, on the other hand, will assert that the peace and joy of those, whose faith withstands the trial, may not equal the most ecstatic vision of his risen Lord that ever gladdened the straining eyes of the Christian martyr at the moment of his supremest anguish?

It is well that the choice of subjects is thus, in one sense, narrowed, at the moment when the multifarious activities of modern life widen the field so indefinitely that selection, necessarily arbitrary, must now appear capricious. History may illustrate something of the debt, which, during the last two centuries, men and women have owed to the Psalms. The mystery of existence forces itself upon our attention. The eternal questions of whence? and why? and whither? have never been more insistent, rolling in upon us like the monotonous surges of the inarticulate sea. With tense nerves and strained senses, men and women ask, what is life, and what is death. No sound of answer comes, except the echo of their own voices reverberating through a cavernous void; and happy are they who, turning in their weariness to the Psalter, find that its words wrap them round like a folding sense which brings them peace. Of all this vast sum of human experience, history takes no account. For every recorded incident, there are millions of cases, unknown beyond the secret chambers of the heart, in which the Psalms have restored the faith, lifted the despair, revived the hopes, steeled the courage, bound up the wounds of the struggling, suffering hosts of humanity.

On the lives of leaders in the various religious movements which mark the period, may be traced the influence of the Psalms.

Here are the words, " And call upon His name, and declare His works among the people " (Ps. cv., verse 1), which are inscribed upon the pulpit at Kidderminster, once occupied by Richard Baxter (1615-92), one of the first and greatest of Noncomformist divines, the eloquent preacher, the voluminous theological writer, patient alike under the lifelong pains of disease and thirty years of almost incessant persecution. A man whose personal holiness was never disputed by his bitterest opponents, and a model parish priest, he so transformed Kidderminster, that " on the Lord's day there was no disorder to be seen in the streets; but you might hear a hundred families singing psalms, and repeating sermons as you passed through them." The use of the Psalms by his parishioners at Kidderminster might well have been the fruit of Baxter's special influence; some may even have been sung in his own metrical version. A *Paraphrase on the Psalms of David* (1692) was among the products of his gigantic literary labours, and his own words show that he found in the Psalms a daily support. In 1662, at the age of forty-seven, he had married Margaret Charlton, a girl of gentle birth and " strangely vivid wit," the faithful, tender companion of whom he paints a loving portrait in his *Breviate of her Life*. " It was not," he writes, " the least comfort that I had in the converse of my late dear wife, that our first in the morning and our last in bed at night, was a psalm of promise, till the hearing of others interrupted it."

Baxter's *Saint's Everlasting Rest* and *Call to the Unconverted* are masterpieces of devotional literature, whose widespread popularity still endures. Scarcely less powerful, though far less popular, has been the influence of the *Serious Call* (1729) of William Law (1686-1761), " a nonjuror, a wit, and a saint, who seems to have believed all that he professed, and to have practised all that he enjoyed." As literature, the book is read for its masterly style and for the keen satire of its portraits. As a call to devotion, it was the first book which made Dr. Johnson think " in earnest of religion." Lord Lyttelton could not lay it down till he had read it through, called it " one of the finest books that ever was written," and only wondered that it " had been penned by a crack-brained enthusiast." On the two Wesleys, on Whitefield, on Evangelicals like Venn, Newton, and Scott, on leaders of the Oxford movement like Keble or Newman, its influence was profound. At the present day, when the churchmanship of Law is again in the ascendant, the ascetic tone of the *Serious Call* finds readers, with whose principles it is more in harmony than with those of Methodist or Evangelical.

At the time when Law wrote, the bare externals of religion were punctiliously observed. But the divorce between precept and practice was absolute. It was on this contrast that Law's logical intellect seized, and the *Serious Call* invites Christians to practise what they professed, to " live more nearly as they prayed." To the use of the Psalms, as an aid to that devotion which dedicates a life to God, one of Law's most eloquent chapters (chapter xv.) is devoted. " Do but so live," he says, " that your heart may truly rejoice in God, that it may feel itself affected with the praises of God, and then you will find, that this state of your heart will neither want a voice, nor ear to find a tune for a psalm." He bids men imagine themselves " with Moses when he was led through the Red Sea." " Do you think that you should then have wanted a voice or an ear to have sung with Moses, ' The Lord is my strength and my song, and He is become my salvation,' etc.?" The chapter closes with a selection of the psalms which are best adapted for devotional use. Psalm cxlv., " I will magnify Thee, O God, my King, and I will praise Thy Name for ever and ever," is his choice for a morning hymn. " The 34th, 96th, 103rd, 111th, 146th, 147th," are such as wonderfully set forth " the glory of God, and, therefore, you may keep to any one of them at any particular hour as you like; or you may take the finest parts of any psalms, and so, adding them together, may make them fitter for your own devotion."

Here are the words of Psalm cxxx., " Out of the deep have I called unto Thee, O Lord: Lord hear my voice," etc., which John Wesley (1703-91) heard sung on the afternoon of Wednesday, May 24th, 1738, as an anthem at St. Paul's Cathedral. The psalm was one of the influences that attuned his heart to receive that assurance of his salvation by faith, which the evening of the same day brought to him in the room at Aldersgate Street. On the foundation of that sure confidence, his intense energy, organising genius, and administrative capacity built up, for the most part from neglected materials, the mighty movement that still bears both his name and the impress of his structural mind. For half a century, as he rode up and down the country, his voice sounded louder and louder, till it penetrated every corner of the kingdom, rousing once more the sense of the need of personal religion, and stirring anew the numbed perception of unseen spiritual realities. On March 2nd, 1791, he died at the Chapel-house in the City Road, London. It was with the words of the Psalms that he met the approach of death. Gathering his remaining strength into the twice-repeated cry, " The best of all is, God is with us!" he lay for some time exhausted. One of the bystanders wetted his parched lips.

"It will not do," he said; "we must take the consequence; never mind the poor carcase." Pausing a little, he cried, "Thy clouds drop fatness!" (Ps. lxv., verse 12); and soon after, "The Lord of Hosts is with us, the God of Jacob is our refuge" (Ps. xlvi., verse 7). Throughout the night he was heard attempting to repeat the words. The next morning he was dead.

With a psalm also died Charles Wesley (1707-88). The first hymn-book compiled for the use of the Church of England was John Wesley's *Collection of Psalms and Hymns*, printed at Charlestown in 1736-7. Wesley regarded hymns as a powerful means both of expressing the devotional feelings and of establishing the faith of his followers. He himself wrote or translated many that are still in popular use. But the great hymn-writer of the movement, and perhaps the greatest hymn-writer the world has ever known, was his younger brother. Of Charles Wesley's 6500 hymns, some are unsurpassed in beauty, and rank among the finest in the English language. Throughout his life, they were the form in which he found the truest expression for his deepest feelings. On his deathbed, in March 1788, the train of thought suggested by Psalm lxxiii., verse 25 ("My flesh and my heart faileth; but God is the strength of my heart, and my portion for ever"), took shape in verse. It was the last exercise of his wonderful gift. Calling his wife to his side, he dictated to her the lines:

> "In age and feebleness extreme,
> What shall a sinful worm redeem?
> Jesus, my only hope thou art,
> Strength of my failing flesh and heart;
> O, could I catch a smile from thee,
> And drop into eternity!"

As Luther's success had stirred the dormant energies of the Roman Catholics, so the Methodists roused the Church of England from her lethargy. A new spirit of life was breathed into the Establishment by men like Newton, Scott, Venn, and Simeon. Of the personal and practical religion of the Evangelicals, William Wilberforce (1759-1833), who moved and finally carried the abolition of the Slave Trade (1807), may be taken as a representative. The brilliant young man, whose gay wit charmed the town, who played faro while

George Selwyn held the bank, gambled with Fox, was the bosom friend of Pitt, flirted with Mrs. Crewe, bandied criticisms with Madame de Staël, or sang ballads to the Prince of Wales, passed in 1785 through that crisis of the mind and character, which men of his school of religious thought call "conversion." The change never turned his natural gaiety into moroseness. He remained the same charming companion, but his purpose in life was fixed: he would devote his time and talents to philanthropic efforts, and especially to the abolition of the Slave Trade.

Numerous passages in his Diary show how largely this hidden life was fed by the study of the Psalms. Granville Sharpe (1735-1813), his predecessor and colleague in the work of abolishing the Slave Trade, sang, night and morning, "a portion of the Hebrew Psalms to his harp." So Wilberforce studied his Psalter. In his Diary for 1803, he writes: "I am reading the Psalms just now, comparing the two versions, and reading Horne's Commentary. What wonderful compositions! What a decisive proof of the Divine origin of the religion to which they belong! There is in the world nothing else like them." In 1807 he had gained two personal triumphs. He had carried his Bill for the Abolition of the Slave Trade, and he had kept his seat for Yorkshire. Neither event elated him. It is in the language and spirit of the Psalms that his reflections on his political successes are expressed, as he meditates on such texts as, "Not unto us, O Lord, not unto us, but unto Thy Name give the praise" (Ps. cxv., verse 1). In 1819, in the midst of the bustle of London life, and the disturbances which threatened the domestic peace of the country, his own mind was serene. "Walked from Hyde Park corner, repeating the 119th Psalm, in great comfort," is the entry in his Diary. A year later, came the king's coronation, and Queen Caroline's claim to be crowned. For taking the unpopular side against the queen, Wilberforce was violently attacked, especially by Cobbett. To a man of his temperament, the pain was bitter. It was to the Psalms that he turned. "The 71st Psalm, which I learned by heart lately," he tells his wife, "has been a real comfort to me."

On the Psalms is based the most popular of all the writings of John Keble (1792-1866), the "true and primary author" of the Oxford movement. His own metrical Psalter (1839) is little used and little known. But though the Psalms supply none of the texts by which the hymns are suggested and prefaced, it is from the Psalter that Keble drew the inspiration of *The Christian Year* (1827). In his " Dedication " he avows his model:

> " O happiest who before Thine altar wait,
>   With pure hands ever holding up on high
> The guiding Star of all who seek Thy gate,
>   The undying lamp of heavenly Poesy.
>
> " Too weak, too wavering, for such holy task
>   Is my frail arm, O Lord; but I would fain
> Track to its source the brightness, I would bask
>   In the clear ray that makes Thy pathway plain.
>
> " I dare not hope with David's harp to chase
>   The evil spirit from the troubled breast;
> Enough for me if I can find such grace
>   To listen to the strain, and be at rest."

A text from the Psalms haunted the memory of Henry Manning as an undergraduate at Oxford, when his religious opinions were yet unformed, and his ambitions still centred on political life. As cardinal and archbishop, the same words bore to him their daily message. "The Psalms and the Lessons," he says in an autobiographical note on the years 1829-31, "were always a delight to me. The verse ' Why art thou cast down, O my soul,' " etc. (Ps. xlii., verse 6), "always seemed a voice to me. Every day in the daily Mass it comes back to me."

In Newman's *Dream of Gerontius*, some striking passages are echoes from the Psalms. Gerontius dies, murmuring the familiar words of Ps. xxxi., verse 6:

> " *Novissima hora est :* and I fain would sleep.
>   The pain has wearied me . . . Into Thy hands,
> O Lord, into Thy hands. . . ."

His " struggling soul quitted its mortal case," and is borne by the angel into the presence of the just and holy Judge. As the soul and its guardian mount upwards, the angelic choirs hymn their Maker's praise in lines, whose opening stanza recalls Psalms cxlviii. and cl.:

> " Praise to the Holiest in the height,
>   And in the depth be praise;
> In all His words most wonderful;
>   Most sure in all His ways!

The great Angel of the Agony pleads with Him whom he had strengthened in the garden, and the soul of Gerontius lies prone at the " dear feet of Emmanuel," . . . happy,

> " For it is safe,
> Consumed, yet quickened, by the glance of God."

Then, as the Angel commits his charge to the temporary keeping of the Angels of Purgatory, the Souls within the golden prison break into a solemn chant, which is a paraphrase of part of Psalm xc.:

> " 1. Lord, Thou hast been our refuge in every generation;
> 2. Before the hills were born, and the world was, from age to age Thou art God.
> 3. Bring us not, Lord, very low; for Thou hast said, Come back again, ye sons of Adam.
> 4. A thousand years before Thine eyes are but as yesterday, and as a watch of the night which is come and gone," etc., etc.

Here are the words—" O give me the comfort of Thy help again; and stablish me with Thy free spirit " (Ps. li., verse 12)—which the great headmaster of Rugby, Thomas Arnold, repeated, as, in June 1842, he lay on his deathbed in the torture of *angina pectoris*. Here is the text—Psalm xvii., verse 16—in which Julius Hare specially delighted. "When," wrote Whewell, his old college friend at Trinity, Cambridge, " the Psalm was read to him before his spirit departed, he thanked those who had thus chosen the words of Scripture which he so especially delighted in; with these sounds of glory singing in his ears, ' I will behold Thy presence in righteousness; and when I awake up after Thy likeness, I shall be satisfied with it,' our dear friend fell into that sleep from which he was to awake in the likeness of Christ." To Neander, Hare and the Cambridge Liberals of his circle looked for the reconciliation of revelation with intellect, and here is the Psalm—" The Lord is my Shepherd; I shall not want " (Ps. xxiii., verse 1)—which was sung by the German students to celebrate the last [1] birthday of the great German theologian (January 6th, 1850). Here, again, is the favourite psalm of Charles Kingsley—Psalm lxxvi. " How strange," he writes, when voyaging up the Rhine in August 1851, and looking on the hills crowned with the ruined strongholds of

---

[1] Neander died July 14th, 1850.

freebooters, "that my favourite psalm about the hills of the robbers (hills of prey) should have come in course the very day I went up the Rhine." Here, lastly, is the favourite text of Dean Stanley, a choice characteristic alike of the man and of his work: "I see that all things come to an end; but Thy commandment is exceeding broad" (Ps. cxix., verse 96).

In the religious history of Scotland, no event since the Reformation created so profound an impression as the secession of the Free Church ministers, May 18th, 1843. Here too the Psalms were at work. Of that movement, Thomas Chalmers (1780-1847) was the leading spirit. In early life he had hovered on the verge of atheism. But in 1810 he had thrown off the spell, and his original, independent mind passed from misery into what he himself described as "Elysium." Henceforward, though, to quote his words, "he could not speak of the raptures of Christian enjoyment: he thought he could enter into the feeling of the Psalmist—'My soul breaketh out for the very fervent desire that it hath alway unto Thy judgements'" (Ps. cxix., verse 20). The depth of his conviction, the intensity of his enthusiasm, the fire of his natural eloquence, triumphed over the rugged uncouthness of his manner. No preacher of his day produced so strong and irresistible an effect.

To secure spiritual independence from civil control in matters which to him and his followers seemed vital, he and four hundred and seventy ministers resigned their livings, and joined the Free Church. With that memorable "Disruption," the Psalms were twice associated. It was from the words, "Unto the godly there ariseth up light in the darkness" (Ps. cxii., verse 4), that Chalmers preached a sermon in Edinburgh (November 17th, 1842), which put fresh vigour into those who dreaded the unknown future. It was from the Psalms, again, that the seceding ministers, on the day of the formal separation, drew courage and hope. On May 18th, 1843, Chalmers presided as moderator over the meeting in Tanfield Hall. A heavy thundercloud darkened the building. But as Chalmers gave out the Psalm (xliii.) to be sung, beginning at the 3rd verse, "O send out Thy light and Thy truth, that they may lead me," the cloud parted; the sun poured forth; the sombre shade became dazzling light.

During two years of Chalmers' ministry in Glasgow (1819-22), he had for his curate Edward Irving, one of the strangest and most pathetic figures in the ecclesiastical history of the last century—the lover of Jane Welsh, the friend of Thomas Carlyle, and the founder of a Church.

In 1822, Irving began to preach at a little chapel in Hatton Garden. Like Byron, he awoke to find himself famous. The most brilliant members of London society crowded to hear him; the mystic eloquence and prophetic outpourings of this impassioned Cameronian were a new sensation; his splendid figure, sonorous voice, and noble features heightened the magnetism that he exercised; fashion fell at his feet. Flattery intoxicated him. He could not endure neglect, and singularity succeeded to singularity. A wave of religious enthusiasm had swept over the country, its tide setting strongly in one particular direction. In the horrors of the French Revolution, in the rise and fall of Napoleon, men saw the fulfilment of Divine prophecies. With senses alert and strained, they watched for signs of the impending end of the world. Poets and painters sought their inspiration in Apocalyptic visions. The current swept Irving from his feet. Hour after hour, he expounded to listening crowds his theories of the Second Advent, his prophecies of "the Coming of the Messiah in Glory and Majesty." In 1831, the "unknown tongues" were for the first time heard in his church at Regent Square, and henceforward they became frequent, if not habitual, occurrences.

In April 1832, the trustees of the Regent Square Church removed him from the pulpit, though the bulk of his congregation followed him to Gray's Inn Road. He was still a minister of the Church of Scotland; but in March 1833, he was deposed from his ministry by the Presbytery of Annan. The tribunal before which he appeared, consisted of homely old men — half ministers, half sheep-farmers — summoned from their rural manses to determine delicate questions of theological orthodoxy. Hours passed in the speeches of the accusers, and in the defence of the most eloquent and brilliant preacher of the day. The trial began at noon. It was dark when Irving was pronounced by the Presbyters to be guilty of heresy. Before the moderator delivered sentence of deposition, in a scene of strange excitement, Irving left the dimly lighted church, in which he had been baptized and ordained, crying to the crowd that obstructed his passage, "Stand forth! Stand forth! What! will ye not obey the voice of the Holy Ghost? As many as will obey the voice of the Holy Ghost, let them depart." He was at least spared the pain of hearing himself cast out by the Church which disowned his service. "I sang in my heart," he says, "'Blessed be the Lord, Who hath not given us as a prey to their teeth'" (Ps. cxxiv., verse 5).

Irving returned to London to find himself forbidden to administer the Sacraments, for the act of deposition was a judicial act, depriving him of his authority as a minister. Though he was re-ordained by the apostles of his own Church, he never recovered from the blow. He accepted it with a humility which was the more touching from his confidence in his extraordinary powers. But his heart was broken. Slowly his life ebbed from him. His faith in his mission was unshaken; he believed in it with all the fervour and strength of his soul, and toiled still to gain for it the ear of the world; but in vain. In September 1834, he left London a dying man. Riding through Shropshire and Wales, and visiting his scattered congregations as he went, he reached Liverpool. In his touching letters to his wife are messages to his little daughter, Maggie, sent in the simply-told stories that he gleaned on his way. When other comforts had failed, and fame had fled, he clung still to his Bible, and made the Psalms his constant companions. "How in the night seasons," he writes on October 12th, "the Psalms have been my consolations against the faintings of flesh and spirit."

At Liverpool he took ship and sailed for Glasgow. The end was near. For a few weeks he was able to preach, though, at forty-two, his gaunt gigantic frame bore all the marks of age and weakness. His face was wasted, his hair white, his voice broken, his eyes restless and unquiet. As November drew to its close, his feebleness increased, till it was evident that his life was rapidly passing away. His mind began to wander. Those who watched at his bedside could not understand the broken utterances spoken in an unknown tongue by his faltering voice. But at last it was found that he was repeating to himself in Hebrew, Psalm xxiii., " The Lord is my Shepherd." It was with something like its old power that the dying voice swelled as it utterred the glorious conviction, " Though I walk through the valley of the shadow of death, I will fear no evil." The last articulate words that fell from his lips were, " If I die, I die unto the Lord. Amen." And with these he passed away at midnight on December 7th, 1834.

Nor is the love of the Psalter confined to those who, in their different ways, and often in bitter opposition, have defended the truths of Christianity. It comprehends, also, many of those who have stood in the forefront of the scientific attack. A vast change has passed over the spirit of the conflict. The combatants no longer fight for victory; both sides respect the convictions of the other; both contend for truth, and learn to welcome it, from whatever source derived. Experience has proved, not only that scientific enthusiasm can raise men to heights of the purest morality, of the most absolute disinterestedness and most austere self-denial, but also that the scientific attitude is not incompatible with religious aspirations or religious convictions. To some men, faith is far harder of attainment than to others; to some, in their profound sincerity of mind, it may even be almost impossible. Yet, probably, few champions of science, driven to take their stand on a point of Nothing in the agnostic abyss of Nothing, have not longed, at some moments of their lives, that their feet were firmly planted on the Rock.

John Locke lived the last fourteen years of his life at Oates, in Essex, an inmate of the house of Sir Francis Masham. In his seventy-third year, his strength failed him fast, and he knew that his end was near. On October 28th, 1704, Lady Masham was reading the psalms for the day, " low, while he was dressing." He asked her to read them aloud, and it was while he was listening to the words, that the stroke of death fell upon him. In the Psalms, Alexander von Humboldt (1769-1859) recognised an epitome of scientific progress, a summary of the laws which govern the universe. " A single psalm, the 104th," he writes, " may be said to present a picture of the entire Cosmos . . . We are astonished to see,

within the compass of a poem of such small dimension, the
universe, the heavens and the earth, thus drawn with a few
grand strokes."

Similar is the testimony of Maine de Biran (1766-1824),
whom Cousin called one of the greatest of French metaphysi-
cians. He had lived through all the storms of the French
Revolution, the Empire, and the Restoration. A soldier, a
politician, an administrator, he had played his part in political life. Yet it was as a solitary thinker, a keen observer
of himself, a deep student of the facts of his inner consciousness, that his chief work was done. In his Journal he lays
bare the mental stages by which he passed from the guidance
of Condillac to that of Fénelon, from the self-interest of the
one to the self-sacrifice of the other. The rapid changes in
all around him forced upon his mind the need of some fixed,
immutable point of support. He could not hold, with his
first master, that man receives, through the channels of the
senses alone, all the elements of his moral and intellectual
nature. Such a theory brought him nothing permanent,
and no repose. For a time he wavered between the creed
of the Stoic and that of the Christian: but gradually Marcus
Aurelius yielded to the teaching of the Bible, the *Pensées* of
Pascal, the *Imitation of Christ*, the *Œuvres Spirituelles* of
Fénelon. Biran became a believer in Christianity. In a
philosophical work, on which he was engaged at the time of
his death, *Nouveaux Essais d'Anthropologie*, a work which
gave a new impulse to the spiritual school of philosophy in
France, he distinguishes three stages in the moral growth of
man. The first stage is animal, governed by instincts and
passions. The second is human, when the will and reason
triumph over the merely animal nature. The third is
spiritual, when the will itself submits to, and is absorbed in,
the guidance of the Divine Spirit. If the second stage is
characterised by effort, the essence of the third is love. The
second is the ideal of the Stoic; the third of the Christian.
The great change in his life took place about 1818. In his
Pensées for March 28th, to April 1st, in that year, he comments
on verse 28 of Psalm cxix.; " the Word that can make me
live, will not come from me nor from my will, nor yet from
anything that I hear or collect from without." In this

conviction he presses forward on his new road. It is religion alone that can help a man to change his nature: it alone gives him, as he says, "the wings of the dove." Without this aid, man would weary of the struggle; and he asks for help, in the words of Psalm vi., verse 2, "Have mercy upon me, O Lord, for I am weak." The last entry in his Diary, May 17th, 1824, made when he already felt the rapid approach of his fatal illness, is a comment on Psalm xxxviii., verse 7: "In my weakness, and in my moral and physical discomfort, I cry aloud upon my cross, 'Have mercy upon me, O Lord, for I am weak. My loins are filled with a sore disease; and there is no whole part in my body.' Woe," he says, "to the man who is alone. Unhappy too is the man, however powerful his intellect, or however great his human wisdom, who is not sustained by a strength and a wisdom higher than his own. The true wisdom, the true strength, consists in feeling the support of God. If he has not this, woe to him, for he is alone! The Stoic stands alone. The Christian walks in God's presence and with God, through this world and the next."

Here are the words of Psalm xxiii., verse 4, "Thy rod and thy staff comfort me," which consoled the dying hours of Sir William Hamilton (1788-1856), "almost the only earnest man" Carlyle found in Edinburgh; a student of colossal learning, yet as original as he was erudite, who did more than any man of his time to release the reflective thought of this country from its insularity, and to bind it to all that was best in the philosophy of Greece, Germany, and France. The insuperable limitations of human knowledge were the essence of his teaching; yet it was on the mysteries which lay beyond the barrier of the Unknowable that he reposed at the moment of his death.

Here are the words which Sir James Simpson (1811-70), in his childhood at Bathgate, knew as his "Mother's Psalm." In times of anxiety and trial, and they were not infrequent in the baker's shop, Mrs. Simpson used to repeat Psalm xx. in the Scottish paraphrase:

"Jehovah hear thee in the day when trouble He doth send,
And let the name of Jacob's God thee from all ill defend:
O let Him help send from above, out of His sanctuary;
From Sion, His own holy hill, let Him give strength to thee."
                                                                    Etc., etc.

The memory of her character and example never faded from her son's mind. Years later, when he was already famous as the discoverer of chloroform, and at the head of his profession, Simpson returned to the impressions of his childhood, and it became his highest ambition to make known to others, in public or in private, the peace which he had found in the Christian faith.

Or, lastly, may be quoted the Sonnet, suggested by Psalm xxvii., which was written by one of the ablest of modern biologists, George John Romanes:

> " I ask not for Thy love, O Lord; the days
>   Can never come when anguish shall atone.
>   Enough for me were but Thy pity shown,
> To me as to the stricken sheep that strays,
> With ceaseless cry for unforgotten ways—
>   O lead me back to pastures I have known
>   Or find me in the wilderness alone,
> And slay me, as the hand of mercy slays.
>
> " I ask not for Thy love; nor e'en as much
>   As for a hope on Thy dear breast to lie;
> But be Thou still my Shepherd—still with such
>   Compassion as may melt and such a cry;
> That so I hear Thy feet, and feel Thy touch,
>   And dimly see Thy face ere yet I die."

Literature has felt the same spell as that which fell upon philosophy and science. Men of letters in their lives or in their writings have acknowledged the universality of the Psalms.

To two paraphrases of the Psalms, Joseph Addison owes no inconsiderable portion of his fame. "David," he writes in the *Spectator*, "has very beautifully expressed this steady reliance on God Almighty in his 23rd Psalm, which is a kind of pastoral hymn, and filled with those allusions which are usually found in that kind of writing." . . . Then follows the well-known version of Psalm xxiii., "The Lord my pasture shall prepare."[1] A month later, appeared an essay on the means of confirming human faith. It closes with the equally famous version of Psalm xix., "The spacious firmament on high."[2] Throughout the English-speaking world, the two paraphrases of the Psalms are known to millions who know nothing of Sir Roger de Coverley or of *Cato*.

[1] *Spectator*, July 26th, 1712. No. 441.
[2] *Ibid.*, August 23rd, 1712. No. 465.

It was with a psalm that William Cowper, a timid, delicate, sensitive child in Dr. Pitman's School at Market Street, Hertfordshire, nerved himself to endure the torture inflicted by an elder boy. "I well remember," he says, "being afraid to lift my eyes upon him higher than his knees; and that I knew him better by his shoe-buckles than by any other part of his dress." Yet, as he sat on a bench in the schoolroom, fearing the immediate coming of his tormentor, he found in the text, "I will not fear what man doeth unto me" (Ps. cxviii., verse 6), "a degree of trust and confidence in God that would have been no disgrace to a much more experienced Christian."

In the language of the Psalms, again, he expressed the despondency which ended in his attempted suicide, and removal to a madhouse. It was a time when, to quote his own description of his state of mind,

> "Man disavows, and Deity disowns me.
> Hell might afford my miseries a shelter;
> Therefore Hell keeps her ever-hungry mouths all
>   Bolted against me."

Placed in Dr. Cotton's asylum at St. Alban's, he recovered. His joy, like his despair, is clothed in the words of the Psalms: "The Lord is my strength and my song, and is become my salvation" (Ps. cxviii., verse 14). "I said, I shall not die, but live, and declare the works of the Lord; He has chastened me sore, but not given me over unto death. O give thanks unto the Lord, for His mercy endureth for ever!" (Ps. cxviii., verses 17, 18, 29). It became his ambition to be the poet of Christianity, and the fruits remain in such hymns as, "God moves in a mysterious way," or, "Hark, my soul, it is the Lord," or, "O for a closer walk with God."

It is by a reference to a psalm that Boswell defends the minuteness of detail with which, throughout the most famous biography in the English language, he has noted the conversations of Dr. Johnson. He quotes from Archbishop Secker, in whose tenth sermon there is the following passage: —"*Rabbi David Kimchi*, a noted Jewish commentator, who lived about five hundred years ago, explains that passage in the 1st Psalm, *His leaf also shall not wither*, from rabbins yet older than himself, thus: That *even the idle talk*, so he expresses it, *of a good man ought to be regarded;* the most superfluous things he saith are always of value."

Of Walter Scott's familiarity with the Psalms, his novels give abundant evidence, and scraps of the Psalms were among the last words which his friends could distinguish from his lips. A tour on the Continent failed to restore his health. But, from the moment when, rounding the hill at Ladhope, he caught his first glimpse of the outline of the Eildons and of the towers of Abbotsford, he revived. Surrounded by his dogs, happy in his home, conscious and composed, he almost seemed to have hope of recovery. On July 17th, 1832, he insisted upon being taken to the study, and placed at his desk. His daughter put the pen into his hand, and he endeavoured to close his fingers upon it; but they refused their office—it dropped on the paper. He sank back among his pillows, silent tears rolling down his cheek. The gallant spirit of the worn-out man had made its last effort. "Friends," said he, "don't let me expose myself—get me to bed—that's the only place." From this time his strength gradually declined. His mind was, for the most part, hopelessly obscured; yet, when there was any symptom of consciousness, fragments of the *Stabat Mater* and the *Dies Iræ* could sometimes be distinguished, mingled with passages from the Bible, or verses of the Psalms in the old Scottish metrical paraphrase. He died September 21st, 1832.

"Half a Scot by birth," Byron spent his childish years at Aberdeen. There, from the teaching of his nurse, he gained a love and knowledge of the Bible which he never lost. Many of the Psalms, beginning with the 1st and 23rd, he learned by heart. Still a mere boy, yet already subject to fits of melancholy, he found expression for his mood in a paraphrase of Psalm lv., verse 6:

> "Fain would I fly the haunts of men—
> I seek to shun, not hate mankind;
> My breast requires the sullen glen
> Whose gloom may suit a darken'd mind.
>
> "Oh! that to me the wings were given,
> Which bear the turtle to her nest!
> Then would I cleave the vault of Heaven,
> To flee away, and be at rest."

On the Psalms, as his mother repeated them to him in

the metrical version of Scotland, James Hogg, the Ettrick Shepherd, nursed his childish imagination, and mingled with them her tales of giants, kelpies, brownies, and other aerial creations of the fairy world. Before he knew his letters, he could say Psalm cxxii., and, as he grew older, he learned by heart the greater part of the Psalter. The Bible was, in fact, the herd-boy's only book. Among the pastoral solitudes of Ettrick, the atmosphere of which was charged with legendary lore, and throbbed with the metrical beat of David's Psalms, he wove into one exquisite vision the ideal and the actual scenes which formed his mental and bodily world.

Here—from the lips of the simple dalesmen whom Wordsworth loved, rising out of the Westmoreland valleys and rolling among the hills whence he drew the healing power of his verse—comes,

" Mournful, deep, and slow
The cadence, as of psalms—a funeral dirge!
We listened, looking down upon the hut,
But seeing no one; meanwhile from below
The strain continued, spiritual as before;
But now distinctly could I recognise
These words: '*Shall in the grave thy love be known,
In death thy faithfulness?*'" [1]

Here, in the mouth, not of one of his mediæval figures, but of a homely rustic, Tennyson [2] places the words of Psalm lxxxvi., verse 15:—

"Sin? O yes—we are sinners, I know—let all that be,
And read me a Bible verse of the Lord's goodwill towards men—
'Full of compassion and mercy, the Lord,' let me hear it again;
'Full of compassion and mercy—long suffering.' Yes, O yes!
For the lawyer is born but to murder, the Saviour lives but to bless."

Here, Matthew Arnold, quoting Psalm xlix., verse 7, expresses his melancholy sense of the dumbness of Christ's death-place, the silence of the sacred land, the isolation of man, and his inability to rise out of philosophic calm into the exaltation of unquestioning faith:

" From David's lips this word did roll,
'Tis true and living yet:
*No man can save his brother's soul,
Nor pay his brother's debt.*

---

[1] *The Excursion:* The Solitary. Psalm lxxxviii., verse 11.
[2] " Rizpah," stanza xiii.

> "Alone, self-poised, henceforward man
> Must labour; must resign
> His all too human creeds, and scan
> Simply the way divine" [1]

Here are the lines which Browning assigns to Pompilia, as, before her flight, she sat at the Carnival, with her tyrant husband crouching behind in the shadow:

> "There is a psalm Don Celestine recites,
> 'Had I a dove's wings, how I fain would flee!'
> The psalm runs not, 'I hope, I pray for wings,'—
> Not 'If wings fall from heaven, I fix them fast,'—
> Simply, 'How good it were to fly and rest,
> Have hope now, and one day expect content!
> How well to do what I shall never do!'
> So I said, 'Had there been a man like that,
> To lift me with his strength out of all strife
> Into the calm, how I could fly and rest!'" [2]

Here is the favourite verse of Elizabeth Barrett Browning, whose confidence in God's government of the world, though tearful, was unshaken:

> "Of all the thoughts of God that are
> Borne inward into Souls afar,
>   Along the Psalmist's music deep,
> Now tell me if that any is,
> For gift or grace surpassing this:
>   'He giveth His beloved—sleep?'" [3]

Or here, drawn from Psalm lxxx., verse 5, "Thou feedest them with the bread of tears, and givest them plenteousness of tears to drink," is her lesson of patience:

> "Shall we, then, who have issued from the dust,
> And there return—shall we, who toil for dust,
> And wrap our winnings in this dusty life,
>   Say, 'No more tears, Lord God!
>   The measure runneth o'er?'" [4]

"It is He that hath made us, and not we ourselves," is the text chosen by Edward Fitzgerald for his tomb. The choice seems the defence for a career that, to many, and perhaps to the man himself at some moments of his life, seemed

---

[1] "Oberman Once More." In the 1888 edition, the first of the two stanzas is omitted. Both are given as printed in the edition of 1867.
[2] *Ring and the Book*. Pompilia, ll. 991-1000.
[3] "The Sleep," stanza i. Psalm cxxvii., verse 3.
[4] "The Measure," stanza ii.

wasted. Yet Fitzgerald had won from Tennyson a generous tribute of praise for his

> " . . . golden Eastern lay,
> Than which I know no version done
> In English more divinely well."

Loving and enjoying leisure, he lived remote from bustle and publicity, admitting into his paradise of music and books nothing that did not "breathe content and virtue." Born with an original mind and character, and never endeavouring to rub them smooth by contact with conventionalities, he remained what he was, and made his life his own peculiar creation.

Outside a narrow circle of his contemporaries Fitzgerald was barely known. But few writers influenced their generation more powerfully than Ruskin and Carlyle. In the purport of their message they differed; in their manner of delivering it, they were absolutely opposed. Yet, apart from the affection which Carlyle bore to his "æthereal" Ruskin, they had many points in common. Both urged the necessity of individuals and nations obeying the commandments of God, Carlyle insisting on the retribution that awaits disobedience, Ruskin emphasising the new powers that glad obedience engenders. Both loved the Psalms. "David's life and history," says Carlyle, "as written in those Psalms of his, I consider to be the truest emblem ever given of a man's moral progress and warfare here below. All earnest souls will ever discern in it the faithful struggle of an earnest human soul towards what is good and best. Struggle often baffled, sore baffled, down as into entire wreck; yet a struggle never ended; ever, with tears, repentance, true unconquerable purpose, begun anew." As both Carlyle and Ruskin felt the power of the Psalms, so the spirit of both was Hebraic. Neither was content to be a mere intellectual thinker; both were, above all, teachers—æsthetic, moral, political teachers. Both were on fire not only to know the right, but to have the right done. They had the intense zeal for action, combined with the undoubting affirmation, of the ancient prophets. Both recognised the effect of a man's life on his opinions and work; both insisted on the intimate connection between the moral conditions under which a man thinks, and the external form or action in which his thought is clothed. It is this perception which gives to Carlyle's historical writing its vivid human interest; it is on this perception that Ruskin founds his view, that only the pure in heart can interpret Nature adequately, or rise to the highest expression of truth and beauty.

To compare the influence of the two men would be scarcely relevant to the subject. It is, however, probably true, that Carlyle taught the thinkers, Ruskin the doers: Carlyle stimulated morals, Ruskin action. Carlyle's gospel of work, force, and strength supplied no additional impulses beyond those by which men of practical energy felt themselves to be already actuated; but theorists were roused by the suggestion of the advent of a leader, who, in his strength, should govern by the profoundest principles that abstract thought could formulate. Ruskin's influence, on the other hand, has been chiefly felt in actual life. In the presence of nature, he gave to ordinary people eyes. In æsthetic criticism, he opposed the spiritual to the sensuous theory of Art. In painting, he gave a new creed to a new school. In architecture, he stimulated the Gothic revival. In the political and social world, his insistence on the moral dignity and destiny of man created new standards as the tests of economic questions, and humanised the iron laws of supply and demand.

Ruskin, as soon as he was able to read with fluency, studied the Bible by his mother's side as few children were ever taught to study its pages. Among the passages that he learned by heart, were Psalms xxiii., xxxii., xc., xci., ciii., cxii. cxix., cxxxix. Of Psalm cxix. he says: "It is strange, that of all the pieces of the Bible which my mother thus taught me, that which cost me most to learn, and which was, to my child's mind, chiefly repulsive—the 119th Psalm—has now become of all the most precious to me, in its overflowing and glorious passion of love for the law of God."

From the Psalms might be collected, so Ruskin taught, a complete system of personal, economical, and political prudence—a compendium of human life. What "Tibullus" in Jonson's *Poetaster* says of Virgil, Ruskin in effect says of the Psalmist's work:

> "That which he hath writ
> Is with such judgment labour'd, and distill'd
> Through all the needful uses of our lives,
> That could a man remember but his lines,
> He should not touch at any serious point
> But he might breathe his spirit out of him."

In *Our Fathers have told us*, Ruskin urges that the first half of the Psalter sums up all the wisdom of society and of the individual. Psalms i., viii., xii., xiv., xv., xix., xxiii., xxiv., well studied and believed, suffice for all personal guidance; Psalms xlviii., lxxii., lxxv., contain the law and the prophecy of all just government; Psalm civ. anticipates every triumph of natural science. On the Psalms is also founded much of Ruskin's æsthetic teaching. The guiding principle of *Modern Painters* is that glad submission to the Divine law which is the keynote to Psalm cxix. Throughout those parts of the Bible which, says Ruskin, people "are intended to make most personally their own (the Psalms), it is always the law which is spoken of with chief joy. The Psalms respecting mercy are often sorrowful, as in thought of what it cost; but those respecting the law are always full of delight. David cannot contain himself for joy thinking of it—he is never weary of its praise: 'How love I Thy law! it is my meditation all the day. Thy testimonies are my delight and my counsellors; sweeter also than honey and the honeycomb'" (Ps. cxix., verse 24). By the love that inspires obedience to law, Ruskin was separated from the rising school of science; by the fruits of that obedience—precision, exactitude, fidelity, realism—he was distinguished from the followers of the expiring romantic school of art. His own teaching was that, by the two qualities in combination, in other words, by docility and faith, men may win back the childlike heart which alone penetrates the mysteries of nature, and regain the power of expressing the beauty and truth with which the external world reveals the Divine law.

Throughout all Ruskin's work there runs this connecting link of glad submission to the law of God. His numerous volumes, touching manifold sides of life, resemble those pious tomes of the Middle Ages into which men wove the totality of their learning and the ardour of their faith. Their design seems, and is, disordered by endless digressions; but all the lines converge on the Divine object of their love. So Ruskin's work is at once a *Speculum Mundi* and a *Speculum Dei*—it is a mirror of the world and of God in the world. Through all his books runs the golden thread of cheerful obedience to the Divine law. Especially is this true of *Modern Painters*, which is not only a beautiful treatise on art, but also the impassioned expression of an adoring faith. The subject is handled as it might have been treated by a mediæval mystic, or a Franciscan poet. Still more is it conceived in the spirit of the Psalmist. As, in his exquisite prose, Ruskin interprets to the nineteenth century God's message of creation, so David sang of God's handiwork, while he shepherded his sheep on the lonely uplands of Palestine. " He who, in any way "—the words are Carlyle's—" shews us better than we knew before, that a lily of the fields is beautiful, does he not shew it us as an effluence of the Fountain of all Beauty; as the *handwriting*, made visible there, of the great Maker of the Universe? He has sung for us, made us sing with him, ' a little verse of a sacred Psalm.' "

CHAPTER XII

1688-1900 (*continued*)

The Psalms in philanthropic movements—Prison Reform and John Howard; in missionary enterprises—John Eliot, David Brainerd, William Carey, Henry Martyn, Alexander Duff, Allen Gardiner, David Livingstone, Bishop Hannington; in ordinary life—Colonel Gardiner, Thomas Carlyle, Jane Welsh Carlyle; in secular history—Brittany and La Vendée, the execution of Madame de Noailles, the evacuation of Moscow in 1812, the Revolution of 1848, Bourget in the Franco-German War of 1870-1, Captain Conolly at Bokhara and Havelock at Jellalabad, Duff, Edwards, and " Quaker " Wallace in the Indian Mutiny, the Boer War.

IN the preceding chapter, the influence of the Psalms during the last two centuries has been illustrated from the lives and writings of leaders of religion, science, and literature. Within the same period, their power may be traced, not only in philanthropic movements or missionary enterprises, but also in ordinary life and secular history.

The religious reawakening which revolutionised England in the latter half of the eighteenth century, inspired numerous efforts towards social progress. The abolition of the Slave Trade, the foundation of the Bible Society, the educational work of Raikes and Lancaster, were the outcome of new and higher standards of life. Among efforts to improve social conditions, an honourable place belongs to the struggle for Prison Reform, which is inseparably associated with the name of John Howard (1726-90). In all the stages of its progress, the Psalms were at work.

In 1755, on Howard's voyage to Lisbon, the *Hanover* packet, in which he was sailing, was captured by a French privateer. Herded together in a filthy dungeon at Brest, he and his companions experienced the horrors of imprisonment. The memory of his own sufferings may well have lingered in his mind. But it was not till 1773, nearly twenty years afterwards, that he began to devote himself to Prison

Reform. While serving as High Sheriff for the County, Howard officially inspected the Bedfordshire jails. Horror-struck at the sufferings of the prisoners, whether criminals or debtors, he began his investigations in England, and gradually extended his visits to Scotland, Ireland, and the Continent. In the damp, unwholesome cells, ill-lighted and badly-ventilated, where prisoners were confined without exercise or employment, jail fever and smallpox raged. Howard's visits were paid in peril of his life. But " Hold Thou up my goings " (Ps. xvii., verse 5) was the text which encouraged him to persevere. The fever had no terrors for him. " Trusting," he says, " in Divine Providence, and believing myself in the way of my duty, I visit the most noxious cells, and while so doing ' I fear no evil ' " (Ps. xxiii., verse 4). Yet he did not always escape. At Lille, in May 1783, he caught the fever. It is in the language of the Psalms that he expresses his gratitude for his recovery: " For many days I have been in pain and sorrow, the sentence of death was, as it were, upon me, but I cried unto the Lord, and He heard me. Blessed, for ever blessed, be the name of the Lord." A deeply religious man, he jots down in his memorandum books his pious ejaculations and secret aspirations. Often his thoughts are couched in the words of the Psalmist. As an example, may be quoted two entries from his Diary, made when he was lying ill at the Hague in 1778: " *May 13th.*—In pain and anguish all Night . . . help, Lord, for vain is the help of Man. In Thee do I put my trust, let me not be confounded. *May 14th.*—This Night my Fever abaited, my Pains less . . . Righteous art Thou in all Thy ways, and holy in all Thy works . . . bring me out of the Furnace as Silver purified seven times."

From a Psalm (lxxix., verse 12) is taken the motto on the title-page of his *Account of Lazarettos*, " O let the sorrowful sighing of the prisoners come before thee," and he chose it because he had himself observed the effect which the words produced on the minds of the prisoners in Lancaster Gaol. In 1789, he left England on the journey which ended with his death at Kherson. He had previously chosen the inscription for his monument, left directions for his funeral, and even selected the text for the sermon which his friend and pastor would preach on the event. The text was Psalm xvii., verse 16. "That text," he says, "is the most appropriate to my feelings of any I know; for I can indeed join with the Psalmist in saying, 'As for me, I will behold thy face in righteousness; and when I awake up after thy likeness, I shall be satisfied with it.'"

Howard's work among prisoners was continued, on different lines, by women like Elizabeth Fry and Sarah Martin. But meanwhile missionary enterprise was taking wider and more daring flight. In June 1793, William Carey and his colleague sailed for India. So opposed to the policy of the East India Company was the idea of a Christian mission, that they were obliged to embark in a Danish East Indiaman, and to settle in Danish territory. Nearly a century later, in April 1874, David Livingstone was buried in Westminster Abbey:

> "Open the Abbey doors and bear him in
> To sleep with king and statesman, chief and sage,
> The missionary come of weaver kin,
> But great by work that brooks no lower wage."

The contrast marks the revulsion of public opinion, and suggests the importance of a movement which is among the marvels of the nineteenth century.

For Protestant England, the history of missions to the heathen begins with John Eliot (1604-90), the son of a Hertfordshire yeoman, an early settler in New England for conscience' sake, and one of the three authors of the metrical version of the Psalms, which was known as the Bay Psalm Book (1640). Few names in American history are more truly venerable than that of the man who gave the best years of his life to the task of preaching the Gospel to the Red Indians. Rising above the special faults which beset the religion of his contemporaries, he was neither sour, nor gloomy, nor fanatical—a kindly-natured, tender-hearted man—who always stored the deep pockets of his horseman's cloak with presents for the papooses. His metrical version of the Psalms in the Indian dialect of Massachusetts (1658) was the first part of the Bible which he published, and in the singing of the Psalms he found the readiest means of arresting the attention of his hearers, and the simplest expression for the religious feelings of the infants of humanity.

Eliot's communities of " Praying Indians " were dead or dying before his successor began his mission work among the Indians of Delaware and Pennsylvania. The Journal of David Brainerd (1718-47), as published in Jonathan Edwards' account of his life (1765), is a remarkable piece of spiritual autobiography. In words which are largely drawn from the Psalms, it traces the inner life of the thoughtful, somewhat melancholy youth, who, growing up in his father's home in Connecticut, or working on his own farm, resolved to devote his whole life, first as a minister, then as a missionary to the Indians of Delaware and Pennsylvania. Five years (1742-7) of toil, anxiety, exposure, and privation, did their work on a sickly, overwrought frame. At the age of thirty, Brainerd died of consumption, with the words of Psalm cii., sung at his bedside by his friends, still ringing in his ears.

The Journal is a forgotten book. It contains few illuminating thoughts; it breathes a theology which to many men is repellent; it speaks a technical language, which, from less saintly and simple lips, might nauseate the modern reader. Yet the picture it presents of utter self-surrender, and of concentrated single-minded effort, is singularly impressive. As a record of religious conflict and spiritual triumph, it may be contrasted with the autobiographies of Bunyan or Henry Martyn. It shows little of the dramatic force and picture-making imagination of the *Grace Abounding;* it reveals scarcely a trace of the natural struggle with human ties and passions, which gives to Martyn's *Journal* so pathetic, and even romantic, an interest. But, bare, simple, detached though it is, it stands apart from similar diaries by reason of its absorption in the one object of Brainerd's life—the strenuous, concentrated effort to attain nearness to God.

The early stages of his progress are common enough. His transient self-satisfaction in doing duty passed away, leaving him so despondent that, like Bunyan, he " begrutched the birds and beasts their happiness," and fancied that mountains obstructed his hopes of mercy. In alternate joy and despair he continued, till, in October 1740, his temper and habit of mind underwent a change. New and higher views of God and His relation to man seemed to take possession of his soul. There was no special call, no vision, no sudden application of some special passage of Scripture to his own particular case. The change came over him quietly, without violent personal impressions. But it was absolute and permanent. Henceforward he had the " full assurance of hope," and retained it " unto the end." But this confidence only made him more humble-minded, more conscious of his own shortcomings. Externally, it impelled him to greater activity in his missionary work; in his inner life, it was the nourishment of his spiritual growth, the source of his love and longing for purity of heart, the spring of that passion for holiness, which banished all motives of fear and self-interest, inspired his eager pursuit on earth of things above, and created his ideal of the beauty of heaven.

The *Journal* is permeated with the power of the Psalms. So much have they become part of his habitual thoughts, that his hopes, fears, and aspirations flow naturally into language which recalls, even when it does not reproduce, the actual words. On the Psalms are based the " five distinguishing marks of a *true Christian*," which Brainerd gives from what he had himself " *felt and experienced*," and the fifth may be taken as some illustration of his character and life:—

" The *laws* of God are his delight, Psalm cxix., verse 97 (' Lord, what love have I unto Thy law; all the day long is my study in it '). These he observes, not out of constraint, from a servile fear of hell; but they are his choice, Psalm cxix., verse 30 (' I have chosen the way of truth; and Thy judgments have I laid before me '). The strict observance of them is not his bondage, but his greatest liberty, Psalm cxix., verse 45 (' And I will walk at liberty; for I seek Thy commandments ')." It is on the same foundation that in the *Journal* Brainerd builds his own assurance of hope. " That holy confidence," he writes, " can only arise from the testimony of a good conscience. ' Then,' says the holy psalmist, ' shall I not be ashamed when I have respect unto all Thy commandments ' " (Ps. cxix., verse 6).

Brainerd's *Journal* is, as has been said, a forgotten book. Yet it would be difficult to measure the magnitude of the results which it indirectly produced. It fired the imagination of William Carey; it stirred the zeal of Henry Martyn;

it inspired the decision of David Livingstone to become a missionary. In his Diary for 19th April 1794, Carey makes this entry:—" I was much humbled to-day by reading Brainerd. O what a disparity betwixt me and him! He always constant, I as inconstant as the wind." Martyn, who repeatedly refers to the same book, made the life of Brainerd his human ideal. Such references as the following might be multiplied:—" 7th November 1803.—I thought of David Brainerd, and ardently desired his devotedness to God and holy breathings of soul." " 23rd September 1803. Read David Brainerd to-day, and yesterday, and find, as usual, my spirit greatly benefited by it. I long to be like him: let me forget the world, and be swallowed in a desire to glorify God."

From Eliot and Brainerd, William Carey (1761-1834) traced his spiritual lineage. The son of the parish clerk and schoolmaster of Paulerspury, in Northamptonshire, he became a Baptist in October 1783. Like Hans Sachs, the poet of the German Reformation, or George Fox, the Quaker, or Jacob Bohme, the mystic, he was by trade a shoemaker. Working at his business, preaching, teaching, a married man and a father, burdened with a debt which he had undertaken for his wife's first husband, he found time to teach himself French, Latin, Greek, and Hebrew. In his daily prayers for slaves and heathen, he conceived the thought, which gradually shaped itself in practical form, that he would convert the heathen world by giving them the Bible in their native tongues. He brought the subject before the assembled ministers of his persuasion, only to be silenced as a fanatic. But his enthusiasm and pertinacity were at length rewarded. At Kettering, in October 1792, in the low-roofed back parlour of Widow Wallis, twelve Baptist ministers formed the *Particular Baptist Society for Propagating the Gospel among the Heathen*. A few weeks later it was decided that Carey should be sent out to Bengal with Thomas, a surgeon who had already worked as a missionary in India. A verse from the Psalms, " O come, let us worship and fall down, and kneel before the Lord our Maker " (Ps. xcv., verse 6), was already inscribed by Christian Friedrich Schwartz (1726-97) over the portal of his Mission Church of

Bethlehem at Tranquebar. It was a psalm (xvi., verse 4), "They that run after another God shall have great trouble," which supplied the text of the sermon preached at the service held to dedicate Carey to his work. Thus was launched, to quote Sydney Smith's sneer, by a few " consecrated cobblers," the first English mission to the heathen in India.

Carey left England, determined never to return. The resolution cost him something. Among the seeds which, years later, he sowed in his garden at Serampore were those of the daisy. "I know not," he wrote, "that I ever enjoyed since leaving Europe, a simple pleasure so exquisite as the sight which this *English* daisy afforded me; not having seen one for thirty years, and never expecting to see one again." During his long, laborious career, thirty-four translations of the Bible were made or edited by him. He himself completed the Bengali, Hindi, Maratti, and Sanskrit versions. His paper factories created a new industry. Not only was he one of the first of Oriental scholars, but he was a scientific botanist, an enthusiastic farmer, an ardent student of natural history. Yet, with him, science was always subordinated to religion. It is a text from the Psalms, " All thy works praise thee, O Lord " (Ps. cxlv., verse 10), that he prefixed to his edition of Roxburgh's *Flora Indica* (1820). It was with the words of a psalm in his mind that he desired to end his life. In December 1823, he lay, as he thought, dying, " I had no joys," he writes; " nor any fear of death or reluctance to die; but never was I so sensibly convinced of the value of an Atoning Saviour as then. I could only say, ' Hangs my helpless soul on Thee,' and adopt the language of the first and second verses of the 51st Psalm, which I desired might be the text of my funeral sermon, ' Have mercy upon me, O God, after Thy great goodness: according to the multitude of Thy mercies do away mine offences. Wash me throughly from my wickedness, and cleanse me from my sin."

Carey survived his illness for nearly eleven years. He lived to see the tone of Anglo-Indian society transformed, and the worst cruelties of the Hindoo religion suppressed. He lived also to see two of his greatest successors among Indian missionaries. In the prime of his manhood, he welcomed Henry Martyn to India; at the close of his own career he blessed Alexander Duff, tottering with outstretched hands to meet the ruddy Highlander—" a little yellow old man in a white jacket."

Both Eliot and Carey had left the Anglican Church before they began their missionary labours; the work of Bunyan, Baxter, Howard, and Wesley was done outside her organisation. But Henry Martyn (1781-1812) lived, laboured, and died a faithful member of her communion. It is this contrast which marks the special importance of Martyn's life and death, as the first Anglican missionary to the heathen, the precursor of a long line of heroes, the spiritual ancestor of men of the type of Bishop Patteson and Bishop Hannington.

Senior wrangler at Cambridge in 1801, a brilliant classic as well as a mathematician, a fellow of St. John's College (1802), Martyn was ordained in October 1803. He had already resolved to devote his life and abilities to missionary work. To this resolution he was drawn, partly by the example of Carey, partly, as has been shown, by the career of David Brainerd. Appointed at the close of 1804 to an East Indian Company's chaplaincy, he sailed for Calcutta in July 1805. The sacrifice was costly. On the one side, were the consciousness of talents, achieved success, a growing reputation, congenial pursuits, material comfort, affection for his home, kindred, friends, and, above all, his love for Lydia Grenfell. On the other side, were exile, solitude, obscure employment among ignorant aliens, possibility of failure, surrender of the comforts and refinements of a scholarly, literary life, separation from kindred and acquaintances, abandonment of his prospects of marriage with the being who was dearest to him on earth. It is this human struggle, chronicled with abundant wealth of detail, which gives to his final victory its pathos, its romance, and, for ordinary men, its vital interest. The Diary depicts, with all the fluctuations of success and defeat, the hard-won conquest of self by a creature of flesh and blood, not the easy triumph achieved over the weak passions of earth by some disembodied spirit.

In his Diary for July 29th, 1804, Martyn speaks for the

R

first time of his love for Lydia Grenfell: " I felt too plainly that I loved her passionately. The direct opposition of this to my devotedness to God in the missionary way, excited no small tumult in my mind." Or again, a month later (27th August): " Reading in the afternoon to Lydia alone, from Dr. Watts, there happened to be, among other things, a prayer on entire preference of God to the creature. Now, thought I, here am I in the presence of God and my idol. . . . I continued conversing with her, generally with my heart in heaven, but every now and then resting on her. . . . Parted with Lydia, perhaps for ever in this life. Walked to St. Hilary, determining, in great tumult and inward pain, to be the servant of God." Martyn tore himself away from the living woman to perfect his union with his exalted ideal of conduct. On the last day of the same year (December 31st), when he was waiting for news of his definite appointment to the Indian chaplaincy, he makes the following entry, clothing his self-surrender in the familiar words of Psalm xxxi., verse 6: " So closes the easy part of my life; enriched by every earthly comfort, and caressed by friends, I may scarcely be said to have experienced trouble; but now, farewell ease, if I might presume to conjecture. ' O Lord, into Thy hands I commit my spirit! Thou hast redeemed me, Thou God of truth!' may I be saved by Thy grace, and be sanctified to do Thy will, and to all eternity; through Jesus Christ."

The struggle was not over. It was renewed again and again. In a sense it ceased only with his life. Few passages in the *Journal* are more pathetic than those which record Martyn's feelings during the detention of his ship at Falmouth and at Mounts Bay. At Miss Grenfell's house at Marazion, on August 10th, 1805, came the final parting. On board ship, throughout his labours among English soldiers and natives at Dinapore and Cawnpore, in the midst of his toil in translating the New Testament into Hindustani and Persian, in his journey through Persia, in his religious disputes at Shiraz, he never swerved from his purpose, never relaxed his efforts to conquer himself—and never forgot his love.

On the eve of his departure from Cawnpore, when the

fatal signs of consumption had declared themselves, and a sea voyage seemed the only chance of life, he makes this entry: "23rd September 1811.—Was walking with Lydia; both much affected; and speaking on things dearest to us both. I awoke, and behold it was a dream! My mind remained very solemn and pensive; I shed tears. The clock struck three, and the moon was riding near her highest noon; all was silence and solemnity, and I thought with pain of the sixteen thousand miles between us. But good is the will of the Lord! even if I see her no more." Side by side with this entry, there are scattered throughout the pages of the *Journal* almost innumerable references to the Psalms, and illustrations of their power to soothe and encourage. In the stress of his struggle in 1804, he found that, by learning portions of the Psalms by heart, he quickened his devotional feelings, and in this way committed to memory Psalm cxix. It was a psalm (x.) that he was reading to Lydia Grenfell when he was hastily summoned to rejoin his ship, and they parted for ever on earth. During his long and tedious voyage, surrounded by uncongenial companions, it was to the Psalms that he turned for comfort. Day after day the entries in his *Journal* of the daily events of his life began with a verse from the Psalms, followed by a short comment. From the Psalms he drew encouragement in his missionary enterprise. Thus (December 10th, 1805) he quotes Psalm xxii., verse 27: " All the ends of the earth shall remember, and be turned to the Lord "; and thus continues, " Sooner or later, they shall remember what is preached to them, and though missionaries may not live to see the fruits of their labours, yet the memory of their words shall remain, and in due time shall be the means of turning them unto the Lord." In failing health, and sleepless nights, assailed by temptation, yet straining after purity of heart, his " hope and trust " is in the words, " Purge me with hyssop, and I shall be clean; wash me, and I shall be whiter than snow " (Ps. li., verse 7). At Shiraz, in the midst of daily disputes with Mahometan doctors, and the laborious revision of his Persian translation of the New Testament, he found " a sweet employment " in translating the Psalms into Persian. The work " caused six weary moons, that waxed and waned since its commencement, to pass unnoticed." It was the Psalms that soothed the fatigue of his headlong ride from Tabriz to Tokat on his homeward journey: " 4th September 1812.—I beguiled the hours of the night by thinking of the 14th Psalm." " 10th September.—All day at the village, writing down notes on the 15th and 16th Psalms."

The closing weeks of his life bring into touching juxtaposition his earthly and his heavenly love. He had resolved to abandon his scheme of translating the Bible into Arabic, and to return home from Tabriz by Constantinople. In one of his last letters, written three months before his death, he tells Miss Grenfell of his plan. " Perhaps," he continues, " you may be gratified by the intelligence; but oh, my dear Lydia, I must faithfully tell you, that the probability of my reaching England alive is but small." The last entry in the *Journal* (October 6th), begins with words which sound like reminiscences of the Psalmist, who remembered the past, and meditated on the works of God. " I sat in the orchard, and thought with sweet comfort and peace of my God; in solitude my company, my friend, and comforter." Ten days later, 16th October 1812, alone among strangers, Henry Martyn passed to his rest.

His epitaph was written by Macaulay:

> " Here Martyn lies. In Manhood's early bloom
> The Christian Hero finds a Pagan tomb.
> Religion, sorrowing o'er her favourite son,
> Points to the glorious trophies that he won,
> Eternal trophies! not with carnage red,
> Not stained with tears by hapless Captives shed,
> But trophies of the Cross! for that dear name,
> Through every form of danger, death, and shame,
> Onward he journeyed to a happier shore,
> Where danger, death, and shame assault no more."

But, in missionary enterprises, there has never been any lack of true spiritual heroes to fill the gaps caused by death. Man after man has come forward, obeying what, in his simple sincerity, he believes to be a call. In doing that work, their own characters have ripened in beauty and nobility. Many have been inspired by the largest views of their country's opportunities and responsibilities; but every genuine missionary has done his best, without self-seeking, in some community, however small, and from each a handful of human beings, at the least, have learned the highest and purest impulses of their lives.

High in the roll of missionaries stands the name of Alexander Duff, the eloquent speaker, the educational statesman, and the first missionary sent out to India by the Presbyterian Church of Scotland. An incident on his voyage confirmed, if it did not shape, his career. On October 14th, 1829, he and his wife sailed from Ryde, on board the *Lady Holland*. Four months later, in rough, boisterous weather, the ship approached the Cape of Good Hope, and made for Table Bay. At midnight, February 13th, 1830, she ran aground. Her back broke; her masts were cut away; waves dashed over the wreck; the position seemed desperate. It was not even known whether the ship had struck on a reef, the mainland, or an island. All around were boiling surf and foam. With great difficulty, one of the boats was launched, manned, and despatched to find a landing-place. Three hours passed. Hope was almost gone, when the boat returned, reporting a small sandy bay. At this haven, which proved to be on Dessen Island, the passengers and crew were safely landed, but all that they possessed was lost.

In the search for food and fuel, a sailor found two books cast by the waves on the shore. One was a Bible, the other a Scottish Psalm Book. In both, Duff's name was written. To the shipwrecked party the books seemed a message from God. Led by Duff, they knelt down on the sand while he read them Psalm cvii., "Whoso is wise will ponder these things," etc. On Duff himself the effect was lasting. All his library was lost. With it had gone all his notes and memoranda, everything that reminded him of his student life. Only the Bible and Psalms were preserved. Henceforth, as he read the message, human learning was to be only a means and not an end. In this spirit he founded his College, to teach in the English language everything that was educationally useful, and to hallow secular teaching with the study of the Christian faith and doctrines. Every morning he and his household began the day by singing together one of the Psalms in Rous's version. On his journeys, the Psalms were ever in his mind. Travelling in 1849 from Simla to Kotghur, his road lay by a narrow bridle-path, cut out of the face of a precipitous ridge of rock. As he rode, he watched a shepherd, followed by his sheep, making his way along the mountain side. The man carried a long rod, at one end of which was a crook, at the other a thick band of iron. If the shepherd saw a sheep creeping too far up the mountain, or feeding too near the edge of the precipice, he went back, caught one of the hind legs of the animal in his crook, and gently pulled it back to the flock. The other end was used to beat off the dangerous beasts that prowled round the places where the sheep lay. "This brought to the traveller's remembrance the expression of David, the shepherd, in the 23rd Psalm (verse 4), 'Thy rod and Thy staff comfort me' —the staff clearly meaning God's watchful guiding and directing providence, and the rod His omnipotence in defending His own from foes. It is no tautology."

Carey and Duff passed away in ripe old age, having lived to see some of the fruits of their labours. Henry Martyn, dying alone in a foreign land, had completed two of the great tasks on which he had set his mind. Very different was the fate of Allen Gardiner (1794-1851). The leader of a forlorn hope of missionary enterprise among the Tierra del Fuegans, he, with his six companions, was starved to death, never wavering in the patient courage or losing the sure trust in God which he drew from the book of Psalms.

After sixteen years' service in the Royal Navy, Commander Gardiner found himself, in 1826, without employment. He was free to devote his life to missionary work. For years he laboured, without any permanent success, among the Zulus in South Africa and the Indians in South America. On September 7th, 1850, he sailed with six companions for Tierra del Fuego, where he hoped to establish a mission. In December the party was landed on Picton Island, furnished with provisions for six months. The natives were hostile and thievish; the climate was rigorous, the country barren and wind swept. They had only a flask and a half of powder between them; the rest had been forgotten: their nets were broken; their food was exhausted, and no fresh supplies reached them from the Falkland Islands. One by one the party sickened and died, the last survivor being Gardiner. In his Diary their story is recorded.

Six months had passed. In the midst of snow, and ice, and storm, the little party prayed for the coming of the expected succour. On June 4th, 1851, Gardiner writes: "Wait on the Lord, be of good courage, and He shall strengthen thine heart. Wait I say on the Lord" (Ps. xxvii., verse 14). A lucky shot, fired with almost their last grain of powder, killed five ducks. It is in the words of the Psalms, that the Diary records the gratitude of the hungry men: "16th June.—He will regard the prayer of the destitute, and not despise their prayer" (Ps. cii., verse 17). ".They that seek the Lord shall not want any good thing" (Ps. xxxiv., verse 10). Three of the band were in a dying condition; and Gardiner himself had realised the prospect of starvation. Still he retained his confident trust: "Be merciful unto me, O God, be merciful unto me, for my soul trusteth in Thee: yea, in the shadow of Thy wings, will I make my refuge until these calamities are over past" (Ps. lvii., verse 1), is his entry for June 21st. A week later was his birthday. "I know," he writes in his Diary for June 28th, "that it is written, 'They who seek the Lord shall want no manner of thing that is good' (Ps. xxxiv., verse 10). And again, 'Cast Thy burden upon the Lord, and He shall sustain thee' (Ps. lv., verse 22). Whatever the Lord may in His providence see fit to take away, it is that which he Himself has bestowed. . . . Still I pray that, if it be consistent with Thy righteous will, O my heavenly Father, Thou wouldest look down with compassion upon me and upon my companions, who are straightened for lack of food, and vouchsafe to provide that which is needful . . . but, if otherwise, Thy will be done." One of the party had now died, and all were very weak. Still their sufferings were endured without a murmur. On July 5th, a hand was painted upon a rock leading to the Pioneer Cavern, in which Gardiner lived, and, underneath it, "Ps. lxii., 5-8." The words referred to are: "Nevertheless, my soul, wait thou still upon God; for my hope is in Him. He truly is my strength and my salvation; he is my defence, so that I shall not fall. In God is my health and my glory; the rock of my might, and in God is my trust. O put your trust in Him alway, ye people; pour out your hearts before Him, for God is our hope." At the end of August, two more of the band had died, and for the rest the end was rapidly approaching. The last entry in the Diary is dated September 5th: " Great and marvellous are the loving-kindnesses of my gracious God unto me. He has preserved me hitherto, and for four days, although without bodily food, without any feeling of hunger or thirst." When a relief ship arrived, October 21st, 1851, the bodies of Gardiner and three of his companions were found lying unburied on the shore.

The death of Gardiner seemed to be an useless sacrifice in a hopeless cause. No results were achieved by him in Tierra del Fuego. The career of David Livingstone (1813-73) was in one respect a striking contrast. It was crowded with triumphs. Nor must his successful labour in the cause of geographical science allow us to invert the order of the objects to which his life was devoted. He was, before all else, a Christian missionary, and, as part of the Gospel message, an apostle of freedom from the horrors of slavery.

Through his mother, David Livingstone seems to have added to the daring of his Highland ancestors the tenacity of the Lowland Covenanter. As a boy of nine, he won a New Testament from his Sunday-school teacher for repeating by heart Psalm cxix. A year later he became a " piecer " in the cotton factory of Blantyre, and grew up, inured to toil, insatiable for books, a keen student of natural history, and an occasional poacher. It was not till he was twenty that his mind took a decidedly religious turn. But, from that time onward, his heart, fired by the examples of Brainerd and of Carey, was set on a missionary life. He offered his services to the London Missionary Society, was accepted, and (November 20th, 1840) ordained. A fortnight later, he started for the Cape.

With a psalm Livingstone bade farewell to his family and home. " I remember my father and him," writes his sister, " talking over the prospects of Christian missions. They agreed that the time would come when rich men and great men would think it an honour to support whole stations of missionaries, instead of spending their money on hounds and horses. On the morning of 17th November (1840), we got up at five o'clock. My mother made coffee. David read the 121st and 135th Psalms, and prayed. My father and he walked to Glasgow to catch the Liverpool steamer." He never saw his father again. His mother had told him that she "would have liked one of her laddies to lay her head in the grave." "It so happened," writes David Livingstone in 1865, "that I was there to pay the last tribute to a dear good mother."

In Africa, for thirty years, Livingstone toiled unceasingly to explore the continent, abolish the slave trade, and evangelise the native races. He early learned the lesson that the spiritual cannot be absolutely divorced from the secular. Some may think that the explorer predominated over the missionary. Yet, throughout his journeys, he maintained, in all its strength and purity, his own inner life of fellowship with God. It was with a psalm that he encouraged himself to face the unknown future which each day might bring. Menaced with death by savages, sickened by the atrocities of the slave trade, often prostrated by fever or gnawed by hunger, tormented by poisonous insects, sometimes moving in such bodily pain that he felt as if he were dying on his feet, he found his daily strength in the words, "Commit thy way unto the Lord, and put thy trust in Him; and He shall bring it to pass" (Ps. xxxvii., verse 5). This was the text which sustained him, as he says himself, at every turn of his "course in life in this country, and even in England."

Livingstone's last expedition started from Zanzibar in 1866. He disappeared into the heart of Central Africa. Only vague rumours of his life or death reached the civilised world. In October 1871, he had arrived at Ujiji a living skeleton; all the stores which he expected had disappeared; he was in a desperate plight; only three of his men remained faithful; the rest had deserted him; starvation stared him in the face. It was then that he was found by Stanley. At Unyanyembe Livingstone halted, while Stanley returned to the coast to send him men and stores. From March to August 1872, he waited. At last the men came, and it is in the words of a psalm that he records his joy. The entry in his Diary for August 9th, 1872, is as follows:—"I do most devoutly thank the Lord for His goodness in bringing my men near to this. Three came to-day, and how thankful I am I cannot express. It is well—the men who were with

Mr. Stanley came again to me. ' Bless the Lord, O my soul, and all that is within me bless His holy name. Amen.' " (Ps. ciii., verse 1.)

With " failing strength, but never-failing will," he pressed on. Weak, bloodless, and suffering excruciating pain, he was, in fact, a dying man. On the morning of May 1st, 1873, he was found dead, on his knees in the hut at Itala. " Kneeling at the bedside, with his head buried in his hands upon the pillow, his last words on earth were spoken, not to man but to God."

In the train of Livingstone followed James Hannington, the first Bishop of Equatorial Africa. In July 1885, he had set out from Frere Town to make his way through the Masai country to Lake Victoria Nyanza. Every morning, throughout his toilsome, dangerous journey, he greeted the sunrise by reading or repeating his " Travelling Psalm," " I will lift up mine eyes unto the hills," etc. (Ps. cxxi.). On October 12th, he left the rest of his party, and, a week later, reached the shores of the lake. He was, in fact, marching to almost certain death. King Mwanga, fearing annexation of his dominions, and believing the missionaries to be the agents of the design, had begun a bitter persecution of the Christians. At a village on the shores of the lake, Hannington was seized, and confined in a miserable prison, surrounded by noisy, drunken guards. Consumed with fever, and at times delirious from pain, devoured by vermin, menaced every moment by the prospect of death, he found strength in the Psalms. On Wednesday, October 28th, he notes in his Diary: " I am quite broken down and brought low. Comforted by Psalm xxvii. Word came that Mwanga had sent three soldiers, but what news they bring, they will not yet let me know. Much comforted by Psalm xxviii." " October 29th, Thursday (eighth day in prison).—I can hear no news, but was held up by Psalm xxx., which came with great power. A hyena howled near me last night, smelling a sick man, but I hope it is not to have me yet." This is his last entry. That day, at the age of thirty-seven, he was killed.

On the influence of the Psalms in the everyday lives of ordinary men and women, it is unnecessary to dwell. The career of Colonel Gardiner (1688-1745) proves, that even the chilling atmosphere of the early years of the eighteenth century did not impair their power over the human heart. Except for his death at Prestonpans, described in *Waverley*, there is little to distinguish Gardiner as in any way remarkable. " A very weak, honest, and brave man," is the testimony of Alexander Carlyle. Philip Doddridge relates that, in July 1719, James Gardiner, then a notorious rake, was " converted " by a vision which appeared to him as he sat in his room at Paris, waiting the hour for an assignation with his mistress, and idly turning the pages of *The Christian Soldier* to find amusement. Alexander Carlyle tells a less supernatural story. But, whatever were the true circumstances, it is not disputed that, from that time forward, Gardiner's character was changed, and that he strove to reform, not only his own life, but the lives of those about him and under his command. A psalm furnished the text (Ps. cxix., verse 158) from which Doddridge preached the sermon that found for him a way to the heart of Gardiner. In his biography of his friend, Doddridge shows how deep was the hold which the Psalms possessed on the colonel's life. That he might at all times command their comfort and encouragement, he learnt several of the Psalms by heart, and, as he rode, alone and in unfrequented places, used to repeat them to himself or sing them aloud. Throughout his letters they are repeatedly quoted. In 1743 he had returned from Flanders, ill, and impressed with the conviction of a speedy death. His intimate friends, and those immediately about him, remembered how his mind dwelt with special delight on the words, " My soul, wait thou still upon God " (Ps. lxii., verse 5), or upon Psalm cxlv., and the version of it by Isaac Watts. The outbreak of the Rebellion of 1745 found him sufficiently recovered to command his regiment of horse at the battle of Prestonpans, fought on the great open field into which the arable land was thrown. Mortally wounded, he was carried past the graveyard of Tranent to the minister's house, where he died. Five-and-twenty years before, he had dreamed a dream in which the place was depicted. " He imagined that he saw his Blessed Redeemer on Earth, and that he was following Him through a large Field, *following Him whom his Soul loved*, but much troubled because he thought his Blessed Lord did not speak to him; till he came up to the Gate of *Burying Place*, when turning about He smiled upon him, in such a Manner as filled his soul with the most ravishing Joy; and on After-Reflection animated his Faith, in believing that whatever Storms and Darkness he might meet with in the Way, *at the Hour of Death* his glorious Redeemer would lift upon him *the Light* of His Life-giving Countenance " (Ps. iv., verse 7).

So habitual a use as Colonel Gardiner made of the Psalms is uncommon. It belonged, perhaps, to the religious views and temperament of a man, who was a " noted enthusiast." Yet in the lives of most men and women, there are moods which only find their natural expression in the familiar language of the Psalms. When Thomas Carlyle sets down his half-humorous, half-bitter contempt for the trivialities of society, he quotes the same verse with which the " judicious " Hooker protested against his wife's shrewish tongue (Psalm cxx., verse 5). Returning in 1835 from a London dinner-party, where he had met Sydney Smith—" a mass of fat and muscularity . . . with shrewdness and fun, not humour or even wit, seemingly without soul altogether," he closes the note with the words—" The rest babble, babble. Woe's me that I in Mesech am! To work." Or again, in a higher and wholly serious tone, it is with a psalm that he encourages his brothers to struggle on. " Courage, my brave brothers, all! Let us be found faithful, and we shall not fail. Surely as the blue dome of heaven encircles us all, so does the Providence of the Lord of heaven. He will withhold *no* good thing from those that love Him (Ps. lxxxiv., verse 12). This, as it is the ancient Psalmist's faith, let it likewise be ours. It is the Alpha and Omega, I reckon, of all possessions that can belong to man." Or, yet again, in one of those moods of despondency, which at times sweep over all of us, it is in the language of a psalm that Jane Welsh Carlyle utters her cry for help. On March 24th, 1856, she had resolved, in spite of weakness and ill-health, neither to indulge in vain retrospects of the past, nor to gaze into vague distances of the future, but to find the duty nearest to hand, and do it. Two days later, she had learnt how much she was the creature of external conditions. " One cold, rasping, savage March day," aided by the too tender sympathy of a friend, brought back all her troubles, and she writes (March 26th, 1856): "Have mercy upon me, O Lord, for I am weak; O Lord, heal me, for my bones are vexed. My soul is also sore vexed; but Thou, O Lord, how long? Return, O Lord, deliver my soul; O save me for Thy mercies' sake" (Ps. vi., verses 2-4).

Few persons of mature years have not, at some time of their existence, proved the adequacy of the language of the Psalms—an adequacy belonging to nothing else in literature—to express, or elevate, or soothe, or solemnise their emotions. For that side of the subject, the everyday, universal experiences of humanity are enough. It only remains to illustrate the ·eternal influence of the Psalms at some of those exciting moments of secular life when modern history has been made.

The French Revolution, and the rise and fall of the Napoleonic Dynasty, may be taken as one example. In Brittany and La Vendée was concentrated all that remained of Royalist and religious enthusiasm. There, at the end of the eighteenth century, worship returned to the simplicity of its primitive conditions. There crowds of armed peasants, fired by the ardour of a childlike faith, knelt at the feet of their proscribed and hunted priests, who stood, under the sky and woods, by the bare rocks which served for the altars of God. There, as they commemorated friends or neighbours who had died fighting the Blues, or as the solemn words of Psalm cxxx., " Out of the deep have I called unto Thee, O Lord," etc., were repeated in alternate verses by priest and congregation, the survivors renewed their vows to fight on for their king and their faith. Nor was the struggle so hopeless as it seemed. High clay banks, topped by beeches, oaks, and chestnuts, intersected the fields, and fenced each side of the narrow, winding roads. Among these natural covers undisciplined peasants met regular troops on equal terms.

Elsewhere in France, the Republicans had gained an easy triumph. During the Reign of Terror, hundreds of men and women died on the scaffold, committing their spirits into the hands of God, in the language of the Psalms. So died

Madame de Noailles, on July 22nd, 1794. With her was executed her father-in-law, the Duc de Noailles-Mouchy, Marshal of France, who, at the age of eighty, mounted the scaffold for his God, as, at sixteen, he had mounted the breach for his king. With her perished also the Maréchale de Noailles-Mouchy, who, fifty-two years before, was married at the Palais de Luxembourg, which had been her birthplace, and was afterward to be her prison.

The touching letters of Madame de Noailles addressed to M. Grelet, the tutor of her two sons, and the guardian of her infant daughter, reveal the beauty of her character and the depth and purity of her faith. " Good-bye, Alexis, Alfred, Euphemia," so, in one of these letters, she writes from her prison, " Keep God ever in your hearts all the days of your lives. Bind yourselves to Him by bonds that nothing can loosen. Pray for your father, and labour for his true happiness. Remember your mother, and never forget that her one longing for all of you was that she might bring you up to the life eternal." With quotations from the Psalms begins the codicil to her will, which she drew up in prison to dispose of her personal effects: " In the name of the Father, the Son, and the Holy Ghost. Accept, O Lord, the sacrifice of my life, Into Thy hands I commend my spirit. My God, haste Thee to help me. Forsake me not when my strength faileth me." (Ps. xxxi., verse 6; lxxi., verses 10, 8.) Her prayer was heard. Few scenes are more striking, even in the history of that dramatic period, than that which is described in the Journal of M. Carrichon, who gave the prisoners absolution on their way to the scaffold. Months before, he had promised that he would do them this last service, and arranged the disguise of a dark-blue coat and red waistcoat, which he would wear. The message came that the ladies were condemned. On the appointed day, he followed the cart in which the prisoners, their hands bound behind them, sat on a rude plank without a back. The crowd was great. He hurried along by-streets to point after point on the road followed by the procession. But all his efforts to make his presence known were fruitless; he watched the eager hopefulness fade into despair. At last, as though by a miracle, a pitiless storm of wind and rain swept bare the crowded street, and left him almost alone and close to the cart in which sat the women. All his irresolution vanished. The prisoners bowed their heads as the disguised priest raised his hand, and, with his head covered, pronounced the whole formula of absolution. The storm ceased; the cart passed on; and the women died with unflinching courage.

In September 1812, the French army entered Moscow. A month later they evacuated the smoking ruins of the city, and began that retreat which proved the turning-point in the fortunes of Napoleon. It was believed by the populace that powder magazines, stored beneath the cathedral of the Kremlin, would explode whenever the gates were opened which separated the altar from the body of the building. A service was held to celebrate the retreat of the French. In spite of the prevalence of this belief, a vast throng, drawn to the spot by awe mingled with curiosity, packed the cathedral from end to end. The Metropolitan of Moscow, who was to preach the sermon, approached the gates, opened them, and passed through unharmed. The fears of the Russian peasants were dispelled, even as the forces of Napoleon were dispersed, and in that supreme moment of triumph the Metropolitan gave out his text, "Let God arise, and let His enemies be scattered" (Ps. lxviii., verse 1).

The power of the first Napoleon was shattered by the disaster of the Russian campaign. Yet once again the imperial dynasty was restored on the ruins of the monarchy. With this second rise and fall are associated two psalms. During the Revolution of 1848, which gave Napoleon III. his opportunity, Psalm xlvi. ("God is our hope and strength") was sung in the streets, not only of Berlin, but of Paris. Twenty-two years afterwards, the German armies were marching on the French capital, chanting Luther's version of Psalm xlvi. Bourget, a little village in the Department of the Seine, was, on three successive days (28th to 30th October 1870), the scene of desperate struggles. When the conflict was ended, there was found, on the bullet-pierced altar of the church, a Psalter. It was open at Psalm lvii.: "Be merciful unto me, O God, be merciful unto me, for my soul trusteth in Thee; and under the shadow of Thy wings shall be my refuge, until this tyranny be overpast."

For Great Britain, it is in India, or on the Indian frontiers, that the romance of nineteenth-century history is mainly concentrated.

In September 1840, Captain Arthur Conolly was sent from Cabul to Bokhara to negotiate the release of Colonel Stoddart. He reached Bokhara in December of the following year, and Stoddart was at once thrown into prison. For many months the two prisoners were kept in a filthy, unwholesome dungeon, swarming with vermin, without change of clothing. In June 1842, both were executed. Several years later, a little book was purchased by a Russian in one of the bazaars at Bokhara. It was Conolly's Prayer Book. Along its margins, and on its blank leaves, are noted the chief occurrences of his long imprisonment. "Thank God," he writes in one place, "that this book was left to me. Stoddart and I did not fully know before our affliction what was in the Psalms, or how beautiful are the prayers of our Church."

It is supposed that the news of the destruction of the Cabul force may have decided the Ameer of Bokhara to execute his prisoners. No disaster of such magnitude had ever before befallen the British arms in the East. On January 13th, 1842, from the walls of Jellalabad, a single horseman was seen riding towards the city. It was Dr. Brydon, the sole survivor of the Cabul force. To the British garrison of Jellalabad, the news meant their own immediate and imminent peril. They knew that within a few days the storm would burst upon them; that, insufficiently provided with ammunition, and scantily supplied with food, fighting behind crumbling walls whose circuit was too vast to be properly manned, they would have to hold their own for weeks against a host excited by previous victory. Such a position might well solemnise the feelings of the most careless. On the next Sunday the whole garrison assembled for Divine service in one of the squares of the Bala Hissar. There was no chaplain, but the Church Service was read to the officers and men by a grey-haired captain, of slight, well-knit figure, whose clear strong voice made every word audible. Instead of the Psalms appointed for the day, he chose the 46th Psalm, "God is our hope and strength," etc., which, as he said, "Luther was wont to use in seasons of peculiar difficulty and depression." The words, well-suited to the desperate circumstances of the garrison, expressed their determination to defend the battlements to the last extremity. They expressed, also, the sublime dependence upon God which was the strength of Henry Havelock, who officiated as chaplain. He was then an unknown man, though he had served with distinction in Burma, in Afghanistan, Gwalior, and the Sutlej. Fifteen years later, when he died at the Alumbagh, after the relief of Lucknow, his name was a household word. His death was worthy of his life. " I have for forty years," he said, " so ruled my life, that, when death came, I might face it without fear." His headlong march, his rapid victories—when the fate of British rule seemed trembling in the balance—had made him the idol of the nation. He had shown by his career, if such an example be needed, that saints can be soldiers, and that those fear men least who fear God most.

When Havelock died (November 24th, 1857), the worst of the Indian Mutiny was over. But the awful weeks which preceded his successes, had strained to the utmost tension the confidence which men and women reposed in the mysterious workings of the Divine purpose. Yet Dr. Duff, writing from Calcutta in May 1857, relied on the promises of the Psalms. In the midst of panic, open mutiny, and secret disaffection, he himself felt " a confident persuasion that, though this crisis has been permitted to humble and warn us, our work in India has not yet been accomplished; and that until it be accomplished, our tenure of Empire, however brittle, is secure." . . . " Never before," he continues, " did I realise as now the literality and sweetness of the Psalmist's assurance—' I laid me down and slept; I awaked; for the Lord sustained me. I will not be afraid of ten thousands of people, that have set themselves against me round about. Arise, O Lord; save me, O my God!' " (Ps. iii., verses 5-7).

Among records of hairbreadth escapes during the Indian Mutiny, few are more striking than the story of Mr. William Edwards, the magistrate and collector of Budaon, in the Rohilkund district. From June 1st, 1857, to August 27th, when he joined Havelock at Cawnpore, he was a fugitive.

With him were a brother collector, Mr. Probyn, Mrs. Probyn, and their four children. Weeks of mental anguish were passed among natives, whose loyalty was doubtful, and who were under the strongest temptation to treachery. At first they were huddled together at Kussowrah, in a cow-house, from which they were forbidden to emerge, hearing at intervals of merciless massacres by natives, and tortured by anxiety for the safety of relations or friends. From Kussowrah they were moved to a village called Runjepoorah ("the place of affliction"), a collection of huts gathered on a bare island a hundred yards square, which rose above floods that stretched almost as far as the eye could reach. Here, during the day, they were so closely packed that the only possible change of posture was sitting up or turning from one side to the other. From Futteghur they heard the bands of the mutineers playing English airs, and from Furruckabad came the sound of guns, which, they learned, were blowing away or shooting down women and children. One gleam of comfort came to Mr. Edwards, but even that was darkened with a moment of despair. His wife and child were at Nynee Tal, ignorant of his fate. A native promised, if possible, to convey to them a note. Mr. Edwards had only a tiny scrap of paper, half the fly-leaf of *Bridges on the 119th Psalm*. On this he wrote his message in pencil, dipped it in milk to make the writing indelible, and set it out to dry. He had hardly done so, when a crow pounced on it and carried it off. But fortunately his native servant had seen what had happened, followed the bird, and recovered the note.

On July 26th, they were able to return to the cow-house at Kussowrah. Their quarters were less cramped. But the heat was terrible; tormented by myriads of flies, starting at every unusual noise, they could only sleep when they had lighted heaps of dried cow-dung, which poured out volumes of acrid smoke and kept the insects at bay. One of the Probyn children died, and then another. The Psalms, however, proved to them a storehouse of comfort. "There is not a day," writes Mr. Edwards in his Diary for August 5th, " on which we do not find something that appears as if written especially for persons in our unhappy circumstances, to meet the feelings and wants of the day. This morning, for instance, I derived unspeakable comfort from the 13th and 16th verses of the 25th Psalm (" The secret of the Lord is among them that fear Him; and He will show them His covenant," and " The sorrows of my heart are enlarged: O bring Thou me out of my troubles "); and in the evening, from the 14th, 15th, and 16th verses of the 27th (verse 16, " O tarry Thou the Lord's leisure; be strong, and He shall comfort thine heart; and put thou thy trust in the Lord ").

After a sleepless night, devoured by mosquitoes, depressed in mind and body, he writes, August 16th: " It is at such times I feel the real blessing the Psalms are. They never fail to give peace and refreshment, when all is dark and gloomy within and without. The circumstances under which many of them were written, seasons of danger and almost despair—David fleeing and hiding from bloodthirsty enemies, as we are—render them peculiarly suitable to our case. This morning I felt the 5th verse of the 68th Psalm most soothing, in the assurance it gives me that, if I am cut off, my God will be with my widow and fatherless children." (" He is a Father of the fatherless, and defendeth the cause of the widows, even God in His holy habitation.") Or again, on August 24th he notes, " Finished to-day, for the second time, that excellent work, *Bridges on the 119th Psalm ;* the sole book in my hands, except the Bible, for the past two months; and fortunate have I been to have had these sources of consolation." They were now in communication with Havelock; but the difficulty of traversing a country infested with mutineers was great. " Nothing new settled," writes Edwards on August 27th, " about our plans, and we are much harassed. Heavy guns firing at Furruckabad to-day, we know not from what cause; but they reminded us painfully of our fearful proximity to that place where are so many thirsting for our lives. Amidst it all, to-day's Psalms are most consoling, and wonderfully suited to our case, especially the 121st." (" I will lift up mine eyes unto the hills, from whence cometh my help.")

Three days later, the party started to run the gauntlet for 150 miles of river way, through the midst of the enemy's country. The journey was successfully made. After three months of hourly suspense and danger, they were safe with the British troops.

From the Psalms the quiet confidence of Dr. Duff drew its serenity; from them also the endurance of Mr. Edwards derived its patient fortitude. The relief of Lucknow showed that the active daring, which not only braves death but courts it, may be equally stirred by the Psalms. " Quaker " Wallace of the 93rd regiment, went into the Secundrabagh, says an eye-witness, " like one of the Furies, if there are any male Furies plainly seeking death, but not meeting it," and quoting the 116th Psalm, Scottish version in metre, beginning at the first verse :

> " I love the Lord, because my voice
> And prayers He did hear.
> I, while I live, will call on Him,
> Who bowed to me His ear."

And thus he plunged into the Secundrabagh, quoting a line at every shot fired from his rifle, and at each thrust given by his bayonet :

> " I'll of salvation take the cup,
> On God's name will I call;
> I'll pay my vows now to the Lord
> Before His people all."

The Indian Mutiny does not afford the latest example of the influence of the Psalms on our secular history. Even in the present century, they have shown their power on the battlefields of nations. It would not be wholly fanciful to compare the struggle carried on by the Scottish Covenanters against seventeenth-century England, with the challenge thrown down by the Boers to the British Empire of the twentieth century. In their pastoral habits, their civilisation, their education, their deep, yet narrow religion, their sturdy independence, Boers and Covenanters stand close together. To us, who regard the conflicts from the vantage-ground of the past, it may seem that the triumph of the large battalions was from the first inevitable. Yet in both cases geographical conditions favoured the smaller force, and foreign aid, or civil discord, was not unreasonably anticipated. Both Boer and Covenanter arrogated to himself the promises of the Psalms. To the dwellers on the solitary veldts of South Africa, the words appealed with the same peculiar force which they had possessed for the inhabitants of the lonely recesses of the Lowland hills, and both Covenanter and Boer fought in the conviction that the Lord of Hosts was on his side.

In President Kruger's frequent appeals to the Psalms, it is unnecessary to discover hypocrisy. Treachery, guile, cruelty, even if such faults could fairly be laid to his charge, are not inconsistent with religious sincerity, when minds of a peculiar type and training are imbued with the spirit of the Old Testament, or convinced that they are fighting the Lord's battle against His enemies. It is as a Cromwellian captain, or as a Scottish Covenanter, that he addresses his burghers in language which goes directly to their hearts. His speech to the Volksraads on October 2nd, 1899, couched in the language of the Psalms, interpreted their promises in favour of the Boers. "Read," he said, "that psalm attentively (Ps. cviii., 'O God, my heart is ready,' etc.), and associate your prayers with that: then will the Lord guide us; and, when He is with us, who shall be against us?" Similar was his speech on May 7th, 1900, in opening the Volksraads. There he applied the words of Psalm lxxxiii. ("Hold not Thy tongue, O God," etc.) to the struggle with the British Empire, and dwelt especially on verse 4, where the enemies of God say, "Come, and let us root them out, that they be no more a people; and that the name of Israel may be no more in remembrance." "Psalm lxxxiii.," argued the President, "speaks of the attacks of the Evil One on Christ's Kingdom, which must no longer exist. And now the same words come from Salisbury, for he too says, 'This people must not exist,' and God says, 'This people shall exist.' Who will win? Surely, the Lord." So again, in his circular despatch to his officers, dated from Machadodorp, June 20th, 1900, he returned to the same passage. "According to Psalm lxxxiii., the enemies of old said that the people shall not exist in Christ's Kingdom. Salisbury and Chamberlain stand convicted by their own words: 'They shall not exist'; but the Lord says, 'This people shall exist,' and Christ is our Commander-in-Chief, Who leads us with His Word." Or, lastly, it is again to the Psalms that he made his appeal a month later, in a final despatch to his officers from Machadodorp: "See," he wrote, "the promise of the Lord in Psalm cviii., where He says, they who fight through God shall do so valiantly, and the Lord will deliver them, and tread down their enemies. Keep courage, therefore, you God-fearing band; the Lord will display His strength to your weakness. . . . Each of ye knows as I do, how unjust and godless the war is, as we were willing to yield almost everything, if we could only keep our liberty and our independence. See Psalm lxxxiii., how the evil spirit of the air said that the valiant fighter named Israel must not exist, and the Lord says, 'He shall exist.' . . . Then the same spirit answered that this nation must not exist, or, to use his own words, 'I will not permit your nation to continue to be a nation.' Dear brothers, through God's Word I am sure of this, that the victory is ours."

A German mystic has said, " He whom God deludes is well deluded." In its entirety, the saying in a hard one; yet it contains a truth. Only the immediate issues in the Boer War have been at present decided. The ultimate effects on the civilised progress of the world and the general interests of mankind belong to the region of the future and of hope. But as it has been with the Covenanters, so it may be with the Boers. Virtues which lent dignity and pathos to the struggle for independence may gain a broader sphere of exercise than the narrow field on which they were previously concentrated. The record of the Cameronian Regiment, raised among the defeated Covenanters, and first commanded by one of the leaders at Drumclog, may be reproduced on a larger scale in the future history of the Boer people.

When the pages of some ancient brown-bound volume are turned, there flutters from between the leaves the withered petal of a rose. The flower is faded, dry, scentless; but it has imprinted something of its shape and colour on the pages between which it has been pressed. As it floats to the ground, the most unimaginative of us is conscious of the desire to read its secret. What moment of joy or sorrow, of despair or hope, did it commemorate in the distant days, when the page was yet unstained, the petal full of fragrance and colour, the hand that placed it there still throbbing with life?

Something similar is the effect of studying the Psalms through human history. There is scarcely a leaf in the Psalter which is not stained by some withered flower of the past. To gather some of these petals and read their meaning, as they fall thick from the pages, has been the purpose of this book. Vain must be the effort to recall to life persons or events divided from us by centuries of change. But as we read the familiar verses, the words bring before us, one by one, the hundreds of men and women, who, passing from tribulation into joy, have, in the language of the Psalms, conquered the terrors of death, proclaimed their faith, or risen to new effort and final victory.

APPENDICES

APPENDIX A

PRINCIPAL AUTHORITIES

CHAPTER I (pages 1-8).

ARCHBISHOP ALEXANDER—*The Witness of the Psalms to Christ and Christianity.* 1877. (Bampton Lectures for 1876.)

C. L. MARSON—*The Psalms at Work.* 2nd ed. 1895.

JOHN KER—*The Psalms in History and Biography.* 1886.
 [See also my Article on " The Psalms in History " in the *Quarterly Review* for April 1897, vol. clxxxv., p. 305.]

JOHN SMEATON—*A Narrative of the Building and a Description of the Construction of the Edystone Lighthouse with stone, etc.* 1791.

Official Description and Illustrated Catalogue of the Great Exhibition of 1851.

MRS. ALFRED GATTY—*The Book of Sundials.* Enlarged and re-edited by Horatia K. F. Eden and Eleanor Lloyd. 4th ed. 1900.

CHARLES LEADBETTER—*Mechanick Dialling ; or, The New Art of Shadows, etc.* 1737.

HERBERT A. GRUEBER—*Handbook of the Coins of Great Britain and Ireland.* (Appendix B.) 1899.

LEOPOLD G. WICKHAM LEGG—*English Coronation Records.* 1901.

SIR PHILIP SIDNEY—*The Psalmes of David, etc. . . . Begun by the noble and learned gent. Sir Philip Sidney, Kt., and finished by the Right Honourable the Countess of Pembroke, his sister. Now first printed from a copy of the original manuscript transcribed by John Davies, of Hereford, in the reign of James the First.* 1823.

FRANCIS BACON—*Certaine Psalmes in Verse.* 1625.

GEORGE SANDYS—*A Paraphrase upon the First Booke of the Psalmes of David.* 1636.

HENRY HOWARD, EARL OF SURREY—*Poems.* 1547.

Appendix A

SIR THOMAS WYATT—*The Seven Penitential Psalmes drawen into English Meter.* 1549. *Poems.* (Aldine edition.)

SIR THOMAS SMITH—*Certaigne Psalmes or Songues of David.* 1549. (MS. Brit. Mus.)

SIR HENRY WOTTON—Psalm civ. in *Reliquiæ Wottoniæ.*

JOHN HOOKHAM FRERE—*Selection of Psalms.* (*Works*, ed. 1872, vol. ii.)

ARCHBISHOP MATTHEW PARKER—*The whole Psalter, etc.*, N.D. [1560.]

BISHOP JOSEPH HALL—*Some few of David's Psalmes metaphrazed in Metre.* 1607. (*Works*, vol. ix. Ed. Philip Wynter. 1863.)

BISHOP HENRY KING—*The Psalms of David from the New Translation of the Bible, turned into Meeter.* 1651.

BISHOP SAMUEL WOODFORD—*A Paraphrase in English Verse, upon the Books of the Psalms.* 1667.

QUEEN ELIZABETH—Psalm xiv. (See *A Godly Meditation of the Christian Soul.* 1548.)

KING JAMES I.—*The Psalmes of King David.* 1631.

FRANCIS ROUS—*The Psalmes of David in English Meeter.* 1641.

THOMAS, LORD FAIRFAX—(unpublished). See Preface to Henry Cotton's *Editions of the Bible and parts thereof in English.* 2nd ed. 1852.

GEORGE WITHER—*The Psalms translated into Lyric Verse, according to the Scope of the Original.* 1632.

PHINEHAS FLETCHER—Six Psalms were published in *Miscellanies*, appended to his *Purple Island.* 1633. [See *Poetical Works.* Ed. A. B. Grosart. 4 vols. 1869.]

RICHARD CRASHAW. *Steps to the Temple.* 1646.

HENRY VAUGHAN—*Silex Scintillans.* (Psalm cxxxi.) 1650.

ROBERT BURNS—Psalms i., xiv. in *Poetical Works.* Ed. 1787. [See Robert Chambers's *Life and Works of Burns*, vol. i., 1856.]

WILLIAM COWPER—Psalm cxxxvii. in *Poems.*

JOHN MILTON—Psalms cxiv., cxxxvi. (1623). lxxx-lxxxviii. (1648). i.-viii. (1653). [See *Poems in English and Latin.* 2nd ed. 1673.]

GEORGE HERBERT—1632. Seven versions first printed in *Fuller's Worthies Library.* Ed. A. B. Grosart. 1874.

JOHN KEBLE—*The Psalter, or Psalms of David in English Verse, by a member of the University of Oxford.* 1839.

Appendix A

SIR RICHARD BLACKMORE—*Version of the Book of Psalms.* 1721.

LUKE MILBOURNE—*The Psalms of David in English Metre.* 1698.

JOSEPH ADDISON—Psalm xxiii. *Spectator*, No. 441. Psalm xix. *Spectator*, No. 465.

CHARLES WESLEY—*The Poetical Works of John and Charles Wesley, etc.* Collected and arranged by George Osborn. 13 vols. 1868-72.

ISAAC WATTS—*The Psalms of David Imitated in the Language of the New Testament, And apply'd to the Christian State and Worship*, by I. Watts. 1719.

ROUSSEAU—*Les Confessions de J. J. Rousseau.* 1781, 1788.

GOETHE—*Aus Meinem Leben—Dichtung und Wahrheit.* 1811.

ST. AUGUSTINE—*Confessions.* Trans. and ed. Charles Bigg, D.D., 1898.

De Imitatione Christi. Ed. John Kells Ingram. (Early English Text Society; Extra Series, No. lxiii. 1893.)

JOHN BUNYAN—*Grace abounding to the Chief of Sinners; in a Faithful Account of the Life and Death of John Bunyan, etc.* 1666.

BISHOP LANCELOT ANDREWES—*Rev. Patris Lanc. Andrews Episc. Winton. Preces Privatæ Græce et Latine.* (Oxonii e Theatro Sheldoniano, MDCLXXV). Ed. Peter Goldsmith Medd. 1892. Trans. by John Henry Newman; "Tracts for the Times," No. 88.

[See also *Lancelot Andrewes*, by Robert Lawrence Ottley. Appendix D. 1894.]

BLAISE PASCAL—*Pensées de M. Pascal sur la Religion et sur quelques autres sujets, qui ont esté trouvées après sa mort parmy ses papiers.* 1669.

CHAPTER II (pages 9-30).

GIBBON—*Decline and Fall of the Roman Empire.* Ed. J. B. Bury. 7 vols. 1896-1900.

CANON BRIGHT—*A History of the Church, A.D. 313-451.* 2nd ed. 1869.
The Age of the Fathers. 2 vols. 1903.

WILLIAM PALMER—*Dissertations on Subjects relating to the Orthodox Communion.* Dissertation xx. 1853.

ALBAN BUTLER—*Lives of the Saints.* 12 vols. 1756, etc.

286 Appendix A

S. BARING-GOULD—*Lives of the Saints*. New Edition. 16 vols. 1897-98.

LAURENTIUS SURIUS—*Historiæ seu Vitæ Sanctorum*. 6 vols. 1581.

SMITH AND WACE—*Dictionary of Christian Biography*. 4 vols. 1877-87.

AMBROSE—*In Psalmum I Enarratio*. (Migne, xiv. 925.) *Hexaemeron*. (*Ibid.*, 223.)

AMÉDÉE S. D. THIERRY—*Saint Jérôme*. 2 tomes. 1867.

CARL ULLMANN—*Life of Gregory of Nazianzum*. Trans. George Valentine Cox. 1851.

ST. AUGUSTINE—*Confessions*. Trans. and ed. Charles Bigg, D.D., 1898.

L'ABBÉ BAUNARD—*Vie de Saint Ambroise*. 1871.

J. H. NEWMAN—*Historical Sketches*. 3 vols. 1872-3.

ATHANASIUS—*Apologia de Fugâ Suâ*.

DEAN STANLEY—*Lectures on the History of the Eastern Church*. 1861.

The Letter of Paula and Eustochium to Marcella about the Holy Places. Trans. Aubrey Stewart. 1889. (Palestine Pilgrims' Text Society, vol i.)

C. F. R. DE MONTALEMBERT—*Moines de l'Occident*. Ed. 1860-77. (References throughout to English edition, with introduction by Gasquet. 6 vols. 1896.)
   [See also my Article, " Rabelais at home," in *Blackwood's Magazine* for April 1894, vol. clv., p. 504.]

J. V. A. DE BROGLIE—*L'Eglise et l'Empire Romain au IVe. Siècle*. 6 tomes. 1856-66.

JOSEPH M'CABE—*Saint Augustine and his Age*. 1902.

AUGUSTUS J. C. HARE—*Studies in Russia*. 1885.

CHAPTER III (pages 31-51).

PROCOPIUS—*De Bello Vandalico ; De Bello Gotthico*.

Flodoardi historia Remensis Ecclesiæ. Ed. John Heller et G. Waitz. (Pertz M. G. H. xiii. 405.)

JOHN PINKERTON—*Vitæ antiquæ Sanctorum Scotiæ*. Ed. Metcalfe. 2 vols. Paisley. 1889.

J. H. NEWMAN—*The Lives of the English Saints, written by various hands at the suggestion of John Henry Newman, afterwards Cardinal.* 6 vols. 1900-1.

JOHN LINGARD—*The History and Antiquities of the Anglo-Saxon Church.* 3rd ed. 2 vols. 1845.

JOHN O'HANLON—*Lives of the Irish Saints.* 1875, etc.

MARGARET STOKES—*Six months in the Apennines ; or, A Pilgrimage in search of vestiges of the Irish saints in Italy.* 1892.
Three months in the forests of France ; A pilgrimage in search of vestiges of the Irish saints in France. 1895.

GEORGE THOMAS STOKES—*Ireland and the Celtic Church : a history of Ireland from St. Patrick to the English conquest in 1172.* 3rd ed. 1892.

THOMAS HODGKIN—*Italy and her Invaders.* 8 vols. 1880-1899.

A. H. HOFFMANN VON FALLERSLEBEN—*Fundgruben für Geschichte deutscher Sprache und Literatur.* 2 Bde. 1830-37.

D. H. STOEVER—*Life of Sir C. Linæus.* Trans. Joseph Trapp. 1794.

C. J. HEFELE—*History of the Church Councils.* Trans. W. R. Clark. Vol. iv. 1871, etc.

STEPHEN BALUZE—*Capitularia Regum Francorum.* Tome i. 1677.

Vita Columbani, auctore Jona Monacho. (Migne, lxxxvii., 1014.)

Tripartite Life of St. Patrick. Ed. Whitley Stokes. (Rolls Series, 89.)

ADAMNAN—*Vita S. Columbæ.* Ed. William Reeves. 1857. (See also trans. and ed. Joseph Thomas Fowler, D.C.L. 1895.)

BEDE—*Vita S. Cuthberti.*

S. Gregorii Magni Vita, auctore Joanne diacono. (Migne, lxxv., 230.)

Vita Hugonis Cluniensis, auctore Hildeberto Cenomanensi Episcopo. (Migne, clix., 867.)

EDUARD WOELFFLIN—*Benedicti Regula Monachorum.* 1895.
Abrégé de la Vie de S. François de Borgia. 1671.

DOM VINCENT SCULLY—*Life of the Venerable Thomas à Kempis.* 1901.

Vita S. Dunstani, auctore Adelardo. Ed. Stubbs. (Rolls Series, 63.)

Appendix A

Chapter IV (pages 52-86).

H. Martin—*Histoire de France.* 4th ed.

L. Sergeant—*The Franks.* (Stories of the Nations.) 1898.

F. R. Guettée—*Histoire de l'Eglise de France.* 1856.

Sir James Stephen—*Essays in Ecclesiastical Biography.* Ed. 1891.

M. Bouquet—*Recueil des historiens des Gaules et de la France.* "Pepin et Charlemagne." Tome V. Nouvelle ed. 1869.

James Bryce—*The Holy Roman Empire.* New ed. Revised. 1866.

J. W. Bowden—*Life of Gregory VII.* 2 vols. 1840.

R. W. Church—*Anselm.* Ed. 1888.

C. De Rémusat—*S. Anselme de Cantorbéry.* 2me. ed.

Dean Stanley—*Memorials of Canterbury.* Ed. 1868.
Lectures on the History of the Eastern Church. 1861.

E. G. Gardner—*The Story of Siena.* 1902.

H. F. Reuter—*Geschichte Alexanders des dritten, und die Kirche seiner Zeit.* 1860-4.

The Pilgrimage of S. Silvia of Aquitania to the Holy Places. Trans. John H. Bernard, 1891 (Palestine Pilgrims' Text Society, vol. i.)

Of The Holy Places visited by Antoninus Martyr. Trans. Aubrey Stewart, 1887 (Palestine Pilgrims' Text Society, vol. ii.)

Theodosius on the Topography of the Holy Land. Trans. J. H. Bernard, 1893 (Palestine Pilgrims' Text Society, vol. ii.)

S. Silviæ Aquitanæ Peregrinatio ad loca Sancta quæ inedita ex codice Aretino deprompsit Joh. Franc. Gamurrini. 1887.

Antonini Placentini Itinerarium. (Corp. Script. Eccl. Lat. xxxiiii., 173.)

Theodosius De Situ Terræ Sanctæ. (Ibid., 135.)

Dean Hook—*Lives of the Archbishops of Canterbury.* Vol. ii.

Itinerarium regis Anglorum Richardi et aliorum in terram Hierosolymorum auciore Gaufrido Vinisauf. Apud Historiæ Anglicanæ Scriptores Quinque. Ed. Thos. Gale. Vol. ii., p. 245. 1687.

Karamsin—*Histoire de Russie.* Tomes ii, v.

Appendix A

J. H. NEWMAN—*The Lives of the English Saints, written by various hands*, etc., vol. i.

Narratio de Fundatione Fontanis Monasterii in Comitatu Eboracensi. Ed. J. R. Walbran. 1863. Vol. i. (Surtees Society, 42.)

Epistolæ Cantuarienses. No. cccxlvi. Ed. Stubbs. (Rolls Series, 38b.)

P. SABATIER—*Life of St. Francis of Assisi.* Trans. L. S. Houghton. 1896.

Speculum Perfectionis; seu S. Francisci Assisiensis Legenda Antiquissima, auctore Fratre Leone. Trans. Sebastian Evans. 1898.

MATTHEW ARNOLD—*Essays in Criticism.* First series. 1865.

C. J. VON HEFELE—*Life and Times of Cardinal Ximenes.* Trans. Dalton. 1885.

ORDERICUS VITALIS—*Historia ecclesiastica*, etc. Apud Monumenta Germaniæ Historica. Ed. Pertz. Scriptores xx., 50.

MOURAVIEFF—*The Church of Russia.* Trans. Blackmore. 1842.

J. COTTER MORISON—*Life of St. Bernard.* 1863.

JOSEPH M'CABE—*Peter Abélard.* 1901.

JOHN PINKERTON — *Vitæ antiquæ Sanctorum Scotiæ.* Ed. Metcalfe. 1889.

P. FRASER TYTLER—*Scottish Worthies.* 3 vols. 1831-33.

F. PERRY—*St. Louis.* 1901.

S. KETTLEWELL—*Authorship of the " De Imitatione Christi."* 1871.
 Thomas à Kempis and the Brothers of Common Life. 2 vols. 1882.

C. WOLFEGRÛBER—*Giovanni Gersen, sein Leben und sein Werk " De Imitatione Christi."* 1880.

DANTE—*Divina Commedia.* Trans. Cary.

W. LANGLAND—*Vision of Piers Plowman.* Ed. Skeat.
 [For the legends of South-Western France, see my Article, " French Stone-Superstitions " in the *Anglican Church Magazine* for October 1888, vol. v., p. 19.]

DRUMMOND OF HAWTHORNDEN—"*A Hymn of the Ascension.*" (Muses Library Edition, vol. ii,)

The Golden Legend. Trans. W. Caxton. (Temple Classics, ed. Ellis.)

Appendix A

CHAPTER V (pages 87-109).

BISHOP CREIGHTON—*History of the Papacy from the Great Schism to the Sack of Rome.* New Ed. 6 vols. 1897.
  John Wyclif at Oxford. Church Quarterly Review for October 1877. Reprinted in " Historical Essays and Reviews." 1902.
  Influence of the Reformation upon England, with Special Reference to the Works and Writings of John Wyclif. A Paper read at the Carlisle Church Congress, 1884. Reprinted in " The Church and the Nation." 1901.

B. NIEHUES—*Geschichte des Verhältnisses zwischen Kaiserthum und Papstthum im Mittelalter.* 1863.

L'ABBÉ J. B. CHRISTOPHE — *Histoire de la Papauté pendant le XVme. Siècle.* 2 tomes. 1863.

J. LOSERTH—*Hus und Wiclif.* 1884.
  [See also my Article on " John Wyclif," in the *Church Quarterly Review* for October 1891 (vol. xxxiii., p. 115), and the authorities there cited.]

J. WYCLIF—*De quatuor Sectis Novellis.* (Wyclif Society, Polemical Works, vol. i., 1883.)

T. WALSINGHAM—*Historia Anglicana.* Ed. H. T. Riley. Vol. ii. (Rolls Series, 28.)

PASQUALE VILLARI—*Life and Times of Girolamo Savonarola.* Trans. Linda Villari. 2 vols. 1888.

MARGARET OLIPHANT—*Makers of Florence . . . and their City.* 1876.
  [See also my Articles on " Savonarola " in the *Edinburgh Review* for July 1889 (vol. clxxix., p. 68), and in the *Church Quarterly Review* for July 1889 (vol. xxviii., p. 426), and the authorities there cited.]

Meditatio pia et erudita Hier. Savonarolæ a papa exusti, supra Psalmos " Miserere mei " *et* " In te, Domine, speravi " *cum præfatione Lutheri.* 1523.

J. C. L. GIESELER—*Ecclesiastical History.* Trans. J. W. Hull. 1853. Vol. iv.

Table-talk of Martin Luther. Trans. and ed. W. Hazlitt. 1890.

Martin Luther's erste und älteste Vorlesungen über die Psalmen. Ed. J. C. Seidemann. 1876.

Appendix A 291

JULIUS KOESTLIN—*Martin Luther; sein Leben und seine Schriften.* 2nd ed. 1883.

FÉLIX KUHN—*Luther, sa Vie et son œuvre.* 2 tomes. 1883, etc.

T. CARLYLE—*Critical and Miscellaneous Essays.* 7 vols. 1889.

SIR W. STIRLING-MAXWELL—*The Cloister Life of the Emperor Charles V.* 3rd ed. 1853.

CLEMENTS R. MARKHAM—*Life of Christopher Columbus.* 1892.

HENRY HARRISSE—*Christophe Colombe, son origine, sa vie, ses voyages, sa famille, et ses descendants.* 2 tomes. 1884.

JUSTIN WINSOR—*Christopher Columbus, and how he received and imparted the spirit of Discovery.* 1893.

Hakluyt Society, vol. ii. (1847); vol. xliii. (1870); vol. lxxxvi. (1893).

BISHOP STUBBS—*Seventeen Lectures on the Study of Medieval and Modern History.* 3rd ed. 1900.

T. E. BRIDGETT—*Life and Writings of Sir Thomas More.* 1891. *Life of Blessed John Fisher.* 1888.

WILLIAM ROPER—*Life and Death of Sir Thomas More.* Ed. S. W. Singer. 1822.

PAUL FRIEDMANN—*Anne Boleyn.* 2 vols. 1884.

JAMES GAIRDNER—*Letters and Papers.* Vols. vii., ix.

J. M. N. D. NISARD—*Renaissance et Réforme.* 3rd. ed. 1877.

F. SEEBOHM—*The Oxford Reformers of 1498.* 1867.

Giovanni Pico della Mirandola, his Life; by G. F. Pico. Also three of his Letters, and his interpretation of Psalm XVI. Trans. by Sir T. More. Ed. J. M. Rigg. 1890.

Erasmi Epistolæ. Ed. Leyden.

Early English Text Society (Extra Series, XXVII.)—*Treatyse concernynge . . . the seuen Penytencyall Psalmes.* Emprynted by Wynkyn de Worde, 12 Iuyn, M.CCCC.IX. (English Works of John Fisher. Part I. Ed. J. E. B. Mayor. 1876.)

LORD ACTON—*Wolsey and the Divorce of Henry VIII.* (*Quarterly Review* for January, 1877.)

A. WOLTMANN—*Holbein and his Time.* Trans. F. E. Bunnett. 1872.

J. M. STONE—*Faithful unto Death. An Account of the Sufferings of the English Franciscans during the 16th and 17th Centuries.* 1892.

J. A. FROUDE—*History of England.* Ed. 1856.

Appendix A

Life and Letters of St. Francis Xavier. Ed. Henry James Coleridge. New Ed. 2 vols. 1886.
 [See also my Article on "St. Francis Xavier" in the *Church Quarterly Review* for April 1889 (vol. xxviii., p. 160), and the authorities there cited.]

Mrs. G. CUNNINGHAME GRAHAM—*Santa Teresa,* etc. 2 vols. 1894.

Life and Letters of St. Teresa. Ed. Henry James Coleridge. 3 vols. 1881.

PARKER SOCIETY—*Later Writings of Bishop Hooper.* Ed. C. Nevinson. 1852.

JOHN FOXE—*Acts and Monuments.* Vol. vii. (Ed. Pratt and Stoughton; 8 vols.) 1877.

JOHN BAYLEY—*History and Antiquities of the Tower of London.* 2nd ed. 1830.

ROBERT SOUTHWELL—*Complete Poems.* Ed. A. B. Grosart. 1872. (*Fuller's Worthies Library.*)

CHAPTER VI (pages 110-136).

Dictionary of Hymnology. Ed. John Julian. See "Old Version." "Psalters, English"; "Psalters, French"; "Scottish Hymnody"; "German Hymnody."

C. E. P. WACKERNAGEL—*Das deutsche Kirchenlied von der ältesten Zeit,* etc. Leipzig, 5 Bde. 1864-7.

CATHARINE WINKWORTH—*Chorale Book for England.* 1863. Nos. 40, 101, 149.
 Christian Singers of Germany. 1869.
 Lyra Germanica. 2nd Series. 1858.

FELIX BOVET—*Histoire du Psautier des Eglises Réformées.* 1872.

E. O. DOUEN—*Clément Marot et le Psautier Huguenot,* etc. 2 tomes. 1878.
 Histoire ecclésiastique des Eglises Réformées du royaume de France. Tome I. (Wrongly attributed to Beza.) 3 tomes. 1841-42.

THOMAS STERNHOLD—*Certayne Psalmes, chose out of the Psalter of David and drawe into Englishe metre by Thomas Sternhold, grome of ye Kyng's Maiestie's roobes.* N.D.
 Al such Psalmes of David as Thomas Sternholde, late grome of the Kynge's Maiestie's roobes, did in his lyfe tyme drawe into English metre. (1549).

Appendix A

THOMAS STERNHOLD (*continued*)

Psalmes of David in Metre, drawen into Englishe Metre by M. Sterneholde. Imprinted in London in Flete Strete at the signe of the Sunne over against the conduit by Edward Whitchurche, the xxii day of June, ANNO DOM. 1551.

One and fiftie Psalmes of Dauid in Englishe Metre, whereof 37 were made by Thomas Sternholde, ad the rest by others, etc. 1556.

The whole Book of Psalmes, collected into English metre by T. Sternhold, John Hopkins and others ; conferred with the Ebrue, with apt notes to sing them withal, etc. John Daye. 1562.

A New Version of the Psalmes of David, Fitted to the Tunes used in Churches, by N. Tate and N. Brady. 1696.

J. STRYPE—*The Life and Acts of Matthew Parker . . . Archbishop of Canterbury.* 1711.

Ane Copendious buik of godlie Psalmes and Spirituall Sangis. 1578.

The Forme of Prayers and Ministration of the Sacrament, etc., whereunto are also added sondrie other prayers, with the whole Psalmes of Dauid in English Meter. Printed at Edinburgh by Robert Lekprevik, MDLXIIII.

The Psalmes of King David, translated by King James. Oxford, 1631.

The Psalmes of David in Meter. Newly translated and diligently compared with the Original Text and former Translations : More plain, smooth, and agreeable to the Text than any heretofore. Allowed by the Authority of the General Assembly of the Kirk of Scotland, and appointed to be sung in Congregations and Families. Edinburgh, 1650.

T. WARTON—*History of English Poetry.* Vol. iv. Ed. Hazlitt. 4 vols. 1871.

The Chronicle of Queen Jane, etc. (Camden Society, Old Series. No. 48.)

JOHN LOTHROP MOTLEY—*The Rise of the Dutch Republic.* New edition. 3 vols. Ed. Moncure D. Conway. 1896.

Accounts and Papers relating to Mary Queen of Scots. (Camden Society, Old Series. No. 93.)

J. A. FROUDE—*History of England.* Vols. viii. and ix.

J. SKELTON—*Mary Stuart.* 1893.

J. HOSACK—*Mary Queen of Scots and her Accusers.* 2nd ed. 2 vols. 1870-74.

Appendix A

ANDREW LANG—*The Mystery of Mary Stuart.* 1901.

HON. M. M. MAXWELL SCOTT—*The Tragedy of Fotheringay*, etc. 1895.

LUCY AIKIN—*Memoirs of the Court of Queen Elizabeth.* 2 vols. Ed. 1818.

JOHN HOLLAND—*Psalmists of Britain.* 1843.

H. A. GLASS—*The story of the Psalters*, etc. 1888.

PHILIP JONES—*A true Report of a worthy fight, performed in the voyage from Turkie, by fiue ships of London, against 11 Gallies and two Frigats of the King of Spaines, at Pantalarea within the streights. Anno* 1586.

> [See p. 285 of the second volume of the *Principall Navigations, Voyages, Traffiques and Discoveries of the English Nation* . . . by Richard Hakluyt. 1599.]

The Casting away of the " Tobie " neere Cape Espartel, corruptly called Cape Sprat, without the straight of Gibraltar on the Coast of Barbarie, 1593.

> [See p. 201 of the Second Part of the second volume of Hakluyt's *Principall Navigations*, as above.]

JAMES SPEDDING—*An Account of the Life and Times of Bacon.* 1878.

WILLIAM STEBBING—*Sir Walter Raleigh.* (Re-issue, 1899.)

JOHN RUSKIN—*Bibliotheca Pastorum.* Vol. ii. (1877.) " Rock Honeycomb."

C. W. LE BAS—*The Life of Bishop Jewel.* 1832.

I. WALTON—*The Lives of* . . . *Mr. Richard Hooker, Mr. George Herbert*, etc. Ed. 1866.

G. HERBERT—*Works.* 2 vols. Ed. 1844.

RICHARD HOOKER—*Ecclesiastical Polity.*

CHAPTERS VII AND VIII (pages 137-172).

F. BOVET—*Histoire du Psautier des Eglises Réformées.* 1872.

E. O. DOUEN—*Clément Marot et le Psautier Huguenot*, etc. 2 tomes. 1878-9.

H. L. BORDIER—*Le Chansonnier Huguenot du XVIe. Siècle.* 1870.

A. COQUEREL, FILS—*Les Forçats pour la Foi.* Etude historique (1684-1775). 1866.

Appendix A

A. COURT—*Histoire des troubles des Cevennes, ou de la Guerre des Camisards*, etc. Nouvelle ed. 3 tomes. 1819.

FLORIMOND DE RÉMOND—*Histoire de la naissance, progrez, et décadence de l'hérésie de ce Siècle.* Rouen. 1623.

J. CRESPIN—*Histoire des Martyrs.* 1582.

F. STRADA—*De bello Belgico.*

N. A. F. PUAUX—*Histoire de la Réformation française.* 1857.

A. CROTTET—*Petite Chronique Protestante de France*, etc. 16me. Siècle. 1846.

G. VON POLENZ—*Geschichte des französischen Calvinismus bis zur Nationalversammlung.* 5 Bde. 1787.

E. BENOIST—*Histoire de l'édit de Nantes.* 1693-5. 3 tomes.

F. DE LA NOUE—*Discours politiques et militaires.* 1587.

F. LEGUAT—*Voyages et Avantures.* 2 tomes. 1708. (And see Hakluyt Society. 1891.)

H. MORLEY—*Life of Palissy.* 2 vols. 1852.

LOUIS PALAYSI—*Bernard Palissy et les débuts de la Réforme en Saintogne.* 1899.

Aulcuns Pseaulmes et Cantiques mys en Chant. A Strasburg. 1539.
    [Calvin's translations were Pss. xxv., xxxvi., xlvi., xci., cxxxviii.)

Les cinquante psaumes de Marot, suivis de la liturgie et du catéchisme et précédés de la préface de Calvin, du 10 Juin, 1543. Genève, 1543.
    [See Bovet, *Hist. du Psautier.* Bibliographie, 1ère. Partie, Nos. 5, 6.]

PAUL HENRY, D.D.—*The Life and Times of John Calvin, the Great Reformer.* Trans. H. Stebbing. 2 vols. 1899.

T. H. DYER—*The Life of John Calvin.* 1850.

BEZA—*Vie de J. Calvin, par Théodore de Bèze.* Nouvelle ed. publiée et annotée par Alfred Franklin. 1869.

Les Censures des théologiens de Paris par lesquelles ils auoyent faulsement condamné les Bibles imprimées par Robert Estienne . . . auec la response d'iceluy. 1552.

Bulletin de la Société d'histoire du Protestantisme. Tome iii.

JEAN DE SERRES—*Inventaire Général de l'histoire de France.* Ed. 1647.

F. A. GASQUET—*Henry VIII. and the English Monasteries.* 2 vols. 1888.

Appendix A

LADY GEORGIANA FULLERTON—*Life of Luisa de Carvajal.* 1873.
[For Coligny, see my Article on " Gaspard de Coligny " in the *Church Quarterly Review* for January 1891 (vol. xxxi., p. 361), and the authorities there cited.]

T. A. D'AUBIGNE—*Histoire Universelle.* 1616-20.

ANGLIVIEL DE LA BAUMELLE—*Mémoires pour servir à l'histoire de Madame de Maintenon.* 1755. (Letter of Madame d'Aubigné.) Also quoted by Puaux, *Hist. de la Réformation Française.* Tome V., and in P. de Noailles, *Hist. de Madame de Maintenon.* Tome I., chap. ii.
[For Henri de Rohan, and the Siege of La Rochelle, see my Article on " Henri de Rohan and the Huguenot Wars " in the *Edinburgh Review* for April 1890 (vol. clxxi., p. 389), and the authorities there cited.]

MONTAIGNE—*Essais.* Liv. I. ch. lvi. (des Prières).

PHIL. DESPORTES—*Les CL. Pseaumes mis en vers français.* 1598.

JEAN METEZEAU—*Les CL. Pseaumes mis en vers français*, etc. 1610.

MICHEL DE MARILLAC—*Les CL. Pseaumes de David,* etc. *Traduits en vers français.* 1625.

ANT. GODEAU—*Paraphrase des Pseaumes de David en vers français.* 1648.

R. F. WILSON—*Life of St. Vincent de Paul.* 1873.

H. HEINE—*Werke.* Ed. Hoffmann und Campe. Romanzero; Hebräische Melodien. Letter to Moser, 23rd May 1823.

BISHOP J. P. CAMUS—*Esprit de St. François de Sales.* Nouvelle ed. 3 tomes. 1840.

S. Francis de Sales, Bishop and Prince of Geneva. 1882. (" Christian Biographies." Ed. H. L. Sidney Lear.)

Mémoire véritable du prix excessive des vivres de la Rochelle pendant le siège. 1628.
[See E. Fournier, *Variétés historiques,* etc. 1855-63.]

Mémoires pour servir à l'histoire de Port Royal, et à la vie de la Révérende mère Marie Angélique de Sainte Magdeleine Arnauld. 3 tomes. Utrecht, 1742.

Histoire des Persecutions de Religieuses de Port Royal écrites par elles mêmes. (Rélation de ce qui s'est passé à Port Royal en 1661.) Chapitre xxii. Ville-Franche, 1753.

EMILE BOUTROUX—*Pascal.* (Les grands écrivains français.)

A. MONASTIER—*Histoire de l'Eglise Vaudoise.* 2 tomes. 1847.

B. MUSTON—*L'Israel des Alpes.* 4 tomes. 1851.

Appendix A

CHARLES COQUEREL—*Histoire des Eglises du Désert*, etc. 2 tomes, 1841. Tome II.

N. PEYRAT—*Histoire des Pasteurs du désert.* 2 tomes. 1842.

Théâtre Sacré des Cévennes (quoted by Douen, *Clément Marot*, etc. Tome I., p. 25).

CHAPTER IX (pages 173-196).

EDWARD ARBER—*The Story of the Pilgrim Fathers*, etc. 1897.

EDWARD JOHNSON—*Wonder-working Providence of Sion's Saviour : being a relation of the First Planting of New England in the Year* 1628. Part III. of Sir Ferdinando Gorge's *America Painted to the Life.* 1659.

The Works of Benjamin Franklin. Ed. Jared Sparks. 10 vols. 1840.

The Works of Jeremy Taylor, D.D. Ed. Heber. 15 vols. 1822.

IZAAK WALTON—*The Life of Dr. Robert Sanderson.* 1678.

The Letters and Journals of Robert Baillie, A.M. Edited for the Bannatyne Club by David Laing, vol. i. 3 vols. 1841-42.

WALTER FARQUHAR HOOK—*Lives of the Archbishops of Canterbury. Laud.* (New Series, vol. vi.) 1875.

SIR HENRY SLINGSBY—*Original Memoirs written during the Great Civil War.* Ed. Sir W. Scott. 1806.

CLARENDON, EARL OF—*History of the Rebellion and Civil Wars in England.* 8 vols. 1826.

JOHN MILTON—*Works.* "Globe" Edition. 1877.

JOHN BUNYAN—*Grace Abounding to the Chief of Sinners*, etc. 1666.

THOMAS CARLYLE—*Oliver Cromwell's Letters and Speeches.* Copyright Edition. 5 vols. 1888.

CHAPTER X (pages 197-224).

PATRICK WALKER—*Six Saints of the Covenant.* Ed. D. Hay Fleming. With a "Foreword" by S. R. Crockett. 1901.

JOHN KNOX—*The History of the Reformation of Religion within the Realm of Scotland.* Ed. Charles John Guthrie. 1898.

A Compendious Book of Godly and Spiritual Songs. Ed. A. F. Mitchell, D.D. 1897.

Appendix A

JOHN HOWIE—*Biographia Scoticana.* Ed. 1796.

Autobiography and Diary of Mr. James Melvill. Edited for the Wodrow Society. 1842.

JAMES DODDS—*The Fifty Years' Struggle of the Scottish Covenanters.* 1860.

ROBERT WODROW—*The History of the Sufferings of the Church of Scotland,* etc. Ed. Rev. R. Burns. 4 vols. 1828-30.

ANDREW CRICHTON—*Memoirs of the Rev. John Blackader.* 1823.

A Cloud of Witnesses for the Royal Prerogative of Jesus Christ, etc. Ed. J. H. Thomson. 1871.

JOSEPH M'CORMICK—*Life of Mr. Carstares.* (Prefixed to *State Papers and letters addressed to William Carstares,* etc.) Ed. 1774.

The Siege of Londonderry in 1689; as set forth in the Literary Remains of Col. The Rev. George Walker, D.D. Ed. Rev. Philip Dwyer. 1893.

CHAPTER XI (pages 225-249).

WILLIAM ORME—*Life of Richard Baxter.* (Prefixed to his *Works.* Ed. 1830.)
[See also my Articles on " Alexander Pope " and " Courthope's Life of Pope " in the *Edinburgh Review* for October 1884 (vol. clx., p. 295), and the *Quarterly Review* for October 1889 (vol. clxix., p. 247)].

WILLIAM LAW—*A Serious Call to a Devout and Holy Life,* etc., 1729.

EDWARD GIBBON—*Autobiographies.* Ed. John Murray. 1896.

[JOHN WESLEY]—*Collection of Psalms and Hymns.* (Charles Town. Printed by Lewis Timothy, 1737.) A facsimile reprint was published, with a Preface by Dr. Osborn, in London in 1882.

CHARLES WESLEY—*The Poetical Works of John and Charles Wesley,* etc. Collected and Arranged by George Osborn. 13 vols. 1868-72.

JOHN WESLEY—*Journal.* 4 vols. 1827.

LUKE TYERMAN—*Life of George Whitefield.* 2 vols. 1876-7.

PRINCE HOARE—*Memoirs of Granville Sharp.* 2nd ed. 2 vols. 1828.

Appendix A

Life of William Wilberforce. By his Sons. 2nd ed. 1843.

JOHN KEBLE—*The Christian Year.* 1828.
The Psalter, or Psalms of David, in English Verse, by a Member of the University of Oxford. 1839.

E. S. PURCELL—*Life of Cardinal Manning.* 2 vols. 1896.

J. H. NEWMAN—*Verses on Various Occasions: "The Dream of Gerontius."* New ed. 1893.

DEAN STANLEY—*Life and Correspondence of Thomas Arnold, D.D.* 2 vols. 1846.

Charles Kingsley; his Letters and Memories of his Life. Edited by his Wife. 2 vols. Ed. 1877.

ROBERT BUCHANAN—*The Ten Years' Conflict, being the History of the Disruption of the Church of Scotland.* 2 vols. 1849.

W. HANNA—*Memoirs of the Life and Writings of Thomas Chalmers, D.D., LL.D.,* 4 vols. 1849-53.

MRS. OLIPHANT—*The Life of Edward Irving.* 4th ed. 1865.

H. R. FOX BOURNE—*The Life of John Locke.* 2 vols. 1876.

F. H. ALEXANDER VON HUMBOLDT—*Cosmos.* Trans. Colonel Sabine. 2nd ed. 1846-58.

JOHN VEITCH—*Memoir of Sir William Hamilton, Bart.* 1869.

JOHN DUNS—*Memoir of Sir James Y. Simpson, Bart.* 1873.

The Life and Letters of George John Romanes. By his Wife. 1896.

ROBERT SOUTHEY—*Life of William Cowper.* (Prefixed to his *Works.*) Ed. 1836.

JOHN GIBSON LOCKHART—*Memoirs of the Life of Sir Walter Scott, Bart.* 10 vols. 1839.

MRS. GARDEN—*Memorials of James Hogg.* 1887.

JOHN GLYDE—*The Life of Edward Fitzgerald, with an Introduction by Edward Clodd.* 1900.

Letters and Literary Remains of Edward Fitzgerald. Ed. William Aldis Wright. 3 vols. 1889.

THOMAS CARLYLE—*On Heroes, Hero-worship, and the Heroic in History.* (See Lectures II. and V.) Ed. 1891.

JOHN RUSKIN—*Præterita.* Vol. i.
        Our Fathers have told Us. Chap. iii.
        Modern Painters. Part vii., Chap. iv.

Appendix A

CHAPTER XII (pages 250-279).

JAMES BALDWIN BROWN—*Memoirs of the Public and Private Life of John Howard.* 1818.

JOHN HOWARD—*An Account of the Principal Lazarettos in Europe,* etc. 1789.

CONVERS FRANCIS—*Life of John Eliot.* (*Library of American Biography*, ed. J. Sparks, vol. v., 1836.)

JONATHAN EDWARDS THE ELDER—*An Account of the Life of David Brainerd . . . chiefly . . . from his own Diary.* 1749.

GEORGE SMITH—*The Life of William Carey, D.D., Shoemaker and Missionary.* 1885.

The Life of Alexander Duff. 2 vols. 1879.

Journals and Letters of Henry Martyn. Ed. S. Wilberforce. 2 vols. 1837.

REV. JOHN SARGENT—*Memoir of the Life of Henry Martyn.* 1819.

REV. J. W. MARSH—*A Memoir of A. F. Gardiner.* 1857.

WILLIAM GARDEN BLAIKIE—*The Personal Life of David Livingstone.* 1880.

The Last Journals of David Livingstone. Ed. H. Waller. 2 vols. 1874.

E. C. DAWSON—*James Hannington, first Bishop of Eastern Equatorial Africa.* 1887.

Autobiography of Alexander Carlyle. 1860.

PHILIP DODDRIDGE—*Some Remarkable Passages in the Life of . . . Col. Gardiner.* 1747.

JAMES ANTHONY FROUDE—*Life of Thomas Carlyle : a History of his Life,* vol. ii. 4 vols. 1884.

Letters and Memorials of Jane Welsh Carlyle. 3 vols. 1883.

HONORÉ DE BALZAC—*Les Chouans ; ou la Bretagne en* 1799. 2nd ed. 1834.

LOUISE H. C. P. DE DURFORT, DUCHESSE DE DURAS—*Journal des Prisons de mon père, de ma mère et des miennes.* 1888.

Appendix A

CAPTAIN JOHN GROVER—*An Appeal to the British Nation in Behalf of Col. Stoddart and Capt. Conolly, now in Captivity in Bokhara.* 1843.

The Bokhara Victims. 2nd ed. 1845.

JOHN WILLIAM KAYE—*Lives of Indian Officers.* 2 vols. 1867.

JOHN CLARK MARSHMAN—*Memoirs of Major-General Sir H. Havelock.* 1860.

WILLIAM EDWARDS—*Personal Adventures during the Indian Rebellion,* etc. 1858.

W. FORBES MITCHELL—*Reminiscences of the Great Mutiny.* 1895.

PAUL KRUGER—*Memoirs, told by Himself.* 2 vols. 1902.

APPENDIX B

INDEX TO THE USE OF PARTICULAR PSALMS

IN this index the historical instances of the use of the Psalter, which in the text are given chronologically, are arranged under the particular Psalms to which they refer.

PSALMS I.-VIII.—Milton, 183
PSALM I.—Byron, 243; Ruskin, 248
   v. 2. Jerome, 19
   4. Boswell, 242
PSALM II.—Luther, 94
PSALM III.—English nation, 128; The Huguenots, 138
   v. 5, 6. Duff (Indian Mutiny), 273
PSALM IV.—Luther, 94
   v. 1. Augustine, 28, 29
   2. Augustine, 29
   7. James Melville, 201; James Gardiner, 268
   9. Gorgonia, 13; Luther, 13, 94; Langland, 83; Ridley, 109
PSALM V.—v. 7. Louis IX., 75
PSALM VI.—Becket, 58; Bishop Hooper, 106; Marot's version, 112 n.; Catherine de Medicis, 137
   v. 1. Florin of Edward III., 3
   2. Maine de Biran, 240
   2-4. Jane Welsh Carlyle, 269
   3. Calvin, 141
   6. Langland, 83
PSALM VIII.—Ruskin, 248
   v. 1, 2. Chaucer, 81
   2. Martin of Tours, 21, 22
   4. Bernard Palissy, 140
   5. Earl of Arundel, 107
   6, 7. Butchers' Company, 3
PSALM IX.—v. 10. Dante, 80
   12. Archbishop Laud, 181
PSALM X.—Henry Martyn, 259

PSALM XI.—Mary, Queen of Scots, 126
PSALM XII.—Luther, 111; The *Tobie*, 129, 130; Ruskin, 248
   v. 6. John Howard, 251
PSALM XIII.—v. 1. Calvin, 141
   3. Saracen, *apud* Gregory of Decapolis, 10
PSALM XIV.—Queen Elizabeth, 122; Ruskin, 248; Henry Martyn, 260
   v. 1. Bacon, 131
   2. Baldwin, 62
PSALM XV.—Ruskin, 248; Henry Martyn, 260
   v. 1. Langland, 82
   6. Langland, 82
PSALM XVI.—Jean Rousseau and Duchess of Orleans, 143; Hugh M'Kail, 206; Henry Martyn, 260
   v. 4. William Carey, 256
   7. Beauchamp family motto, 3
   12. James Melville, 201
PSALM XVII.—John Gibson, 216
   v. 5. John Howard, 251
   16. Julius Hare, 234; John Howard, 252
PSALM XVIII.—v. 10. Shakespeare, 133
   18. Shakespeare, 133
   25-27. Rev. George Walker, 222
   28. James Melville, 201
   29. Mause Headrigg, 205
   39, 40. Clovis, 53

Appendix B

PSALM XIX.—Joseph Addison, 241; Ruskin, 248
v. 5. Shakespeare, 133; Milton, 184
13. Bunyan, 187
PSALM XX.—Gwynlliu and Cadoc, 43; Sir James Simpson, 240
v. 7. Antony, 16, 17; Patrick, 37; Adelme, of Chaise-Dieu, 63
9. National Anthem, 2
PSALM XXI.—Henry of Navarre, 150
PSALM XXII.—Bishop Hooper, 106
v. 1. Richard I., 62
12. Shakespeare, 132
21. Royal supporters, 2
27. Henry Martyn, 259
PSALM XXIII.—Chosen by Augustine as the hymn of martyrs, 10; Bishop Hooper, 106; George Herbert, 135; Isabel Alison and Marion Harvie, 216; Edward Irving, 238; Joseph Addison, 241; Byron, 243; Ruskin, 247, 248
v. 1. Neander, 234
4. James Melville, 201; Sir William Hamilton, 240; John Howard, 251; Alexander Duff, 262
6. Benedictine Rule, 45; father of Richard Cameron, 210
PSALM XXIV.—Legends of South-West France, 84; Ruskin, 248
v. 1. Great Exhibition of 1851, 3
7-10. Langland, 83; The *Golden Legend*, 85; Milton, 183
8. Alfred, Neot, 50
PSALM XXV.—Margaret Wilson, 217
v. 1. Louis IX., 75
6. Pico della Mirandola, 98
13. William Edwards (Indian Mutiny), 275
14. François de Sales, 159
16. William Edwards (Indian Mutiny), 275
PSALM XXVI.—v. 2. Abelard, 74

PSALM XXVI.—v. 8. Paula, 20; Hugh of Cluni, 47
10. Langland, 82
PSALM XXVII.—Rev. George Walker, 222; G. J. Romanes, 241; James Hannington, 266
v. 1. Oxford University, 3; Savonarola, 93; François de Sales, 158; James Melville, 201
9. Gregory the Great, 44
14-16. William Edwards (Indian Mutiny), 275
14. Allen Gardiner, 263
16. Lady Jane Grey, 117
PSALM XXVIII.—James Hannington, 266
v. 8. Coins of Black Prince, 3
PSALM XXIX.—v. 8. George Herbert, 135
PSALM XXX.—Bishop Hooper, 106; James Hannington, 266
PSALM XXXI.—Savonarola, 92, 93; Charles V., 96; Fisher, 101; Bishop Hooper, 106
v. 1. Xavier, 104; Mère Angélique, 163
1-8. Dante, 81
6. Our Saviour, 5; Stephen, 5; Basil, 14; Charlemagne, 54, 55; Becket, 58; Hus, 89; Jerome of Prague, 89; Luther, 93, 97; Melancthon, 93; Tasso, 97; Columbus, 97; Charles V., 97; Fisher, 102, 107; John Haughton, 102; Thomas Cromwell, 107; Hooper, 106, 107; Ridley, 107; Robert Southwell, 109; Lady Jane Grey, 119; Duke of Suffolk, 119; Egmont, 122; Horn, 122; Mary, Queen of Scots, 127; George Herbert, 135; Wishart, 199; John Knox, 199; Hugh M'Kail, 206; Donald Cargill, 211; James Renwick, 215; Newman — *Gerontius*, 233; Henry Martyn, 258; Madame de Noailles, 270

Appendix B

PSALM XXXII.—Augustine, 29; Ruskin, 248
  v. 1. Dante, 81; Langland, 82.
  2. Izaak Walton, 177
  7, 8. Alexander Peden, 212
PSALM XXXIII.—v. 2. Benedictine Rule, 46
  17, 18. Madame Prosni, 161
PSALM XXXIV.—William Law, 230
  v. 1. Theodore the Martyr, 10
  5. Fisher, 101
  10. Columba, 39; Allen Gardiner, 263
  11. Baithen, 40
  12-15.—Benedictine Rule, 45
PSALM XXXV.—v. 3. Thomas à Kempis, 77
  10. Thomas à Kempis, 77
  23. The Armada, 61, 127, 138
PSALM XXXVI.—v. 7. Langland, 82
PSALM XXXVII.—v. 5. David Livingstone, 265
  16. Jeanie Deans (Scott), 205
  25. Jeanie Deans, 205; Baillie of Jerviswood, 214
PSALM XXXVIII.—Bishop Hooper, 106
  v. 7. Maine de Biran, 240
  15. George Herbert, 135
PSALM XXXIX.—Ambrose, 29
  v. 1. Pambo, 17; Benedictine Rule, 46
  8. Shakespeare, 133
  10. Calvin, 141
PSALM XL.—v. 1. François de Sales, 158
  2. Francis of Assisi, 69; Robert Southwell, 108
  5. François de Sales, 158
  6. Cromwell, 195
  21. Queen Elizabeth, 122
PSALM XLII.—Daniel M'Michael, 216
  v. 1. Early Christians, 9, 10; George Beisley, 108; Henry II., 137
  2. François de Sales, 159
  6. Manning, 233
  14. Vladimir Monomachus, 73; Jeanie Deans, 205
PSALM XLIII.—Baptism of Augustine, 29; Anthony of Navarre, 137
  v. 3. Thomas Chalmers, 235

PSALM XLIII.—v. 5. Luther, 94, 95; Jeanie Deans, 205
PSALM XLIV.—James Melville, 200
  v. 23. Ambrose, 14
PSALM XLV.—Coronation Services, 2; Philip Nicolai, 111
  v. 8. Gregory VII., 56
PSALM XLVI.—Demetrius of the Don, 63; Luther and Melancthon, 95; Luther and Thomas Carlyle, 95; Luther, 111; Cromwell, 190, 196; Napoleon III., 271; Havelock, 272
  v. 1. Turstin of York, 67
  1-3. Rev. George Walker, 221
  4. Bernard and Fountains Abbey, 68
  5. Cathedral at Kieff, 30; Mediæval cosmogony—The Holy City, 76
  7. John Wesley, 231
  7-11. Rev. George Walker, 221
  10. Vincent of Lerins, 47; Richard Cameron, 210; James Renwick, 215
PSALM XLVII.—Ruskin, 248
  v. 13. Shakespeare, 133
PSALM XLIX.—v. 1. Gregory Nazianzen, 29
  7. Matthew Arnold, 244
PSALM L.—v. 16. Origen, 15
PSALM LI.—Savonarola, 92, 93; More, 97, 100, 107; Lady Jane Grey, 118; Duke of Suffolk, 119; Egmont, 122; Wolfgang Schuch, 145; Jacques Roger, 171; François Benezet, 171; Bunyan, 186; Wishart, 198, 199.
  v. 1. Neck-verse, 3
  1, 2. William Carey, 256
  7. Langland, 83; Shakespeare, 132; Henry Martyn, 259
  10, 11. Teresa, 105
  12. Thomas Arnold, 234
  13. Savonarola—Michel Angelo's picture, 93
  17. Augustine, 27; Langland, 83; Teresa, 105
  18. Henry V., 62

Appendix B

PSALM LII.—Charles I. and the Scottish Camp, 183
PSALM LV.—Darnley, 125
   v. 6. Jerome, 19; Byron, 243; Browning, 245
   6, 7. Benedictines at York 66
   7. Turstin of York, 67
   8. Fountains Abbey, 67
   15. Hooker, 115
   18. Benedictine Rule, 46
   22. Allen Gardiner, 263
   25. Burghley, 130
PSALM LVI.—Charles I., 183
PSALM LVII.—v. 1. Allen Gardiner, 263; altar at Bourget, 271
   8. Robert Sanderson, 177
PSALM LVIII.—v. 4. Shakespeare, 132; Milton, 184
PSALM LX.—v. 1. John Haughton, 102
   2. Bishop Hall, 175
   11. John Howard, 251
PSALM LXII.—Bishop Hooper, 106
   v. 1, 2. Augustine, 27
   5. James Gardiner, 267
   5-8. Allen Gardiner, 263
PSALM LXIII.—Beza, 141; Chrysostom, 141
   v. 9. Thomas à Kempis, 77
PSALM LXV.—v. 11. Robert Southwell, 108
   12. John Wesley, 231
PSALM LXVI.—v. 14. Bunyan, 185
   18. Thomas à Kempis, 77
PSALM LXVIII.—Antony, 17; Browning, 17; Charlemagne, 54; Savonarola, 92; The Huguenots, 138, 141, 147, 151, 152, 161; Beza, 141, 147; Cromwell, 195; Moscow, 271
   v. 1. National Anthem, 2; Cromwell, 194; Alexander Peden, 213; Rev. George Walker, 221
   4. Shakespeare, 133
   5. Shakespeare, 132; Alexander M'Robin, 216; William Edwards (Indian Mutiny), 275
   15. Shakespeare, 132
   18. Bunyan, 187

PSALM LXIX.—Bishop Hooper, 106
   v. 12. Archbishop Laud, 181
PSALM LXXI.—Mary, Queen of Scots, 127; Bishop Jewel, 134; William Wilberforce, 232
   v. 1. John Howard, 251
   8. George Herbert, 135; Jewel, 135; Robert Sanderson, 177; Madame de Noailles, 270
   10. Madame de Noailles, 270
PSALM LXXII.—Athanasius, 22; Ruskin, 248
   v. 10, 11. Christian Art, 2, 3
   19. Thomas à Kempis, 77
PSALM LXXIII.—Early Christians, 9; Bishop Hooper, 106
   v. 1. Bishop Hooper, 106; Coligny, 149
   24. Jerome, 20
   25. Charles Wesley, 231
PSALM LXXIV.—Vaudois, 165; Covenanters, 206
PSALM LXXV.—Ruskin, 248
PSALM LXXVI.—English Nation (Spanish Armada), 128; Robert Bruce, 128; Huguenots, 147; Covenanters, 208, 209; Kingsley, 234
   v. 2. John Endicott, 174
   11. Turstin of York, 67
PSALM LXXVII.—Bishop Hooper, 106
   v. 3. François de Sales, 159
   7-9. Bunyan, 187, 188
PSALM LXXVIII.—v. 30. Turstin of York, 67
PSALM LXXIX.—Huguenot prisoners, 146; The Jews, 146; The Puritans, 146; The French Revolution, 146; Carthusians of Woburn, 146; Jean Rabec, 147; James Melville, 200
   v. 1. Jerome, 31
   1-4. Bede, 42
   2. Parsons, 146; Luisa de Carvajal, 146
   5, 8. Augustine, 27
   9, 10. Crispin and Crispinian, 10
   12. John Howard, 251

Appendix B

PSALMS LXXX.-LXXXVIII.—Milton, 183
PSALM LXXX.—*v.* 5. Elizabeth Barrett Browning, 245
   8. Theodosius, 60
   13. Origen, 15; Shakespeare, 132
PSALM LXXXII.—*v.* 1. Bishop Andrewes, 175
PSALM LXXXIII.—Benedict, 48; President Kruger, 277, 278
   v. 4. President Kruger, 277
PSALM LXXXIV. — Benedictine Rule, 46; Isabel Alison and Marion Harvie, 216
   v. 1. Paula, 20
   1, 2. François de Sales, 158
   2. François de Sales, 159.
   11. Paula, 20; Thomas Aquinas, 46, 47
   12. Carlyle, 268
PSALM LXXXV.—Cromwell, 190, 196
   v. 8. The *Imitatio Christi*, 77
   9. Robert Southwell, 108
   10. Langland, 83
PSALM LXXXVI.—*v.* 7. David I. of Scotland, 75
   13. Casaubon, 142
   15. Tennyson, 244
PSALM LXXXVII.—Bishop Hooper, 106
   v. 1. University of Durham, 3
   2. Augustine, 29
PSALM LXXXVIII.—*v.* 7-10. Henry of Navarre, 150
   11. Wordsworth, 244
   18. Henry of Navarre, 150
PSALM LXXXIX.—*v.* 1. François de Sales, 159
   8. Cromwell, 195
   47. Shakespeare, 131
PSALM XC.—Charles V., 96, 97; John Hampden, 182, 183; Newman — *Gerontius*, 234; Ruskin, 248
PSALM XCI.—Beza, 141; Casaubon, 142; Ruskin, 248
   v. 1. Henri de Rohan, 160
   4. François de Sales, 158
   9. Savonarola, 92
   13. Augustine, 27; Barbarossa and Pope Alexander III., 59

PSALM XCII.—Casaubon, 187
   v. 4. Dante, 80
PSALM XCIII.—The Covenanters, 204, 205
   v. 2. Mediæval cosmogony, 76
PSALM XCV.—Battle-cry of the Templars, 61
   v. 6. Christian Friedrich Schwartz, 255
PSALM XCVI.—William Law, 230
PSALM C.—Shakespeare, 114; Longfellow, 114; William Kethe, 114; Louis Bourgeois, 114
   v. 2. Edward Fitzgerald, 245
PSALM CI.—Death of Monica, 14; Columba, 38; Nicephorus and Vladimir Monomachus, 72; Ridley, 105; Bacon, 131
   v. 6, 7. Bacon, 131
   10. Bacon, 131
PSALM CII.—David Brainerd, 253
   v. 6. Christian Art, 2, 3
   6, 7. Robert Southwell, 109
   11. Sundials, 3
   13. Fisher, 100
   17. Allen Gardiner, 263
PSALM CIII. — Sanderson, 177; James Renwick, 215; William Law, 230; Ruskin, 248
   v. 1. David Livingstone, 266
PSALM CIV.—Mediæval cosmogony, 76; Humboldt, 238; Ruskin, 248
   v. 3. Shakespeare, 133
   5. Mediæval cosmogony, 76
   26. Mediæval cosmogony, 76
   28. Langland, 83
   29-30. Lady Jane Grey, 117
   30. Wilfrid, 49
   32. Becket, 58
PSALM CV.—*v.* 1. Baxter's pulpit, 228
PSALM CVI.—*v.* 3. Louis IX., 75
PSALM CVII.—Alexander Duff, 345
   v. 8. Cromwell, 190
   16. The *Golden Legend*, 85; Bunyan, 186
   20. Wishart, 198
   43. Alexander Duff, 261
PSALM CVIII.—President Kruger, 277, 278
PSALM CIX.—*v.* 6-20. Bunyan, 188

Appendix B

PSALM CX.—Luther, 94; Cromwell, 192, 195
PSALM CXI.—William Law, 230
v. 4, 5. Dunstan, 51
10. Charles Bailly, 107
PSALM CXII.—Ruskin, 247
v. 4. James Melville, 201; Thomas Chalmers, 235
PSALM CXIII.—Calvin, 140
PSALM CXIV.—Francis Borgia, Duke of Gandia, 47; Dante, 80; Huguenots on the Loire, 149; Milton, 183
v. 3. Antoninus the Martyr, 60
4. Theodosius, 60
PSALM CXV.—John Sobieski, 61, 138; Cardinal Ximenes, at siege of Oran, 63
v. 1. Agincourt, 62; Henry IV., 62; Shakespeare, 132; Bernard Palissy, 140; William Wilberforce, 232
4-8. Jean Leclerc, 145
4, 5. Early Christians, 10
8. Cromwell, 191
16. Burghley, 130
PSALM CXVI.—" Quaker " Wallace, 276
v. 13. Bernard, 61
PSALM CXVII.—Cromwell, 196
PSALM CXVIII.—Basil in Pontus, 17, 18; Luther, 94; Charles V., 95, 96; Huguenots, 147; Landing of William of Orange, 218; Rev. George Walker, 222
v. 6. Cowper, 242
14. Donald Cargill, 211; William Law, 230; Cowper, 242
16-end. Donald Cargill, 211
17. Wyclif, 87; Luther, 93, 94; Cowper, 242
18. Baldwin, 62; Cowper, 242
23, 24. Cromwell and the Scottish troops, 193
23. Queen Elizabeth, 122
24, 25. Huguenots, battle of Courtras, 151; d'Aubigné, 152; Louis Rang, 170; Jacques Roger, 170; Rochette, 172
26. Charlemagne, 54

PSALM CXVIII.—v. 29. Cowper, 242
PSALM CXIX.—Augustine, 29; " Little Alphabet of the Monks," etc., 78; William Wilberforce, 232; Ruskin, 247, 248; Henry Martyn, 259; David Livingstone, 264; William Edwards (Indian Mutiny), 275
v. 6. David Brainerd, 254
20. Thomas Chalmers, 235
24. Ruskin, 248
25. Theodosius, 25; Nicasius of Rheims, 32; Dante, 80
28. Maine de Biran, 239
30. David Brainerd, 254
36. Pascal, 163
45. David Brainerd, 254
62. Benedictine Rule, 46
65-70. François I., 145
71. François I., 145
96. A. P. Stanley, 235
97. David Brainerd, 254
105. Shakespeare, 133
116. Benedictine Rule, 45
121. David I. of Scotland, 74, 75
137. Emperor Maurice, 11
148. Izaak Walton, 177
158. Philip Doddridge and Col. James Gardiner, 267
164. Benedictine Rule, 46
175. Silvia, mother of Gregory, 44
PSALM CXX.—v. 4. Cromwell, 189
5. Benedictines at York, 66; Bacon, 131; Hooker, 268; Carlyle, 268
PSALM CXXI.—The Covenanters, 205; David Livingstone, 264; James Hannington, 266; William Edwards (Indian Mutiny), 275
v. 1. Dante, 79, 80
3. Coghill family, 3
4. François de Sales, 159
PSALM CXXII.—The Ettrick Shepherd, 244
v. 1. Gregory and Nonna, 12; The Huguenots, 139
PSALM CXXIV.—Justus Jonas, 111; John Durie, 200
v. 5. Edward Irving, 237
6. Huguenot seal, 139

PSALM CXXVI.—James Melville, 201
   v. 1. Robert Estienne, 142
PSALM CXXVII.—Pope Clement III., 61, 62
   v. 1. Compton family, 3; City of Edinburgh, 3; Eddystone Lighthouse, 3; Huguenot house at Xainton, 144; Benjamin Franklin, 174
   2. Madame Guyon, 164
   3. Elizabeth Barrett Browning, 245
   4-6. Bunyan, 189
PSALM CXXVIII.—Henry II., 137
PSALM CXXIX.—Henri Arnaud, 165
   v. 3. Alexander Peden, 213
PSALM CXXX.—Luther, 111, 133; Hooker, 133; P. Fletcher, 134; Diane de Poitiers, 137; John Wesley, 230; French Royalists, 269
   v. 3. Beza, 141; Bunyan, 187
PSALM CXXXII.—*v.* 15. Gall, 37; Anselm, 57
   18. Paulinus, 14
   19. Shilling of Edward VI., 3
PSALM CXXXIII.—*v.* 1. Langland, 83
PSALM CXXXV.—David Livingstone, 264
   v. 7. Mediæval cosmogony, 76
PSALM CXXXVI.—Athanasius, 23; Milton, 183
PSALM CXXXVII. — Vincent de Paul, 156; Camoens, 157
   v. 4. Jerome, 19; John II., 156
   8. Calvin, 172; Sir Robert Hamilton, 209
PSALM CXXXIX.—O.H. German fragment of 9th century, 35; Linnæus, 35; Thomson, 35; Ruskin, 247

PSALM CXXXIX. — *v.* 6. More, 99
   24. Port Royalists, 162, 163
PSALM CXLI.—Early Christians, 9
   v. 2. Shakespeare, 132
PSALM CXLII.—Francis of Assisi, 70
PSALM CXLIII.—*v.* 8. Savonarola, 91
PSALM CXLIV.—Bernard, 61
   v. 1. Philip Jones, 129
   4. Sundials, 4
PSALM CXLV.—Paul Gerhardt, 111; Milton, 184; James Gardiner, 267
   v. 1. William Law, 230
   3. Augustine, 25
   9. Langland, 82
   10. William Carey, 256
   13. Mosque at Damascus, 29, 30
   17. John Howard, 251
PSALM CXLVI. — William Law, 230
   v. 2. Strafford, 180
   3. Ordericus Vitalis, 71
PSALM CXLVII.—William Law, 230
   v. 5. Augustine, 25
   9. Shakespeare, 132
   18. Victory over Spanish Armada, 128
PSALM CXLVIII.—Francis of Assisi—Canticle of the Sun, 69; Newman—*Gerontius*, 233
   v. 4. Mediæval cosmogony, 76
   8. Mediæval cosmogony, 76; Alexander Peden, 212
PSALM CXLIX.—Thomas Müntzer, 115; Caspar Schopp, 115
PSALM CL.—Benedictine Rule—Bell-casting, 46; Newman—*Gerontius*, 233
   v. 6. John VIII., 34

INDEX

Abelard and Heloïse, 71; account of [M'Cabe, chap. xi.], 73, 74; the "Historia Calamitatum," 73, 74; letters quoted, 74
Acre, Baldwin dies at, 62
Adamnanus, his "Life of Columba" cited [Fowler, 134], 40
Addison, Joseph, 6; quoted, 241; his paraphrases of Psalms xxiii. and xix., 241
Adelme, abbot of Chaise-Dieu, at the passage of the Tagus, 63
Ælla, king of Northumbria, 44
Ælred, of Rievaulx, cited [Pinkerton, ii. 281-283], 74
Agincourt, battle of, 62
Agnes, St., mosaics at Ravenna, 5
Aidan, bishop of Lindisfarne, death of [Montalembert, iv. 127, 134 n.], 41
Aignan, St., saves Orleans, 32
Aigues Mortes, St. Louis at [Martin, iv. 326], 75; Vincent de Paul at [Wilson, 22], 156; the Tour Constance at, 165
Ainsworth, Henry, of Amsterdam, his version of the Psalms, 174
Airs-moss, 210
Aix-la-Chapelle, capitulary of [Baluze, i., col. 714], 35; death of Charlemagne at [Guettée, iii. 238], 54
Alais, treaty of, 162, 164; the Camisards at [Peyrat, i. 350], 168
Alaric, sack of Rome by [Gibbon, chap. xxxi.], 31, 32
Alaric II., killed by Clovis at Vouglé [Martin, i. 447], 53
Alba, St. Teresa dies at [Coleridge, iii. 369], 105
Alberic, prior of Molesme ["Life of Stephen Harding," Newman, vol. i.], 64
d'Albret, Jeanne, mother of Henry of Navarre, 152
Alençon, Henry of Navarre at, 150
Alexander III., Pope, and Barbarossa, 58, 59
Alexandria, Cyril, bishop of, 14; return of Athanasius to, 22
Alfonso the Valiant, of Castile, 63
Alfred, King, and St. Neot ["Life of St. Neot," Newman, iii. 133], 50
Alison, Isabel, 205; her death [Wodrow, book iii., chap. 5; vol. iii., 277; "Cloud of Witnesses," 117 seq.], 216
Alnwick, James Melville at, 201
"Alphabet of the Monks" [Kettlewell, "Brothers," ii. 119-124; see Appendix A, chap. iv.], 77, 78
"Alte fage," 166
Alva, Duke of, and St. Teresa [Cunninghame Graham, ii. 259], 104; and Egmont, 120; and the Huguenots, 148
Amasea, Theodore of, 10
Ambrose, St., 8, 22; quoted [Migne, xiv. 925, 223], 11; quoted by Casaubon, 142; introduces antiphonal chanting [Baunard, 324 seq.], 14; death of [Bright's "History," 223; Baunard, 594], 14; and Theodosius [Bright's "Fathers," i. 519; Baunard, 448-456], 25; and Augustine, 13, 26, 29; on the Duties of the Clergy, 29
American Constitution, the, Benjamin Franklin on, quoted [Works, ed. Sparks, v. 155], 174, 175
Amiens, Martin of Tours at, 21

Andrewes, Lancelot, bishop, 6, 7, 175
Angers, Jean Rabec burned at, 147
Angoulême, Place du Mûrier at, 143
Angoumois, the ("Huguenotes"), 143
Anne Boleyn, her marriage, 99
Annecy, François de Sales born at, 157
Anselm, Archbishop, account of [Church; Montalembert, vi.], 56, 57; his "Cur Deus Homo?" [Montalembert, vi. 170], 57, 58
Anthem, the National, 2
Anthony, king of Navarre, his Psalm [Douen, i. 709], 137
Antiphonal chanting, see *Ambrose*
Antoninus, of Placentia, the Martyr, cited [see Appendix A, chap. iii.], 60
Antony, St., account of [Newman's "Historical Sketches," ii. 99-102; Baring-Gould, January 17th]; Alban Butler, January 17th], 16-18; Life of, by Athanasius [Migne, lxxiii. 126], 18; and Augustine, 28
Antrim's regiment [Walker], 218
"Apologetical Declaration, The," 217
Aquileia, Jerome at, 19
Aquinas, St. Thomas, 46, 47
Arbroath, sundial at, 3
Ardusson, the river, 73
Argenteuil, Héloïse at, 73
Armada, the, motto of, 61, 127; account of [Froude, xii.], 127, 128
Armagnac, valet to Henry of Navarre, 150
Arnaud, Henri [Monastier, ii. 126], 165
Arnauld, Antoine, learns the Psalms by heart, 163
Arnauld, Mère Angélique [see Appendix A, chap. viii., "Mémoires pour servir," etc.; "Histoire des Persécutions," etc.], 162, 163
Arnold, Matthew, quoted, 244
Arnold, Thomas, death of [Stanley, chap. x.], 234

d'Arques, Château, battle at, 152
Arundel, Philip, earl of, in the Tower [Bayley, i. 135], 107
Arundel, Earl of, at Strafford's trial [Baillie], 178
Ash, Thomas, on siege of Londonderry, quoted [Walker, ed. Dwyer, 210], 222
Assisi, see *Francis*
Athanasius, St., 8; at Rome [Bright's "Fathers," i. 169, 180; Thierry, i. 22, 23], 18; returns to Alexandria [Bright's "Fathers," i. 199; Stanley's "Eastern Church," 274; Greg. Naz. orat., xxi.], 22; at church of St. Theonas [Bright's "Fathers," i. 240; "History," 76, 77; Stanley's "Eastern Church," 283], 22, 23
Attila, 32
d'Aubigné, squire to Henry of Navarre, 150; cited [Livre 17, cap. xx.], 150; death of [Puaux, v. 224; Noailles, i. 66], 152
Augustine, St., of Canterbury [Bede, i. 25; Montalembert, iii. 186 *seq.*], 43, 44
Augustine, St., of Hippo, 6, 7, 8, 10; his baptism [Conf., ix. 6], 13, 29; his death [Possidius, xxi.; Bright's "Fathers," ii. 306], 14; account of his conversion, 25-29; his "City of God," 29, 30
Avila, St. Teresa born at [Coleridge, i. 4], 104
Avranches, Henry II. at, 58

Bacon, Francis, 5, 8; his "Essays" quoted, 130; his "Certaine Psalms," 131, 135
Baillie of Jerviswood, death of [Wodrow, iv. 110 *seq.*], 214
Bailly, Charles, inscription in the Tower [Bayley, i. 149], 107
Baithen and Columba, 40
Baker, Major, at siege of Londonderry [Walker, April 19th], 219
Baldwin, Archbishop, at Crusades [Epist. Cant. cccxlvi.; Vinisauf, i. 66; Hook, ii. 572], 62
Bangor [Montalembert, ii. 397], 42

Index

Bangor Iltyd [*ibid.*], 43
Barbarossa and Alexander III., 58, 59
"Barebones Parliament, The," Cromwell and [Carlyle, iii. 201, 225, 227], 195
Barlow, Joel, versifier of the Psalms, 174
Bartholomew, St., massacre of [Crottet, 322], 150, 200
Basil, St., 8, 22; his death [Bright's "Fathers," i. 393; "History," 163], 14; in Pontus [*ibid.*, i. 368; "History," 88; Basil Ep., 19], 17, 18; and Emperor Valens [*ibid.*, i. 373; Greg. Naz. orat., xx., xliii.], 24
Basing House, siege of [Carlyle, "Cromwell," i. 209-213], 191
Basle, Council of, 90
Bass Rock, the, prisoners on, 205, 210
Baxter, Richard, account of [Orme], 228, 229, 257
Bay Psalm Book, the, 174, 252
Bayles, the martyr [Southwell, ed. Grosart, p. 52], 108
Beaton, Cardinal, and George Buchanan, 197
Beauchamp family, the, motto of, 3
Bec, Anselm at, 57
Becket, Thomas à, murder of [Stanley, Canterbury, 122 *seq.*], 58
Bede, the Venerable, 8, 42; account of [Montalembert, iv. 239 *seq.*], 48
Bedfordshire, John Howard in [Memoirs, 124], 251
Beisley, George, priest, in the Tower, 108
Bellamy, Anne, betrays Robert Southwell [Poems, ed. Grosart, liii.], 108
Bellot, Cavalier, besieged at [Peyrat, i. 451], 168
Bemerton, George Herbert at, 134, 135
Benedict Biscop, account of [Montalembert, iv. 172-186], 48, 49
Benedict, St., of Nursia, founds Monte Cassino [Montalembert, i. 400], 32, 33; Rule of, see *Rule*

Benezet, François, his death [Coquerel, ii. 50; Peyrat, ii. 420], 171
Benignus and St. Patrick, 38
Bernard, St., 8; preaches Crusade, 61; enters Citeaux [Newman, "Life of Stephen Harding"], 65; abbot of Clairvaux [*ibid.*], 66; and Fountains Abbey [Narratio, etc., p. 35], 68
Berwick, death of James Melville at [Diary, xxviii. *seq.*], 201
Beza, Theodore, account of, 141; his translation of the Psalms, 112; his translation of the Psalms quoted, 147; his translation of the Psalms prohibited, 155
Bible Society, the, founded, 250
Biran, Maine de, see *Maine*
"Bishops' Bible, The," 110
"Bishops' Drag Net, The," 203
Black Prince, the, coins of, 3
"Black Tom Tyrant" (Strafford), 178
Blackader, John, quoted, 203
Blackmore, Sir Richard, his version of the Psalms, 6
Blantyre, cotton factory at, Livingstone in, 264
Blednoch, the (Wigtown martyrs), 217, 218
Blesilla, daughter of Paula [Thierry, i. 32, 159-160], 18; her death [Thierry, i. 219], 19
Boer War, the, 276-278
Böhme, Jacob, 255
Bokhara, Conolly and Stoddart at [Grover], 272
Bordeaux Pilgrim, the (Itinerary), [Thierry, i. 37], 19, 60
Borgia, Francis, Duke of Gandia [Abrégé de sa vie, 29], 47
Borgia, Roderigo (Pope Alexander VI.), and Savonarola [Villari, i. 152, and *passim*], 91
Boswell quotes Archbishop Secker [ed. Hill, i. 33], 242
Bothwell, Earl, and Wishart [Knox, book i.], 199
Bothwell Bridge, battle of [Wodrow, iii. 106, 107], 209
Bougés Mountain, 166
Bourgeois, Louis, sets the Psalms to music, 112, 114

Bourget, Psalter found at, 271
Boussac, legendary treasure at, 84
Boyne, the, battle of, 218
Brady, Nicholas, and Nahum Tate, 113
Brainerd, David [" Life, Remains, and Letters," ed. Jonathan Edwards, 1845, Aberdeen], 174, 257, 264; his death [*ibid.*], 253; his journal [" Diary of David Brainerd," 2 vols., London, 1902], 253, 254
Brantôme, cited, on Condé [Discours, lxxx. 1], 148; quoted, on Coligny [Discours, lxxix.], 149, 150; at La Rochelle, 151
Breagh, plain of, St. Patrick at, 37
Breda, Charles II. at, 192
Bregenz, Columban and Gall at [Montalembert, ii. 272], 36
Brest, John Howard at [Memoirs, 19], 250
Bretigny, the peace of, 151
Britain, invasion of [Bede], 42; early colleges in [Montalembert, iii. 146, 152], 42; described by Procopius, 43; the Danes in, 50
Brittany and La Vendée, insurrection in [Les Chouans, ii. 135 *seq.*], 269
Brittia, island of, described by Procopius, 43
Browne, Ezekiel, Hampden dies in his house, 182, 183
Browning, Elizabeth Barrett, quoted, 245
Browning, Micaiah, captain of *The Mountjoy* [Walker, July 27th], 223, 224
Browning, Robert, his " Ring and the Book " quoted, 17, 245; " Pambo " quoted, 17; " Strafford " quoted, 180
Bruce, of Earlshall, and the Covenanters at Airs-moss [Knox, book iii., chap. 4], 210
Bruce, Robert, the preacher, at Edinburgh, 128
Brussels, Egmont at, 120
Bryant, William Cullen, versifier of the Psalms, 174
Bridges on the 119th Psalm, 274, 275

Brydges, Sir John, Lieut. of the Tower, 118
Brydon, Dr., survivor at Cabul, 272
Buchanan, George, his Latin version of the Psalms, 197
Buckingham, George Villiers, first Duke of, driven from Rhé, 161; Bacon's advice to [Spedding, " Life and Letters," vi. 24], 131
Bullinger, Heinrich, Bishop Hooper and, 105
Bunyan, John, 6, 7, 253, 257; his " Grace Abounding," 185-189, 253
Burghley, William Cecil, Lord, 8, 130
Burns, Robert, 6
Butchers' Company, the, motto of, 3
Byron, Lord, and the Psalms, 243

Cabul, destruction of British force at, 272
Cadoc the Wise, abbot of Llancarvan [Montalembert, ii. 406], 43
Calvin, John, account of, 140, 141
" Calypso's Island," Basil's retreat in Pontus, 17
Cameron, Michael [Wodrow, iii. 212] 210
Cameron, Richard [Wodrow, iii. 212, 220], 210
Cameronian Regiment, the, 278
Cameronians, the, 204, 210, 214, 215, 217, 218
Camisards, the, 168-170
Camoens, Luiz de, 6; his exile, 156, 157; " The Lusiad " quoted, 157
Camus, Bishop, his " Esprit de St. François de Sales," 157
Canossa, Henry IV. at [Bowden, ii. 174; Montalembert, v. 364], 56
Canterbury, Augustine of, see *Augustine*; Benedict Biscop at, 48; Wilfrid at, 49; Dunstan, archbishop of, 50; Anselm, archbishop of, 57; murder of Becket, 58; penance of Henry II., 58; pilgrimages to, 61

Index

Capitulary of Aix-la-Chapelle, see *Aix-la-Chapelle*
Carey, William, 257, 262, 264; sails for India, 252; account of, 255-257; quoted, 255
Cargill, Donald, 205, 214; account of [Wodrow, book iii., chap. 4; " Six Saints," vol. ii.; " Cloud of Witnesses," 6 *seq.*], 210; quoted [" Six Saints," ii. 8], 202
Carlyle, Alexander, on Col. Gardiner [Autobiography, p. 16], 267
Carlyle, Thomas, 6, 236; quoted, 249, 268; on Sir William Hamilton, 240; and Ruskin, 246, 247; his " Luther's Psalm " [Critical and Misc. Essays, iii.], 95
Carlyle, Jane Welsh, see *Welsh*
Caroline, Queen, 232
Carrack, Peden preaches at [" Six Saints," i. 90], 213
Carrichon, M., and Madame de Noailles, 270
Carrickfergus, Peden's escape from, 212
Carstairs, William, at Torbay [Life, p. 34], 218
Carvajal, Luisa de, quoted [Life, Lady G. Fullerton, p. 254], 146
Casaubon, Isaac, 8; story of [M. Pattison, 335], 142
Caswall, Edward, 103
Cataldus of Tarentum, [Montalembert, iii. 157], 34
" Cathac, The," Columba's Psalter [Stubbs, 261, 262], 39
Catherine of Arragon, the divorce, 98, 102; Forest, her confessor [Lingard, v. 107 *n.*; " Faithful unto Death,"] 101, 102
Catherine de Medicis [Douen, i. 709], 8, 137, 148, 150
Caussade, Rochette captured at, 171
Cavalier, Jean, account of [Peyrat, i. 350, 451; ii. 85], 168, 169
Cawnpore, Henry Martyn at, 258
Caxton, " The Golden Legend " quoted, 84, 86
Certosa, the, Francis I. at the church of, 145
Cervantes, 6

Cesarea, death of Basil at [Bright's " Fathers," i. 393; " History," 163], 14; Basil and Valens at, 24
Cesarius, bishop of Arles [Montalembert, i. 353], 32
Cévénols, the, 61, 165, 168
Chablais, François de Sales at, 158
Chaise-Dieu, Benedictine abbey of, 63
Chalcedon, death of Emperor Maurice at, 11
Chalcis, desert of, Jerome in, 19
Chalgrove Field, death of John Hampden at, 182, 183
Chalmers, Thomas, account of [see Appendix A, chap. xi.], 235, 236; preaches at Edinburgh [Hanna, iv. 309, 341], 235
Chantal, Madame de, 154, 157
Charenton, Casaubon at, 142
Charlemagne, 8; at Rome [Martin, ii. 262, 263, 328], 54; death of [Martin, ii. 364; Guettée, iii. 238], 54, 55
Charles I., sanctions the Psalter, 114, 180; and Strafford, 175, 178; at Newark, 183; and Scottish Kirk, 201
Charles II., and Scottish Kirk, 192; accession of, and Cargill, 202
Charles V., of Spain, 8, 90; and Marot, 95; abdication and death [Stirling-Maxwell], 96, 97
Charles IX. of France, 150
Charlton, Margaret, wife of Richard Baxter [Orme, i. 296], 229
Charterhouse, the, monks of, executed [Froude, ii. 342-362], 101, 102
Chaucer quoted, 81
Chayla, François du, account of [Peyrat, i. 287 *seq.*], 166, 167
Cherson, see *Kherson*
Choczin, battle of, 138
" Christian Year, The," 233
Chrysostom, St. John, his favourite Psalm, 141
Cistercians, the, founded by Stephen Harding [Life, in New-

man, vol. i.], 64; in England [*ibid.*, vol. v. 108, 167 *n*.], 66
Citeaux, foundation of [Newman, vol. i.], 64
Clain river, 21
Clairvaux, monastery of [Newman, vol. i.], 66, 68
Claverhouse at Drumclog [Wodrow, iii. 69], 205
Clement of Alexandria, "Stromata" quoted, 11
Clement III., Pope, and Crusades, 61
Clement VII., Pope, and Henry VIII. [Lingard, v. 2, 13, 19-20], 99
Clifford, Lord, 75
Clovis, his baptism, 52; at battle of Vouglé [Martin, i. 447], 52, 53
Cluni, Hugh of [Vita, apud Migne, clix. 867], 47
Clyde, the, apparition on the banks of [" Six Saints," i. 33], 204
Cobbett, William, and Wilberforce, [" Life of Wilberforce," v. 68], 232
Coburg, Luther at, 13, 94
Cod, Cape, landing of Pilgrim Fathers at, 174
Coghill family, the, motto of, 3
Coins, of Black Prince, of Edward III., of Edward VI., 3; struck to commemorate defeat of Armada, 128
Coligny, Andelot de, 148
Coligny, Gaspard de, Admiral of France, 138, 147, 153; account [Brantôme, iii.], 147-149
Colme-kill, 40
Columba, St., 8; account of [Montalembert, iii. 1-133; Life, by Adamnan, III. xxiii; and Reeve's Introduction, xxxiii.], 38-41
Columban, St., 34; account of [Montalembert, ii. 272, etc.; Life, apud Migne, lxxxvii., 1014], 36
Columbus, Christopher, 8, 90; account of, 97; his habitual signature [Markham, 295; Irving, iv. 437], 97
Commet, M. de, Vincent de Paul writes to, 156

Compostella, pilgrimages to, 61
Compton family, the motto of, 3
Condé, Prince de, 138, 148, 149
Conolly, Capt. Arthur, death of, at Bokhara [Kaye's "Indian Officers," 139, 144], 272
Constance, Council of, 89, 90
Constance, Tour, at Aigues Mortes, 165
Constantius, Emperor, and Athanasius, 22
Corneille, translates the Psalter, 155; his "Heraclius," 11
Coronation offices, the, based on the Psalms, 2
Corsairs, Barbary, 155, 156
Cotton, Mr., of Boston, Cromwell writes to [Carlyle, iii. 172-3], 194
Cotton, Dr., his asylum, Cowper at, 242
Council, of Basle, 90; of Constance, 89, 90; of Milan, 22; of Toledo [Hefele, iv. 471], 35; of Toulouse, 110
Courtras, battle of [Douen, i. 11], 151
Cousin, Victor, on Maine de Biran, 239
Covenant, The National, signed at Edinburgh [Wodrow, i.], 202
Covenant, The Solemn League and, 202; prohibited [Wodrow, i. 423], 202
Covenanters, the, and Boers compared, 276-278
Coverdale, Miles, his version of the Psalter, 110
Cowper, William [see Appendix A], 6; and Madame Guyon, 163; account of, 242; quoted [Southey's "Life," chap. vi.], 242
Craig, John, versifier of the Psalms, 113, 114
Craigmad, apparition at [" Six Saints," i. 35], 205
Cranmer, Thomas, 99; and the Psalter, 110
Crashaw, Richard, 6
Crespin, his martyrology, 144
Crewe, Mrs., afterwards Lady, and Wilberforce [Life, i. 47, 48, etc.], 232

Index

Crispin, and Crispinian, SS. [Surius, Alban Butler, Baring-Gould, October 25th; Hasted's Kent, iii. 514], 10
Cromwell, Oliver, 61; account of [Carlyle], 189-196
Cromwell, Thomas, death of, 107
Cross, "Invention" of the, see *Helèna*
"Crossing the Bar," 211
Cruithnechan, priest, and Columba [Reeve's "Adamnan," Introd., xxxiii.], 38
Crusades, the, 61, 62
Cuthbert, St., account of [Montalembert, iv. 127-155; Bede, cap. xxxvii.-xl.], 8, 40, 41; his "beads" ["Marmion," II. xvi.], 41
Cyran, St., suspected of heresy, 162
Cyril, of Alexandria, death of [Bright's "Fathers," ii. 424; "History," 370], 14
Cyril, see *Methodius*

Dalzell, General, at Rullion Green, 205
Damascus, mosque at, inscription on, 30
Damour, Pastor, at Château d'Arques, 152
Dante, 6; on Anselm ["Paradiso," xii. 137], 57; "Divina Commedia" quoted, 33, 78-81; on the Penitential Psalms, 79
Darnley, Earl of, death of [Froude, viii., ix.], 123-126
Dartmouth, The, at siege of Londonderry [Walker, July 30th; ed. Dwyer, 211], 223
David, King, his harp, 1; Henry IV. compared with him, 154, 155
David I. of Scotland, 71; his death, [Pinkerton, ii. 281-3], 74, 75
Daye, John, publishes complete version of the Psalter, 113
Deans, Jeanie ("Heart of Midlothian"), 205
"Declaration, The Sanquhar" [Wodrow, iii. 212 *n*.], 209, 210
Defensor, Bishop [Baring-Gould, Martin, November 11th, p. 246], 21
Demetrius of the Don [Stanley, "Eastern Church," 402 *seq.*; Karamsin, iv. 377 and v. 78-86], 63
Deo Gratias, bishop of Carthage [Gibbon, chap. xxxvi.], 32
Derry (Londonderry), siege of [Walker, see Appendix A, chap. x.], 218-224; William and Mary proclaimed at [Walker, March 20th], 219
Desportes, Abbé, translates the Psalter, 154
Dessen Island, Alexander Duff at, 261
Diane de Poitiers [Douen, i. 709; Bordier, ix.], 137
Diarmid, King, and Columba, 39
Diarmid, attendant of Columba, 40
Dié, Louis Rang dies at, 170
Dieppe, Château d'Arques at, 152
Diocletian, persecution of, A.D. 288, 10
Dnieper, the, 72
Doddridge, Philip, cited, on Col. Gardiner, 267
Domenico, Fra, and Savonarola, 91
Donatus, of Fiesole, 34
Donskoi, monastery, 64
Doon Hill, at Dunbar, 193
Douglas, Capt. Andrew, of *The Phœnix* [Walker, July 30th], 223
Dragonnades, the, 164
Druids, the, and St. Patrick, 37, 38
Drumclog, 205, 279; account of, 208, 209
Drummond of Hawthornden, quoted [ii. 21], 84
"Drunken Parliament, The," 202
Dudley, Lady Jane, account of, 116-119
Dudley, Lord Guildford, death of, 117
Duff, Alexander, 8, 257; account of, 261, 262; (Indian Mutiny), 276; quoted, 273
Dunbar, Wilfrid imprisoned at, 49; battle of [Carlyle, iii. 28 *seq.*], 193-194

Dunottar, prisoners at, 205
Dunstan, St., 8, 48; account of, [Lingard, "A.S. Church," ii. 267, etc.; Vita, ed. Stubbs, 61, 355], 50, 51
Durham university, motto of, 3
Durie, John, account of [Melvill's Diary, 134], 200, 201
Dwight, Timothy, versifier of the Psalms, 174

Eddystone Lighthouse, the, inscription in [Smeaton, p. 183], 3
Edgar, King, 50
Edinburgh, motto of, 3; John Knox dies at, 199; John Durie at, 200; National Covenant signed at, 202; Cargill executed at, 211; Renwick executed at, 215
Edward VI. and Sternhold, 112
Edwards, William, his escape, 272-276; his Diary quoted, 274, 275
Egmont, Count of, his trial and death [Motley, part iii., i. and ii.], 120-123; his letter to Philip II. [*ibid.*, chap. ii.], 120, 121
Eleyn, Mistress, and Lady Jane Grey, 118
Eliot, John, missionary, 174, 255, 257; account of, 252, 253
Elizabeth, Queen, 6; the "Geneva jigs," 113; on death of Mary, 122; her version of Psalm xiv. quoted, 122
Elwy Monastery founded [Montalembert, ii. 396], 42, 43
Ely, Cromwell at [Carlyle, i. 81], 189
Endicott, John, Pilgrim Father, 174
"Enfants de Dieu," Cévenols [Peyrat, i. 271, 314], 165
Epiphanius, bishop of Pavia, 32
Episcopacy in Scotland, 201 *seq.*
Erasmus, 61, 90; Luther on ["Table-talk," dclxxi., dclxxii.], 97; on Luther [Epist. vi. 4], 98; and Fisher [Bridgett, 98; Erasm. Ep., 109], 100
Estramadura, Charles V. in, 96

Essex, Earl of, his death, 130
Estienne, Robert, and the Sorbonne [Douen, i. 13], 142
Ethandun, battle of, 50
Ethelred, coronation of, 51
Ettrick Shepherd, the, see *Hogg*
Etzel (Attila), 32
Euodius, friend of Augustine, 14
Eustochium [Thierry, St. Jérôme, i. 32, 159, 160], 11, 18; at Bethlehem [*ibid.*, i. 298, etc.], 19, 20; death of [*ibid.*, ii. 240], 21
Exhibition of 1851, the, motto of, 3

Fage, Durand, quoted [see Douen, i. 23], 220
Fairfax, Thomas, Lord, 6
Farne Island, Cuthbert on [Montalembert, iv. 137], 41
Feckenham, abbot of Westminster, and Lady Jane Grey, 117, 118
Fénelon, archbishop of Cambrai, 154; and Madame Guyon, 163
Ferdinand the Catholic, his death foretold [Stirling-Maxwell's "Charles V.," 266], 96
Feuillants, the, 153
Finnian, St., and Columba [Montalembert, iii. 20], 38, 39
Fisher, John, bishop of Rochester, 90; account of [Bridgett, see Appendix A, chap. v.], 100-101
Fitzgerald, Edward, 245, 246
Fitzurse, murderer of Becket, 58
"Flagellum Dei" (Attila), 32
Flanders, Dunstan in, 50
Fletcher, Dr., dean of Peterborough; and Mary, Queen of Scots, 126
Fletcher, Phinehas, 6; quoted [Poet. Misc., Psalm cxxx., stanza 3], 134
Florence, Spinello's frescoes at, 32; Savonarola at, 90-92
"Forçats de la Foi" [see Appendix A, chaps. vii., viii.], 139
Forest, John, Confessor to Catherine of Arragon [Lingard, v. 107 *n.*; "Faithful unto Death" chap. iii.], 101
Fotheringay, Mary, Queen of Scots, executed at, 126

Index 317

Fountains Abbey, foundation of [Narratio, etc., see Appendix A, chap. iv.], 66-68; deputation to Clairvaux [*ibid.*, p. 35], 68

Fox, Charles James, and Wilberforce ["Life of Wilberforce," i. 17], 232

Fox, George, the Quaker, 255

Fox, John, the Martyrologist, quoted [1555, 1554], 107, 119

Franc, Guillaume, sets the Psalms to music, 112

Francis I. of France, and Marot, 112; at the church of the Certosa, 145; his death, 145

Francis of Assisi, St., 8; his "Canticle of the Sun" [Sabatier, 304-305; M. Arnold, "Essays in Criticism," 212-213], 69, 70; account of [Sabatier; Spec. Perfectionis, chaps. iv., cxiii., cxviii.], 68-70

Franciscans at Greenwich, 101

François de Sales, St., 154; account of [Lear, 27-28; 259-265, etc.], 157-159; and the Port-Royalists, 162, 163

François Xavier, see *Xavier*

Frankish Kingdom, the, 53, 54

Franklin, Benjamin, on the American Constitution [Works, ed. Sparks, v. 155], 174, 175

Free Church, the, founded, 235

Frere, John Hookham, 6

Frisians, the, Wilfrid and, 49

Fry, Elizabeth, 252

Fuller, Thomas, cited ["Church Hist.," book vii., 31, 32], 113

Furruckabad, Edwards and the Probyns at, 274, 275

Gall, St., 34; at Bregenz [Montalembert, ii. 272], 36; founds monastery [*ibid.*, 293], 36, 37

Gandia, Duke of, see *Borgia, Francis*

Gardiner, Allen Francis, Commander, account of [Marsh's Memoir], 262-264; his Diary quoted [*ibid.*, 363 *seq.*], 263, 264

Gardiner, James, Colonel, account of [Doddridge, "Remarkable Passages," 30 *seq.*], 266-268;

his vision [*ibid.*, 84, 85], 267, 268

Gardon river, Lalande defeated at, 169

Geneva, Calvin introduces chanting of Psalms at, 140; François de Sales at, 158

"Geneva Jigs, The," 113

Genevieve, St., and Paris [Alban Butler, January 3rd], 32

Gerhardt, Paul, his hymn, 111

Germanus, bishop of Auxerre, in Britain [Bede, I. xvii. and xx.], 42

Ghent, monastery of St. Peter at, Dunstan in, 51; Egmont and Horn at, 120

Gibson, John, death of [Wodrow, iv. 243], 216

Gioacchino di Fiore, the Calabrian seer [Sabatier, St. Francis, 46-50], 68

Gladstone, W. E., 8

Glasgow, Edward Irving at, 236

Glastonbury, Dunstan, abbot of, 50

Goa, Camoens at, 156

Godeau, bishop of Grasse and Vence, his Preface to the Psalms quoted [2nd ed., p. viii.], 155

Godfrey, abbot of St. Mary's, York, 67

Goethe, 6

"Golden Legend, The," quoted [ed. Ellis, vol. i. 98], 84-86

Gorgonia, sister of Gregory Nazianzen, her death [Ullmann, 136, 137], 13

Goute, Madame de la, sister of the widow Prosni, 161

Goudimel, Claude, sets the Psalms to music, 112

Greenwich, Franciscans at ["Faithful unto Death," see Appendix A, chap. v.], 101

Gregory of Decapolis, cited [Migne, c. 1210; Galland, Bibl. Vet. Pat., xiii. 513], 10

Gregory the Great, account of [Vita, ap. Migne, lxxv., 230; Greg. Epist. I. v.; *ibid.*, lxxvii. 448], 44; and conversion of England [Montalembert, iii. 186 *seq.*; Bede, I. xxv.], 44, 45

Gregory Nazianzen, account of [Ullmann], 12; against Julian, 29
Gregory, father of the preceding [Ullmann, 17, 19, 302], 12
Gregory VII., Pope, see *Hildebrand*
Grelet, M., and Madame de Noailles, 270
Grenfell, Lydia, and Henry Martyn [Sargent's Memoir; Journal], 257-260
Grenoble, 170, 171
Grey, Lady Jane, see *Dudley*
Grey, Lady Katharine, sister of Lady Jane, 117
Groningen, James Renwick at, 215
Guilds, mottoes of, 3
Guiscard, Robert, and Salerno [Bowden, I. 156], 55; and Hildebrand [Bowden, II. 312; Montalembert, v. 365], 56
Guise, Duc de, 147, 148
Gustavus Adolphus, watchword of, 61
Guthrun, the Dane, 50
Guyon, Madame, her imprisonment [Upham's "Life," 379], 163, 164
Gwynlliu, the Warrior [Montalembert, ii. 409-410], 43
Gytha, wife of Vladimir Monomachus, 72

Hadrian I., Pope, and Charlemagne, 54
Hague, the, John Howard at, 251
Hæmmerlein, Thomas, see *à Kempis*
Hall, Bishop, 6; preaches at Whitehall, 175
Hamilton, Sir Robert, on giving quarter at Drumclog [Wodrow, iii. 70 *n.*], 209
Hamilton, Sir William, 8; his death, 240
Hammond, Col. Robert, Cromwell writes to, 192
Hampden, John, death of, at Chalgrove Field, 182, 183
Hampole, Richard Rolle of, 110
Hannington, Bishop, 8, 257; death of, [Dawson, 443], 266;

his Diary quoted [Dawson, 440, 441], 266
Harding, Master, Lady Jane Grey writes to, 117
Harding, Stephen, founder of the Cistercians, 46; account of [Life, in Newman, vol. i.], 64, 65
Hare, Julius, death of, 234
Harold of England, father of Gytha, 72
Harvie, Marion, death of [Wodrow, iii. 277; "Cloud of Witnesses," 135 *seq.*], 205, 216
Haslerigg, Sir Arthur, governor of Newcastle, Cromwell writes to [Carlyle, iii. 30], 193, 194
Hatton Garden, Irving's chapel in, 236
Haughton, Sir Gilbert, his son killed at Marston Moor, 182
Haughton, John, prior of the Charterhouse, account of [Froude, ii. 342-362], 101, 102
Havelock, Henry, 275; at Jellalabad, 272; death of, 273
Headrigg, Mause ("Old Mortality"), 205
Heine, Heinrich, 6; quoted, 1; and Psalm cxxxvii. [Romanzero, book iii., Jehuda Ben Halevy, ii.; Werke, xviii.; and Letter to Moser, Werke, xix., p. 71], 157
Helena, The Empress, her "invention" of the True Cross, 60
Henry II. of England, and Becket, 58
Henry II. of France, and Marot [Douen, i. 709; Bordier, viii., ix.], 112, 137
Henry IV. of England, 62
Henry IV. of France (Henry of Navarre), 8; and the Huguenots, 147, 150; Metezeau dedicates version of the Psalter to, 154
Henry IV. of Germany, at Canossa [Bowden's "Gregory VII.," ii. 174; Montalembert, v. 364], 56
Henry V. of England, 8, 62
Herbert, George, 6; and Francis Bacon [Walton, ed. 1866, 269; Bacon's Works], 131, 135; ac-

Index

count of [Walton, 273, 307], 134, 135
Herder, Johann Gottfried, 6
Herefrith, abbot of Lindisfarne, cited [Bede's " St. Cuthbert," chaps. xxxvii.-xl.], 41
Herles-how, hill of, 67
Hexham, Wilfrid at, 49
Higginson, Francis, teacher at Salem [" Wonder - Working Providence "], 174
Hilary, St., bishop of Poitiers, 21; church of, at Poitiers, 53
Hildebrand (Pope Gregory VII.), 8; account of [Bowden; Montalembert, vol. v.], 55, 56
" Hill Folk, The," 204
" Hind Let Loose, The," engravings of Covenanter martyrs in, 216
Hippo, death of St. Augustine at [Bright's " Fathers," ii. 306; Possidius], 14
Hobbs, abbot of Woburn, 146
Hoffmann, Aug. Heinr. von Fallersleben, quoted [" Fundgruben," pt. i., p. 3], 35
Hohenstaufen, the, at Salerno, 55
Hogg, James (the Ettrick Shepherd), his boyhood, 244
Holbein, Hans, his portrait of Fisher, [Woltmann, p. 313], 100
Honorius, The Emperor, and the taking of Rome [Procopius, Bell. Vandal, i. 2; Gibbon, chap. xxix.], 31
Hooker, Richard, cited [Eccl. Pol., book v., chap. xxxix. 1], 115; his " Ecclesiastical Polity," 134; quoted [book v., chap. xxxviii. 2], 136; his death [Walton, ed. 1866, p. 213], 133
Hooper, John, bishop of Gloucester; account of [Later Writings, Parker Society, and Introduction], 105-107; quoted [ibid., xxxii. 176, 373, 294-5, 583, 584], 105, 106
Hooper, Anne, wife of the preceding, 106
Hopkins, John, translator of the Psalms, 112, 113

Horn, Count, friend of Egmont, account of [Motley, pt. iii., chap. i., ii.], 120-122
Horner, the martyr [Southwell, ed. Grosart, p. 52], 108
" Hortensius," of Cicero, the, influences Augustine [Conf., III. iv.], 26
Howard, John, 257; account of [J. B. Brown, Memoirs], 250, 252; his Diary quoted [Ibid., 270], 251; preparations for his last journey [Ibid., 592, 593], 251
Hugh of Cluni [Vita, apud Migne, clix. 867], 47
Hugh of Kirkstall, see *Kirkstall*
Hugo, Victor, his " Légende des Siècles " quoted (xxvi., La Rose de l'Infante), 127, 128
" Hugon, Le Roi," 144
" Huguenotes," utensils so called, 143
Huguenots, the, 138 seq.; houses of, 144; " Marseillaise " of, 61, 138; persecutions of, 146, seq., 217 seq.; poetry of, 143; proverbs, etc., concerning, 144
Huguenot seal, device on, 139
Humboldt, Alexander von, 8; quoted, 238, 239
Huns, the, invasion of, 32
Hunter, his Diary during siege of Londonderry quoted [Walker, ed. Dwyer, p. 200], 220
Hus, John, 8, 88; death of, 89
Hypatia, the murder of, 14

Iley, Alfred at, 50
" Imitatio Christi," the (and see *Thomas à Kempis*), 76-78
Indians, South American, Allen Gardiner and the, 262
Ingliston, cave at [Wodrow, iv. 243], 216
Iona, Columba at [Montalembert, iii. 37, etc.], 39; importance of, 40
Ireland, Cromwell in, 192
Iris river, in Pontus, 17
Irongray, Minister Welsh at, 203; M'Robin hanged at, 216
Irving, Edward, account of, 236-238; his death, 238

Index

Itala, death of Livingstone at [Last Journals, ii. 308; Blaikie], 266
Ivan the Terrible, 63

James I. of England, 6; his version of the Psalter, 114, 175; and the Scottish Kirk, 201
Jarnac, Condé killed at [Puaux, ii. 279], 149
Jarrow, monastery of, 48
Jellalabad, siege of, 272, 273
Jerome, St., 8; account of [Thierry], 18-21; revises Septuagint and Psalms [Thierry, i. 142]. 19; his letter to Marcella [Thierry, i. 350], 20; on the boyhood of Origen, 12; on the taking of Rome, 31; quoted by Raleigh, 128
Jerome of Prague, 8, 88, 89; his death, 89, 90
Jerusalem taken by Saladin, 61
Jesuits, the, 153
Jewel, Bishop, cited [Works, ed. Jelf, viii. 141], 114; his "Apology," 134; his death, 134
Jews, the lamentation over Jerusalem, 146
John II. of France, prisoner in England, 156
John VIII., Pope, and Cyril and Methodius [Stanley, "Eastern Church," 368 seq.], 34
John, abbot of St. Salvator, and Anselm, 57
Johnson, his "Wonder-Working Providence" quoted, 174
Johnson, Dr., on Law's "Serious Call" [Boswell, ed. Hill, i. 68], 229
Joinville, Sire de, cited [Hist. de St. Louis, 2me. partie, xv.], 75
Jonas, Justus, his hymn, 111
Jones, Philip, quoted [see Appendix A, and *Turkey merchantmen*], 129
Jonson, Ben, his "Poetaster" quoted (Act. v., sc. 1), 248
Joyeuse, Duc de, at Courtras, 149, 150
Julian, The Emperor, and Gregory Nazianzen, 29

Keble, John, 6, 229; his metrical Psalter [see Appendix A, chap. xi.], 233; his "Christian Year" quoted, 233
Kempen, 77
Kempis, Thomas à, 6, 7; account of, 47, 76-78; his "Soliloquy of the Soul" [Kettlewell, "Brothers," i. 181 seq.], 77
Ken, Bishop, 6
Kennedy, Jane, and Mary, Queen of Scots, 126
Kentigern, venerated as St. Mungo [Montalembert, iii. 164], 42; recites the Psalter [Life, by Jocelyn, xiv., Pinkerton, ii. 29], 41; founder of Elwy [Montalembert, ii. 396], 42
Kethe, William, versifier of the Psalms, 113, 114; his "All people that on earth do dwell," 114
Kettering, the "Particular Baptists" founded at, 255
Kherson (Cherson), St. Vladimir baptised at, 72; death of John Howard at [Memoirs, 629], 251
Kidderminster, Richard Baxter at [Orme, i. 169 n.], 228, 229
Kieff, baptisms at, 72; cathedral of St. Sophia at, 30
"Killing Times, The," 215-218
King, Bishop, 6
Kings, the Three, see *Wise men of the East*
Kingsley, Charles, quoted [Letters and Memories, i. 292, 293], 234, 235
Kingston, Ethelred crowned at, 51
Kirke, Major-Gen., at siege of Londonderry [Walker, June 15th], 219, 222
Kirk-o'-Field, the, described, 123; death of Darnley at, 123-126
Kirkstall, Hugh of, cited (History of Fountains), see *Fountains*, 66 seq.
Knox, John, introduces Genevan Psalter into Scotland, 114; quoted, 197, 198, 199; death of 199
Koulikoff, defeat of Tartars at, 63

Kremlin, the, sermon of Metropolitan in, 271
Kruger, President, quoted, 277, 278
Kussowrah, William Edwards and the Probyns at, 274-276
Kyle, Alexander Peden preaches in, 213

La Chaise, Père, 164
Lacknacor, stone of, Columba born on, 38
Lady Holland, The. wreck of, 261
Laeghaire, King, and St. Patrick, 37, 38
Læta, stepdaughter of Paula, St. Jerome addresses his treatise to her, 19
La Ferté, monastery of, 66
La Jonquire, General, defeated by Camisards at the Bridge of Salindres, 168, 169
Lamartine, Alphonse de, 6
Lammermoor hills, Cuthbert on, 41
Lancaster, Joseph, 250
Lancaster Gaol, John Howard and prisoners in, 251
Lanfranc, Archbishop, and William the Conqueror, 56
Langen Schwalbach, sundial at, 3
Langland, 61; "Piers Plowman" quoted, 82-84
Langres, diocese of, 64
La Noue cited, 138
Laud, Archbishop, trial and death, 180, 181; his Prayers quoted, 181, 182
Lauderdale quoted, 207
Laval, du Chayla, prior of, 166
Law, William, 229; his "Serious Call" quoted [Works, iv. 148-9, 159], 229, 230
Leake, captain of *The Dartmouth*, 223
Leclerc, Jean, death of [Crespin, p. 85], 145
Lefèvre d'Etaples, translation of the Psalter, 143
Legnano, battle of, 59
Leguat, François, on the island of Rodrigues [see Appendix A, chap. vii.], 139
Leighton, Robert, archbishop [Wodrow, i. 237; ii. 175], 203

Leignes river, 64
Lennox, Duke of, and Durie, 200
Leo, St., and Rome [Gibbon, chap. xxxvi.], 32
Leo III., Pope, crowns Charlemagne, 54
Leo, Brother, cited [Speculum Perfectionis, chap. iv.], 69
Leonides, father of Origen [Thierry, St. Jerome, i. 354], 15
Lerins, 33, 48
Lerins, Vincentius of, 47
Les Devois de Martignargues, battle of [Peyrat, ii. 85], 168
Leslie, Alexander, Covenanter, 202
Leslie, General David, defeated by Cromwell at Dunbar, 193, 194
Lestrange, comrade of Coligny, 149
Leyden, Separatists at, 173
Ligugé, monastery at, 21
Lille, John Howard at [Memoirs, 418], 251
Lindisfarne, Cuthbert at, 41; Wilfrid at, 49
Lindsay, Sir David, translates the Psalter, 198
Linnæus, inscription on his lecture-room [Stoever, 269], 35
Livingstone, David, 8; buried in Westminster Abbey ["Personal Life," 452-455], 252; account of, and death [Blackie's "Personal Life"; "Last Journals,"ii. 308], 264-266
Llancarvan, monastery at [Montalembert, ii. 406], 43
Locke, John, 8; his death, 238
Locmenach, monastery of, 73
Londonderry, see *Derry*
Longjumeau, treaty of [Crottet, 302], 147
Lorraine, Schuch in, 145
Louis IX. (St.) 8, 71; account of, and death [Martin, iv. 326-330; Perry's "St. Louis"], 75
Louis XIII. and Godeau, 155
Louise of Savoy, regent of France, 145
Loup, St., saves Troyes [Alban Butler, July 24], 32; in Britain, see *Lupus* (*infra*), 42

x

"Loyalty House" (Basing House) [Carlyle, "Cromwell," i. 213], 191
Lozère, caves of, 143
Lucknow, relief of, 273, 276
Ludlow, Col. Edmund, his interview with Cromwell [Carlyle, iii. 5], 192
Lundy, Col., at Londonderry, 219
Lupus, of Troyes (and see *St. Loup*), in Britain [Bede, I. xvii. and xx.], 42
Luther, 8, 90, 93; writes to Ludwig Seuffel, 13; account of, 93-95; his hymns, 111
Lutterworth, death of Wyclif at, 87
Luynes, at Montauban, 161
Lydd, Church of SS. Crispin and Crispinian at [Hasted's Kent, iii. 514], 10
Lyons, Wilfrid at, 49
Lyons, gulf of, Vincent de Paul captured in, 156
Lyttelton, Lord, on Law's "Serious Call," 229

Macao, Camoens at, 156
Macaulay, Lord, his epitaph on Henry Martyn quoted, 260
MacBriar, Ephraim, ("Old Mortality"), Hugh M'Kail prototype of, 206
Machadodorp, President Kruger's despatches from, 277, 279
M'Kail, Hugh, 205, 215; death of [Wodrow, ii. 53, 58, 59 *n.*], 206, 207
Mackay, Alexander Murdoch, 8
Mackenzie, quoted on siege of Londonderry, 223
Maclachlan (McLauchlison), Margaret, death of [Wodrow, iv. 248, 249], 217, 218
McMichael, Daniel, death of [Wodrow, iv. 239, 240], 216
McRobin, Alexander, death of [Wodrow, iv. 240], 216
Maes-Garmon, battle of [Bede, I. xvii., xx.], 42
Magus Moor, murder of Archbishop Sharp on, 208
Maine de Biran, account of, 239, 240
Maintenon, Madame de, 164

Male, William von, friend of Charles V., 96
Mamai, defeated at Koulikoff, 63
Manichees, the, Augustine and [Conf., III. v.; IX. iv.], 26, 29
Manning, Cardinal, quoted [Purcell's "Life," i. 68], 233
Mantes, William the Conqueror killed at, 71
Marazion, Henry Martyn at, 258
Marcella, letter of Paula and Eustochium to, 11; her community on the Aventine [Thierry, St. Jerome, i. 29, 350], 18, 19, 20; letter of Jerome to, 20
Margaret, Countess of Pembroke, see *Pembroke*
Margaret, Countess of Richmond, see *Richmond*
Marguerite de Valois, and Marot, 112
Marillac, Michel de, versifier of the Psalter, 154
Marmoutier, monastery of, 22
Marot, Clement, and Charles V., 95; his "sanctes chansonettes [Bordier, viii., ix.; Douen, i. 709], 112, 137; his version of the Psalms [Douen, i. 289], 139, 140, 141, 146, 166; his version of the Psalms prohibited, 145, 155; Francis I. and, 145
Marston Moor, battle of, 182
Martin, St., of Tours, church of, 52, 53; account of [Newman's "Historical Sketches," ii. 186-190, 203; Baring-Gould, November 11th], 21, 22
Martin, Sarah, 252
Martyn, Henry, 8, 253, 262; account of [Kaye's "Indian Officers," i. 459 *seq.*; Sargent's Memoir], 257-261; his Journal quoted [Journal, i. 67, 162, 145, 152], 254, 257, 259
Martyrs, hymn of (Augustine's) [sermo ccclxvi.], 10
Mary, Queen of Scots, 8; and Darnley, 123-126; death of, 126, 127; lines written before execution, 127
Mary I., queen of England, 122
Mary II., queen of England, 219

Index

Masham, Sir Francis and Lady, 238
Mather, Cotton, versifier of the Psalms, 174
Maurice, The Emperor, death of [Gibbon, chap. xlvi.], 11, 210
Mayenne, Duc de, 152, 161
Mayflower, The, 174
Mazel, Camisard historian, quoted, 170
Meaux, Leclerc, wool-comber of, 145; the prisoners of [Crespin, p. 169], 146
Mediæval art, Jerome in [Thierry, ii. 243], 21
Mediæval science, 76
Mekong river, Camoens at, 156
Melancthon, 8, 90; death of, 93; and Luther, 95
Melrose, Cuthbert at, 41
Melville, Andrew, 199; death of, 201
Melville, James, quoted [Diary, 22, 27], 200; death of [Diary, xxviii. *seq*.], 201
Metezeau, Jean, versifier of the Psalms, 154
Methodists, the, 226, 231
Methodius and Cyril, translation of the Bible in Sclavonic [Stanley's " Eastern Church," 368 *seq*.], 34
Metz, Jean Leclerc dies at, 145
Michel Angelo, his picture of Savonarola, 93
Milan, death of Ambrose at, 14; Council of, 22; Theodosius and Ambrose at, 25; Augustine at, 26-29
Milbourne, Luke, versifies the Psalms, 6
Milton, 6; versifies the Psalms, 183; the Psalms in his poetry, 183-185
" Mirror for Magistrates, The " (Psalm ci.), 131
Moir, David Macbeth, quoted (Night Hymn of the Cameronians), 208
Molesme, monastery of, 64
Monasticism, spread of, 17, 22; in Rome, 18; in Gaul, 21; in Western Europe, 34
Monica, or Monnica, death of [Aug. Conf., ix. 12], 13, 14

Monkton Farleigh, Bishop Jewel dies at, 134
Monmouth, Duke of, and Cargill, 210
Montaigne quoted [Essays, I. lvi.], 154
Montauban, 139; siege of, 161, 162; Rochette at, 171
Montcontour, battle of, Coligny wounded at [Douen, i. 13; d'Aubigné, I. v., xvi.], 149
Monte Cassino, founded by Benedict, 33
Montpellier, death of Benezet at, 171
Montrose, psalm-singing introduced at, 200
Moors, the, in Spain, 62
More, Sir Thomas, 90; Luther on [" Table-talk," dcclxix.], 97; account of [Bridgett], 98-100
Morimond, monastery of, 66
Moscow, threatened by Tartars, 63; Napoleon at, 271; Metropolitan of, his sermon, 271
" Mouchard," 144
Mountjoy, Lord, 218
Mountjoy, The, at siege of Londonderry [Walker, July 30th], 223, 224
Mulla, the white stag of, 38
Mungo, St., of Glasgow (Kentigern), 42
Müntzer, Thomas, 115
Musselburgh, Cromwell at, 193
Mutiny, the Indian, 272-276
Mwanga, King, and Bishop Hannington [Dawson, 440], 266

Nancy, Schuch burned at, 145
Nantes, Edict of, 152, 154; revoked [Puaux, vi. 87 *seq*.], 164, 165
Napoleon, at Moscow, 271
Napoleon III., and Revolution of 1848, 271
Naseby, battle of [Carlyle, "Cromwell," i. 192], 190
Neander, 234
" Neck-verse, the," 3
Nelson, servant to Darnley, 125, 126
Neot, St., account of [Newman's " English Saints," iii. 109-187],

50; recites the Psalter daily [*ibid.*, 109, 110], 50
Newman, Cardinal, 229; his "Dream of Gerontius" quoted ["Verses on various occasions," 323-370], 233, 234
Newport (Monmouth), St. Woolos, 43
Newton, John, 229, 231
Nicasius, bishop of Rheims, his death, 32
Nicephorus, Patriarch, instructs Vladimir [Palmer's Dissertations, 92-3], 72
Nicolai, Philip, his hymn, 111
Niebelungenlied, the, 32
"Night Hymn of the Cameronians, The," quoted, 208
Nisbet, John, death of [Wodrow, iv. 235; "Cloud of Witnesses," 466], 215
Noailles, Madame de, quoted [Duras, "Journal," etc., 192, 203], 270; death of [*ibid.*, 284-97], 270
Noailles-Mouchy, Duc de, death of [*ibid.*, 183], 270; Maréchale de [*ibid.*, 223, 4, 5], 270
Nola, Paulinus dies at, 14
Nonna, mother of Gregory Nazianzen [Ullmann, 17], 12, 13
Noyers [Puaux, ii. 273], 148, 149

"O Deus, ego amo Te" (Xavier's hymn), translated, 103
Odoacer and Severinus [Montalembert, i. 374; Gibbon, chap. xxxvi.], 32
Oran, capture of, 63
Ordericus Vitalis quoted, on death of William the Conqueror [Hist. Eccles., VIII., xiv. and xvi.], 71, 72
Origen, 8; his boyhood [Thierry, St. Jerome, i. 354], 12, 15; account of [Thierry, 354-360], 15; his apostasy and remorse [Epiphanius Hær., lxiv. 2; apud Migne, xli. 1072-3], 15
Orleans, cathedral of, 143
Orleans, Duchess of, and Jean Rousseau, 142, 143
Ormiston, Wishart at, 198
Orthez, bridge of, 143

Ostia, Augustine and Monica at, 13
Oundle, Wilfrid dies at, 49
Oxford University, motto of, 3

Padua, St. François de Sales at, 158
Paiges, Sebastian, court musician to Mary, Queen of Scots, 124
Palissy, Bernard, account of [Morley, II. 242-246; Palaysi, 36, 37], 140
Pambo [Socrates, Eccles. Hist., IV. xxiii.], 17
Paraclete, the, oratory of, 73
Parker, Archbishop, 6; his Diary quoted, 113; falls from his horse [Strype, book i., chap. vii.], 113; his translation of the Psalms, 113
"Particular Baptist Society, The," founded at Kettering, 255
Pascal, Blaise, 6, 7; quoted [Pensées XXIII. viii.; XIV. vii.], 162, 163
"Pastors of the Desert, The" [see Appendix A, chap. viii.], 170 seq.
Paterson, Bishop, and Marion Harvie ["Cloud of Witnesses"; Wodrow, iii. 277], 216
Patrick, St., at Tara [Tripartite Life, i. 41 seq.; ii. 455; O'Hanlon, iii. 554 seq.], 37, 38
Patteson, Bishop, 257
Paul and Silas at Philippi, 5
Paul III., Pope, creates Fisher a cardinal, 101
Paula (the elder), account of, and death [Thierry, St. Jerome, i. 32, 159, 160, 225-310, 312, 335; ii. 85-88], 18, 19, 20; and Eustochium, letter to Marcella [Thierry, i. 350; Pal. Pilgrims' Text Society, vol. i.], 11, 12
Paula (the younger) [Thierry, ii. 61, 241], 18, 21
Paulina, daughter of Paula the elder [Thierry, i. 159, 160], 18
Paulinus, Bishop of Nola, death of [Bright's "History," 334], 14
Pavia, battle of, 145

Index

Peden, Alexander, 205; quoted [" Six Saints," i. 70, etc.], 209, 211, 216, 218; account of [" Six Saints "], 211-214; specimens of his preaching [Six Saints," i. 59; i. 90], 213, 214
Pelican, the, as the symbol of Christ, 3
Pembroke, Margaret, Countess of, 5; translates Psalms, 129
Penitential Psalms, the (*i.e.*, vi., xxxii., xxxviii., li., cii., cxxx., cxliii.), Augustine [Possidius, 31], 14; Dante [Gardner's " Dante," 40], 79; Fisher [Bridgett, 106], 100; Spenser [Works, ed. Payne Collier, i., lxxv., ed. Todd. i., clxxi. *n.*], 129
Pentland Rising, the, account of [Wodrow; Blackader, " Six Saints "], 205, 206, 211
Pepin, of France, 53, 54
Persecution, of Diocletian, 10; of Severus, 15
Peters, Hugh, quoted [Carlyle, " Cromwell," i. 213], 191
Philip I. of France, 71
Philip II. of Spain, and the Netherlands [Motley, pt. iii., chap. i., etc.], 119
Phillips, Edward, quoted, 113
Phocas, and the Emperor Maurice 11
Phœnix, The, at the siege of Londonderry, 223
Pico della Mirandola, quoted [Seebohm, 117], 98; account of [Seebohm, 9; Villari, 1-77, 88, 244], 98
Picton Island, Commander Gardiner at [Marsh's Memoir, 348], 262
Piers Plowman, see *Langland*
Pilgrim, the Bordeaux [Thierry, i. 36], 19, 60
Pilgrim Fathers, the, 174
Pilgrimages, 60-61; satirised, 61
Pitman, Dr., his school, Cowper at, 242
Pitt, William, friend of Wilberforce [" Life," *passim*], 232
Plymouth, U.S.A., 174
Poissy, Henry of Navarre at, 150
Poitiers, 21, 53

Poitiers, Diane de, see *Diane*
Poitou, Bas-, wolves called " Soubises " in, 144
Pont de Montvert, affair of [Peyrat, i. 287 *seq.*], 166, 167
Pontigny, monastery of, 66
Pope, his " Eloïse to Abelard " quoted, 73
Possidius, biographer of Augustine, quoted [" Vita," Aug. 31], 14
Port Royal, abbey of, 162, 163
Port-Royalists, the, 153, 162
Prague and Wyclif, 89
Prague, Jerome of, see *Jerome*
" Praying Indians," Eliot's, 253
Pré-aux-clercs, the, 112
Prelacy, Scottish feeling against, 197, 215
Prestonpans, death of Col. Gardiner at [Doddridge, 179 *seq.*], 267, 268
Primers, mediæval, 110
Prison reform, 250, 251
Privas, 143
Probyn, Mr. and Mrs., and their children, 274-276
Procopius cited [Bell, Gotth., iv. 20], 43
Prosni, widow, at La Rochelle [Puaux, v. 187 *seq.*], 161, 162
Psalms, the, the early Christians and [Palmer's Dissertations, 285 *seq.*], 9, 10; antiphonal chanting of, introduced by Ambrose, 14; revised by Jerome, 19; Athanasius' " Exposition " and " Titles," 22; Methodius and Cyril translate, 34; in monastic life, 35, 46; recited by Kentigern, 41; by St. Neot, 50; by pilgrims, 60; by Stephen Harding [Newman, i. 12], 64; Wilfrid and, 49; Savonarola on, 92, 93; Luther and, 93, 98; Bishop Hooper on, 106; Council of Toulouse and, 110; Prayer Book version of, 110; in public worship, 111, 140, 200; Huguenots and, 138 *seq*; Calvin introduces chanting at Geneva, 140; Antoine Arnauld and, 163; singing of, in Scotland, 200; translation in Persian, 259

Index

Psalms, metrical versions of, Addison, 241; Ainsworth, 174; Bacon, 131; Barlow, 174; Baxter, 228; Beza, 112, 147, 155; Blackmore, 6; Brady, 113; Bryant, 174; Buchanan, 198; Calvin, 140, 141; Carlyle, 95; Corneille, 155; Craig, 113, 114; Daye, 113; Desportes, 154; Dwight, 174; Eliot, 252; Elizabeth, Queen, 122, 131; Fletcher, 131; Godeau, 155; Heine, 157; Hopkins, 112-114; James I., 114, 131; Keble, 233; Kethe, 113, 114; Lindsay, 198; Luther, 94; Marillac, 154; Marot, 95, 112, 137 *seq.*, 155; Mather, 174; Metezeau, 154; Milbourne, 6; Milton, 183; Parker, 113; Pembroke, Countess of, 129; Racine, 155; Rous, 114, 261; Sandys, 6; Sidney, Sir Philip, 129; 131; Spenser, 129, 131: Sternhold, 112-114; Surrey, Earl of, 131; Tate, 113; Waldis, 111; Wedderburns, the, 198; Whittingham, 113; Wisedome, 113; Wyatt, 131
Psalter, battle of the [Montalembert, iii. 20-26], 39
Puertocarrero, Tomas de [Stirling-Maxwell, "Charles V.," 323], 96

Quercy, François Rochette in, 171

Rabec, Jean, death of [Crespin, p. 374], 147
Rabelais at Ligugé [see Appendix A], 21
Racine translates the Psalter, 155
Raikes, Robert, 250
Raleigh, Sir Walter, 128; quoted [" Hist. of the World," book ii., chap. xvii.], 128
Rang, Louis, 170; death of [Peyrat, ii. 405], 170
Regent Square, Edward Irving in, 236
"Reign of Terror, The," 269
Religion in the eighteenth century, 225-228

"Remnant, The," 204, 210
Rémond, Florimond de, quoted [see Douen, i. 3], 138, 172
Remy, St., blesses Clovis, 52
Renard, Spanish ambassador, 116
Renard, Rues du, 144
"Reynard the Fox," 61
Renwick, James, 205; account of [Wodrow, iv. 446-454; "Cloud of Witnesses," 483 *seq.*], 215, 216
Revolution, the French, and Irving's preaching, 236
Rhé, island of, 161
Riccio, David, 123, 125
Richard I. at the Crusades, 62
Richard, prior and sacrist of St. Mary's, York, 66 *seq.*; first abbot of Fountains, 67
Richelieu, Cardinal de, 161
Richelieu, Duc de, 172
Richmond, Margaret, Countess of, and Bishop Fisher, 100
Ridley, Bishop, death of [Fox, 1555], 107
Rievaulx founded [Newman's "Saints," v. 108], 66
Ripon, abbey of, 49, 67
Robert, abbot of Molesme, 64
Rocamadour, pilgrimages to, 61
Rochelle, La, 139, 149; siege of [Puaux, v. 180 *seq.*; and see Appendix A, chap. viii.], 151, 160-162
Rochester, Earl of, quoted, 113
Rochette, François, account of [Peyrat, ii. 435], 171, 172
Rodrigues, island of, François Leguat at, 139
Roger, Jacques, death of [Peyrat, ii. 406], 170, 171
Rogers, Samuel, his "Italy" quoted, 59
Rohan, Henri, Duc de [see Appendix A, chap. viii.], 160
Roland, Camisard leader [Peyrat, ii. 91 *seq.*], 169
Rolle, Richard, of Hampole, 110
Romanes, G. J., 8; quoted, 241
Rome, monasticism in, 18 *seq.*; taken by Alaric [Gibbon, chap. xxxi.], 31
Romney Marsh, 10
Roper, Margaret, 99
Rostislaf, 73

Index

Rouen, death of William the Conqueror at, 71
Rous, Francis, his version of the Psalter, 6, 114, 261
Rousseau, Jean, the painter, and the Duchess of Orleans [Douen, i. 21], 142, 143
Roxburgh's "Flora Indica," 256
Royal arms, the, supporters of, 2
Rule of Antony, 33; of Basil, 33; of Benedict [Montalembert, i. 417; Bened. Regula], 33, 45, 46, 48, 51; of Cistercians [Newman, "Life of Harding," chap. xvii.], 65; of Isidore, 33; of Macarius, 33; of Reformed Carmelites, 104
Rullion Green, battle at [Wodrow, ii. 30 seq.], 205, 206; inscription at, 206
Rump, the, 195
Runjepoorah, William Edwards at, 274
Rupert, Prince, at Chalgrove Field, 182, 183
Ruskin, 6; on Sir Philip Sidney, 129; and Carlyle, 246, 247; account of, 247-249
Rye, the river, 66
Rye House Plot, the, 214

Sachs, Hans, 255
St. Agnes' Mount, monastery of, Thomas à Kempis at, 7, 77
St. Andrews, Wishart at. 199
St. Angelo, Gregory VII. a prisoner in, 56
St. Apollinare Nuovo, church of, at Ravenna, 5
St. Brelade's, sundial at, 4
St. Gervais, abbey of, William the Conqueror dies at, 71
St. Germain-en-Laye, treaty of, 150
St. John, Mrs., cousin of Oliver Cromwell, 189
St. Gildas de Rhuys, abbey of, 73
St. Sophia, cathedral of, at Kieff, inscription [Hare's "Russia," 447-450], 30
Saintes, 21; Palissy at, 140
Saladin, Jerusalem taken by, 61
Salem, U.S.A., Pilgrim Fathers at, 174

Salerno, tomb of Hildebrand at, 55
Sales, St. François de, see *François*
Salindres, bridge of, battle at [Peyrat, ii. 91 seq.], 169
Salmasius, 8
San Chan, island of, death of Xavier at, 102, 103
Sanderson, Robert, bishop of Lincoln, account of [Walton], 176, 177
Sandys, George, versifier of the Psalms, 6
San Michele, sundial at, 3
Sanquhar, "Declaration" read at, 210
Saracen, the converted [Gregory of Decapolis, Serm. Hist., xxix.], 10
Savonarola, 90, account of [see Appendix A, chap. v.], 90-93; portraits of, 90, 93
Scheffer, Ary, his picture of Augustine and Monica, 13
Schlavia, Anselm at, 57
Scholastica, St., sister of Benedict, 46
Schopp, Caspar, his "Classicum Belli Sacri," 115
Schuch, Wolfgang, burned at Nancy [Crespin, p. 88], 145
Schwartz, Christian Friedrich, his mission church at Tranquebar, 255, 256
Science, mediæval, 76
Scott, Thomas, 229, 231
Scott, Sir Walter, 6; quoted ("Marmion," II. xvi.), 41; characters in his novels, 205; his death [Lockhart, vii. 389], 243
Scottish Kirk, the, see *Charles I.* and *Charles II.*
Scrooby, Separatists at, 173
Seal, old Huguenot, 139
Secker, Archbishop, quoted by Boswell [Works, i. 223], 242, 243
Sedan, death of Andrew Melville at, 201
Selwyn, George, and Wilberforce ["Life of Wilberforce," i. 16], 232
"Separatists, The," at Scrooby

[Arber, p. 329], 173; at Leyden [*ibid.*], 173
Serampore, William Carey at, 256
Sergius, the hermit, 63
Serlo, the monk, history of Fountains, 66
Seuffel, Ludwig, correspondent of Luther, 13
Severinus, of Noricum, 32
Severus, persecution of, 15
Sévigné, Madame de [Letter 342, ed. 1838], 162
Shakespeare, 6; quoted, 40, 62, 114, 173, 180; the Psalms in, 131, 133
Sharp, James, Archbishop of St. Andrews [Wodrow, iii.], 202, 203; and Hugh M'Kail, 206; his murder, 208
Sharpe, Granville, colleague of Wilberforce, 232
Sherborne, Stephen Harding at, 64
Shiraz, Henry Martyn at, 259
Shrewsbury, Earl of, and Mary, Queen of Scots, 126
Sidney, Sir Philip, 5, 128; his translation of the Psalms, 129
Sidonius Apollinaris cited, 11
Siena, Spinello's frescoes at, 59
Sigismund at Council of Constance, 89
Silvia, mother of Gregory the Great [Greg. Vita, iv. 83; apud Migne, lxxv. 230], 44
Silvia of Aquitaine [see Appendix A, chap. iv.], 60
Simeon, Charles, 231
Simonoff monastery, 64
Simpson, Sir James, his "Mother's Psalm," 240
Skell, the river, 67
Skene, James, Cargill's letter to [" Cloud of Witnesses," 13], 211
Slave-trade, abolition of, 231, 232, 250
Smith, Sydney, on the Baptists, 256; Carlyle on, 268
Smith, Sir Thomas, 6
Soana, Gregory VII. born at, 55
Sobieski, John, war-cry of, 61, 138
Soissons, Crispin and Crispinian at, 10
Sorbonne, the, and Robert Estienne, 142; and Clement Marot, 145
Soubise (Le roi des Parpaillaux), 144; " Soubises," " Pierres de Soubise," 144
Southwell, Robert, account of [Works, Introd., ed. Grosart, xliv.-lix.], 108, 109; quoted [*ibid.*, 62, 84, 103, ed. Grosart, p. lii.], 109
" Spectator, The," quoted, 241
Speedwell, The, at Delft [Arber, 329], 173
Spenser, Edmund, his version of the Penitential Psalms [Works, ed. Payne-Collier, i., lxxv.], 129
Spinello, his frescoes at Florence [Montalembert, i. 410], 32; at Siena, 59
Staël, Madame de, and Wilberforce [" Life of Wilberforce," iv. 158, 167], 232
Stanley, Dean, his favourite psalm, 235
Stanley, H. M., finds Livingstone, 265
Steinach, the, Gall at, 37
Stephen, the martyr, 5
Sternhold, Thomas, 112-114
Stewart, Sir Thomas, uncle of Oliver Cromwell [Carlyle, i. 81], 189
Stoddart, Colonel, death of, at Bokhara, 272
Stones, Druidic, names for, in France, 144; superstitions concerning, in S.W. France [see Appendix A, chap. iv.], 84
Strada cited [de Bello Belgico, Libb. iii. and v.], 138
Strafford, Earl of, his trial and death, 177-180
Strasburg, Bishop Hooper at, 105
Stridon, birthplace of Jerome, 19
Suffolk, Duke of, 119
Sundials [see Appendix A], 3
Sussex, Wilfrid in, 49
Swift, the, Wyclif's ashes thrown into, 88
Symonds, servant to Darnley, 125

Tagus, the, passage of, 63
Tanfield Hall, Chalmers at [Hanna, iv. 341], 235

Index 329

Tanlay, Coligny at, 148, 149
Tarn, the, 167
Tartars, the, in Russia, 63
Tasso, death of, 97
Tate, Nahum, 113
Taylor, page to Darnley, 125
Taylor, Jeremy, 175, 176; quoted [Works, vol. xv., p. 97], 175, 176
Telesia, monastery at, 57
Tellier, Michel le, chancellor [Puaux, vi. 87 seq.], 165
Templars, the, battle-cry of, 61
Tennyson, his "Crossing the Bar" 211, quoted ("Rizpah"), 244; on Edward Fitzgerald, 246
Teresa, St., 90; account of [Coleridge, i. 4, 8; ii. 362, 369-70], 104, 105
Thebaid, the, 18
Theodore the Martyr ["Dict. Christian Biography," iv. 956], 10
Theodore of Mopsuestia, quoted, 11
Theodosius, The Emperor, and Ambrose [Bright's "Fathers," i. 519; Baunard, 448-456], 25
Theodosius, De Situ Terræ Sanctæ [See Appendix A, chap. iv.], 60
Theonas, St., church of [Bright's "Fathers," i. 240; "History," 76, 77; Stanley's "Eastern Church," 283], 23
Thessalonica, massacre at, 24, 25
Thomas, "Little Alphabet of the Monks," etc. [see Appendix A, chap. iv.; Kettlewell, ii. 119 seq.], 77, 78
Thomas, Surgeon, friend of William Carey, 255
Thomas Aquinas, St., 46, 47
Thomas, St., of Villanova, 8
Thomson, his "Hymn" quoted, 35
Tiberius II., 11
Tierra del Fuego, Allen Gardiner at [Marsh's Memoir, 346], 262, 263
Tobie, The, wreck of [see Appendix A, chap. vi.], 129, 130
Toledo, Council of, 35

Topcliffe, the executioner [Southwell, ed. Grosart, liv.], 108
Torquemada, 136
Torwood, Cargill at, 210
Totila and Benedict [Montalembert, i. 410], 32
Tours, Martin at, 21; Clovis at, 52; "Le Roi Hugon," 144
Toulouse, Council of, 110; Rochette at, 172
Tower of London, the, 107
Tracy, murderer of Becket, 58
Tranent, Col. James Gardiner at [Doddridge, 188], 267
Tranquebar, church at, 256
Treasure, hidden, superstitions in S.W. France [see Appendix A, chap. iv.], 84
Tulliver, Maggie ("Mill on the Floss"), 7
Tunis, death of St. Louis at, 75; Vincent de Paul, slave at, 156
Turkey merchantmen, the five [see Appendix A, chap. vi.], 129
Turstin, archbishop of York, 67
Tylney, Elizabeth, with Lady Jane Grey, 118
Tyndall, his version of the Psalter, 110
Tyrconnel, Lord, at siege of Derry [Walker, ed. Dwyer], 219

Ujiji, Livingstone at [Last Journals, ii. 155], 265
Unyanyembe, Livingstone at [*ibid.*, 229], 265
Urban II., Pope, and Anselm, 57
Uzés, cathedral at, 143

Valens, The Emperor, and Basil [Bright's "Fathers," i. 373; Greg. Naz. orat., xx. xliii.], 25
Valladolid, death of Columbus at, 97
Vassy, massacre at, 147
Vaudois, the [Monastier, ii. 91, 126; Douen, i. 23 n.], 164, 165
Vaughan, Henry, the Silurist, 6
Venice, Barbarossa at, 59
Vendée, La, insurrection ["Les Chouans," ii. 135 seq.], 269
Venn, Henry, 229, 231

Index

Victoria Nyanza, Lake, Bishop Hannington at, 266
Vienne river, Clovis at, 53
Vililla, bell of [Stirling-Maxwell's " Charles V.," 266], 96
Vincennes, Madame Guyon at, 163
Vincent de Paul, 153; account of [Wilson, 18-22], 155, 156
Vincentius of Lerins, 47
Virgilius, Celtic saint, 34
Vladimir St., baptism of [Stanley's " Eastern Church," 359; Mouravieff, 14, 15], 72
Vladimir Monomachus, 8, 71; account of [Stanley's " Eastern Church," 359; Palmer's Dissertations, 92-3; Mouravieff, 31, 363], 72, 73; dying injunctions to his son [Karamsin, ii. 203-9; Stanley, 372 seq.], 72, 73
Voltaire, " Henriade " quoted [Chant. II., 121-4], 148
Vouglé, battle of, 52, 53

Waldis, Burkhard, of Hesse, versifies Psalter, 111
Walker, George, at siege of Derry, 219, 220, 221; quoted [ed. Dwyer, 20, 37], 219. 221, 223; his sermon [ed. Dwyer, 105 seq.], 221, 222
Walker, Patrick, on Prelacy, quoted [" Six Saints," ii. 4], 197; his " Six Saints " quoted, 205, 209, 212, 213, 214
Wallace, " Quaker," at the Secundrabagh [Forbes-Mitchell, 56], 276
Wallace, William, 71; death of [Tytler, i. 279-80], 75
Wallis, Widow (the Particular Baptists at Kettering), 255
Walsingham, pilgrimages to, 61; Thomas of [Rolls Series, 28, Ib, p. 119], 88
Walton, Izaak, his " Life of Sanderson " quoted, 176, 177
" Walton, young," killed at Marston Moor [Carlyle, " Cromwell," i. 167], 190
" Wanderers, The," account of, 207, 208
" Wandering Willie," his saying [" Redgauntlet," Letter xi.], 208
Watts, Isaac, 6
Waverley, Cistercians at [Newman's " Saints," v. 167 n.], 66
Wearmouth, monastery at, 48
Wedderburns, the, their " Spiritual Sangis," 198; quoted, 199
Welsh, Mr., " outed " minister, at Irongray [Blackader], 203
Welsh, Jane (Carlyle), 236; quoted, 268, 269
Wesley, Charles, 6, 229; account of, 231; death of, 231; hymns of, 231
Wesley, John, 257; and Law's " Serious Call " [Journal, i. 94], 229; account of, 230; death of, 230, 231; his " Collection of Psalms and Hymns " [see Appendix A, chap. xi.], 231
Whewell, William, quoted as to Julius Hare, 234
Whitby, sundial at, 3
Whitefield, George [Tyerman, i. 16], 229
Whitehall, Cromwell's speeches in the Painted Chamber [Carlyle, iv. 218, 220], 190, 195, 196
Whittingham, versifier of the Psalms, 113
Wight, Isle of, Wilfrid in, 49
Wigtown Martyrs, the [Wodrow, iv. 248, 249; " Cloud of Witnesses," 440], 216-218
" Wild Whigs, The," 204
Wilberforce, William, account of [see Appendix A, chap. xi.], 231, 232
Wilfrid, St., 8, 48; and Psalter [Montalembert, iii. 376-378], 63; account of [ibid., iii. 376-381, 412; iv. 33, 48, 72, 108], 48, 49
Wilkie, James, primarius of St. Andrews [Melville's Diary, 27], 200
William the Conqueror, and Lanfranc, 56; death of [Ordericus Vitalis, VIII., xiv. and xvi.], 71
William Rufus and Anselm [Montalembert, vi. 158 seq.], 56, 57
William of Orange, landing of, in England, 218.

Index

Wilson, Margaret, 205; death of [Wodrow, iv. 248, 249], 217, 218
Winchester, Marquis of, at Basing House, 191
Winslow, Governor, quoted [Arber, "Pilgrim Fathers," 329], 173
Wise men of the East, the, in Christian Art, 3
Wisedome, versifier of the Psalms, 113
Wishart, George, account of [Knox, i. 125 seq.], 197-199
Wither, George, versifier of the Psalms, 6
Woburn Abbey, Carthusians of, 146
Wodrow, Robert, cited, 210; quoted, 216
Woolos, St., at Newport (Mon.), 43
Worcester, battle of [Carlyle, iii. 172-3], 194, 195
Wordsworth, 6; quoted [Ecclesiastical Sonnets), 59, 180; quoted ("Excursion"), 244
Worms, Diet of, 95
Wotton, Sir Henry, 6
Würtemburg, Roger ordained at 170
Wyatt, Sir Thomas, versifier of the Psalms, 6, 131; insurrection of. 116
Wyclif, John, 8, 61, 93; death of, 87

Xainton, inscription at, 144
Xavier, Francis, 8, 90; death of [Coleridge, ii. 572], 102-104; his "O Deus, ego amo De" translated [Latin text in Coleridge, i. 315], 103
Ximenes, Cardinal, 8; at Oran [von Hefele, transl. Dalton, p. 419], 63

Yaroslaff, builds church of St. Sophia at Kieff, 30
York, Duke of, and Cargill [Wodrow, book iii. chap. 4], 210; and Peden ["Six Saints," i. 90], 214
York, St. Mary's Abbey at, 66
Yuste, Jeromite convent, Charles V. at, 96

Zanzibar, Livingstone at [Last Journals, i. 1 seq.], 265
Zulus, the, Commander Allen F. Gardiner and [Marsh's Memoir, chap. iv.], 262
Zurich, Bishop Hooper at, 105
Zwingli, 111

THE TEMPLE PRESS, PRINTERS, LETCHWORTH

Other Related Titles

In addition to *Psalms in Human History* we are happy to offer the following related titles:

A Pathway into the Psalter by William Binnie is a masterful study of the Book of Psalms by a master teacher. Spurgeon said, "A highly valuable work. Supplies a desideratum."

The Psalms in History and Biography by John Ker is a perfect compliment to *Psalms in Human History*.

Notes on Galatians by J. Gresham Machen is a precise and practical exposition of Paul's Epistle that opens up the glorious doctrine of justification by faith alone in Christ alone. It is very timely.

Biblical and Theological Studies by the professors of Princeton Seminary in 1912, at the centenary celebration of the Seminary. Articles are by men like Allis, Vos, Warfield, Machen, Wilson and many others.

Theology on Fire: Vols. 1 & 2 by J.A. Alexander is the two volumes of sermons by this brilliant scholar from Princeton Seminary.

A Shepherd's Heart by James W. Alexander is a volume of outstanding expository sermons from the pastoral ministry of one of the leading preachers of the 19th century.

Evangelical Truth by Archibald Alexander is a volume of practical sermons intended to be used for Family Worship.

The Lord of Glory by Benjamin B. Warfield is one of the best treatments of the doctrine of the Deity of Christ ever written. It is simply masterful.

The Power of God unto Salvation by Benjamin B. Warfield is the first book of sermons ever published of the expositions of this master-theologian.

The Scripture Guide by James W. Alexander is a helpful guide to lead young people and new converts into a deeper appreciation of the Word of God.

My Brother's Keeper by James W. Alexander is a book of letters Alexander wrote to his 10 year old brother. It is full of sound advice on a wide variety of subjects.

Mourning a Beloved Shepherd by Charles Hodge and John Hall is a little volume containing the funeral addresses for James W. Alexander. Very informative and challenging.

Call us Toll Free at 1-877-666-9469
Send us an e-mail at sgcb@charter.net
Visit us on line at solid-ground-books.com

SGCB Titles for the Young

Solid Ground Christian Books is honored to be able to offer over a dozen uncovered treasure for children and young people.

Bible Warnings: *Sermons to Children on Dangers that lie along their Path and How to Avoid Them* by Richard Newton is the sequel to *Bible Promises* that you hold in your hand. Fifteen brilliant chapters. Newton at his very best!

Bible Promises: *Sermons to Children on God's Word as our Solid Rock* by Richard Newton directs children to rest in the certain promises of God.

Heroes of the Reformation by Richard Newton is a unique volume that introduces children and young people to the leading figures and incidents of the Reformation. Spurgeon called him, *"The Prince of preachers to the young."*

Heroes of the Early Church by Richard Newton is the sequel to the above-named volume. The very last book Newton wrote introduces all the leading figures of the early church with lessons to be learned from each figure.

The King's Highway: *Ten Commandments to the Young* by Richard Newton is a volume of Newton's sermons to children. Highly recommended!

The Life of Jesus Christ for the Young by Richard Newton is a double volume set that traces the Gospel from Genesis 3:15 to the Ascension of our Lord and the outpouring of His Spirit on the Day of Pentecost. Excellent!

The Child's Book on the Fall by Thomas H. Gallaudet is a simple and practical exposition of the Fall of man into sin, and his only hope of salvation.

The Child's Book on Repentance by Thomas H. Gallaudet is a simple and practical exposition of the Fall of man into sin, and his only hope of salvation.

The Child's Book on the Soul by Thomas H. Gallaudet is a simple and practical exposition of the Fall of man into sin, and his only hope of salvation.

The Child at Home by John S.C. Abbott is the sequel to his popular book *The Mother at Home*. A must read for children and their parents.

My Brother's Keeper: *Letters to a Younger Brother* by J.W. Alexander contains the actual letters Alexander sent to his ten year old brother.

The Scripture Guide by J.W. Alexander is filled with page after page of information on getting the most from our Bibles. Invaluable!

Feed My Lambs: *Lectures to Children* by John Todd is drawn from actual sermons preached in Philadelphia, PA and Pittsfield, MA to the children of the church, one Sunday each month. A pure gold-mine of instruction.

Truth Made Simple: *The Attributes of God for Children* by John Todd was intended to be a miniature Systematic Theology for children. Richard Newton said that Dr. Todd taught him how to teach children. Practical and crystal clear!

The Young Lady's Guide by Harvey Newcomb will speak directly to the heart of the young women who desire to serve Christ with all their being.

The Chief End of Man by John Hall is an exposition and application of the first question of the Westminster Shorter Catechism. Full of rich illustrations.

Call us Toll Free at 1-877-666-9469
Send us an e-mail at sgcb@charter.net
Visit us on line at solid-ground-books.com

www.ingramcontent.com/pod-product-compliance
Lightning Source LLC
Chambersburg PA
CBHW022049160426
43198CB00008B/171